Some Rain Must Fall

Some Rain Must Fall

AUTOBIOGRAPHY 1907–1995

Isabelle Bendon

ISABELLE
MUNDAY

First published in 2003 by Isabelle Munday
15 Eastern Road, Haywards Heath
West Sussex RH16 3NG

Distributed by Gazelle Book Services Limited
Falcon House, Queen Square
Lancaster, England LA1 1RN

British Library Cataloguing in Publication Data
A catalogue record for this book is available from the British Library

ISBN 0-9544388-0-9

Typeset by Amolibros, Milverton, Somerset
This book production has been managed by Amolibros
Printed and bound by T J International Ltd, Padstow, Cornwall, UK

Chapter One

What my mother told me.

My parents rented two upstairs rooms in a house in Pownall Road, Dalston, a then slightly upmarket area in North East London. The large terraced houses were uniform. All stonework was painted a deep cream. Street doors were grained and varnished, as was all woodwork around window frames. Starched white lace curtains were tastefully draped to show an aspidistra plant or pretty ornament. Each morning housewives shone the brass fittings on street doors and the black leaded foot scrapers shone beside whitened doorsteps. Dirt from the pavement outside the house was swept into gutters. Later men came sweeping roads and scooping up the dirt into their handcarts.

Mother worked as an outdoor machinist, stitching uppers for a children's shoe factory. The pay was 4s 6d per twelve pairs of uppers and all shoes were leather-lined. After finishing his service with the Royal Navy, Father worked as a French polisher or as he grandly stated, "I'm a beautifier of foreign wood."

On a bitterly cold February day in 1907 I was dragged into the world by forceps delivery, after forty-eight hours of painful labour, weighing 11lbs 10oz. The delighted doctor beamed, "She's beautiful, there's enough flesh and bone there for two babies." A little later when Father saw my bruised swollen face he remarked, "What an ugly brat." Mother said she cried herself to sleep.

Two years later baby Jimmy arrived. The landlady told Mother that with two children she would be unable to stand the noise over her head and asked Father to find other accommodation. They finally rented a two-roomed flat in Guinness's Buildings, Columbia Road, Bethnal Green.

Slowly, as time passed, I became aware of things. I played with Jimmy while Mother machined. She did the housework, cleaned windows, did washing and ironing. Strapping Jimmy in his pushchair we went shopping each day, and when the machining was finished she tied us both in the pushchair, taking us to the shoe factory to collect her wages. We were bathed and fed and put to sleep before Father returned from work. He always seemed to be shouting and if Mother shouted he hit her. It must have been weekends when he didn't work that were the times he shouted most.

This morning, Father was raving as usual. Mummy had fed Jimmy and had peeled my egg. What Mummy said, I've no idea, Father suddenly picked up a Bentwood chair and slammed it against Mummy's back. She lurched against the table, my egg toppled and the yolk spilled onto the tablecloth. I screamed and getting off my chair ran to Father's leg and bit him hard through his trousers. He slapped me hard across my face and I fell against the iron gas cooker and the day went dark. Mummy was crying as she smoothed my forehead. "It hurts by my ear," I said and began crying.

"I said she was all right," Father said. He began putting on his jacket and left us. Mummy told me I was knocked out for twenty minutes.

Some time later, I don't know how long, two strange men came and began moving the furniture. Father pointed to items and the men took them away. They rolled up the oilcloth in the bedroom while Father threw out things from the chest of drawers.

"Are we moving, Mummy?" I asked.

"No, just be a good girl." Father flung some money on the floor. He came to the machine.

"Please leave my machine, Jim."

He punched her in the face, raving all the time.

Mother said later that he left five shillings for us saying he would pay five shillings to keep us kids and Mother could collect it from his parents each Thursday. Mother could work to pay the rent and keep herself.

Mother was seated on the bed when Father came back into the room. I don't know what she said, but he punched her in the face. I kicked his leg hard and he threw me on the bed then left. I cuddled Jimmy as he began to cry. It made me want to cry too. Mummy picked up the clean washing and clothes, and holding them she said, "Your father has left us for a lady."

"Why does he want another lady when he has us?"

"I'll tell you when you're older," she smiled. "I'll prepare some lunch, at least he has left food."

In the living-room, the cream-painted dresser was a fitment of the rented flat. There was crockery on the shelf and beneath the drawers a floral curtain hid the shelf for pots and pans. There was oilcloth on the floor, the table and two chairs, Mummy's machine, Jimmy's high chair and pushchair. The room looked so empty. Later we had some tea.

"This evening we will see Uncle Harry, he will help me."

Uncle Harry was Mummy's younger brother and was married to Aunt Lucy for some time. It was past our bedtime when we arrived at Uncle's house. Jimmy was already asleep. I walked the short distance and was feeling sleepy, so Aunt Lucy sat me in an armchair and I slept.

It must have been a Saturday afternoon. In those days one could hire a barrow for two pence an hour and this was how Mummy and Uncle moved our belongings. The upstairs back room into which we settled had two half-cupboards, one each side of the fireplace. In one Mummy put pots and pans, crockery and food. In the other she stored clothes and clean washing. I remember all this as if it occurred yesterday. Mother told me about her family; she was the eighth child, Harry was the last. There was Fred, Edith, Alice, Lizzie, George, Agnes, Minne, Isabella (my mother) and Harry. Her father was a railway guard; he had an accident getting a toe crushed between buffers. Gangrene caused his death at forty-seven.

He had worked for the London and North Eastern Railway for thirty years. The railway gave his wife a weekly pension of six shillings. My mother was four years old at that time. The three eldest were working, Fred for a firm of packing-case-makers and Edith and Alice worked as dressmakers. Mother never knew Lizzie, who died from measles, or George, who at the age of twelve caught pneumonia and died.

Uncle Fred had a fine tenor singing voice and at nineteen sang at clubs and in pubs each night. He received three shillings for singing two songs… quite a sum in those days.

Christmas-time was a lively time for us and as my birthday was in February, I began school when the school reopened after the holiday. I was almost five years old. I liked school and learned quickly.

Mother told me she began piano lessons when she was six years old, the cost was sixpence an hour.

Chapter Two

Granny Boast (Mum's mother) saw her children marry. Mother knew Father at school. Granny Boast did not like him and when at seventeen he joined the Royal Navy, she was pleased and hoped that Mother would forget him.

They resumed "walking out" when he finished his service. When Mother left home to marry, Granny Boast warned, "He will never be any good to you, he comes from a family of drunkards. Bella, you have made a mistake."

When Harry married and took over the house, Granny Boast went to Suffolk to live with her widowed sister.

Now, back to the day I began school. We sat two children to a small desk and wrote on slates with a crayon-type pencil. We copied the words from the blackboard on which the teacher had written, "The cat sat on the mat; the dog sat on the mat; the cat and dog sat on the mat." We repeated the words parrot fashion. The teacher wiped the board clean, told us to turn our slates over and write the words from memory. We had playtime, then went home for dinner. Back in the afternoon, we had to put our arms on the desktop and go to sleep, each day the same.

There wasn't much space to play in our back room. We played on the bed, that was a ship; and we played under the table, that was a tent. On dull days the room was lit by a single finger-type burner that made a fan-shaped glow. We stayed with Aunt Lucy when Mum took her finished work to the factory.

Aunt Lucy worked as a fancy box-maker and brought home strips of coloured paper for us to play with.

Then came the day of the magic lantern show. We sat on the floor in the darkened hall. There were pictures of animals, birds and flowers. If we knew the species we called out. Then came the picture of a man asleep in a chair, his mouth wide open. On a shelf a mouse was looking at the sleeping man and suddenly jumped into the open mouth. I screamed with fright and was led out of the hall. "It's just a picture," I was told.

"The mouse was biting the man's tongue," I insisted, still crying.

It was Easter-time when tragedy struck at our house.

Uncle Harry belonged to a cycling club and had crashed and a few hours later died. Aunt Lucy was devastated and kept saying, "We have been married just four years, why me?" Mother was crying too. I loved Aunt Lucy, she was so kind to me. The accident happened at Herne Hill. I imagined he rode his cycle up the hill and fell off at the top.

A blackboard was put up at the window and neighbours pulled their blinds down. The coffin was put in Aunt Lucy's parlour, and the house was very quiet. Mum went out some days with Aunt Lucy and she didn't do much machining. Mrs Copes looked after Jimmy and me while Mum was out.

On the day of the funeral I wore a black dress and a white pinafore.

Granny Boast came from Suffolk, and all the aunts and uncles.

The blackboard was taken away from the window and the coffin was pushed out through the window because the passage was too narrow. There were wreaths hung all round the hearse. The black horses had high feathers on their heads and long velvet drapes hanging from their backs almost to the ground. There were three carriages in which all the family rode. Members of the cycling club followed slowly behind the procession, wreaths were on each handlebar. The street seemed full. Neighbours stood quietly at their doors, men took off their caps as the carriages passed. It was so sad.

"Why are all the horses wearing hats?" I asked Mrs Coles.

"Not hats, they are called plumes." She called to Gracie, "Come, children, I'll get you all some dinner."

We had mashed potatoes mixed with egg and a slice of bread and jam for afters. Then we were sent out to play and we told each other we were going to have a funeral like Uncle Harry's.

When the mourners returned, Mrs Coles sent Jimmy and me home. Everyone was quiet. My mum and Aunt Alice were making tea and Aunt Edith was handing round plates and sandwiches. "Have you both been good?" she asked as she reached us. We took a sandwich and nodded. I was staring at my mum's mother. It was the first time I had seen Granny Boast. She wore a kind of bonnet with wide black ribbons tied in bows under her chin, and although all the ladies took off their hats, she kept her bonnet on. She wore a black cape trimmed with shiny black beads. I have never seen anything like it; those beads fascinated me.

"Come here, little Belle," she said. I went to her and she lifted me on her knees. "This is the first time I have seen you since you were a baby, and I have never seen Jimmy before today."

"I like Aunt Lucy's hat," I told her. I didn't know what to say to her. "It's got a lace curtain down the back."

She shook her head. "That's not a curtain, it's made of special net, called 'widow's weeds'."

"I'm going to have a hat like that when I grow up," I replied.

"No, no, don't say that."

Mum and Aunt Alice came in with cups of tea. The men were all standing and talking… it was more like a party.

"So you go to school now?" Granny Boast asked. "Have you learnt the ABC?" I nodded. "When your mother and her brothers and sisters went to Columbia Road School, it was School Board of London and I had to pay for them to be taught their lessons.

It was a penny a week until the age of seven, and after that it was two pence a week for each child."

After the holiday we returned to school and as weeks passed by we played in the street while Mum machined the shoes, and Mrs Coles took care of us when Mum took the finished work to the factory and to get paid.

Chapter Three

About three times a year a herd of bullocks would be driven through Ravenscroft Street on the way to the slaughterhouse, accompanied by many drivers shouting for people to close street doors, and barking dogs adding to the noise. It was in the afternoon after school and I was looking in the sweet-shop window, half-way up the street, at a black and white cat asleep on a tray of broken rock sweets. Hearing the noise I turned to see the herd of bullocks rushing into the turning. I dashed for home reaching our house as Mum came along the passage to close the door. I fell down the two steps into the passage as Mum shut the door over me, seeing a bullock skid to a stop. I have been scared of bullocks ever since.

Mother told me much later that Father began to come round in the afternoons after Uncle Harry's funeral. It wasn't too often, but if there was a knock on the door she never knew if he would be there. She said he told her he was a changed man, and how much he missed his children. He said his mother told him how we were keeping and he was so sorry to learn about Uncle Harry. When Mum asked him about the woman he had sold the furniture to, leaving us with nothing, he said she had gone back to her husband.

Every week on Thursday Mum would go round to Granny Munday to collect the five shillings Father sent for our keep. Sometimes she took Jimmy in his pushchair, sometimes she took both of us, but she would never enter the house because Father may be there.

One Thursday when Mum took both of us to collect the money, Gran said, "Why don't you come to tea on Sunday with the children, yes?"

"No thank you, Mother."

"Jim won't be here, if that's what you think."

Grandfather came to the door. "I'd like to see the children for an hour or so, Bella. After all they are our first grandchildren, so please, just this once. I'll make sure Jim isn't here, if that is what worries you."

So we went to Gran's to tea. There was jelly and custard, winkles, bread and jam and cakes all spread out on the table. We didn't know where to start. Mother picked the winkles out of their shells... Jimmy didn't like them; I thought they tasted funny, but we loved the jelly and custard.

The table cleared, Jimmy and I played on the floor while the grown-ups chatted. Very soon their voices became a little louder. Granny looked angry and Mum got the pushchair and put Jimmy in it.

"Don't go like this, Bella," said Grandfather.

"She won't hear a word said against him... after all he has done to me and the children."

"He has changed, really he has. I think you should give him another chance, if only for the children's sake. They do need their father."

Mother told me much later that it all began by Gran saying, "Why do you always keep my son talking on the street?"

Mother answered saying, "Did he tell you what he did to me last time we were behind closed doors? He sold the furniture and punched me in the eye, so I speak to him in the street because it's safer for me. People can see then."

But Father still came round occasionally. Mum also told me she and Aunt Lucy had a very long talk about him.

Mother told Aunt Lucy that Father was learning cellar work because a Mrs Blacket had put his name forward to manage a public house owned by West's Brewery Company, but it had to be run by a man and wife.

"So that's why he's been trying to get round you, Bella."

"The children do need a father, Lucy."

"Not one who shouts and frightens them. You've told me how he's knocked you about, it's not good for the kids to see that happening."

"He said he's changed, he won't act like that again."

"Don't believe him, Bella. A leopard cannot change its spots or a tiger its stripes."

Mother told me the conversation was something on those lines. She said Lucy tried her hardest to make Mother change her mind.

When Mother said she felt a little sorry to be leaving, Lucy told her, "My sister's getting married in July, so she'll come to live with me."

When Mother told Father that she had decided to give him another chance he was delighted, promising her she would have no regrets and the kids would want for nothing. When mother asked about furniture, he told her the pub was fully furnished and there was also a piano for her to play. Mother wanted to know what would happen to her machine.

"Sell the stuff you have, you won't need that rubbish anymore."

"You pay Lucy half-a-crown each week to store my machine and bed in her small box-room." Reluctantly Father agreed.

"Jim said there's a piano there," Mum told Aunt Lucy as they packed up our few clothes prior to leaving.

"Well, Bella, looking after the children and serving in the bar, what time do you think you'll have for playing the piano?"

Mother told me at this point she wondered if she was doing the right thing.

When Mum told me we were going back to Daddy, I didn't want to go.

"No, Mummy," I said, "he will hit you again... I saw him hit you."

"No, he won't do it anymore."

I cuddled my brother. "We don't want to go to Daddy, do we, Jimmy?"

My brother shook his head, "No. Dad, don't like him."

Mother said we were silly and took us in to say goodbye to Aunt Lucy. I cried, I loved her she was so kind. I insisted on taking the doll's bed Grandfather Munday had made for me for Christmas. He had made Jimmy a chair with a flap in the front, it had a ridge round the flap and nothing could slip off. He had made Mother a what-not, a corner unit with shelves to put things on. Jimmy's chair and Mum's what-not were stored with the other furniture in the box-room.

So, in May, three months after my fifth birthday, we moved into the pub called The Two Crowns on the corner of Holm Street and Edith Street.

I was taken to the nearest school, Maidstone Street. I was put straight into the girls' school and my new teacher's name was Miss Mathas.

This teacher had a large doll with a light brown face, dressed in Eastern fashion with a yashmak, lots of beads and thin trousers you could see the legs through. I had never seen anything like that before.

Chapter Four

Miss Mathas taught me a love of poetry. We all learned by repetition, parrot fashion. Scripture was the first lesson every morning after assembly.

Then came learning the multiplication tables. We read aloud as Miss Mathas pointed them out and thus by repetition we knew them by heart. We had lessons in spelling, copybook writing, history, geography, needlework and painting and drawing. We had a morning and afternoon break of fifteen minutes as a playtime. We had a two-hour break for dinner and the day's school finished at 4.30.

I liked school and learned quickly.

Let me tell you about the pub as I remember it. It had two large frosted glass windows with the two crowns etched into the glass. The entrance door in Holm Street was marked "Jug and Bottle", the corner was marked "Public Bar". Entering the "Jug and Bottle" bar you saw wooden bench-like seating. The bar was small, there was a long passage leading to the large tap-room. A large open fireplace was on the right. There was a skittle alley, a long table and at one end of the table was a slate inset for the game shove ha'penny. A dartboard hung at the far end of the room and there was a door leading to a small yard, which was kept locked.

In the long passage was a staircase leading to our living accommodation, which comprised a long living-room at the top of the stairs. There was a large kitchen range on the right, a tall dresser against the wall on the left, a highly polished table in the centre surrounded by six high-backed chairs, one of which had wooden arms. This chair Father called his. At the end under the window was a wooden bench. Along the landing, a door on the right was a bedroom for Jimmy and me and we had a narrow bed each on either side of the room. There was a blanket box against the wall between the beds and a chair for our clothes; there was no room for anything else. On the left was our parents' bedroom; we were not allowed in there so I never knew what it was like. The end door led into a large parlour. The oilcloth was brown with autumnal leaves, there were two low cupboards beside the chimney recess, and there was a piano and a black horse-hair couch with two matching armchairs. A small round table, around which were four padded chairs, stood in the centre and a brown rug was placed in front of the couch. I had never seen so much furniture before and when we first moved in Jimmy and I kept walking round in amazement.

The scullery led off from a door in the living-room. It was small with a yellow stone sink in one corner next to a gas cooker. Under the sink various cleaning things were stacked and also there hung a long galvanised bath. A door led to an iron stairway... six steps down was a landing and the toilet or WC, as it was then called. There were more steps down into the yard behind the tap-room.

The public bar led into a large bar with wooden seating round the walls and another door leading to a small room, a favourite for a cosy chat.

The bar itself had four engines: beer, stout, light ale and bitter. Beer was at that time four pence a pint, bitter was more expensive. On the bar counter stood a glass jar containing arrowroot biscuits, quite big and sold for a penny each.

The greatest event at that time in our young lives was that we had a nanny... a Mrs Renick. She was a lovely person.

She was tall and slim, she wore a black skirt that reached the ground, mostly grey blouses and pinned at her throat was a brooch with the word "Mother". Her dark hair had some grey streaks and was plaited and coiled on top of her head, and there were six tiny curls resting on her brow. She had nice blue eyes, a thin nose and an oval face. She cleaned, cooked and looked after Jimmy and me from eight o'clock in the morning until eight o'clock at night, when she left for her home. For all this work Father paid her the princely sum of 7s 6d per week. Mother worked in the bar from nine in the morning until twelve o'clock at night and when the pub closed, washed glasses. For this work, Father paid Mother five shillings weekly.

Mother told me that when she protested that five shillings wasn't much pay for fifteen or sixteen hours' work each day, he replied, "You have board and lodging, remember."

We also had a pot man named Mr Poulton. He was a short man with rosy cheeks and a thatch of black hair. He worked hard, sweeping out the bars each morning and shovelling sawdust into the dustbin. There was no wall-to-wall carpets in those days, just wall-to-wall sawdust. Mr Poulton went to the sawmills in Tuilerie Street once a week and bought a sack of sawdust for the bars. The bin was put out for the dustmen to empty. The open-topped yellow-painted horse-drawn cart came down the streets regularly. On windy days as these men emptied the bins, paper and some sawdust would blow back along the road. There were always road sweepers to clear up and they would shovel the dirt into little handcarts. The streets were kept very tidy and housewives would sweep pavements outside their street doors and whiten their doorsteps.

Mr Poulton would sweep and dust the tap-room each morning and in winter he would light a fire and keep it stoked up all day. Father would stand a bag of potatoes beside the fireplace; Mr Poulton would fill the oven shelves with medium-sized potatoes to bake. These, when cooked, were free to customers using the tap-room. If men wanted salt on the potatoes, Father would smother them. “Makes them thirsty,” he would say laughing.

Chapter Five

Three times a week, Nanny lifted the bath from the wall in the scullery and heaved it onto the bench in the living-room. She would boil up two large kettles, empty them into the bath and add cold water. Jimmy and I would be bathed together then, wrapped up in nightdresses, we would be taken down to the bar to say goodnight to our parents. Each night we had a hug and kiss from Mum and a quick peck on the forehead from Father.

Nanny would put us to bed at seven o'clock, clear up and leave for home at eight o'clock. She really slogged for her pittance.

The classrooms in school were large. All desks faced the teacher, there were five rows of desks and five desks in each row and we sat two to each desk. There were forty-two to forty-six children in our class and it was the same in the rest of the nine classes on our floor. The infant classes were on the ground floor, the girls' classes on the next floor and the boys' on the top floor. The entire wall behind the teacher was lined with blackboards.

All the boys wore short trousers and flat caps. When they reached the age of fourteen they wore long trousers.

Ladies wore skirts reaching the ground, and they always wore hats, pinned to their hair with hat pins with a decorated knob.

Chapter Six

So the days merged into summer and with six weeks holiday from school, poor Nanny was rushed off her feet. She never lost her temper, she tended our needs and kept our clothes washed and cleaned and we always looked tidy. We also had a big Airedale dog named Floss, she was lovely but Father wouldn't let us pet her, he insisted she was a working dog and had to look after the pub when it was closed. Father had Thursday afternoons and evenings off and took Floss for walks on London Fields. Mother had Mondays free from two o'clock until eight o'clock in the evening.

On an August day during school holidays, I was bouncing my ball outside the pub. The cellar flaps were open, Father had washed down the fascia. I looked up at the gold lettering edged with black, "West's Brewery", all on a green background. "Looks clean, Father."

"I've just scrubbed it, haven't I?" he shouted.

The dog came into the street. I bounced the ball and she jumped for it, hitting the ball with her nose, it went into the cellar.

The dog rushed into the pub through the bar parlour where the door leading to the cellar steps was open. In the cellar she banged against the beer pipes in her eagerness to retrieve the ball. Father went berserk. "I'll kill that bloody dog," he bawled. The dog bounded happily towards him, dropping the ball at his feet. He grabbed her collar and dragged her through the tap-room into the yard and chained her up, swearing all the while.

"Don't hit her," I screamed as he took off his belt. As he raised his arm, I threw myself over the dog's body, and received all the force of the belt. I screamed the place down, running in circles with pain. Mum rushed out from the bar and Nanny came running down the iron steps. All talked at once while I screamed continuously. Finally I sobbed, "He belted me." Mum cuddled me while Nanny boldly told Father, "You should be ashamed of yourself, Mr Munday, the dog doesn't understand what she has done wrong."

"Mind your own business and you're sacked."

Mum was helping me up the steps. She turned to Father, "You sack Nanny and you'll be potty."

Nanny bathed my back and smeared on some soothing oil and told me, "You have a pretty mauve and pink stripe from your shoulder to your little bum." And Nanny stayed.

I was told later that Floss had knocked against the bitter pipe and as a result the bitter came up cloudy and could not be sold for thirty-six hours, and as bitter was the most expensive drink Father was bad tempered for a couple of days and the dog gave him a wide berth.

One very dull Monday in October, after school, Mum took me and Jimmy to have tea with Aunt Lucy. It was after five o'clock and getting dark. As we turned into Ravenscroft Street a lamplighter was lighting the street lamps. I watched as he pushed the long pole into the globe and the light flared.

"Where does the gas come from, Mummy?" asked my brother.

"There is a small bar in the globe that he pushes up and the gas comes through the pipes and the light at the end of his pole lights the lamp." We watched as yet another lamp was lit. "When I was a little girl," said Mum, "gas came to Ravenscroft Street in about 1890, the roadway was dug up and gas pipes put into the houses. We were told we had five hours' gas for a penny. The burner was finger-shaped and shone a fan-shaped light. It was lovely, you could see into every corner of the room, much nicer than a candle or an oil lamp that we'd used previously." Then we arrived at Number 35.

We had a lovely tea, jam sandwiches and a slice of homemade cake, and Aunt Lucy gave us lots of coloured strips of paper to take back to the pub.

We were told the lamplighter earned some extra money knocking up people who wanted to get up early. He charged two pence a week and kept knocking at doors until he was answered; that way he made sure people were up. Mother paid Aunt Lucy the half-crown for storing our bits of furniture in her box-room, then we left for home in time for Nanny to put us to bed and for Mum to be in the bar by eight o'clock. The pub was lit by gas mantles that gave a white incandescent light, which Mum told us came much later.

Nearer Christmas I came home from school to find Mum crying. Asking why she was crying, Nanny said, "Be a good girl and don't worry your mother."

Christmas came at last. We hung our socks at the end of our beds as Nanny instructed. In the morning there was so much to look at. I had two dolls, a new pair of boots and a new dress, a Christmas stocking filled with sweets and small toys; we were so excited. Jimmy had a clockwork train set; it went round in circles on shining rails. He too had a new pair of boots, a large Christmas stocking, a box of bricks and a new sailor suit. We had never had so many presents before. "I wonder where these things came from," asked Jimmy. "Perhaps it's because we're rich," I replied thoughtfully.

Nanny and Mr Renick came and stayed with us all that day.

Although the pub opened in the morning, it closed at two o'clock. It opened again at 5.30, so in the evening we were left with Nanny and her husband. We had a lovely dinner that day, which Nanny cooked, a big turkey and Christmas pudding, which I don't remember ever having before, and Nanny cut slices of iced cake. We went to bed that night very happy and contented.

Chapter Seven

About a week after Christmas, Nanny and Mr Renick took me to a pantomime. They told me Jimmy was too small to understand – apart from that Mum said Nanny would have to nurse him all the time and it would not be very enjoyable for her.

Nanny's black skirt reached the ground, and over it she wore a short green coat that had a fur collar and small brown hat with a hat pin that had a large green bauble. She looked lovely. Mr Renick wore a long brown overcoat and a black bowler hat.

I wore my red coat, a red bonnet and carried my brown muff, which had a furry lining and kept my hands warm. We walked up Tuilerie Street and boarded a tram to Shoreditch Church. Leaving the tram we crossed the road and waited for a bus. We got off the bus outside the Britannia Theatre, Hoxton. It was an afternoon matinee of the play *Sleeping Beauty*. Many people were queuing on each side of the entrance, but having reserved tickets, we went straight in. I marvelled at the splendid curved staircase before me… all red carpet and shining brass. The wide staircase led to a wide landing where, at an open door, stood a man dressed in a red coat and black trousers. Mr Renick handed the man our tickets, "Front row, sixth on the left, sir."

There was more red carpet on the stairs leading to our seats, and Mr Renick led the way. We had front seats in the circle, I was told.

Mr Renick took off his overcoat and folded it carefully and

put it on my seat for me to sit on. Thus I was able to see the stage clearly as I sat between Nanny and her husband. The orchestra was playing quietly as people took their seats.

"I see there is electric lighting," said Nanny.

"Yes, dear, but I don't think it will ever replace gas," replied Mr Renick. "It's controlled with a switch and anything can go wrong, whereas gas is continually in the pipes."

He produced a bag of dolly mixtures, which he gave me, saying, "Don't eat them all at once." I thanked him and handed the sweets to Nanny. "Presently, dear," she said. She then helped me out of my coat and hung it over the brass rail in front of our seats and did the same with her own coat. Then the lights went out and the orchestra began a lively tune, with the drapes swinging open to a most magnificent court scene, the christening of the little princess.

The king and queen wore gold crowns, and jewels sparkled on their robes. The courtiers blew trumpets and a proclamation was read out.

The court jester pranced around, the bells on his costume tinkling as he moved. Then came the fairies, small children, offering gifts of grace, beauty and all the virtues. They danced round the beautiful, large draped crib; the king made a speech and suddenly a figure draped in misty black seem to float in from nowhere.

The audience began to boo. I asked Nanny why and she told me she was a wicked fairy. Funny, I always thought fairies were good.

The wicked one prophesied the princess would prick her finger on a spindle. The little fairies shooed her away and the audience applauded. There was more singing and dancing by all the courtiers and the fairies together said, "Farewell, we shall again be seen when Princess Mayflower is sixteen," and the drapes swung closed to be raised twice more to the applause of the audience.

The next scene introduced Prince Charming. Nanny said he was a lady, but he was dressed in blue satin with matching trousers and lots of sparkle and his hair was white, which Nanny said was a wig. I wondered how she could see from this distance.

When Prince Charming left the stage two comics told jokes and tap danced. After their act came the interval.

A white board slowly came down in front of the stage. Mr Renick said it was the safety curtain. He explained to me it was fireproof and if the stage caught fire people in the theatre were safe.

Nanny insisted on taking me to the WC and we had to wait in line. After rinsing our hands we returned to our seats with the drapes swinging apart. The scene was a dim garret and at the front of the stage was a spinning-wheel at which a nice lady sat weaving. The princess, now grown up, entered. She was dressed in a lovely long pink dress and had long fair curly hair; she had diamonds round her neck, and bracelets on her arms.

She chatted to the lady as she watched the weaving and the nice lady was showing the princess how to use the spinning-wheel. The princess was weaving at the wheel when she suddenly screamed.

"I've pricked my finger, Dame," and suddenly the nice lady was in the misty black of the wicked fairy and she shuffled off the stage with a cackling laugh. Two little fairies led in the king followed by his queen, who wept loudly when she saw the princess lying on the floor. The king was saying the old witch had finally killed his daughter when all the fairies came in and said the princess was only sleeping and all the court would sleep too – until Prince Charming came and kissed the princess awake. I was impatient for that to happen. The drapes closed. A man came in front of the curtain and did some talking. When he went behind the drapes, Nanny said now we would see the transformation scene, and after asking what that was she replied, "You just wait and see."

When the drapes parted, I was amazed. It was all shades of mauves and light browns. Deep at the back of the stage a waterfall cascaded down. High up on what looked like rocky ledges stood some of the little fairies, some posed centre-stage. I questioned Nanny about the waterfall, thinking maybe it would overflow the stage, but she said, "No, dear, that is silver paper, very cleverly moved to make it look like water." Nanny knew everything.

Suddenly the fairies were flying about high above the stage. They held hoops with silver and coloured strips floating around them as they flew in formation, posing with the hoops. It all looked very unreal.

I wondered at that moment if I could be a stage fairy. The final scene was a glittering array of courtiers dancing and singing, all this after Prince Charming had kissed the princess awake and the audience clapped and called for more and the curtains were raised four times until a gentleman came and thanked the audience for their patronage.

We arrived back at the pub at 6.30. Mr Renick had a drink at the bar but Nanny came straight upstairs and rushed around preparing tea. Father was served first. He soon went back to the bar and Mum came in for her tea and I told her how lovely it had all been. She said although my birthday was a month away, the visit to the theatre had been Nanny and her husband's present to me, so I gave Nanny a great hug and a kiss of thanks.

Chapter Eight

For days I raved about the flying ballet in the transformation scene and on returning to school after the Christmas holiday I wrote about it for a composition story, and I had to read it aloud in front of the class. Most of the kids thought I was lying… people just could not fly. I told them my mother said the fairies were on wires. Asked if I could see the wires, I had to say no.

It was the first Saturday in February that Granny Munday came into the pub to ask if she could take me shopping with her… she did this a few times. Usually she did her shopping in the street markets.

Today she was really dressed up. She wore a black hat trimmed with curly feathers and a navy blue coat trimmed with a lot of braid over a black skirt. She wore a spotted veil over her face and black gloves. She told my parents, after they had given their consent, she was shopping for underclothes. We left the pub by the public bar. I turned to say bye to Mr Poulton, who was brushing out the gents' WC. Gran grabbed my arm saying, "You don't speak like that to menials." It was a very cold, frosty day.

We boarded a tram in Hackney Road outside the Children's Hospital; there were four other ladies who wore veils like Granny sitting on long seats each side of the tram. It seemed quite a long ride and we alighted at Hackney Station. We walked under the archway, crossed August Road and after a short walk along Mare Street we came to the large departmental store, Matthew

Rose. Right next door was Parnells, another large store. The windows of these stores were large, reaching almost to the pavement. The beautiful clothes and furs on the dummies standing or sitting in the windows took my breath away, as I had never seen such a wonderful array. We looked in the windows of both stores. I was mesmerised by the clothes and curtains and materials. It was nearly as breathtaking as the pantomime.

Then we entered Matthew Rose. A long counter stretched down one side of the department, and behind this, along the wall, were numerous drawers filled with merchandise. There were three assistants; two were serving customers. A long carpet-type runner covered part of the well polished oilcloth. Ranged opposite the counter, dummies clothed in the latest fashion stood elegantly posed. I was fascinated by the small tube-like containers that ran along overhead wires and disappeared round a corner. Asking Gran what they were, she replied, "They carry money to the cashier."

She lifted me onto one of the many chairs placed outside the counter and told me to sit still and not fidget.

As Gran sat down, an assistant greeted her, "Good morning, madam, can I help you?"

Madam; I looked at Gran, fully expecting her to be on her high horse, but no. She smiled sweetly, "Yes. I would like to see some whale-boned stays, with back lacing, please."

"And your size, madam?"

I didn't hear Gran's answer clearly, it sounded like twenty-two.

From a drawer behind her the assistant spread on the counter a khaki-coloured garment, white lacing in the centre and with embroidery of small blue flowers. Gran turned the stays over and felt the white flannel lining. The price was 7s 11¾d. "Could I see the next price," she enquired. The assistant smiled, and turning to another drawer produced another pair of stays more elaborately embroidered than the first pair. They appeared to have more seams and stitching to me and were priced at 8s 11¾d, and Gran decided on these. I watched the cash boxes flying along wires as Gran asked to see nightdresses and chemises. Duly produced, Gran selected chemises with lacy tops threaded through with pink and blue ribbon. Then we went right to the end of the department for long underpants for Grandpa. She chose three pairs of socks for him and two shirts that were priced at 7s 6d each. Back at the first counter she purchased two pairs of black stockings for 6¾d per pair. Jotting down the items on the cash docket, the assistant remarked, "The nightdress was 9s 6d, madam, and the chemises were 4s 6d each." The bill came to over two pounds and Gran placed three folded sovereigns on the counter. The assistant stuck a penny-red stamp and wrote across it, then she folded the money neatly in the bill, reached up for the cash box and unscrewed the lid. In went the money, replaced in a socket. She pulled a lever and the cash flew along the wire to disappear round a corner… so that money was posted.

"They have posted your money, Gran," I gasped.

"Don't be so stupid," she snapped.

"But she put a stamp on your bill."

"That was because madam spent over two pounds," the assistant said smiling. As we sat awaiting the return of some change the assistant neatly wrapped the purchases. It was quite a sizeable parcel and a handle was made of twisted string.

We left the store and crossed the road to wait for a tram. Gran said while we waited, "I think I'll ask your mother if I can get your name put on a list for you to work there when you grow up and leave school. Matthew Rose is a very prestigious place to work. You get board and lodging and five shillings a week pocket money." I never did find out how she knew all this.

"I don't want to work there, I want to be an actress," I said stubbornly as the tram came into sight.

The look on Gran's face was a picture as she pushed me into

the tram. When we were seated she said, "You can get that idea out of your head in double-quick time, your father would never consent to that, young lady." I stared at her sulkily.

"I'll do what I like when I grow up, I don't care what Father says, besides, he swears all the time at Mum, he even swears at Nanny."

"Now I know you're telling lies."

"You're not there all the time," I answered back.

I refused to speak to her no matter what she said. She had called me a liar when I was telling the truth.

When we got off the tram she took me into Duke's, a large linen draper's at the corner of Columbia Road, and bought me a yard of two-inch-wide ribbon for my hair. "An early birthday present," she smiled.

I murmured a polite thank you. Thus we arrived home. Nanny made us tea, we ate some scones and tiny fruit-drop cakes and Gran left. Father came up for his tea and I told him about our shopping.

"My mother said you were sulky, what do you mean by that?"

"Just some hair ribbon," I answered.

"Well that's better than nothing."

I began to unwrap the small bag to show him my gift.

"No time now, later," he said, leaving the room to get down to the bar.

When Mum came in for her tea I was able to tell her about our trip and to tell her I didn't want to work at Matthew Rose when I grew up. She said, "You have many years yet before you leave school behind, so don't let what your grandmother said worry you," and Nanny agreed.

They thought the blue ribbon would look pretty on my dark hair.

Come bath time and Nanny did her usual chore heating up the water and we had a great time playing with the soap trying to blow bubbles through our fingers.

Finally we were ready to be taken down to the bar to say goodnight to our parents. The pub was always very noisy on Saturday nights.

With my blue ribbon in my hand, I ran down the stairs ahead of Nanny into the bar parlour while Nanny carried Jimmy. There was a lot of shouting. I opened the bar door in time to see a man smash a glass on the counter and ram it into another man's face. Blood spurted onto the sleeve of my mother's blue blouse.

"He's cut his head off," I screamed.

Father appeared from nowhere and hustled us into the bar parlour. "Get these bloody kids upstairs," he yelled at Nanny.

I kept screaming, "He cut his head off, I saw him, I saw him and the blood went over Mummy's blouse." I was inconsolable and Jimmy was crying too. Nanny had an awful time getting me to sleep that night, I cried myself to sleep.

This was a day I remember clearly so many years later.

Nanny didn't come on Sundays so next morning I kept asking Mum what had happened to the man's head. Telling me not to worry about it and to try and forget what I saw, she had to get down to the bar because Sunday was the day for the beer pipes to be cleared.

We amused ourselves with our toys and Mum came to prepare dinner. The pub closed at three o'clock after a short morning session and opened again at five o'clock. At seven o'clock, Mum dashed up to put us to bed, she always left the light on for us because we were left alone without Nanny there. And that night I wet the bed.

Mother was furious. "Why did you do it?" she demanded. "It will give Nanny so much more work. Washing and drying things is much harder and takes longer on wet days."

"I couldn't help it, Mummy. I didn't mean it, I'm sorry."

The nightmares began the next night. The head rolled after me, covered in sawdust from the bar floor. I was in a corner and couldn't get away. I woke screaming. Mother came into me and told me to stop it. I woke Jimmy and he began crying but all I could say was the head was running after me. Eventually I slept and next day at school I forgot about my dreams. I came home from school to find Mum crying and Nanny comforting her. After asking why Mummy was crying, I was told to be a good girl and not worry Mummy too much.

And the nightmares and the bed wetting went on and the screaming sessions. One morning Father smacked my bottom, he rubbed the wet sheet all over my face, hair and arm, he swore calling me filthy names.

"I can't help it, don't, don't." I cried loudly as Nanny appeared in our bedroom.

"Mr Munday, that child is ill, please don't punish her like that. She needs a doctor."

"Mind your own bloody business," yelled Father.

"Don't you bloody well swear at me."

Father stopped wiping the wet sheet over me. I looked at her. Nanny swearing, she must be angry.

Mum came into the room, she had been polishing the bar counter, she said, and came up to see what the noise was about.

I was still trying to wriggle away from Father's grip on my wrist. So I bit his hand. He clouted me across the head and I fell onto my bed crying.

"That's right," stormed Mum, "now start on the kids, they're just about your mark." He lifted his arm to hit Mum but Nanny screamed at him, "Don't you dare, don't you dare."

Mum cuddled me tightly. "You think I should take her to see a doctor?"

Nanny nodded. "Last night she told me she was afraid to go to sleep. She keeps dreaming about that fight in the bar."

That evening we waited our turn to see the doctor.

Two steps led to Doctor Simpson's surgery. Mother briefly told him why we had come to him. I sat quietly on a chair.

He turned towards me, leaning forward. "Now suppose you tell me just what happened," he spoke softly.

And I gave him the full detailed description, including Father's disgusting treatment. Psychiatrists hadn't been invented in those long-ago days. He was kind to me. His white curly hair, white moustache and his slightly pink face, gave me the urge to confide in him.

He chatted to Mother over my head for some while, then he spoke to me, "How would you like to go away for a while?"

"Not without Mummy and Jimmy," I answered.

"Your Mother tells me you have an auntie living in the country."

I looked at Mum.

"Your Aunt Alice, remember?"

For a small round bottle of tonic his fee was a shilling.

"I'm not ill, Mummy," I said when we stepped outside the surgery. "What did he say about me, and why do I have to go away?"

"You need to be away from the pub for a while, that will make you forget those dreams you have."

My sixth birthday came. I received cards from Mum and Nanny but no presents (Father's orders) because I was a lazy, dirty kid. I began to dislike Father very much.

Mother told me she had written to Aunt Alice; there were no phones in those days. One day towards the end of February, Mum came to school with me to explain the reason why I would be absent for a while, and the next day my cousin Florence collected me to take me to Aunt Alice. Florence was her nineteen-year-old daughter.

West Ham in those days was considered "in the country". It was a long journey entailing two tram rides and two bus rides. We walked down a tree-lined road and in front of each house was a low brick wall topped by fancy iron railings, behind which were neat privet hedges. Florence let us in using a key and a black dog bounded along the passage to greet us, stopping short and growling when he saw me.

"It's all right, Tosh," she said, "sit." The dog sat sniffing at me as I edged past him. Aunt Alice appeared between curtains at the end of the passage.

"Come on, little Belle, he won't hurt you and we are going to make you better."

"I'm not ill," I protested as she gave me a bear-like hug.

"Are you still having those nasty old dreams?" she asked as she led me into a cosy living-room.

I nodded. "And I'm still making the bed wet," I admitted shamefaced. "But I can't help it, Aunt Alice, that head rolls after me and I scream and Father gets cross."

"I suppose that's natural," she mused.

Aunt Alice was tall but fatter than my mum; she too had black hair and had a bun at the back of her head. She had laughing blue eyes and a rosy face; she also sang a lot as she worked around the house. She was also my godmother.

Florence worked in an office and Uncle Bill worked at Tilbury Docks as a ganger – a type of foreman.

When Uncle Bill came in from work that first evening, he hugged me and swung me into the air – a thing Father had never done. He kissed Aunt Alice and Florence and having said grace we had a nice dinner of meat and vegetables and jam pudding and custard afterwards. They chatted and laughed over the meal... all so different from meals at the pub where Nanny forbade any speaking at table from us children.

Uncle Bill was a very tall man and very thin, he had a long face and a long straight nose and a wide mouth, and most of all he had brown twinkling eyes. He always seemed to be laughing.

And in Aunt Alice's house there was a bathroom. The large white bath filled one end of the room; next to it was a toilet basin and a WC with a lid. This fascinated me; I went there often, just to lift the seat up and down. I went to bed early that night in a small room by myself. Florence turned the gas burner low and saying goodnight closed the door. I stared at the dim light and began crying quietly for my brother Jimmy, then I was asleep. I was awakened some time later by Florence who sat me on a small potty. That night I did not wet the bed and had no bad dreams.

It was my first dry night for nearly a month.

My dresses and changes of underclothes were packed into a soft cane case, and now Aunt Alice was finding me a dress after she had bathed me. There were two taps at the end of the bath. I held my hands under the warm running water and asked my aunt where the hot water came from. "There is a small boiler behind the fire grate and when the fire is lit, we get hot water very quickly."

"Nanny boils water in the big kettle for our baths," I told her as she sponged me.

"Yes, I know. It must be very trying for your parents." I hadn't thought much about that.

She found a dress with pink flowers printed all over the material, then she found the blue ribbon Granny Munday had bought me. "This will look nice with that dress." She smiled at me as I shuddered.

"Now what was that for?"

"I don't like that ribbon… it's blue."

"It will look nice on your dark curls."

"Please, Aunt Alice, you have it, I don't like it, it's like Mummy's blouse with blood on it."

"Come now, don't be silly, it's pretty," and she insisted on cutting the ribbon in two. She tied a bow each side of my hair.

Florence sat me on the potty again that night, but the nightmare was more vivid. I woke screaming and the bed was soaked.

Uncle Bill came into the room already dressed for work.

"Come on, Belle, we can't have this, you know. Look how you're frightening Florence and your aunt." I was inconsolable.

"That head came after me," I sobbed.

"You mustn't scream in the night like this, your uncle has to get up very early and had you cried earlier you could have disturbed his rest. How often does this happen?"

"At home? Every night," I answered miserably.

I sat in a dry part of the bed while Aunt Alice told me to go to sleep as it was too early for me to get up. I was crying quietly. When would the dream stop and more importantly, when would I stop wetting the bed? I never did this dirty thing until I saw that man's head off. That was clear in my reasoning. I was sure of that because the head always rolled after me in the sawdust.

Chapter Nine

So the winter passed into spring and summer. On the days of sunshine and hot weather, when the fire was lit twice a week for baths, the house became really too warm. Doors and windows were opened for coolness. Before Florence left for the office she arranged papers for me to keep up with my schooling in arithmetic and writing. She did a list of sums, additions, subtractions and division. She would cut a paragraph from the newspaper for me to copy and also a composition on a subject she thought I knew something about. She corrected these papers each evening and commented, good or not good. Aunt Alice did dressmaking at home for different neighbours and taught me to sew. She taught me to darn. She didn't think I did this too well and said my stitches were like cat's teeth. I played a lot with Tosh too.

Some Sundays we went for bus rides to a park and we had a picnic lunch. I liked that very much and gradually the dreams became less frequent and slowly the bed wetting ceased.

I always insisted on never wearing the blue hair ribbon, I didn't like the colour and Aunt Alice didn't press me for that reason.

Mother wrote every week, sometimes enclosing a short note from Nanny who always reminded me to be a good girl, do as I was told and to remember my manners and say my prayers. Sometimes my aunt read passages of Mum's letters to me and some of her answers to the letters.

At the end of August Auntie thought I was ready to go home. For nearly three weeks the bed had been dry and I had only one bad night.

I was sorry to leave, but as Auntie reminded me, I had school to go to. And so I returned home to a big surprise.

Mother wasn't in the bar, and saying a brief hello to Father Florence and I went upstairs to find Mum feeding a baby.

I stared at the baby, at Mum and at Nanny.

"How long have you had it?" I asked in amazement.

"It isn't an it, it's your baby brother, Billy."

"When did Billy come?"

"He was born on the 17th of July." Mum smiled. "I asked Aunt Alice not to tell you, to give you a surprise."

Mum wiped the baby's face and held him towards me saying, "Have a look at him, he's so lovely."

I went closer, he had a small round face and a small button nose, as I looked at him he opened his eyes then yawned.

"He hasn't any teeth." I looked at Nanny. "Are you going to look after him too?"

She laughed. "Of course I am, I'm his nanny too."

Florence held the baby while Mum prepared tea. Florence asked me, "Were you surprised to see your baby brother?"

I nodded asking, "Were Mummy and Father surprised too?"

"Not really," she replied, and after tea she left. Mother told me Uncle George had died at work and Aunt Minne had moved from her house in York Street into buildings and had signed the twins into care to foster parents. "I could never do that to my children," said Mum.

"When are the twins coming back to Auntie?" asked Jimmy.

"When they are fourteen." At that time George was ten, the twins were seven and Will was four (these were our cousins). I don't think there was a widow's pension in those days. Returning to school in September after the summer holiday, Mother explained the reason I had missed school. I was shown into a large classroom, my new teacher was Miss Bernes. She was tall and fair-haired. There were five rows of desks and in each row were five desks. We sat two to a desk and I counted forty-three girls in this class. Lessons began with decimals. I hadn't a clue. Despite Florence teaching me spelling and arithmetic I was far behind the other girls. The teacher called me to her table, explaining and giving me simple decimal sums and adding homework I began learning quickly. Then we learned percentages and fractions.

After almost two weeks back at school, in the quietness of the morning lesson came the sudden ringing of the school bell. The girls rushed into the playground followed by our teacher and we formed drill lines, teacher at the head. The playground was filled with crowds from the infants' classes too. "Fire drill," my friend said as the teacher began calling our names. We answered.

Telling Nanny about the fire drill, she thought it a good idea.

"Nanny, have you seen my train engine?" asked Jimmy.

"Where did you last play with it?" Nanny asked. "Look there."

A few weeks later I had the nightmare dream again. The bloodied head came after me, I screamed, sobbing. Father came into the room and smacked by bottom hard, saying: "Now you have something to scream about. Are you happy now you've woken the baby?" I cried myself to sleep.

My baby doll disappeared, just like Jimmy's train engine.

Father organised brake outings and on this sunny second Sunday in September a gaudily painted brake, drawn by four brown horses waited outside the pub, as did ladies and gents, dressed in their Sunday best and carrying packages of sandwiches. They began finding seats in the brake. Nanny and her husband, Mr Renick, were taking Jimmy and me along for the ride. Streamers were tied to the side lamps, the horses had paper flowers tied in their hair. Men sitting with the horse driver cheered as the ride began and a trumpeter blew long blasts of music. The brake was open-sided with shining brass rails round. We sang songs as the trumpeter played and people stared as we bowled along the Hackney Road. We were going to The Rising Sun, Epping Forest, I was told. We stopped where there was a large pub and a pond from which the horses drank thirstily. "Are we in the forest?" I was told this was The Green Man pub, Leytonstone, where the horses were changed. A new team of horses was quickly harnessed and we were off again. Finally we reached our destination. The horses, released from the harness, roamed into the forest. Everyone was happy to stretch legs and wander into the pub. We sat on a bench while Nanny brought us some lemonade and we ate sandwiches. There were swings, coconut shies, roundabouts and hoopla tables under the trees. It looked so pleasant. "I wish Mummy was here," said Jimmy. Mr Renick won a coconut and gave us pieces to eat. Jimmy and I slept in the afternoon in the brake. Time for home. We again stopped to change horses and arrived home at about eight o'clock. Nanny gave us a quick wash and we went to bed contented. Next day at school we had to write a composition about what we did over the weekend. I went to town about the brake outing and received top marks for detail and expression. On the last Sunday of that September came an event that changed our lives.

On Sundays the pub opened at 9.30 a.m., and was closed from 2.00 until 5.00 p.m. Father coped with the help of our pot man, a Mr Poulton. Mother cooked dinner and tended our wants and dinner was eaten while the pub was closed. After the meal Father slept. Nanny never came Sundays.

After dinner on Sundays, Mummy used to take us to a small park in Ion Square. This Sunday from Thulleries Street we turned into Busk Street where Nanny lived. She was waiting at her door and told us to hurry inside. "You managed it then?" she asked.

Mummy nodded. "His last words were, be back at five sharp."

"Then he's in for a shock," laughed Nanny. The room was bright with sunshine and on the shelf I saw my baby doll beside Jimmy's train.

Mr Renick helped us with our coats and we ate a lovely tea with jelly and custard and small cakes. They chatted, some words I heard, like "furnished", "the best I could find", "it's near". Mummy and Nanny washed the dishes. "Now, be good, do as Mr Renick says, we won't be too long."

We played with our toys, Baby Billy was sleeping in an armchair.

When Mum and Nanny returned we dressed and left, walking along the darkening streets. I asked, "When are we going to the pub?" Mum sighed.

"Not anymore, darling, I hope." What did she mean? I was six, Jimmy was four and the baby just ten weeks old. We finally came to a house and Nanny let us in with a key. "Go quietly upstairs," she said to Mummy. Mum had carried the baby while Nanny had the pushchair piled high with a large bundle. We entered a large room. A bed faced the door, a table stood between two long windows. There was a couch and two armchairs, two half-cupboards in fireside recesses and a wash handstand against a wall on which stood a large basin and water jug. Nanny didn't stay too long. She undid the large bundle that held sheets, blankets and linen and some of our clothes.

The house, 7 Holmes Street, was in the same area as the pub. If we were running from him, he would soon find us, I thought.

Mum opened the door to a knock. The lady of the house introduced herself. She was Mrs Snowcill. Mum asked where the gas meter was as she needed hot water to bathe the baby. It was outside the door on the landing. Mum cranked in some pennies, filled a kettle and lit a gas ring standing on the hearth in the fireplace.

While Mummy bathed the baby, Nanny made the bed with bed linen from the bundle brought with us. In those days, babies wore long calico robes adorned with wide embroidered lace; underneath there was a long flannel wrap. Comfortable in a clean nappy and long nightdress, Nanny laid him on the bed.

"I'll bring you food early in the morning," she told Mother and saying goodnight to us left. Mummy washed me, then Jimmy. He lay next to the baby and Mummy put me at the bottom of the bed.

"How long are we living here?" I asked.

"I hope we will find something better soon, darling. Go to sleep now, maybe tomorrow you can stay home from school."

Sitting up in bed, I watched Mummy empty the water into a bucket, which she took with her from the room. Back, she filled the kettle, asking, "Would you like some tea?" I nodded. I looked at the green blinds that Nanny had drawn as soon as we entered the room. They covered pretty lace curtains tied back with cords. There was crockery on the half-cupboards and there was a clock on the mantel-shelf that was not ours. It was all so different from the pub. I drank the tea Mummy gave me.

"When are we going back to the pub, Mummy?"

"Never, I hope. Your father has been too cruel to me."

I had often seen him hit her, never on the face. She had to serve in the bar next day. He was always friendly to customers and they all seemed to like him. Mummy said he showed off.

Nanny came next morning with lots of groceries, saying, "This lot should last you a few days, so I think you should stay inside for a time and keep her from school. He could follow her from there."

"I shall never be able to repay you for all your help, you will have lost your job too now the children are with me."

Nanny laughed. "It is about time I retired, I think. I'll see you again." Mummy hugged her and she left.

I woke next morning wondering where I was. Mummy was already heating water for tea. I had washed when Jimmy woke. We had breakfast, just bread and jam. On the wash handstand was a large enamel jug. This Mummy used to fill with water. After breakfast Mummy said, "Come, I'll show you where the WC is." It was downstairs across a small yard. It was clean and there were squares of newspaper hanging by cotton on the wall.

"My teacher will be angry if I miss school, Mummy."

"I'll write you a note to give her, don't worry."

"Is Nanny coming today?" asked Jimmy.

"I'm not sure, play with your train while I bathe and feed Baby." He lay on the bed, pink and clean in just a nappy, kicking his legs in the air.

"How old is he, Mummy?" asked Jimmy. "He has no teeth."

"A couple of days over ten weeks." Mummy sounded sad.

We stayed in the room for a week; Nanny brought food twice. On Saturday we visited Aunt Minne in the buildings. She was pleased to see us, as were our cousins, George and Gill. Auntie and Mummy talked for a long time. When it was dark we returned to our own one room.

I returned to school on Monday, taking a note from Mum and my finished homework. My teacher said, "Thank your mother for writing."

Living like this must have been difficult for Mother. Looking back, I remember standing in that large basin and being washed down, and then it was Jimmy's turn for washing. All water was heated on the gas ring and the bucket emptied each time. I had not had my hair washed all that week, so different from Nanny keeping us clean at the pub.

On the Saturday at Auntie's, Cousin George was sketching an ornament, Gill was showing Jimmy letters he had learned after he began school's summer break. "Do you like living in these buildings, George?"

"Yes, there are big baths in the bath house, it's good."

"I wish we had a bath. What else is there?"

"Well, there's lots of kids and there are large grounds all round the blocks where you can play. Now, shut up, I'm sketching."

"Where has Auntie gone?"

"Bethnal Green market, I expect."

"Will she be long and where is my mum?"

"My mother will be home when her money runs out and that won't be long. I don't know where your mother is so shut it."

The baby woke and began crying. "Can I make Baby a sugar dummy?"

"Do what you like," he snapped. I looked into Baby's bag and found a piece of clean linen. With a small ball of margarine then a spoonful of sugar, I tied it securely into a small ball and pinned it safely to the baby's bib. He stopped crying immediately I put the sugar dummy into his mouth.

A lovely look of contentment came over his small pink face.

A little later Auntie came home with two filled shopping bags.

"My poor arms really ache, I'll put away the shopping then get you kids a sandwich. Anything happened?" she asked. George shrugged; I shook my head, but wondered at the question.

"I'm hungry, Auntie," said Jimmy. "We only had bread and jam for breakfast."

Auntie laughed. "Well, that's better than nothing."

About an hour later Mother returned without Nanny and the pushchair.

"Everything go all right?" Auntie asked Mummy.

"I'll have to wait three or four days," Mummy answered. "We'll talk about it when the kids go to sleep. I hope I'm lucky."

We were into our third week at Mrs Snowcill's house.

I must describe the flat where Auntie lived. The room was large and L-shaped. In a deep recess was a large red and gold settee, and there were two matching armchairs. A table stood in the centre of the room and there were six chairs to match the settee. A tall cream-painted dresser stood against one wall. Auntie's machine was beneath the window. She stitched shoe uppers. Two wide cupboards, the top one for food, the lower one for coal, were next to a closed-in kitchen range, and next to that was an iron, black leaded cooker. While we stayed with Auntie, Mummy and the baby slept on the settee and Jimmy and I slept in the two armchairs, the seats facing.

Water was drawn from a tap over a yellow stone sink on the landing. Auntie sent me to fill a jug. I looked out of the window to see the block of buildings facing. I saw the thick iron railings that surrounded the roof opposite and saw washing flapping in the breeze.

Mother and Auntie got busy with housework. George said suddenly, "I'm pleased my mother is thinking of moving. Your father had you turned out from Mrs Snowcill's. If he finds out your mother is here, he'll come round and frighten *my* mother, so I hope she finds somewhere else to live soon." He looked at Auntie as she came into the room. "How soon will we be moving, Mum?" he asked. "I've told Belle we're moving."

"As soon as I find somewhere suitable, I'll let you know."

The next Saturday, Auntie cared for the baby while we played with our toys. We didn't see Mother until late evening. When she came in she said, "Thanks, Minne, for your help. Everything is ready. Have they been good?"

I heard Mother say, "I've seen Lucy and she is so pleased."

After dinner we all set out, Auntie locking her door. We went up the stairs, round landings and more stairs. On the top landing Mother opened the door of Number 79 and there was all our furniture from Aunt Lucy's. It seemed Mother had had removals men help her shift the furniture and get the room straightened ready for us to settle in. We had some tea then Auntie and my cousins left. I went into the other room; there were just two rooms. Our bed was there, the high chair Jimmy sat in when a baby and the pushchair. Wall-to-wall bare boards and the small fire grate completed that room. There was a large window that looked out onto another block of buildings and miles and miles of chimney pots. The playing grounds looked a long way down.

I took a note to my teacher giving our change of address.

"So you're not living at the public house?" she queried. "Has your mother given you the reason?"

I shook my head. "We've been staying with my auntie for a few days."

"Give me your homework and go to your desk. Don't ever go near the pub, Belle. Promise me, and if ever you see your father in the street, run like mad away from him."

We were together and Mum resumed her machining and household chores. She went to Granny Munday's each Thursday to collect the five shillings. She never went inside that house fearing Father would be there.

Cousin George and Bill went to the same school as I did. I had their company mornings; we went home separately.

One day I said to Mum, "George told me Father came to Mrs Snowcill to kill us. Is that true?" It was then that Mum told me what happened.

Mother went to Granny Munday. She told me she was asking for ten shillings weekly for our keep. She came back triumphant, waving a ten-shilling note. "I threatened to take him to court and Grandfather gave in immediately." The money was ready each Thursday. There were very many children playing in the grounds. We played hopscotch and many ring games. I played whip and top, peg top, five stones (gobs and bonsters), statues, and we had skipping ropes. A man with a barrel organ played in the street and we danced to the music. We were healthy, happy but often hungry as Mum tried to make ends meet. Always she paid the rent first, 4s 6d weekly. If it wasn't paid by nine o'clock Monday night, a notice to quit was pushed through the letter box. Mother often said Aunt Lucy's words. A leopard doesn't change its spots or a tiger its stripes.

As Jimmy was nearly five years old, Mum had been able to get him placed in school two weeks previously. It was now the first week into November. I collected my cousin Bill and Jimmy at midday and we could not get home quickly enough to see our flat. There were five flights of sixteen stone stairs to reach our landing. The door opened straight into the room. Sausages were frying on the cooker, which was just inside the door. Potatoes were boiling and a bright fire burned in the kitchen range, which could be entirely enclosed. Oilcloth was on the floor and the table in the centre of the room, devoid of a cloth, was set with plates and cutlery. Originally we had two chairs, now there were four more and Auntie said Mum had bought them from a second-hand shop "up the road".

"That's nice, or we would have to sit on the floor," Jimmy said.

I looked round the room as I ate my dinner. Next to the fireplace were two large cupboards, the top one was for use as a pantry, the one beneath was used for coals. At right-angles to the cupboards was a wide window that overlooked Columbia Road. All the woodwork was painted a pale cream and the walls painted a mid-pink distemper. Looking into the next room, there was just our bed and Jimmy's baby high chair and wall-to-wall floorboards. Mum's machine was beneath the window, and so far there were no curtains, but we were not overlooked being so high up.

While we were at school during the afternoon, Auntie had taken Mum to the factory and Mum became an out-door machinist the same as Aunt Minne.

Home from school in the afternoon I found Mum already stitching the uppers of small sizes of shoes and the baby fast asleep in the bedroom. She left the machine immediately and got some tea ready for us and I felt it was good to be home and warm. There was now some short curtaining at the window and it was very cosy and it was our home. Asking questions, Mum told us we could buy cheap coal from the coal shed in the buildings and she had bought twenty-eight pounds for sixpence, the price being two shillings for a hundredweight.

Auntie had said there was a tearoom where, if you put your tea into the teapot, it would be filled with boiling water. This was free and there were baths opened on different days for the tenants to bathe and when we came home tomorrow (Tuesday) she would take us to have a lovely bath. We couldn't wait for the next day to come. The one who was bathed each day was Baby Billy and Mum always sat with her back to us when she breast-fed him. Next morning she took the finished work to the factory and was given a large bundle of uppers to stitch and a pay book.

Before we had tea on the first Tuesday, Mum packed towels, soap and some clean clothes into a bag and down we went to the bathrooms. The lady attendant (Mrs Ruler) spoke to Mum and she took our baby into a small room then showed us into a room of white glazed bricks, a small window near the ceiling, a huge white bath, a wooden seat fixed to the wall and a cork mat on the stone floor. Mrs Ruler controlled the water from outside and a copper tap poured water into the bath. Mum began quickly to undress us, Jimmy was afraid, he said it was too big, but Mum lifted us in and with a soapy flannel soon had us liking the big bath. I had never seen such a big bath. I thought about the long galvanised bath Nanny had to use and wondered how and when my parents had bathed when we were at the pub. My hair had been washed too and given a towel I dried myself while Mum towelled Jimmy. Dressed, we waited outside near Mrs Ruler's room while Mum bathed and I kept rubbing my hair dry. Other mothers came in with small children, I think there were eight or nine bathrooms and this was all free.

There were seven flats on each landing, one-room lets and five two-room lets. Each landing had three toilets, two sinks, a laundry and a rubbish shoot. White glazed bricks were half-way up the walls, the top half being the same mid-pink distemper as in the rooms. The sinks were a shallow yellow stone beneath two large windows. The doors to the toilets were brown-grained and varnished and there were rules regarding cleaning.

Mum told us the caretakers were a Mr and Mrs Upton, living in F Block, and a Mr and Mrs Ruler, who lived in C Block and were "on call" during the day. The rota for using the laundry was agreed among the tenants themselves. Once in seven it was Mum's "turn" to scrub the stone stairs and once in each three weeks her "turn" came to clean our half of the landing, the two toilets and the windows over the sink, the brass tap and sink.

Home from school we were having tea. Mum had cut slices of bread and I was toasting them before the nice fire. It was dark outside and the fan-like flame from the small finger-like gas burner shone a pinky light over the room and suddenly Jimmy said, "Do you think Daddy will like living here after being at the pub, Mum?"

"Oh, Jimmy, Jimmy," she said, "don't ask that question."

I put the toasted slice on a plate ready for Mum to butter.

"Sit down and listen," she said quietly. "I have to tell you this, although I had hoped to talk about it when you were a little older. Your father doesn't love us anymore, so we have left him. He has found a lady he loves much more than he does us."

Jimmy began crying and Mum went to him, giving him lovely cuddles. I think I was glad, I am sure it didn't sink in that now we were on our own.

"Mummy, we don't want him, he was spiteful, wasn't he?"

"Yes, dear, and I became tired of being a punching bag."

"What's a punching bag?" asked Jimmy.

"Never mind," said Mum. "Now listen to me."

What she said next I am sure did not register too clearly at that time, but as time passed we understood better.

It was a few weeks before Baby Billy was born. Some ladies who drank at the pub had told Mum they had seen Father with a lady when they had gone to Southend on an outing from their Mothers' Meeting Club one Thursday. The lady told these friends she was Mrs Munday.... Mother didn't tell us then that the woman was pregnant – something else we learned later. So with Nanny's help, every Thursday, which was Father's day off, Nanny had collected some bed linen, a few clothes for us and nappies for the baby and had taken them to her house. Then she found a room at Mrs Snowcill's house, which was at the end of the same road as the pub. Being that Mum was in such a desperate hurry, this was the best Nanny could do. Everyone who rented a house let one or two rooms those days but it had to do for the time being. Mum told us she couldn't go to Aunt Lucy, that would be the first place Father would visit. Mum and Nanny both prayed the Sunday she chose to leave would be fine and give her an excuse to take us to the park. And it was.

Of the five shillings weekly Father paid Mum, she had managed to save £13 7s 5d. There wasn't very much left of that now.

Father had soon found out where we were and on the Thursday night, four days after we had left and when the pub closed, he had begun throwing stones at the window. Finally Mum had to let him in. On entering the room, he said he had come to shoot Mum and levelled a revolver at her. She said if he shot the kids first she wouldn't care what happened to her. She told us he pointed the gun at Jimmy then said he couldn't do it and put the gun on the table. Then Mum said she rushed downstairs and woke Mr Snowcill for help. He turned Father out of the house saying if Father came back he would have him locked up.

Next day Mrs Snowcill asked Mum to leave at the end of the week because she would not have her children upset by the "goings on".

That is how we came to Mum's sister, Aunt Minne, and she suggested filling in a form to try for a flat in the buildings, so here we were.

Mum finished by saying, "I have told Granny Munday I want

ten shillings weekly for you three kids, he can pay it to her and I'll collect it Thursdays, then he can't say he has paid the money when he hasn't."

"Is that ten shillings for each one, Mum?" I asked.

"Heavens, no, ten shillings to keep three of you."

The one thing that I realised was that Father had attempted to kill us and Mother was frightened of him, so we had to be afraid too.

"I want you to be good kids and do as I say. I'll look after you and work for you. Jimmy, you will be five in December and Belle, you will be seven in February, so you are both old enough to be told this."

She smiled and ruffled Jimmy's hair. "It will soon be Christmas, but there won't be any toys. There isn't a Father Christmas, parents fill children's stockings, so as I haven't too much money I'll buy a blanket for our bed and you will get a new pair of shoes each. I'm sorry, but at least while we live here we will be happy together, and I'll do my machining and earn some money. We'll get by, you'll see."

"No Father Christmas and no toys," said Jimmy dismally.

I am sure we did not understand fully all Mum told us until she said, "If ever you see your father in the street, run home as quickly as you can. I don't want him to find out where we live, and don't tell Granny Munday if she asks you." We solemnly promised.

And so we settled down to our new way of living, but like everything we soon forgot Mum's warning.

Chapter Ten

We soon learned the names of the many children that lived in the buildings and as we played in the grounds surrounding the blocks, spring rolled into summer, it never seemed to rain.

The games we played

There were phases for different games. Times for wooden hoops that we bashed with sticks to send them bowling along the pavements, then we sat on the kerbs to play five stones (gobs and bonsters), then whip tops we slashed along or peg tops at which my brother could, with a flick of a finger, pick up and keep spinning along his arm. Although I could flick the top into my hand, I could never run it along my arm. Then there was the spinning Diablo; this I was good at throwing into the air and catching still spinning. There was shuttlecock. For a half-penny you could buy a cork with a few feathers stuck into it and with a piece of cardboard knock it into the air. There were ball games and skipping games, follow my lead, higher and higher, double Dutch and bumps. Then there were games where we formed large rings singing songs to each one: *In and Out the Windows, I Sent a Letter to my Love, Poor Jimmy is Weeping, The Farmer's in his Den.* Then in straight lines we would sing *On the Mountains* or *Do you Know the Muffin Man?* and *Oranges and Lemons.* We played statues and blew over cigarette cards on low windowsills. Sometimes we would try to climb lamp-posts trying to reach the bar just to hang on to, then drop to the pavement, and as the evenings began to get dark we would wait for the lamp lighter and watch him poke his long pole through the small opening to light the street lamp. I feel sorry for the children of today, television has robbed them of so much happiness playing with other children, and then streets were safe for children, we did not live in fear of what might happen if one was out late. Our caretaker would come round the grounds at nine o'clock at night calling, "Upstairs or in the street." Tenants were not annoyed after that time at night and they made quite sure the grounds were cleared by that time.

After we had lived in the buildings for about six months, Aunt Minne moved to Goldsmith's Row. She had three rooms and a scullery over a tool shop. We missed playing with our cousins, but as Auntie said, "The boys needed a room to themselves." Meanwhile, we were still sleeping four in our bed; Mum, Baby and Jimmy at the top, me at the bottom. Apart from small general shops, nearly every other shop had a small printed card in the corner of the window reading, "weekly payments taken", where you could select goods and the shop keeper would store the goods, give you a card and on the final payment you collected the goods. This way Mum purchased quite a few clothes for us. Looking out of our window, rooftops and chimney pots stretched to the horizon. The summer was hot and school holidays were enjoyable. Four of us kids danced round a barrel organ that "did the pubs" on Fridays. We began opposite the buildings at a pub we called Crumps, then on to the Baxendale, next the Old Oak, next the Birdcage then over to The Planter. At each pub one of us kids would go round with his cap, we usually had some onlookers as we did high kicks and one girl, Emily Western, could kick her legs out sideways while down on her haunches.

We always gave the money to the organ grinder and when we left him at The Planter, he always gave us a penny each. This I always took home to Mum. I could eat lemons like most people eat oranges and I would save two farthings to buy a lemon, other kids would buy sweets. One day a trumpeter was playing outside Crumps. He was playing *Nellie Dean.* I stood on the narrow pavement listening to him, noisily sucking my lemon, and I thought he was playing very funnily. He suddenly stopped playing and putting his hand in his pocket said, "Here's a penny, go and suck that bloody lemon in the next street." I grabbed the penny and ran in case he changed his mind. Giving it to Mum, she wanted to know where it came from. When I told her she laughed, saying, "By golly, you must have made his mouth water so much he couldn't play his trumpet."

Now there was something else in the sky; great sausage-like balloons, barrage balloons. Mum told us that the war – World War I – wouldn't last too long. "Be over by Christmas," people said... but so much for that. It lasted four terrible years and thousands of brave men died.

There were some sporadic raids by German Zeppelin airships. When the siren sounded all the tenants locked their doors and descended to the lower landings and stairways in total darkness, chatting until the sirens sounded the all clear. We heard a bomb had fallen in Holmes Street.

When I arrived home from school lunch time, Mum asked me to go to Auntie's to borrow sixpence until Thursday and on the way home to buy half a pound of sausages and two pounds of potatoes and to hurry back as she had to cook dinner for us. As the sausages cost four pence, I would have a penny change. I decided to walk down Tuilerie Street and see the house in Holmes Street that had been damaged by the bomb. Half-way down Tuilerie Street was a large removals van, drawn by two burly horses. I stood as a wardrobe was being lowered to the pavement, tied by ropes held by three men from an upstairs window. The polished 'robe gleamed in the sunlight. "I'm going to have one of those when I grow up," I thought. I was so deep in speculation.

I spun round as a heavy hand gripped my shoulder. I turned, ready to lash out, to face Father. I stared at him uncertainly.

"What are you doing here?" he asked smiling.

"I'm going to Auntie's to borrow sixpence," I replied unguardedly.

"Still at the same school?"

I nodded and said, "You never come to see us, do you?"

"Now how can I? I don't even know where you live."

"We live in Guinness's Buildings, number seventy…." Too late I remembered Mum's warning: "If you see your father, run home."

He handed me a shilling saying, "Take this, no need to go to your aunt's now." I ran away quickly and collecting the sausages and potatoes rushed in to tell Mum what had happened.

"What did he say, tell me, and what did you say, for him to give you a shilling?" She sounded so angry.

"I don't remember," I said.

"Come on, you repeat word for word. You are always reciting that poetry, you remember all right, so tell me?"

I slowly repeated the conversation; she put her hands to her head.

"Oh, Belle, what have you done? We have lived here in peace for just over eighteen months. That is one reason why I always went to your gran's myself to collect the ten shillings, knowing she wouldn't ask me where we lived now… God knows what will happen. After all I said, the way I have warned all of you. I could smack you, I really could."

"I didn't tell him the number."

"Don't be so stupid. He only has to ask at the superintendent's office, now we have to be on our guard always."

She began preparing our dinner in silence. I stood close to her.

"Mummy, I am sorry, truly I am." I just could not understand her anger.

Now every time Mum took her finished work back, she locked us in, always taking the key with her. We had to knock on the door to be let in from school and if we went for an errand, again the door was locked. Slowly her need for caution communicated itself to us and we became a little scared to play in the grounds with the other kids.

During the time we had lived there I became a real little street rake. Gone were all the refined manners Nanny had taught me. I fought and scratched like an alley cat. If I got scratches and bruises, I made sure the kid I was fighting had scratches and bruises too. In the East End it is the survival of the fittest and I made sure Jimmy and I survived. Mum said we must learn to fight our own battles; she had to work to feed us and keep a roof over our heads.

After about a month it happened.

Chapter Eleven

It was Saturday and it had been raining. I was playing on the landing near the door with two friends from a lower landing when I heard a noise. I looked through the railings and saw Father staggering drunkenly on the stairs. "Is your mother in?" he demanded.

I rushed in to Mum before he was half-way up the stairs. "Father," I screamed, "and he's drunk."

Billy, now nearly two years old, was sitting on the table and Mum was tying his shoe laces. He was a sturdy little boy with fair curly hair.

Father entered, rolled against the table and fell onto a chair near the window between the machine and the wall. Mum snatched up Billy.

"What do you want?" she said. "We don't bother you."

"Come and give your daddy a kiss," he said to me.

I stood well away from him but Mum pushed me towards him. I still hung back, he put out an arm to grab me as I saw a knife in his right hand. I screamed just as the door burst open and two men dashed in.

"Run, Missus, and take the kids, he's drank half a bottle of whisky, so get out now."

Mum needed no telling twice, and pushing me in front of her she asked, "Where is Jimmy?" We ran down the stairs just as Jimmy was coming along the next landing. A Mrs Bevan said as we hurried down the stairs, "Go into my flat, you'll be all right." Her number was 77 and in a small recess. There was loud shouting and swearing coming from our flat and the neighbours were all agog. We listened behind Mrs Bevan's door at Father, shouting, "I'll kill them all" – with swear words thrown in.

Mrs Bevan came into her flat a little later. "He asked where you had gone and we pointed down the stairs." She went to her window and looking out said, "They have reached the grounds, those men are very helpful."

"I cannot thank you enough, Mrs Bevan, if you'll keep an eye on the kids, I'll get some coats for them and Billy's pushchair and take them to my sister's place for the weekend… and thank you again."

Mum came back with coats and soap and towels and strapping Billy in his pushchair we set off for Aunt Minne's. I fully realised the mistake I had made giving Father our address. Supposing those men hadn't followed him. I had been completely absorbed in the furniture removals and off my guard. Father's hand on my shoulder, him being at that place and forgetting Mum's warning, how could I have forgotten, and now what?

A side door next to the tool shop led to a passage and up a flight of stairs into Auntie's flat. At the top of the stairs was the scullery and another door to the toilet.

A short flight of stairs led to two rooms, one the boys' bedroom and the large room over the shop was the living-room. More stairs led to Auntie's bedroom. Mum was telling Auntie the reason we had arrived so suddenly. I heard Auntie say, "Don't worry, we'll manage."

We had sandwiches for our lunch and later fish and chips for dinner. Mum slept with Auntie and I lay on the settee with Billy. Jimmy slept in the two armchairs pushed seat-to-seat together. I couldn't sleep, this was all my fault. I lay thinking about the two years we had lived at 79, of the lovely grounds we had played in, of the triangle by the first gate along the railings that bordered Columbia Road, along by the bathrooms where we could play hop-scotch (the one place in the grounds kids were allowed to chalk) and of the games we played. We had been happy, sometimes naughty and smacked, but loved and cuddled by Mum when we were good. I thought how Mum had managed with so little money… how many times we had dinners that had cost just three ha'pence and that had fed the four of us: a penny saveloy and a half-pence-worth of pease-pudding bought from the German pork butcher. The saveloy was cut lengthwise into four and the pease-pudding spread on two slices of bread for each of us.

Who out there can remember the soup kitchens? One entrance in Columbia Road and the other one in Virginia Road? Here one could buy a pint of thick pea soup for three ha'pence, take your own jug or for a penny, one could sit at a table and be served a small basin of soup and a thick slice of bread. We often had that in winter. Mum would add a cup of water and boil it again and it was shared, the chopped vegetables tasted delicious. The work Mum did, machining shoe uppers, was not paid too well. Three shillings and sixpence for one dozen pairs for best work and sometimes as low as two shillings for the same number if the sizes were smaller.

Perhaps now Father had found us he would make us go back to the pub. I didn't want that… stop thinking… go to sleep. My eyes felt full of smoke and I realised I was crying. Why had I been so stupid? Why?

I awoke, Billy was patting my face. "Wake, Belle. Was that man our dad? I never knew we had a dad."

"He isn't a good dad, Billy, he… he…." I couldn't tell my small brother how spiteful Father was or how he had hit Mum.

Mum came into the room. "Come on, up you get, all of you." We followed Mum into the scullery, she was carrying a kettle of hot water and very quickly we were washed and dressed. Cousin George was out. He had a paper round. He delivered papers before school and again in the evenings. He received three shillings weekly and extra on Sundays. Auntie gave him sixpence for himself. A whole sixpence, that would take ages to spend. Auntie told Mum the money helped. We all had toast for breakfast, stew for dinner and bread and jam for tea. George and Cousin Billy, Jimmy and I left for school from Auntie's Monday. Mum said to come home to the buildings dinnertime.

It would be good to be home once again. I collected Jimmy and arrived home to find Mum very upset, she was frying bacon and eggs for our dinner.

Billy was seated in his high chair. "Wash your hands and sit down," Mum said crossly. We went out to the sink on the landing and ran cold water through our fingers. "Mum is cross about something," I told Jimmy.

Back in the flat, at the table, there was a small rasher and an egg on each plate. We began in silence. Suddenly Mum banged down her knife and fork. "Through you opening your big mouth we now have to move. The super screwed a tag over the keyhole and I couldn't get in. I had to go to the office and he wouldn't take my rent. Instead he's given me one week's notice to leave." She glared at me looking very angry. "We'll be put out on the street all through you."

"I'm very sorry, Mummy, I didn't know I...."

"I warned you both what would happen, I warned you, I know your father."

"Can we go back to Auntie?" asked Jimmy.

"Of course not," Mum said sharply. "I'll have to find somewhere, and I can't work if I'm out searching for a place to live."

As we kissed goodbye before returning to school, she hugged me saying, "I can't help feeling cross with you, Belle, I didn't think you could be so silly. Now hurry or you'll be late."

"I'm sorry, Mummy, truly I am."

"Ah, well, as one door closes another opens... I hope."

I could not concentrate on my lessons. We had to move, that was all I could think about. To say goodbye to our neighbours on our landing, Mrs Gee and her four-year-old son Harry at Number 78, Mr and Mrs Lawrence at 80. Along the landing the laundry room, the concrete copper and the small fire hole that when lit boiled up the clothes. The two large wooden rectangular tubs on wooden stilts where Mum rubbed the clothes up and down the washboard to get them clean, the wooden airer, high in the ceiling, which let down on the pulley to hang washing on wet days and the vast space on the roof to blow washing on fine days. Then to Number 81; Alice lived there alone after the loss of her baby.

Mr Dixon, a widower at 82, lived with two small children cared for by his teenage sister while he worked. Mr and Mrs Bacon at Number 83 and their son Billy, aged twelve, who sucked his thumb, and at the last flat in our block lived Mr and Mrs Howard with two grown-up daughters, Number 84.

My teacher called me to task several times during that Monday and finally I told her we would soon be moving.

When we eventually left 79, all our neighbours waved us farewell with many wishes of good luck, and “Do come back to see us sometimes, don’t forget.” Need I say we never went back?

Very many years later we heard the buildings had been modernised.

Home from school that afternoon, Mum told us she had found a place. It was just one room, but it would have to do. She quickly prepared tea and then began machining. “I want to get finished and get this work to the factory,” she said, and about an hour later, putting on her coat and hat, she locked us in saying, “Be good and if there’s a knock, don’t answer.”

Now I realised why Mum always locked us in when she went out and why the flat door was kept locked. The thought that Father would find us must always have been at the back of her mind.

Chapter Twelve

We moved into a small back room in Mansfield Street. The lady's name was Mrs Mignotte. Her husband had recently been killed in France; there were two children, Rosie and Joe. The front room upstairs was let to a Mr and Mrs Stuart, and every Saturday night they got drunk and quarrelled.

On the landing was a gas cooker, which we shared with them, also a penny-in-the-slot gas meter. Mr Stuart went to work, but Mrs Stuart spent her time knitting socks for her husband. Billy soon endeared himself to her and she would call, "Come and see Auntie Jean, wee Billy," and I think Mum was glad Billy was in good hands while she machined.

Christmas was a trying time for Mum. Work was very slack; sharing the few orders among the outdoor machinists meant just less money for the bare necessities. Mrs Mignotte went to relatives for Christmas and the Stuarts had the loan of our large table because we hadn't the room for it and we sat at a very small table for our meals. The Stuarts were out all day. Our Christmas dinner was made up of three pennyworth of bacon bones, a two-penny packet of Foster Clark's pea soup powder, two pounds of potatoes for a penny and some carrots and onions, and Mum made some dumplings. It was delicious and we ignored what little meat there was on the bones.

And we had a Christmas tree. Probably picked up from the gutter, Mum put this small branch of a tree into a bottle with pieces of silver paper pressed loosely into balls and stars. She had threaded these on cotton and twisted them round the bit of tree. Resting on a plate with four small fancy candles alight round it, it was the most beautiful sight a child could imagine. Of all the many Christmas trees, more ornately decorated with tinsel and coloured glass balls, that small twig stands out most in my memory. After dinner we sat round the fire watching the bacon bones burn and splutter. We had no toys but a bright new penny each and we felt rich.

We still went to the same school but it was quite a long way. A highlight of our Saturday mornings was to go to the gasworks in Whiston Street to buy coke. At 28s 6d it was really something for us. We took the pushchair and when it was our turn to be served, we stood on the weighbridge and were weighed, then our sack was filled, we paid our money and left. Once a man said, "Tell your mother you're all getting fatter." Mother said, "That's a laugh."

One Sunday we had tea with Mrs Mignotte. We had watercress sandwiches and a small cake. We sat in front of the fire on the floor and our mum explained our predicament. I heard Mrs Mignotte say, "Your husband probably knew you lived in the buildings, but not the number, he could have followed the kids home from school."

"Oh God," said Mum. "I'll have to find somewhere right away from this district. If he comes here I'll be so sorry."

"Well, I'll miss the two shillings you pay rent, but...."

"I'll write to my sister in Hackney, maybe she can help."

There were sporadic Zeppelin raids and the many searchlights roamed the night sky picking out these airships, but the shells fired always missed.

We lived with Mrs Mignotte for roughly six months. Aunt Agnes came to see us and arrangements were made for us to move once more.

I gradually learned that Aunt Agnes had shifted her furniture upstairs so Mum could have two rooms downstairs. The scullery was shared, also the gas cooker. Auntie's husband, Uncle Charlie, worked in the Surrey and Commercial Docks and went out very early each morning. Also with Auntie lived Uncle Charlie's mother, Granny Clifton. This old lady frightened me. She always wore a bonnet that went to a point in the centre with a posy of artificial flowers to one side and tied under her chin with black ribbon. I never saw her without her bonnet and wondered if she went to bed in it. Mum found out the nearest school for us was Plough Lane School and after a week we set off with Mum to get enrolled there. From the beginning I didn't like that school. To begin with, the playground was on the roof and at playtime I always stayed near the railings because I thought the roof might cave in with the weight of all the children tearing around. One other thing, we had a different teacher for each lesson and we sometimes changed classes. All the time I wondered if the roof would fall in… stupid.

The first occasion when Granny Clifton scared me was when I took Auntie three small cakes up to her to have with a cup of tea. As I turned to leave, Granny shouted, "Little Belle, what shall we see when the veil is lifted?"

Aunt Agnes said, "You're frightening the kid… take no notice of her, Belle, stay and listen to her song." And Granny croaked:

> "Some of the ghosts were long and some of the ghosts
> were short.
> There they sat in a ghastly row upon the churchyard
> wall.
> Some gave a loud ha ha, some gave a loud he he.
> I tried to bid them all goodnight but they would not
> let me be."

I listened and as time went by I gradually learned the words.

Perhaps she thought she was amusing me, but I was glad to get out of the room.

Auntie did shoe machining like Aunt Minne and Mum and Granny Clifton sewed on buttons and did trimming of the excess lining of the uppers. All shoes, however cheap, had a soft buff-coloured lining: this was, said Aunt Agnes, how Granny earned her keep.

In a Zeppelin raid in 1916 an airship was brought down at Cuffley, Billericay, in Essex. We watched from Auntie's back-room window. Uncle Charlie was shouting, "Get them… get them."

Suddenly a small ball of fire was visible over the top of the airship. "That came from the air," said Uncle. The Zeppelin burst into flames, broke into two and fell slowly to earth. Uncle Charlie cheered like mad. "If they lose a few more like that, the war will soon be over," he said laughingly.

Mum told us that a young airman, a William Leif Robinson, had been awarded the VC for shooting the Zeppelin down.

Chapter Thirteen

Is there anyone out there who can remember Blind Fred? He sat in Hackney churchyard where the paths crossed leading to Sutton Place. He sat there every day, in all weathers. A tray across his knee contained shoelaces, matches, pipe cleaners and collar studs. A small enamel mug on a cord hung round his neck and a thick Braille bible rested on top of the tray. He was always cheerful and passers-by hailed him on their way to work. All the children spoke to him on the way to school. He knew many of us by name and said he could remember us by the sound of our voices. He had a fantastic memory. He sat in the churchyard for many many years. I have been told a plaque has been let into the wall near where he sat. I don't know if this is true, I have never been back to see.

Aunt Agnes said the house had been condemned as unfit, but the war had begun and so delayed the place being pulled down. There were twelve houses where we lived in Clarence Mews, a cul-de-sac off Clarence Road, and they were all due for demolition.

In one house lived a lively Jewish family. There were two sisters and Esther taught my brother Jimmy the verse and chorus of *Ragtime Cowboy Joe* and they would sing it together to entertain us.

On the corner of Clarence Road was a cinema and that Christmas of 1916 there was a children's programme of fairy stories. At a penny entrance fee the cinema was crowded. There we saw a short coloured film, *Cupid and Psyche.* I remember a green leafy background and Cupid wore a yellow dress with a very short skirt. He waved his hands into the air and grabbed a purple dress and slipped it over Psyche's head... magic. The next film was the story about a princess who was born with half her face black and whoever would kiss her, her face would become white, but when her veil was lifted all the would-be suitors would not kiss the black half of her face, until a shy shepherd lad kissed her and immediately the king made him a prince and he married the princess and they lived happily ever after... more magic.

And each child was given a bar of chocolate to take home... even more magic. We sent Mum and Aunt Agnes crazy telling about the films.

Towards the end of 1917 Granny Clifton died; she had a very bad cough. Meantime I kept on about how much I disliked that school, how much the playground on the roof scared me and despite assurances, nothing would make me feel safe there. Naturally it was silly but at that time I was sure the roof would cave in.

Every Thursday Mum went to Granny Munday to collect the ten shillings. She never stayed too long and the money was always ready for her. As Granny lived in Shipton Street, Mum sometimes called to see Aunt Minne. On her way there she saw a notice of a flat to let in Goldsmith's Row. She decided to see it and luckily thought it suitable. She paid a week's rent to secure it and arranged to move on Saturday in nine days' time. When Mum broke this news I was so pleased. Now I could go back to my old school, renew old friendships... I counted the days, they would not go past fast enough for me. Aunt Agnes told us she too was looking for somewhere to live. Moving day came and as Mum wouldn't tell us anything about the new place it came as a surprise to find it was two rooms with a large kitchen, a first-floor flat in a three-story house. The rooms were large and our bits of furniture looked lost. Mum said there was a bedroom for the boys and a bedroom for me and her. While living in Hackney she had been paying off a bed having the boys in mind.

Our oilcloth was placed in the centre of the rooms with the floorboards as edging and after all sleeping as usual in the one bed for a week, Mum made the final payment and the new bed was delivered. The problem now was bedding. A mattress came with the bed – that was all – so we shared a pillow and one blanket and managed that way until Aunt Minne introduced Mum to her tallyman. This way you chose goods and on the first payment the goods were delivered. So Mum chose two pillows, a pair of sheets and a quilt – the whole lot cost 32s 6d, to be repaid at the rate of a shilling a week at least, more if you could manage it.

Mum moaned and worried that she hoped she could keep up the payments.

She came up with the bright idea of teaching me to help her. She taught me to cut off cottons, sew on buttons and carefully trim seams. We had newspaper on the floor to collect the mess we made. She never machined after 7.30 and all the quiet work was done after that time. The cottons and clippings were collected on the newspaper and rolled up and stored in a cardboard box in a recess near the fireplace ready to light fires in the winter. Nearly ten years old, I now took her finished work to the factory and she got on with her work. Her only treat was the Sunday newspaper, *The News of the World.* It was a large broadsheet of forty-eight pages and cost two pence. She called it the scandal sheet.

On one page in the paper were printed the words and music of the latest songs. This Mum would read and using her fingers play on the table as if she was sitting at a piano. "When I grow up, Mum, I'll buy a piano," I promised. "Then you will be able to make real music."

"Pianos cost an awful lot of money, so forget it."

The rent of the flat was ten shillings weekly, so the money Mum collected from Granny Munday took care of that and the money Mum earned machining kept us clothed and fed. After having rice for dinner three days running, I moaned, "I don't like rice, can't we have something different?"

"Eat it up and be thankful. It's good for you. Look at the Chinese, that's all they eat, and they are strong."

"But I don't want to be a Chinese," I told her. How she laughed. My brothers spread jam on the rice and loved it. I shook pepper on mine.

Our gas was a penny-in-the-slot and the meter was fixed near the front door, and I was able to crank a penny into it when the need arose. One Friday the gasman came to empty the meter. He shook the pennies onto the table; I had never seen so much money. He counted it out into piles and put it into small blue bags marked "Five Shillings Copper". He gave Mum a small green receipt showing amount of gas burned and amount of cash returned. He gave Mum 1s 10d back. Mum was pleased.

Next day, Saturday, she sent me to the pork butcher in Columbia Road for three faggots. They were about a three-inch cube of a greyish-looking concoction, very spicy and tasty. So we were going to have faggot stew for dinner that day… we loved this and off I went. I walked along the railings of Guinness's Buildings to watch for any of the children I used to know. I knew none of the children playing in the grounds. After making my purchase I decided to look in Stock's toyshop window. I walked up Ropely Street and at the first house I stopped. Sitting on the doorstep, reading a comic was a playmate I had raced round the buildings with. She wore a white pinafore over a black dress. "Hallo, Kitty," I said.

She looked up, all smiles when she saw me. "What are you doing round here?" She stood up, coming down four steps to the pavement.

"When did you move from the buildings?"

"Well, Fred and Gus were growing and Mum said we needed more room, so here we are." She took my hand, "Come up and see Mum." We went to the upstairs flat. "Look who is here, Mum."

Mrs Perryment was nursing a baby; it was nearly asleep.

"Why, Belle." She hugged me. "Where have you sprung from?"

I explained where we now lived and she said we must get together for a cup of tea and a chat. "Ask your mum and brothers to come tomorrow for a cup of tea, now promise me?" I thanked her and left, I couldn't get home fast enough with the message. Mum and Mrs Perryment had been great friends when we lived at the buildings. Kitty was my age and a younger brother, Cyril, was Jimmy's age, and there were two older brothers, Fred and Gus, who both went to work, one at a printer's and one at a sawmill (we learned later). So we all arrived at Mrs Perryment's flat on Sunday at four o'clock.

We all chatted nineteen to the dozen, we had so much to say. The sadness was, Mr Perryment had been wounded by shrapnel and had had four months' leave, then had been sent back to France and had been killed at a town named Albert. Baby Walter had been born three months later and was now four weeks old.

We had muffins and shrimps for tea and with the promise to visit regularly we left at 7.30. Mum was very happy now she had a friend living near. And Mrs Perryment came often, she chatted as Mum machined.

Aunt Lucy paid us a surprise visit. She was leaving Ravenscroft Street because she was remarrying and then was leaving for Canada. She had met a nice Canadian soldier and had fallen in love again.

It was a few weeks later when Mum came home from Granny Munday with the news. Father had obtained the management of a pub The Lady Owen in Goswell Road, and as the pub did meals Grandfather and Granny were going to live with him to help out. Father was going with Mary Bransgrove and they now had three children. Mum was elated. She said, "Now I won't have to keep looking over my shoulder, thank God he has packed up with her."

"How will we get the money, Mum?" asked Jimmy.

"I have told Grandpa where we live and he has promised he will bring me the ten shillings every week, then I won't have to worry. I have told Grandfather, as long as his precious son stays away from us he can do as he likes. Now we can get on with our lives in peace."

Chapter Fourteen

One day Mrs Perryment visited us and outside our house on the pavement she had found a ten-shilling note. We arrived home from school and Fred and Gus joined us. That was when we heard about the find.

"Let's all have a bust up," said Mrs Perryment. She turned to me, "Go to Daultry's and get nine two-penny pieces of skate and sixpenny-worth of chips and we'll share the change, Belle," she told Mum.

"No, you found the note," Mum insisted, "the change is yours."

So off I went to Daultry's, the best fish shop around. The shop was full. In the lull I yelled, "Nine two-penny skates and sixpenny-worth of chips." All eyes turned in my direction.

"Where's your money?" demanded Lizzie Daultry suspiciously.

I produced the note from the small bag Mum had made for me to put her wages in when I sometimes collected money for her finished work from the factory. She held the orange-and-red-printed note to the light. In those days there was no metal stripe in notes, one looked for the watermark. She put the note in her till and continued serving other customers while I waited for my order to be cooked. When it was ready she placed first the fish in the straw bag I had then the large parcel of chips on top.

"Now you hurry straight home," she said.

"Where is my change?" I asked.

"It's wrapped separately in the bag."

I scooted home, excited at the thought of having a big piece of fish to myself. Having sent Kitty with a note for Fred and Gus to come to our flat, the table was set with our six dinner plates and four knives and six assorted forks. Jimmy, Billy and I had tea plates and the long pieces of fish hung over the edges so Mum cut the fish in half and, adding chips, we tucked in, the vinegar and salt doing a great trade. A cup of tea and we were all sated. The change, three half-crowns and a sixpence, were argued over by Mum and Mrs Perryment, and they finally settled; Mrs Perryment had five shillings and Mum had three shillings. That was true friendship between them.

Kitty and her brothers Cyril, Jimmy, Billy and I sat one day later talking on our doorstep. Cyril wanted to know all about living in Hackney. Jimmy told them about the playground on the roof and how scared I had been. I spoke about Blind Fred and then told of the time Mum had taken us to the Hackney Empire. How we had lined up behind the theatre to get a seat in the gallery (the gods). We sat on hard wooden seats and the entrance was just three pence. The play was *The Bing Boys Are Here.*

As it was wartime, the play was naturally about the war. While we waited for the curtain to rise we admired all the red plush and ornate gold paintwork. To us kids it was out of this world. The orchestra played, the curtains parted and on stage soldiers marched around singing "Soldiers of the King", and the audience joined in lustily. The next scene soldiers were in trenches, the stage was darkened and there were shells bursting and guns off-stage fired noisily, the entrenched soldiers showing a derisive disregard for the enemy. The stage gradually lightened and all hell broke loose. The officer gave the command, "Over the top!" and the actors charged about the stage, some falling, supposedly killed or wounded, then back to the trenches dragging their wounded comrades with them. A weak cry for help was heard. "That's the captain," they cried, "let's try to get him."

"I'll go," cried one man leaping out of the trench, and he crawled into the wings, returning with the wounded captain over his shoulder, to the thunderous applause and cheers from the audience. We kids cheered like mad but Billy cried. "Are they dead?" he asked, seeing some actors still lying on the stage. "Don't cry, Sonny," called a man behind us, "it's all pretend."

I think that spoiled our evening. Until then it had all appeared very real. Kitty and Cyril listened excitedly. Then we spoke of Mark's Penny Bazaar, right next to the Empire. Everything sold there cost a penny or half-penny. Boxes of coloured crayons, chalks, small boxes of paints complete with a brush, tins of cleaning polishes, dusters, feather mops, small brushes, two candles for a penny, two sheets of pins for a half-penny, shoelaces, studs, boxes of drawing pins, toy soldiers and various small toys, too numerous to mention. Who can remember Marks?

A few weeks before we had been turned out of Guinness's Buildings, I had attended Sunday school at St Augustine's Church in York Street, a turning off the Hackney Road… I think the name has been changed to Yorkton Street.

The high Gothic arch led to a small patio, then to the church doors. A short distance from the church was the priory; the entrance was in Dunloe Street. It was a type of convent, I think, because the sisters who took classes in the church dwelt there. When we moved to Hackney I had missed the Sunday school and now we had moved back to Goldsmith's Row I resumed attending. The sisters were pleased to see me back and again I was in Sister Alice's class. Under her coif she had a round face and ruddy cheeks. She was very strict and maintained silence while the preacher spoke. On Mondays there was a play class at the priory. There was a huge doll's house, if I remember rightly it must have been five foot tall. There were four floors and an attic I had never seen before. All the rooms were beautifully furnished and in detail scaled down to size with small exquisitely dressed dolls. In the kitchen were tiny pots, pans and dishes.

Whoever had donated this gift, or made it, was a craftsman of great skill. We loved to play with this and rearrange the furniture and a sister always hovered near to make quite sure nothing was broken. We children always wanted this type of house when we grew up. Of such stuff dreams are made.

Going to church on Sunday I read the text. I thought about it throughout the lesson. I stood reading it again when I left church memorising it. Reaching home I repeated it to Mum, who listened intently as I recited:

> "Into each life some rain must fall,
> Some days may be dark and dreary"

"I think, Belle, into my life there have come many storms."

Mum received a letter from Aunt Agnes saying she had moved to Number 10 High Street, Homerton, and because, despite wearing glasses, she was not doing machining and had taken a lodger, a young lady named Florence Fish, aged twenty-two, with her money would help to pay the rent. This lady worked in a factory doing war work, she was a tailoress, and they wanted machinists and would Mum like to try for a job there?

Aunt Agnes was one of Mum's elder sisters. She was eight years older than my mum. After reading the letter Mum said, "I'll certainly have to get work from somewhere, the shoe trade is in the dumps and we're getting hungry." I posted a letter to Auntie later.

Meantime, as Aunt Minne lived a short distance farther along the road, we saw her and our cousins often. Aunt Minne had received a letter from Aunt Agnes too and did not like the idea of a young girl lodger. "Charlie's got a wandering eye," Auntie said.

It was a long time later I found out what a wandering eye was.

The tenants on the ground floor were a Mr and Mrs Wood. They had priority over the small garden and Mr Wood spent all his spare time in it. Every Sunday he was off to the flower market in Columbia Road. This flower market had been held for years. Mum said it was held when she was a small child. It was a riot of colour throughout spring, summer and autumn, and in winter trees, shrubs and bulbs were on sale. Everything needed to make a good garden was on sale; all the implements needed could be bought. People came from miles away and every Sunday the road was crowded.

Mum told us there was a large vegetable market beneath the Columbia Buildings when she was small. The buildings were erected at the cost of £250,000, money donated by Baroness Burdett-Courtts. She died in 1906.

Ornately moulded spires rose above a row of Gothic arches that led to small shops of one-man businesses mostly allied to the furniture trade. The baroness donated to many charities that helped the needy.

So life and the war went on. We saw more dinner-times than dinners. I remember the small tin box kept on the back of the cooker. In it all used matches were put to be packed back into the empty match box and stored in the fire oven during summer ready to burn in the winter and the many scraps of trimmings off the shoe linings collected and wrapped and stored in the box by the fireside recess. Nothing was wasted. Mum would unpick two dresses of mine and make me a new dress out of the best pieces. The tallyman called each Saturday and the next purchase Mum made was two nightdresses for herself and me and two pairs of pyjamas each for the boys; the cost was £2 5s 9d, and Mum hoped she would keep well and work to pay the bill. We were so thrilled with our new nightwear we paraded around in it long before it was our bedtime.

Aunt Agnes and Uncle Charlie came to visit and with them came their lodger, Florence Fish. Florence, when she took off her coat, wore a grey dress and a wide-brimmed hat, black and trimmed with silk ribbons and two pink artificial roses, and when

Auntie and Uncle divested themselves of their outer clothing, the gear was taken to the bedroom and laid on the bed. I couldn't take my eyes off this grey dress. It had two skirts, one narrow and the overskirt hung to four points, two at the front and two at the back. The overskirt was edged with a pink braid. She made a great fuss of us kids and asked Mum to call her Flo. Mum had made cheese and corned beef sandwiches, the slices cut into four, and we were warned before they came not to be greedy and only take two pieces each of the sandwiches. We were on our very best behaviour. The adults chatted and chatted.

I heard Flo say, "We need machinists at the factory, why don't you give it a trial, Bella?"

"But I don't know anything about tailoring," Mum replied.

"Trousers are just straight machining," Flo told her.

"There are girls who do pockets, others do flies and waistbands. All you would do would be legs; why, little Belle could do that."

"You could make tea for your brothers if Mummy went out to work, Belle, couldn't you?" asked Auntie. "Mummy could earn more money if she went out to work and she could buy things for all of you."

"What sort of things?" asked Jimmy.

"Things to wear I suppose and things to eat, that would be nice, and you would all like that." Auntie smiled at us in turn.

"Who will look after Billy while we're at school?" I asked.

"Yes, Aggie," said Mum. "That's just what I'm thinking about."

"Perhaps you could take him to Minne's, give her a couple of bob for her trouble, Belle could collect him after school, and you would be much better off in the long run. Why not think about it?"

"I'll think about it," replied Mum. "I don't want her having accidents with boiling water. I'd never forgive myself."

Eventually they left and while clearing away, Mum was very quiet. She had never left us before and was always there when we arrived home from school and what about our dinners and our teas? I couldn't cook dinners. Needless to say we didn't want her to leave us all day and my brothers kept asking her what she was going to do. Billy didn't want to go to Aunt Minne's.

It wasn't long before she made up her mind. She told me of her decision and said, "When you come home from school at dinner-time, you can make tea and have bread and butter and when I come home each night, I'll make you all a nice dinner."

The problem of caring for Billy was solved when Mrs Wood, the lady on the ground floor, said she would look after him. "It's only for a short while each day and he can play in the garden. Just give me half-a-crown each week and I'll be quite happy with that. He's a dear little soul."

And so it was all arranged with satisfaction and Mum began her war work. I found it strange at first and Billy came in for his dinner of bread and marge. After school, it was more bread and marge until Mum returned each evening at seven o'clock. She worked until one o'clock on Saturdays and her first week's wages was £1 2s 6d. My goodness, we had never had so much money, and what did we have for dinner on that first Saturday? A penny meat pie each, which I went for while Mum cooked potatoes. Well, if we were to have treats like this Mum could go out to work. The second week, on Saturday afternoon, a man delivered a long galvanised bath like Nanny used at the pub. Now we had a bath each, every Saturday night instead of a wash down; it was lovely. I bathed first, and then with great difficulty Mum, Jimmy and I lifted the bath to empty it into the brown stone sink. The boys bathed together and again the bath was emptied. Mum bathed when we went to bed and the bath was emptied next morning, and for Sunday dinners we now had meat and cabbage as well as potatoes, and dinner every night. Truly, we were leading the life of Riley.

My teacher called me and a girl named Hughes to her table one morning. "I am thinking of putting forward your names for a scholarship," she said. "You both have very retentive memories, you both learn easily and remember all you are told, read and observe. Just tell your parents what I have said."

"I don't think I want to try," said Ethel.

"And you," said our teacher, "don't you want to try? You have the opportunity to go to a grammar school. It will serve you better when you leave this school." She turned to Ethel. "Grasp this opportunity, and you won't regret it, I assure you."

"I don't want to leave this school and my friends," I answered her.

"I'll give you both plenty of homework and that will be a great help to you," the teacher went on. "I'll speak to the headmaster, he has told me he will be coaching four boys, so between you, you should achieve something."

The thought of more homework than I already did loomed large. "I do have to look after my brothers," I told my teacher. "My mum has to go out to work and I have to help her."

"Well, do your homework first, then help your mother."

It was quite certain; Miss Barnes, our teacher, had made up her mind.

"You both will be well under the age limit of twelve years old by the 13th of April, so I have no worry about that."

Mum didn't think too much of the idea when I told her about the scholarship. "Never mind the homework, looking after your brothers comes first."

It would soon be the Whitsun holiday and as Billy would be five in July, he could begin school after the holiday. Jimmy had been teaching him easy words and counting and to me I thought he was clever because he could remember.

So I marched home with reams of homework. I cared for my brothers, I helped Mum washing up, shopping and, when I could, helped with cooking and as the summer break from the school holidays came I wasn't so rushed.

The war went on, there were still some air raids and we all rushed to Guinness's Buildings for shelter. People from the small houses flocked into the buildings, sitting on the stairs, all feeling secure. There were a few raids that September of 1917.

Grandfather Munday brought the money every Thursday evening; he gave us a half-penny each. Needless to say we were all very pleased to see him and he never ever spoke about Father, nor did Mum.

Mum was now earning more than twenty-five shillings each week and was paying money off different things to improve our home. Just before Christmas a roll of linoleum was delivered. It was a pretty green decorated with lemon scrolls. Mr Wood helped Mum cut it to fit corners and our kitchen dining-room looked very smart when the furniture was in place. We were told never to tell Grandfather that Mum went out to work. The week leading to Christmas Grandfather came, Mum always made him cocoa. On this evening he had a cold and it was raining heavily. Mum hung his overcoat round a chair in front of the fire.

Mum liked Grandfather very much and after some chat, she said:

"Dad, will you ask Jim to send a few bob more? The kids are growing and their clothes cost more. This ten shillings pays our rent, so what I can earn has to feed and clothe us. I haven't bothered him before, Belle will be eleven in February and Jimmy had a birthday recently, he's nine. So I'm not asking for a fortune and he has deprived them all along the line... never a penny extra at Christmas or even a card. I don't know what you think of him."

Grandfather was silent. Finally he said, "I'll do what I can for you, Bella, but you know what he's like."

"Oh yes," Mum replied bitterly, "I know what he's like, too well."

We went down to the door to kiss Grandfather goodbye. It was snowing tiny flakes and he said it was very slippery underfoot and so with a cheery merry Christmas we waved him off to The Lady Owen, Goswell Road.

Our Christmas dinner was out of this world. A small chicken, roast potatoes with Brussels sprouts and a currant pudding for sweet and we each had a bar of chocolate. The boys had a new pair of knickerbockers each and I had a new pinafore. It was a wonderful Christmas.

A week after Mum received a registered letter. Mrs Wood signed for it; the postman said I was too young. She gave it to me, telling me to put it in a safe place until Mum came home. What could it be about I wondered.

The registered envelope contained a ten-shilling note. Mum looked at the orange-red lettering, then shook the envelope but that was all it contained. For the next few weeks the registered letter came regularly and Mum wondered about it. At the end of February she received a black-bordered envelope with a letter from Grandmother. She wrote saying as Grandfather got off the tram near Goswell Road, he had slipped and had broken his back in two places and also had head injuries and sadly had died, and again there was no address given.

Mum assumed poor Grandfather had not passed on her request for more cash. So for some time the registered envelopes arrived each Thursday.

Billy did well in the infants' school and after joined the boys' school. Now Jimmy could see him in the playtime break.

Looking back, I now wonder how my mother coped. Some evenings she would come home, feed us and then begin some washing. Coloureds one evening and maybe the next evening the white things, slapping them up and down the rubbing board then boiling them in a bucket on the cooker. She bought a room airer that Mr Wood fixed to the ceiling for her. There always seemed to be washing hanging on the airer. She taught me to iron and dust, I helped as much as possible between the homework and my studies. In May Ethel and I sat exams for the scholarship. We were taken to a school somewhere in Hoxton. I think we both had butterflies in our tummies but would not admit it.

We both passed and received our framed certificates from the mayor at Shoreditch Town Hall. It was a St Leonard's scholarship with a grant for uniforms. Kids never wore a school uniform in those days; we went to school in clothes our mothers could afford. When eventually we attended the grammar school in a navy blue drill dress, box-pleated from a square-necked yoke and a blazer trimmed at the edges with a dark green braid, topped with a hard straw hat, Ethel and I didn't feel too happy but gradually conformed to the new curriculum. Teacher became Miss or Sir. Arithmetic became maths, scripture became religious instruction, composition essays, painting and drawing art, and the sewing class needlework, and those French verbs! I yearned for my old school. At this new school Empire Day passed unnoticed, and I thought about the half-day holidays I was missing.

Chapter Fifteen

Each child attending the school wore a red, white and blue ribbon for Empire Day, the 24th of May.

I think our headmaster at my old school must have been a very patriotic man. Of the six years I spent there, it never once that I can remember rained on Empire Day. Well, it wouldn't dare to, not with Mr Nye organising things. For two weeks before the day we practised the songs we would sing. If the 24th fell on a Saturday or Sunday, it was celebrated on the Friday.

With 40 to 45 children to a class and nine classrooms to each floor, there were roughly 1,100 children assembled in the boys' playground. In the large rectangular space, the boys would be in lines on the far side, the infants would be in line along the wall and the girls facing the boys, and we all had a good view of Miss Crouch, the music teacher, with her red and white pointer conducting. I think we all had in mind the half-day holiday when it was over. Miss Crouch would bang her tuning fork on the iron rail in front of her as she stood on the top step and we would all sing "Ahhhhhhhh."

The singing always began with *God Bless the Prince of Wales*, followed by *Ye Mariners of England*, *Soldiers of the King*, *Sons of the Sea*, *Rule Britannia* and *Land of Hope and Glory*. After assembly we would have a scripture lesson then arithmetic, and at ten precisely we would file into the boys' playground ready for the off. Mr Hye would be prowling around seeing all was in order.

On this particular day, I think I was nine years old, a few of my friends had learned a parody of *Land of Hope and Glory.*

We sang at the top of our voices: "Land of soap and water, Mother wash my feet."

Three girls suddenly appeared in front of me, and then I felt a poke in my back. I turned to see Mr Hye, he motioned me to join the other girls and eventually had seven of us in the front row. The singing went on while we wondered why we had been selected. He marched us to the steps and when the singing had stopped, he told the whole school of our misdemeanour.

"So," he finished, "instead of enjoying your half-day off, you will spend the time copying out for me, in your best writing, mind, the two verses and chorus of *Land of Hope and Glory,* twenty times." He grinned at each of us sardonically. "To be on my desk at nine o'clock Monday morning sharp. That way you will remember the correct words to the end of your days." He was right; I can still reel off the two verses and chorus to this day.

Needless to say, my mum was furious that I had less time to help her that weekend. My new school did not celebrate the 24th of May.

The comics we read, costing a penny each: there was *Comic Cuts, Funny Wonder, Film Fun,* very popular showing the capers of Charlie Chaplin, Harold Lloyd, Ben Turpin, the cross-eyed comic. There were Fatty Arbuckle, the Keystone Cops and the Mack Sennet Bathing Beauties with Mabel Norman. There was also the two-penny coloured *Rainbow* and the *Magnet* with the escapades of the Famous Five and the antics of the tat boy, Billy Bunter at the Greyfriars Boarding School.

Sometimes we went to the cinema – Saturday morning cinema for children, admission one penny, to see our heroes, Eddie Polo and William S Hart, fight the Indians and herd together stampeding animals. They were our favourite cowboys. Wallace Reid raced fast cars along wide roads to rescue damsels in distress, and we all read subtitles aloud. Then our heroines: Pearl White in *The Perils of Pauline*, in the series left either tied to a chair, the villain tying her to the chair and gloatingly threatening to toss a bomb into the room or, the next week, leaving her tied to the railway line with the train thundering closer and closer as the words on the screen read, "Continued next week."

Marie Wallcamp: bravely she acted with wild animals, always being chased by lions or falling into animal traps. And for drama, Nazimove, Marie Dresler, Ethel Clayton, and Nita Naldi, the vamp *par excellence.*

Later there was Mary Pickford with the long golden curls and her husband Douglas Fairbanks Senior, and the never-to-be-forgotten Lillian Gish and Richard Barthomew in the tear-jerking *Broken Blossoms.*

At first, I wasn't too happy at my new school, but I studied hard and received high marks, and so progressed.

At the end of September 1918, Mum came home and told us the contract for war work would not be renewed and she had to leave the factory, so it was back to the shoe work. So Mum began working at home again and it was very nice to return from school and find her there to welcome us and as it was getting colder, a warm fire was a great comfort. Alas, the money Mum now earned was less than the war work she did, so a little more scrimping was quite in order. One day Mum received an open letter, envelope flap tucked inside with a half-penny green postage stamp. It was from Granny Munday. She was now living at Number 8 Great Cambridge Street (this was just three streets away from where we lived), and the ten shillings would be there each Thursday evening. So Jimmy and I went to collect the money. Gran was living in one room. A bed was against the wall on one side of the room; on the small table stood a large cage, inside was an African grey and pink parrot. She was pleased to see us and commented on how much we had grown. I wanted to know where Father was. She said he was at the pub, "So don't ask questions."

"Is Father coming here?" Jimmy asked.

"No, but he's thinking of buying this house for me soon."

I put four half-crowns into the small bag I had round my neck, which Mum had made for me to carry money, Gran gave us a farthing each and we hurried home. Telling Mum what Gran had said, we were full of the parrot.

"Gran said she lets him fly round her room each morning," Jimmy said.

"And your father is going to buy her that house?" Mum questioned. "At her time of life, what does she want with a big house?"

That of course we could not answer. Life went on, the shoe work, school and the war. There was talk of the war soon ending, but I think it went over our heads. It had gone on so long the thoughts of peace were very remote.

A drab November day; talk of an armistice. Suddenly streets were being decorated with bunting. Everyone hung out flags, except us... we didn't have flags to put out, but we joined in the mood of happiness that prevailed.

Mrs Perryment came and Aunt Minne and she brought with her some cakes, tea and sugar and we had a high tea. People were dancing in the streets and I think at night many people got drunk. The 11th of November... a date remembered to this day. Next day life was back to normal but everyone smiled more.

Our usual scrimping went on and Christmas came with frugal meals. We spent Boxing Day with Aunt Minne and Cousin George and Bill.

Chapter Sixteen

After Christmas, Mum said she would look for work, going to a job where she could earn more money. She said she was paying the tallyman less money, but he was quite nice about it. "It would be great if I could pay for things as I wanted them and I pray that day will come soon."

At the end of January she began going to work and the task of caring for my brothers began, but they were older now and more helpful and gradually we began to forget the war and the thoughts of air raids. We played with Kitty and Cyril, visiting each other's houses. Mrs Perryment told us she was moving back to Farnham, in Surrey. She said she grew up in a village there. We had a farewell tea together.

Flo often came to see us and one day, it was a Sunday, she told Mum Aunt Agnes was upset and said Uncle Charlie was seeing another woman.

"Goodness, who would have him?" asked Mum. "He must be sixty if he's a day. Is Agnes sure?" and Flo nodded.

"Aggie knows the docks finish around four o'clock and he's not getting home until about seven o'clock and he's getting home sober. That is what makes her so sure." Flo went on, "They were having words when I arrived home from work one night, but stopped when they heard me coming up the stairs, I felt in the way."

There was some quiet talk for a while.

During the summer, street parties were held for children. Goldsmith's Row was a narrow road with much through traffic. Now there were a few cars and trucks as well as the horse-drawn carts, so a street party in the road was completely out of the question.

A few times we had tea with Aunt Minne and our cousins. George had now left school and had a job with a decorator and builder and was paid good wages. Although he came home very dirty sometimes, she was pleased.

Mum paid up the tallyman who said he was sorry to lose her. Mum said the girls where she worked held clubs. Numbers were put into a small box and you took your turn to buy goods from the shop where the club was held.

Flo brought her young man to see us. His name was Patsy and Flo said she was fed up with the quarrelling at Auntie's and was going to live with Patsy and get married later. Mum was shocked.

Now we had more underclothes and shoes, meals were varied and we had better food. One Saturday she came home with a tea service she had bought in the market.

She put them in a bowl intending to give the china a good wash. She poured in the boiling water and some soda. "We'll have everything to match on the table now," she told us smiling. "I'll wipe, Mum," I said. I began with the small plates. The first cup I picked up the handle came off. Mum was a bit cross. "Leave them, I'll finish," but as she began to wipe, the next handle came away from the cup, and the next and we ended with six cups without handles. "Well, it was cheap, I suppose that's all I could expect for a half-crown," she said philosophically. But at least we had saucers and small plates that matched. Mum made some weekly payments at shops and gradually built up our home. She told us a lady where she worked had joined her in a Christmas club and we would have some Christmas food, and so 1919 sped along.

I was doing very well in my new school and my brothers too were getting good reports from their teachers and Mum and her fellow-workmates had all had rises in wages but Mum said prices were going up in the shops.

We were off school for the Christmas holiday and on the evening of the 22nd of December Mum gave us instructions as to what we would do next day, which was the day the Christmas club she had joined earlier in the year shared out food.

She said, "I am told by Laura to take two very big bags. Now I have made bags from sacking with strong handles. Take Billy's old pushchair, that will take the weight. There is a large hall in Brookby Walk, that's in Homerton High Street, and if you walk to the end of Wells Street the place is almost opposite. Now you all know your way there. It opens at twelve, so Laura tells me, and you line up and take your turn. Do you understand all that?"

We nodded, we all knew High Street Homerton, that was where Aunt Agnes lived and we often visited her there. "I'll give you money for your dinners. Go to Cook's and get a pie and mash each and I know you will not be hungry."

She made us repeat her instructions word for word and with thought of pie and mash to eat in the pie shop we went to bed happy. Mum dashed off to work next morning after repeating all she had told us and we were to start out at midday. We did. It was cold and the boys' thin overcoats were barely thick enough to keep them warm. We tied our scarves tightly round our necks. The pies and mash we enjoyed, for three ha'pence it was a filling meal for us and off we marched to Brookby Walk. Billy was in the pushchair, I covered his bare knees with the bags Mum had made. The short socks and knickerbockers left the boys' knees bare. I did have stockings, but we hurried along trying to keep warm. Eventually we arrived at the hall to find a long queue of people. We tacked ourselves on the end. I asked the man in front, "Please, Mister, what's the time?"

"Nearly two o'clock, if we're lucky we might get in there by four o'clock."

"They'll be sold out by then," Jimmy said dismally. Someone laughed.

So we moved slowly along and still people lined up behind us. By three o'clock the sky darkened and it began to snow, we were frozen. Suddenly Billy wanted to pee. "Do it in the road, Sonny," said a lady kindly. I pushed him towards the gutter. The job done he said, "The snow got on my tassel," and everyone who heard him laughed. I hoped I wouldn't want to. It was all right for the boys, but I could not see myself watering the road. Don't think about it, I told myself. When we reached the entrance to the hall it was snowing thick flakes, then we were inside. The bright lights dazzled us. There were long rows of trestles piled high with food of all kinds. We had never seen so much. Billy got out of his pushchair and we were at the first trestle. "Bird?" questioned the man in a straw hat. I nodded and a turkey dropped into the bag held open. Next a box about eighteen inches square was pushed towards us and Jimmy and I loaded it on the pushchair and Billy pushed it along, and at the place where a man or woman served, things were pushed towards us. Soon both bags were overflowing. Someone found another bag for me and at the last counter, the lady asked, "How many in family?"

"Four, Miss," and into my bag she dropped four Christmas stockings.

Then we struggled into the street and the blinding snow. "How can we get home with all this stuff?" I asked my brothers. I gave Billy the lightest bag to carry, the box took up the room in the pushchair, so I put one bag on the top and with Jimmy holding one handle of the other bag and me holding the other handle, and pushing the pushchair with the other hand we set off home. Needless to say, we didn't get too far before we wanted a rest and we were getting wet. The boys' flat caps were snow-covered, so was my woollen bonnet. We brushed each other free of snow and off we went. The shop lights brightened our way along Wells Street. As we neared a greengrocer's a man came out of the shop.

"Good Lord, kids, you're loaded, been to the club?" We nodded, too cold to speak. "Come in the shop, I'll find you a sack," and he helped carry our bags into the warm shop.

We stood there, three skinny kids, frozen and wet. He produced two long sacks. "Now," he said to Billy, "if you sit in one of these sacks, you can have a ride home. Open the sack, Ma," and a lady held the sack.

"No, no," yelled Billy, "don't put me in the bag, no."

"Now, listen, Son. You sit in the sack in your pushchair, I'll pack some of these things round you and you'll be warm. He tucked Billy into the sack, packing some of the goodies round his legs. He tied the box on Billy's lap and round the sides of the pushchair. He wheeled the lot outside his shop and told me to rest the handles of my bag over the holds of the pushchair. He cut holes in another sack and covered it over Jimmy. He then gave us sixpence, and with Jimmy carrying a bag we started for home with the snow still falling thickly. I was a little scared, the horses and carts appeared suddenly and everywhere seemed so silent. We didn't speak much and I wondered if we would get home safely. I depended on street lights to guide me. As we neared the top of Wells Street the snowing eased suddenly. We stopped to brush the snow from our clothes; the boys' caps were soaked, so was my bonnet and my hair was wet too. We heard a passing couple say the buses were not running; that was the reason no buses had passed us in Wells Street going to Hackney Wick and why I thought I had taken the wrong road. "My feet are frozen, I can't feel them," Jimmy said.

I felt tired; Billy was six and all the goods packed round him plus the bag hanging on the handles made it hard for me to push him along. Getting up and down kerbs was difficult too and Jimmy couldn't help very much.

Carefully we crossed Mare Street into Lamb Lane. Here I kept to the road. We reached London Fields and the going was smoother. "We'll soon be home now," I said trying to sound cheerful.

"Will Mummy be home?" asked Billy.

I had no idea of the time; it had been dark for so long, I thought it must be very late. "I think so and I hope so because we have to get these things upstairs."

The lights of the Broadway market loomed nearer and unconsciously I quickened my steps. In the market the snow had turned to a brown slush underfoot and we plodded on. The paraffin flare lights on the stalls made it seem a little warmer and certainly more cheerful. We crossed the canal bridge and I nearly slipped as the weight of the pushchair pulled me quickly down the slope. We passed the Standard Cinema, not much farther, past Aunt Minne's, The Goldsmith Arms. "Can you run on home, Jimmy, and see if Mum can help me?" He went on but it was too slippery for him to run and we arrived at our gate almost together. Mum came through the door as I stood waiting for some help. As she came towards me I said, "Oh Mummy," and burst into tears, "I'm so cold."

She told Jimmy to bring scissors. We cut the box free and put it in the passage, and lifted Billy out of the sack. I almost crawled upstairs only to rush down again… I just made it to the toilet. Back in the warm room, I saw the time was ten minutes to eight.

"Get off your wet clothes and shoes quickly, all of you." She was filling the kettle, and then lifted down the long bath. The fire was bright sending out warmth. Mum put the bath in front of the fire and poured in some cold water, then poured in a little of boiling water. "Put your feet in, it won't be too hot at first, when you can feel your feet, I'll add the hot water. I don't want you all to get chilblains." She made us a cup of hot cocoa each and we sat, feet in hot water, a steaming cup of cocoa, and we gratefully warmed our hands round the cups while Mum unpacked the bags.

One by one the goods were put on the table. A frozen turkey, the tab on it read 7lbs 3oz; five pork chops in one piece, six oranges and six tangerines, eight apples, a box of dates, a large bag of mixed nuts, a piece of cheese, about half a pound, Mum thought, a box of Christmas crackers, the four stockings, a packet of cocoa, a tin of boiled sweets, half a pound of butter, a pound of sugar, six bananas and a box of cream biscuits. That was the bags emptied. "What's in the box, Mum?" Billy asked.

The box was stuck up with some brown sticky paper that Mum cut through with scissors. Inside was a pound pudding in a white basin, an iced cake, a tin of jam, a tin of marmalade, half a pound of tea and a small box of crystallised fruits, all packed in torn paper shavings and neatly folded in the bottom a fancy paper tablecloth. "Golly," said Billy. "That will last us forever."

Mum surveyed the laden table, then suddenly sat down and burst into tears. We went to her, wet feet damping the mat. I had never seen my Mum cry, yet there must have been many times that she had shed tears.

"Don't cry, Mummy, please," said Billy, "it's Christmas, and all this food." I began to cry too. My feet were so painful. Jimmy said his toes were burning. Billy was the one with dry shoes but had insisted he had his feet in the bath too. Mum encircled us in her arms and told us to stop making her cry. "I came home in the thick snow, hoping you were all home. I got so worried, I was thinking about meeting you but thought I might miss you." She gave me a towel. "Dry your feet, just rinse them again first."

The boys dipped their feet into the bath again, then Mum dried their feet saying, "Here's clean socks, and I bought you all a present for Christmas. I didn't know it would snow so hard, now you will have your gifts tonight." She left the room and came back with three small boxes. Inside were slippers... slippers... the last time Jimmy and I had slippers we were at the pub and they had been left behind. Mum had bought them a size larger saying our feet would grow into them.

The food was packed away and the turkey was placed on two plates on the draining board, the body on one plate and the head and neck on the other.

While doing this we told Mum about the kind greengrocer and she said she hoped we knew our manners and thanked him.

When the turkey had thawed, Mum asked Mr Wood to pull out the insides for her. He told us he and Mrs Wood would be away for Christmas and to be sure to bolt up doors back and front, and with thanks and best wishes he left.

Then came a surprise. From the fire oven she had kept hot fish and chips for each of us. “Oh, thank you, God,” I thought. This was going to be a most wonderful Christmas, all that food would last us ages.

Needless to say we made the most of it and we had a wonderful and happy time. We sang carols and some very old songs Mum had taught us and there was Boxing Day next day too. The Christmas cake was rich with fruit but the icing was like china. Mum broke it into pieces and we ate it like sweets; the icing lasted us kids for days.

The books and puzzles and small toys in the Christmas stockings were kept in one of the shoeboxes and amused Billy for hours and we were back to normal after the holiday.

Chapter Seventeen

Two or three weeks after the holiday, taking off the hated blue serge drill dress, we three kids set off to Gran's to collect the ten shillings.

The door was opened by a young lady; she was crying and ran upstairs leaving us to close the street door. Gran seemed very cheerful; the parrot was walking round the outside of his cage, much to Billy's delight. Gran asked us if we had been good and what we had done at school that day. This was her usual question. She seemed to me to be very cheerful.

"I've finally got the title deeds to this house. Your father has bought it for me, isn't he a kind man?" No reply from us kids.

"What's title deeds?" asked Jimmy.

"It means I now own this house entirely, and now I want you to do something for me. You take that chair, Jim, down to the scullery, wait a sec." She went to the table drawer and taking out a hammer and a long nail, she told me, "Down in the scullery there is a copper. Stand on the chair and knock the nail into the bottom of the copper bowl."

"I can't do that, Gran, people won't be able to boil their clothes."

"Exactly," she said. "That's what I want. I'm not having the smell of washing all over my house. The wash baths are down the bottom of the road, they can go there. Do as I ask."

"I mustn't do that, the landlord will be annoyed," I said scared.

"I'm the landlord, so don't worry."

"The lady was crying when she opened the door," said Jimmy.

"That's right, she is having a baby, so she has to find somewhere else to live. I want no prams scraping my hall wallpaper."

"I can't knock a nail through iron," I protested.

"It's not iron, it's a thin metal," she assured me.

"Does Father come to see you, Gran?" asked Jimmy.

"Yes, but not too often, he's a very busy man."

"All right," said my brother, "the next time he comes to see you, you ask him to knock the nail in. I'm not taking any blame."

"You're all ungrateful kids," she snapped. "Look at all the farthings I've given you for doing my errands. I'll keep my money in future. Here's your money." She threw four half-crowns on the table. "Pick it up and go and don't lose it then say I never gave it to you."

As we turned to leave, she demanded, "What about a kiss for your gran?" Dutifully we in turn kissed the proffered cheek and left.

Repeating all Gran had said and asked us to do, Mum said in amazement, "Your grandmother is a wicked old bitch and in heaven's name, what does she want with a big house at her age? She must be nearly sixty."

After tea, I did my homework then helped Mum, snipping cottons and sewing on buttons while Mum trimmed off excess lining and neatened all edges, packing pairs together as she cleared and packed the finished work. All trimmings and cottons were collected and rolled in newspaper, ready to help light the fire next day.

Aunt Minne and our cousins had tea with us one Sunday and Auntie told us the twins, Fred and Bert, would soon be home for good. They were nearly fifteen years old and it would be nice to be all together again.

Flo visited us with her young man, saying they were marrying at a registry office in a few weeks' time and it would be very quiet and Mum was invited.

We visited Aunt Agnes for tea one Sunday and when Uncle Charlie went to buy cigarettes, Auntie said to Mum, "She must be married. The husband must be home weekends because Charlie stays here." She looked at Jimmy and me, then said, "Little piggies have got big ears," and laughed.

On the Saturday Flo was married it rained and Aunt Agnes, Uncle Charlie, Mum and Flo and her new husband came to our house in a taxi. I was sorry the neighbours couldn't see my mum get out of the cab. We had a really great tea and a big white wedding cake decorated with silver balls and shoes was produced from our cupboard. It had been kept a secret from us and when they left there was confetti all over the floor and Flo had left a large piece of the cake for us.

The twins were to spend four days with Aunt Minne and Cousin George and Bill to see if they would "fit in" – Auntie's expression. She invited us to tea on Easter Monday. We had never met the twins. In profile they were alike as two peas. Full face they looked so different. Bert was lantern-jawed, Fred had a round face. Auntie said Bert was like his father's family while Fred took after my side of the family.

The twins left immediately after tea and Cousin Bill said he had a jigsaw and we followed him into the kitchen to help fit in the small pieces.

We left Cousin George, Auntie and Mum chatting. Suddenly voices were raised. Cousin Bill said, "That's Mum and George rowing again."

I went back to ask why they were shouting and as I opened the door, I heard George say, "Did you know about this, Aunt Bella?"

"No, she doesn't, it's my business." Catching sight of me in the doorway, Auntie shouted, "Get back with the boys and shut the door."

So Easter Monday ended unhappily and Mum was very quiet as we walked the short distance home. Once indoors we wanted to know about why she began to quarrel immediately the twins had left, then, changing the subject, she asked us in turn what we thought about the twins.

We said we thought they were all right, they were our cousins and when they were home for good, we would see more of them and get to know them better. They were older than we were and we saw George and Bill more often.

At the end of May when we came home from school Mum was not there to greet us. I made tea for us and was spreading margarine on toast when Mum returned. She looked tired. When asked where she had been, she said she had been with Aunt Minne and had been very busy all afternoon. She thanked me for caring for my brothers and I thought this strange. I always prepared tea if she was busy or out.

I think it was about a week later, Mum told us Aunt Minne had a baby boy. His name was Harry. We didn't give much thought to the news. Sex was an unheard of word and we hadn't a clue where babies came from or how they were conceived. We were truly ignorant of such matters and Mum never spoke to us about such things; that was for grown-ups. When we went to collect the ten shillings, Mum said, "Don't tell Granny about Auntie's baby."

Tea at Auntie's next Sunday was our introduction to the new baby. We thought he was pink and ugly and he cried most of the time. Our Billy remarked that the baby had no teeth, so how did he eat? After tea George spent the rest of the evening in the kitchen on his own.

Auntie said, "He's upset, but he will have to get used to it."

Harry was christened in August 1920.

One Thursday Billy and Jimmy went to collect the money from Gran. Billy had fallen down on the way there and badly grazed his knees, and Gran had smeared some of her green ointment on the wound. This ointment went on cuts, grazes and bruises and was very soothing. She made it herself.

Gran would send us to Lawrence's in Hackney Road for a quarter-pound of bladder lard. "Make sure the man serves it from the bladder," she insisted, "the other sort won't do." The lard was scooped from large pigs' bladders; it was soft and creamy and cost three pence. She had a large copper kettle and hung it on a hook in her coal cupboard. I never knew how long it stayed in the coal cupboard, but when taken out it was a bright green colour. She then proceeded to finger it off into small jars with tight screw-on lids. That was Gran's green ointment.

During the summer break from school I helped Mum with her work in the evenings. She was teaching me quite a lot about the trade. I was given a huge pile of homework from school and did this when I felt like doing it and we were happy together. Mum was earning more money, with my help, she said, and the weather was warm and like the other kids around we ran about without shoes or socks. We took a bottle of water and a few bread and butter sandwiches and played in the park all day, going home when we were tired and hungry. Streets and parks were safe places in those days and mums never had to worry about kids being abducted or molested. Thoughts like that were never entertained.

Aunt Agnes came to see us and we were sent out to play. Going in for tea, we saw Aunt Agnes had been crying and Mum didn't look too happy. After tea the boys went out to play and I washed the dishes while Mum was machining.

"Listen, Belle," she said suddenly, Uncle Charlie is the father of Aunt Minne's baby. Now you know, keep it to yourself."

"Is Aunt Agnes pleased?" I asked.

"No, she is not, she is very angry. You don't know this, but my sister had six children, three of them were stillborn, and the others died soon after being born. There was one who lived just three months, so try to understand how Aggie feels and why she is angry." I listened but it was all unintelligible to me. I was so naive. Mum was speaking in riddles. The baby was christened Harry Clifton-King. The only one in our family with a hyphen to his name, Mum said. I thought he was a nice little baby.

In September I joined an amateur drama group; there still lurked the idea that I would like to be an actress. I was chosen as Fairy Rose, the play *Sleeping Beauty*, and I remember how the real actresses behaved many years ago when Nanny took me to the Britannia Theatre, Hoxton. I had lines in most scenes and a fair-haired girl wanted the part I had been given. At the christening scene, in rehearsals, I had to say, "I give her beauty, none in this wide world will be as fair as she." This girl said to the director, "Mr Gates, I am much prettier than she is, I want to be Fairy Rose," but Mr Gates said, "Listen, Hannah, you give the princess grace and that is just the same, so be good, do as I say." She poked her tongue out at me so I put my thumb to my nose and wagged my fingers at her, and Mr Gates told me, "Fairies don't make rude gestures at each other." Her jealousy continued and at times she tried to trip me up. The play ran three nights before Christmas and if some of us fluffed our lines the audience applauded the final curtain.

Christmas 1920 for us wasn't a bit like the 1919 one when we had a table filled with the goodies from the Goose Club, but we had chops in batter pudding and roast potatoes and bread pudding with custard for a sweet. Collecting the ten shillings from Gran a few days before Christmas, she gave us a penny each saying, "Don't spend it all at once, remember, every mickle makes a muckle." I never ever found out what a mickle was, or a muckle.

After Christmas, Mr Gates thought he might try to put on *Aladdin* for next year and thought I would make a good little genie. Needless to say this upset Hannah and after I had learned some of the lines, three months later I left the group. If the pettiness was like this in an amateur group, it must be worse on the real stage, so goodbye to becoming an actress.

Now I decided to become a hairdresser, that's what I wanted to be.

Before I finally decided to leave the drama group, an event occurred in our road. Soon after Christmas men brought long thin metal pipes into the houses. Electricity had arrived with 1921. Slots were cut into skirting boards, holes were bored into floorboards and these metal pipes were fixed to walls from a switch, then across the ceiling with small U-shaped metal brackets. A small wooden circle was fixed in the centre of the ceiling from which dangled a thin flex, at the end of which hung a light bulb. A small meter was fixed in the side cupboard; I think it was a shilling slot meter. It was about a week before we could use the lighting and when light flooded the room, Mum said, "My goodness, now I've seen it all; from candles to lamplight and gas and now this. Whatever will they think of next?"

In February I was fourteen and went to Gran a few days after my birthday to collect the money. She gave me two half-crowns.

"Only five shillings, Gran. Where's the rest of the money?"

"You're fourteen now, so you will be starting work."

"But I don't leave school until I'm sixteen, and maybe not then."

"When I was thirteen, I went to work learning to make men's ties," she said, "and you should be thinking about getting a job and less of school."

"I don't know what Mum will say," I said picking up the half-crowns.

"What can she say? The money has always been paid regularly."

When I told Mum of the conversation with Gran, she was furious. "Get my hat and coat, I'm going to tell her a few things she won't like."

When we arrived at Gran's Mum was seething. The parrot was crawling round the outside of his cage squawking loudly.

"Where is the rest of the money?" Mum demanded. "Have you kept it?"

"No, I haven't," Gran said crossly, "that's all he sent this week. He said Belle should start working for her living."

"He did, did he?" Mum said angrily, as she threw the two half-crowns on the table. "Well you tell him from me, unless there is a pound here next week I'm taking him to court and I really mean it." Gran said nothing as I followed Mum out of the room. Mum walked quickly. "I could have hit the old crow," said Mum. "I really believe she has the rest and is trying it out."

"What are we going to do, Mum?" I wondered about the rent being paid.

"We'll manage somehow, and the rent man will have to wait a week."

And the next week a pound note was waiting. If Gran didn't argue with Mum, she certainly had plenty to say to me. She shouted how the money had been paid each week, never missed, how good her son was, some men would have left the country, then where would we be? Her tirade went on and on, sooner or later she would have to come up for air, then I would tell her what I thought of her precious son. When she stopped, I started. I hardly remember all I said. I shouted at her as she had shouted at me and in between the old parrot squawked. I remember saying Jim is twelve and Billy is eight. Could she keep two boys that age fed on five shillings and what about clothes? I thought her son was a mean old Scrooge, a miser. I so liked the sound of those words, I repeated them two or three times, finishing up with, "I wish Mum would take him to court, he is a rich man and I'm sure we could get more money then."

"Your mother walked out, she left him taking away his children. That would go against your mother and you're getting too big for your boots."

"He used to hit her," I shouted.

"Don't tell such wicked lies, now sling your hook." She got up very quickly, I thought she was going to hit me, but she opened the door and I left. But I had the pound note and was happy that Mum could now pay the rent.

At the end of March I left the drama group. Aunt Minne's baby grew very quickly and Auntie borrowed Billy's baby high chair.

At Whitsun-time Auntie's twins came home for good. Fred found work with an engineering firm and Bert found a job with a pawnbroker. Cousin George came and redecorated our kitchen and covered the electricity pipes with wallpaper and whitewashed the ones when he did the ceiling, quite smart.

In July Flo had a baby girl and named her Florence Irene.

Breaking up school for the summer holidays, our teacher (Miss) told us when we resumed school we would be taught sex lessons.

Telling Mum about this, she said, "Whatever next? I have never heard of such a thing. Time enough to learn about that when you're married. Soon they'll build maternity homes next to schools. Curiosity killed the cat," she said. Many years later, so many very young girls became gymslip mums, there seemed to be some truth in her forebodings.

During the school holiday, I helped Mum with her work and her earnings soared a little. I took her work, when finished, to the factory and sometimes I saw my cousin Bill there as Aunt Minne worked at the same factory. Bill was nearly nine years old and on this day he told me Aunt Agnes had visited them and had had a row with his mother and it was about Harry and when they had finished rowing they were both crying. He wanted to know if we had seen Aunt Agnes.

A nurse came to give the sex lesson, it lasted half and hour. She told us how the womb worked, drawing a slight pear-shape on the blackboard, how it had a monthly cycle, collected eggs then discarded them causing a period. It was very mysterious to me; at that time I hadn't yet had a period. I had heard snatches of conversations by other girls but didn't take much notice and my mum never said a word when I explained what the nurse had told us. If there ever was an opening for Mum to talk to me, she ignored it and as these lessons were just once a month, most of the lesson was forgotten by the next one. And so on to Christmas 1921.

It passed quietly; Aunt Minne and the boys came to tea on Boxing Day. Harry was now walking around and talking. All I noticed was that Cousin George ignored him completely. And the days and weeks into 1922 sped past.

I think it was towards the end of April, Jimmy came from Gran with the money and told Mum Father wanted to see her next Thursday at two o'clock. Beyond that, Jimmy repeated that was all Gran said.

That next Thursday, Mum kept me home from school and I went to meet Father with her. We arrived at three o'clock, purposely late.

Gran opened the door with the remark to Mum, "You're late," and leaving me to close the door, we followed her into her room. Father was standing, his back to the fireplace. Catching sight of me he asked, "What is she doing here, I thought she was still at school?"

"Your mother is here, I suppose as your witness, Belle is here to listen to what you have to say, and yes, she is still at school."

"You're both looking well," said Father. Mum made no comment.

"I want a divorce," Father began. "It can be done quietly and I'll pay."

"You amaze me," Mum said, "and if that's what you want we'll have it noisily. And why have you suddenly decided on divorce?"

"I want to give my children a name," he replied.

"You should have thought about that when you were busy making them."

"Listen, I'll give you fifty pounds, that's a lot of money," he said.

"Is that all the value you put on your kids' names?" queried Mum.

"One hundred pounds then."

"My religion does not countenance divorce," Mum answered quietly.

"You and your bloody religion," he shouted at Mum.

"Come along," Mum said to me, "we're going."

"I'll take you to court, you'll see. You took the kids away from me."

"You do that. I'll see you there." Then we left.

I cannot remember the conversation word for word, but that was the gist of it. We heard him shouting swear words as we closed the street door. Once outside I said to Mum, "Why don't you divorce him? We could do a lot with £100, we could buy things."

"And how long do you think that amount would last, eh? No, I have something all his money can't buy. She will never be Mrs Munday while I live and I'll see him out. Had he treated us fairly, I might have had thoughts about it, but he has deprived you kids too long and that's something I can't forgive."

"But he is taking you to court, he threatened."

"Don't worry yourself about that. He hasn't a chance."

Life went on for the rest of the year. I did lots of homework for the matriculation. I helped Mum all I could and we still scrimped and scraped. We visited our aunts and Flo, or they came to see us. Sex lessons continued and gradually the enormity of what Aunt Minne had done to her sister Agnes caused me to want to ask Mum lots of questions.

"What kind of man was Uncle Charlie?" A few times I had called at Aunt Minne's with some message from Mum, to find Uncle Charlie there playing with his son Harry and I always wondered why he was not with Aunt Agnes. On these occasions when I told Mum all she would say is, "He's a rotter."

Mum's 1922 Christmas present to my brothers was a single bed each. She had been paying off for them almost two years.

Linen for them was sparse but gradually she brought sheets and blankets and so as time passed Mum added to our home and Jim now worked evenings on a paper round and received 3s 6d weekly. It all helped. So that year passed.

Chapter Eighteen

The matriculation exam and my sixteenth birthday loomed near. I had studied hard and hoped I would pass, but I knew I would have to leave school.

Mum was adamant, saying, "You are growing up, you will want nice clothes, you must work and help me, your brothers need coats and they don't grow on trees, so put any idea of staying at school out of your head."

I could understand her viewpoint, though I did at times argue with her, and in the end had to come round to her way of thinking.

She was called before the school governors, two men and a woman. Mum stated what she thought and finished. "She has no father to help, I have worked for her and now she must work and pull her weight. I'm sorry but that is the situation and she is leaving at the end of the term."

They let Mum have her say, and then the woman asked, "Have you finished, Mrs Munday?" She spoke quietly to the two men and then she turned to Mum.

"I think you are behaving in a selfish manner."

Mum's temper flared. "Don't you dare call me selfish. It won't be what she knows but who she knows that will get her by in life, you believe me," and no matter what they said, Mum stuck to her guns and I left school at the end of the term and began immediately at a shoe factory to learn the trade, earning the princely sum of nine shillings weekly, out of which Mum gave me a shilling. I worked from eight o'clock in the morning until six o'clock in the evening, with an hour off for lunch; no Saturday as I was a junior. I decided to try for a Saturday job in a hairdresser's. Now more than ever I wanted to cut hair. I trailed around all the barber shops and hairdressers and drew a blank. After about six weeks of trying, I walked into Ben's, a tobacconist opposite Shoreditch Church. I spoke to a young lady, enquiring if she was the manageress. She went into the gents' salon and said, "This is Mr Ben." I told him I needed a Saturday job, but he said I had to be apprenticed, but would I like a receptionist's job, and how was I at figures and could I supply a reference? At that moment I would promise anything. I got a reference from Aunt Minne. She just had to say I was honest. So I had one foot in towards becoming a hairdresser, but it took a long time.

Mr Ben was a Jewish man of indeterminate age and his accent was as thick as a London fog. He scanned my reference briefly.

"Who wrote all this for you, a relative?"

"Yes, my auntie," I answered.

"Well, at least you're honest. Can you work Sundays?"

"I don't know. Must I?"

"If you want this job, yes." He smiled. "It's just mornings, nine till one o'clock, and Saturdays nine in the morning until nine at night; one hour off for lunch. I'll pay 7s 6d wage. If you think you would like the work, start next week, Saturday, sharp at nine o'clock."

Walking home I worked out that I would be getting sixpence an hour, and working nine hours a day and five days a week for just nine shillings weekly, that was just a fraction over two pence an hour; the sooner I left the factory the better. Unfortunately Mum had signed papers for three years.

At Mr Ben's that first morning he asked me, "Can you play the Yiddish piano?" I thought, this will lose me this job, as I shook my head.

"I'll show you." He came into the small reception cubicle.

"This is it," he smiled, pointing to a National Cash Register (NCR). He pressed down keys numbered in pounds, shillings and pence and up came small white discs relating to the price of keys pressed.

"It's quite easy, just be careful not to over-ring."

He erased all the prices he had shown me and said, "Now you begin, clear."

The girl on the tobacco counter said her name was Anna and between sales she told me that Mr Kaufman was the first hand in the gents' salon at street level and upstairs in the ladies' salon there were two men, a lady and a girl learner.

The day was busy; each assistant came with a client to my window to see that money was paid. I had to put ladies' dockets onto a separate file from the men's and I really had to keep my wits about me more so to play the Yiddish piano correctly. A tall fair-haired man came to my window with his clients quite a few times; I thought he stared at me intently each time.

Anna didn't work Sundays and Mr Ben served behind the tobacconist counter. The ladies' salon was also closed on Sundays.

The gents' salon was very busy and sometimes Mr Kaufman gave me dockets marked "goods, three and sixpence, but no money". When I asked for the cash, he smiled saying, "That's OK, you don't need to worry."

It was one o'clock before I realised it. Mr Ben gave me my wages, patted my head and said, "Till's right, see you next Saturday, don't be late." I stared at him.

"Don't you mean Friday afternoon, Mr Ben?"

"Yes, of course I do, sorry, I wasn't thinking. Bye."

I hurried home, eager to give Mum my wages. She was pleased for me and gave me 2s 6d for myself.

Then my thoughts turned to cosmetics. Tokalon foundation cream in a small white pot cost 1s 6d. Next week I would buy a lipstick. Mr Kaufman's dockets worried me.

Next Friday I resumed working and felt a little important as I seated myself in my cubicle.

Both salons were at their busiest Fridays and Saturdays and I had to keep my wits about me playing the Yiddish piano correctly.

On this, the second Friday of my working, Mr Kaufman's dockets totted up to forty-two shillings. I was scared stiff.

Forty-two shillings to me was a fortune. Suppose Mr Ben asked me to pay for this discrepancy in the till; he'd probably send me to prison for theft. I decided to ask someone for help… but who?

Sometimes I walked home with Len.

I decided to ask his advice. On Saturday I walked with him along Hackney Road.

"Len. I think Mr Kaufman is robbing Mr Ben," I began.

"Whatever has given you that idea?"

I explained about the dockets, "And this week I'm forty-five shillings short in the gents' till."

"You know what that cash is for, don't you?" I shook my head. "It's for this." With his right hand his fingers stroked down the forefinger of his left hand, saying, "You know?"

I watched the action, then said, "Yes, but why couldn't he tell me they were for finger stalls."

He burst into uncontrollable laughter.

"Belle, you are priceless, don't ever change."

It wasn't until I was married years later that I understood the meaning of his actions.

As work at the shoe factory became more demanding of my attention, I decided to leave Mr Ben. We were both sorry, but he said, "Come to get your hair cut sometimes, I'll always be very pleased to see you and to know how you're getting on."

As I slid into womanhood, Mother said, "You're a bit late, but don't worry, now keep away from boys," and nothing more was said on the subject.

I began suffering from biliousness. The attacks would begin without warning. The doctor prescribed bismuth and peppermint and down through the years I have drunk pints of the stuff. Finally Mother decided she would have me examined to find the cause of these attacks.

I had had a couple of bad attacks while working at the factory. There had been quite long intervals between. On this morning I felt awful. I asked the forewoman if I could go home, I felt ill.

"Get back to your seat, I think you just want days off." Instead I rushed from the workroom and made for the toilet. I sat on the chair beside the bath momentarily exhausted. After a while, Mollie, who sat next to me, came in. "You look terrible," she began. "She has sent me to bring you back to your work." I made another dash to the toilet.

What Mollie said I don't know, but when I returned to the workroom, the forewoman said, "I don't know how often this will happen, but if you were not an apprentice I would be sacking you." I went home feeling very resentful.

That bout decided Mother. She took me to the Mildmay Hospital, Shoreditch. The doctor's questions were intimate and embarrassing and the examination most unpleasant for me. And I remember the doctor's verdict. "This sickness is the result of the body's system rejecting anything it doesn't like, maybe two meals not agreeing, perhaps fruit. This girl is perfectly healthy and while there is biliousness she will never suffer any illness. The bismuth and peppermint her doctor prescribes acts as a soothing agent, so, Mother, you have nothing to worry about, and you," he said turning to me, "try to notice what you eat."

We thanked him. To me it seemed it was something I had to live with, I did wonder for how long. Always after these attacks I wanted something with vinegar, usually a tomato.

I rested the rest of the morning and after eating some toast I decided a walk in the fresh air would be ideal. I walked along the Hackney Road, round Shoreditch Church, down Calvert Avenue into Virginia Road. Passing a shoe factory a notice in the window caught my eye. It read, OUTDOOR MACHINIST WANTED. BEST WORK ONLY APPLY. There was no way Mother's children's stitching could be called best work, but the factory where I worked was first class. I entered a small cubicle and rang the bell. A window flapped open, a tall man snapped:

"Yes, be quick, I'm busy."

"You need outdoor machinists."

"Can you do bound work?" As I nodded he continued: "Run and turned, turning in?"

I replied quickly: "If I didn't know the trade I would not have applied in the first place."

He placed a small roll on the window frame.

"This sample is a pair of bound court shoes. Everything is supplied, we use rubber solution not paste, and there is a small reel of matching cotton. We pay a shilling for each pair of samples. That's all. Good day."

In the street I crossed fingers. I could help Mum after I finished work at the factory. I left there at six o'clock evenings and being an apprentice did not work Saturdays like the other ladies.

Suddenly my thoughts were interrupted by someone calling, "Little Belle." Turning I saw Mrs Gee. It was nice to see her after so long.

"Come home with me," I said, "Mum will be pleased to see you."

"Where are you living now?"

"We have a flat in Goldsmith's Row," I replied.

We sat chatting; there was much to speak about. She worked as a cook at Leman Street Police Station with the help of two ladies. She left, promising to visit again.

I began telling Mum of the sample and that I would help her with this new work if the sample was satisfactory. I showed

Mum how to make an invisible join in the binding, then I knocked over the binding, Mum machined in the lining and I taught her to use points of scissors to trim excess lining a fraction below the binding. Next morning Mum and I went to the shoe factory with our work. The tall man whose name we learnt later was Mr Wright examined the work minutely then smiled.

"Have you got a notebook?"

"No, I'll get one," answered Mum. He placed three bundles on the wicket flap, then scribbling on a piece of paper handed it to Mum. She showed it to me. On it was written, "Three dozen courts at seven shillings." I stared, and then pushed the bundles back.

"No, thanks, you can keep your work at that price."

"What's the matter?"

"The price. Why, it's less than 2s 6d per dozen pairs."

"You're mistaken. The price is seven shillings for each dozen pairs."

"I'm sorry… I thought…." I was trying to hide my surprise.

"You should never jump to conclusions, young lady."

In the street, Mum said, "I was ready to turn down the work too."

After lunch I returned to the factory, telling Mum to do what stitching she could until I returned from work.

The forewoman greeted me, "Have you come to work after your rest, and when is the next sickness to start?"

"Your guess is as good as mine," I retorted then sat down to work.

I helped Mum whenever I could with housework and the shoe work and did shopping. Between us we were earning good money.

About this time we were called "flappers" – the word "teenagers" had not yet been invented.

With Mum we always finished evenings at eight o'clock. Some nights I went out with my friend Louisa. We strolled along Mare

Street, Hackney, eyeing out the local talent. Mare Street was then nicknamed Monkey's Parade.

"We don't speak to flat caps, only trilbies," said Louisa referring to men's headgear. "And we stay together, no separating."

A new star appeared on cinema screens; his name was Rudolf Valentino. His Spanish style caused a new style of hats for women.

A stiff-brimmed flat-crowned hat, trimmed with a bunch of artificial cherries and two long black ribbon streamers hanging down the back. These hats were everywhere, worn whether they suited you or not.

I still wanted to cut hair and once told Mum I would be glad to end the apprenticeship and try to find work in a barber's shop.

"I've said so before, Belle. If you have a good trade in your hands, you will never want for a shilling or two. You can always work with me at home. We're doing all right at the moment."

We were eating better and we all had decent clothes, this I had to agree, but I still had that ambition.

Now I had a trade, if I was unable to get work cutting hair, I had something to fall back on. I had no worries; I could pay for things I wanted.

A few months previously, my brother Jim left the shoe factory because he said he was fed up doing the same thing day after day. He immediately landed a job in a shop that sold motorcycles and gramophones and records. A young lad of about fifteen kept the records in order and the young manager was very helpful to Jim. The repairs to motorcycles were a busy sideline in this shop and Jim, always mechanically minded, quickly learned how to dismantle a motorcycle and find the faults, and his wage was now thirty-five shillings weekly. It seemed in 1925 our luck was turning. Mum was given a three-dozen bundle of bound court shoes from the new factory and a tin of thin rubber solution. There were a dozen pairs of white shoes and two dozen pairs of brown. That first day she waited for me to get home before she tackled the binding. Tea over, we settled down to some serious stitching and by eight o'clock Mum was feeling a little more confident, and at 7s 6d for a dozen pairs and my help each evening, the first week's wages she earned were £2 15s 6d. She was elated, she had never earned so much before.

One Sunday Mrs Gee came to see us. She was going to move into a large house in Scawfell Street and she asked Mum if she would move in with her. The rent was two pounds weekly and they could pay one pound each. The important thing Mrs Gee wanted was the question of sharing the bath, which was in the lower kitchen, and the cooker and sink were also in that kitchen, and it was a question of agreement about using the bath. Mum would have four rooms and a kitchen so....

Mum was dubious. "Do let's move, Mum," we chorused, "we are earning more money now and we could afford the extra rent." Mrs Gee was delighted when Mum agreed and on a hot June Saturday we moved into Scawfell Street.

The rooms were large and beautifully decorated. We had never seen such pretty wallpaper. Mum had a little money saved and went shopping for floor covering and later a large roll of linoleum was delivered and gradually out of the chaos some order was restored. Now we had a bedroom for the boys.

The most remembered event of 1926 was the General Strike. It began with the miners. All negotiations broke down and in the middle of May, the transport workers joined them. There were no trains, buses or trams... soon the tramlines rusted over and as the strike dragged on throughout the summer, newspapers became scarce.

Travelling did not affect us. Bill was at school, Jim always walked to work, so did I, and Mum walked to the shoe factory with the finished uppers.

I remember the army was summoned to drive buses to get people to work.

Although they did not issue tickets, people gladly gave them their fare money. The drivers stopped wherever people wanted to alight.

I think the strike finally ended about October, and whatever the opposing conclusion came to I have long forgotten.

All I know was that the population was very pleased and as life became more normal, people settled down to resume living their own lives again.

Chapter Nineteen

One Friday evening in November Jim brought his manager home. Jim introduced him as Alf. He was very polite and adapted easily. He called Mum "Ma". He was about five feet eight, black hair sleeked back and dark brown eyes set in a rather thin face.

He stayed for a sandwich and pickle supper. The evening passed pleasantly as we chatted generalities.

"You must come again, Mr…?" said Mum.

"Call me Alf. Yes, I'd like to visit again and my thanks for a very nice evening." He turned to me, "Goodnight, Belle, I'll be seeing you, soon if I may."

I suppose at nineteen I should think about finding a boyfriend and that is how I began "walking out" with Alf Cox.

I finished my apprenticeship at the shoe factory and happily left, and worked full time at home with Mum. We were earning over five pounds weekly and Mum was slowly buying furniture and adding to our home.

Then she decided to buy a gramophone from Alf's shop.

It was an ornate table model in light oak. When the lid was opened it disclosed the turntable with a goose-necked tone arm. Two fancy doors opened in front to allow a sound outlet, and the first record we played was a song called *Marketa.* We listened enthralled. Each evening we sat and listened to the musical addition to our home.

This began my brother Bill's interest in records and

gramophone catalogues. He went round shops collecting leaflets as advertised by the different companies, and soon became very knowledgeable on the subject.

Alf let us have records at cost price and beforev long we had quite a collection.

Mum paid me wages for working with her and I now had some nice clothes. I had five pounds saved and decided to buy a piano. Mrs Gee had one and Harry was a very good player. We were introduced to Harry's friends and their small parties. Lizzie was Harry's girl. There was Charlie Steven and his girl Renee, John Williams and his girl Millie, my brother Jim and his girl Hilda and our cousin Bill King and his girl Sadie. Mum played the piano "to make a change", she said, and I was amazed how much she could remember after not playing for so long a time.

Sometimes a tall fair chap would come round and join us. He was Harry's friend. I thought him a little aloof, but came to the conclusion that maybe he was shy. He too could play the piano.

With my five pounds savings, I marched into a shop and surveyed the pianos on show. The salesman struck chords on some of them and although I hadn't a clue, I pretended I knew about music. I chose a pleasant sounding one for sixty-five guineas and of course, I needed a stool. That was 35s 6d. The bill, totted up, came to seventy pounds.

"Do you understand the meaning of hire purchase?" he asked.

"I promise to keep up the payments, is that so?"

"If you don't pay regularly, we can take the goods back and you lose all monies paid. So long as you understand." I nodded. He handed me a form. "Fill this in and get a guarantor to sign it. By the way, you are over eighteen?" I assured him I was.

"OK, bring back the form, duly signed and we will deliver the goods." I could not get home fast enough. Explaining to Mum, she hit the ceiling.

Had I gone raving mad? Did I want my brains tested? Do you realise what would happen if I couldn't pay? She went on and on. In this mood I knew she would never sign her name to the form.

"I'll ask Mrs Gee to sign for me," I threatened.

"You'll do no such thing. Belle, I could hit you for not telling me what you were thinking of doing. Why?"

"I want to learn to play like you, that's why."

"You're a bit old to begin learning. There is so much to memorise."

"I have a good memory and I promise I'll do all you tell me if you will teach me, Mum. Please sign the form, it will make me happy."

"What about Alf? Have you thought about him?"

"What about him? I won't ask him to stand security for me."

I sulked a little most of Sunday. At tea-time Alf came and after tea we strolled along Lea Bridge Road. I didn't speak much, I told him about the piano. He said he would willingly sign the form for me, but I thought that would make Mum even more angry. Monday morning she said, "For goodness' sake, stop mooning around, I'll sign the bloody form for you and woe betide you if you miss any payments. I dashed off to the shop elated. The salesman entered details into a ledger, gave me a payment book and said the piano would be delivered Wednesday afternoon. I couldn't wait for Wednesday.

I went to Sully's music shop and bought *Smallwood's Pianoforte Tutor* for £2 6d. I was determined to learn to play.

I helped Mum with the shoe work all I could. Really I could not do enough for her, I was so grateful to her for standing security for me.

Twenty-three Scawfell Street was a large semi-basement corner house with its entrance in Dunloe Street. Five steps, built on the side of the house, topped by an L-shaped iron rail, led to a grained and varnished street door. A short distance along a twelve-foot-high wall, a wooden green painted door opened to a concrete yard and two toilets. The street door opened into a square hall with doors leading to rooms. Immediately left of the entrance a stairway led to upstairs accommodation. Five stairs led to the yard and a small landing led to the semi-basement, a large living-room and a kitchen. In the kitchen was a tall cupboard holding saucepans and other kitchen utensils, a cooker and a sink and bath. The bath had only a cold tap. Hot water was supplied by a gas geyser and putting sixpence into a slot meter a nice bath was the result and by an amicable agreement with Mrs Gee we all managed two or three baths each a week. We were one big happy family. Mum called Mrs Gee Lil, and naturally she called Mum Bella. Harry had a dartboard that was nailed to one of the toilet doors and the boys enjoyed their dart-playing.

Mrs Gee worked at the Leman Street Police Station, Whitechapel, as cook, and while she worked there we could always obtain the bug blinder to keep the pests under control and they gradually vanished.

I spent every spare moment practising scales, my foot on the soft pedal, as I didn't want to annoy our neighbours with so much repetition. Harry helped me too, but his large hands could easily span ten notes. However, Mum said practice would make my fingers nimble, so I practised.

One day I told Mum I was going to get a job. She was very surprised.

I said, "I know you can manage this work now without my help and I still want to be a hairdresser. It's something I have always wanted to do."

The more she argued with me, the more adamant I became and on a morning in April 1927 I set out, hopes high.

I walked along the Hackney Road into the best-looking salon.

Driers were whirring in two cubicles. A young lady greeted me. "Can I help you, madam?" Madam said she would like to speak to the manager.

A good-looking Jewish man came out of a cubicle, comb in hand. He smiled.

"I wish to learn this trade," I began. "Could I become an apprentice?"

He shook his head. "I am fully staffed at the moment, two young ladies are having their elevenses. Why not try a hairdressing school? There are quite a few of them in the West End." I thanked him and boarded a bus to Liverpool Street Station. Down the tube I booked to Oxford Street.

Walking down Regent Street I came to Galleries Lafayette, a large departmental store. The windows were beautifully dressed. I walked past and came to Raynes, a shoe shop. Staring at the display I stood trying to find any faults in the shoes. They were all perfection personified. I entered the shop.

Again I asked to speak to the manager. A tall man dressed in a pin-striped suit smiled. I quietly asked if he needed an assistant. He nodded and said, "Sorry, not at the moment, leave your telephone number at the desk, good morning," and left me standing there. I marched out. Where next? I turned back into Oxford Street. I came to Bond Street and slowly did some window-shopping; most goods displayed were not priced. Now I was admiring more shoes, mostly of the evening variety. I walked slowly into this shop.

I enquired of the assistant if I could speak to the manager. Unconsciously I crossed my fingers, saying to myself, "Third time lucky."

A very black-haired brown-eyed man stared hard when I asked if he needed an assistant. "What do you want to work here for?"

"I like the style of your window." I could think of nothing else to say.

"Have you worked with shoes before?"

"Yes, for quite a long time." I was speaking in the poshest way I know.

He frowned. "How old are you?"

"Twenty."

"Twenty, and you've worked with shoes a long time?" His tone was filled with disbelief. "And you are twenty?"

"My mother stitched shoe uppers," I told him. It seemed to me I was losing ground. I cast furtive glances at the three assistants as they attended to their customers' needs.

"Have you a black dress?" he queried.

"Yes, sir," I lied. I'd soon get one, I promised myself.

"Oh, by the way, can you speak French?"

My heart sank to my feet. "I learned it at school, those verbs were a trial to me, I think I have forgotten some of the language."

He smiled, "Oh well, at least you're honest about it, but if I take you on my staff, will you promise to brush up on the language?"

I'd have promised him anything; instead I nodded.

"Good. Be here 8.45 sharp, Monday morning. Your pay will be twenty-seven shillings weekly, payable every ten days; there will be commission on sales when you're on the floor. Good afternoon, Miss...."

"Munday, Isabelle Munday."

He nodded.

Outside the shop I could have turned a cartwheel. I had started at the top, I was so pleased with myself. Farther along the street I saw Revelle's Hairdressing Academy. I couldn't believe my eyes. It was all coming my way.

"Steady, Isabelle," I told myself, "learn to crawl before you walk."

Telling Mum my luck, I don't think she was too pleased, however, she hoped I would succeed, but said, "Don't build your hopes too high."

I went to dancing class one night a week with my friend Louisa and when I told her I was going to work in the West End, she said, "You'd better be careful up there, remember there are lots of pitfalls for the likes of soppy dates like you, but you might learn a thing or two if you keep your eyes open."

I think Louisa's mother was very open-minded and discussed

many problems and ways of growing up with all the family, while my mother shut up like a clam.

Mother's comment as I started off on Monday was, "Be careful, Belle, and watch what you do and say. Some people take things the wrong way."

In the tube train we packed in tighter than sardines. At each station along the line more and more people squeezed in. I was pressed on all sides by men and girls and I almost fell out of the train at Oxford Circus. I hurried along to Bond Street breathing fresh air after the stuffy tube and just managed to make it at 8.45.

As the door opened for me one girl was already hoovering the carpet in the showroom. She greeted me politely and asked my name, and in return said her name was Betty. She pointed to stairs. "Put your hat and coat in the closet in the stockroom, the other girls are down there."

In the stockroom two girls were powdering their faces. They said their names were Miss Bennet and Miss Wardley and asked what they should they call me.

They thought my name was a laugh. "Do you ever get called Tuesday or Wednesday?" they asked good-naturedly. I replied, "I did when I was small."

A bell tinkled. "That's the manager," one said. He entered the stockroom and said good morning quite pleasantly to us. "Upstairs, girls, and Munday, you stay here." I was left alone. "Now, Munday," he began briskly, "here are your duties. For a week you will stay down here learning the stock, and I'll give you our trade code, which you will learn by heart and never divulge outside the shop. After a week you'll be on the floor to serve, if you know the stock and the code. Each one of the girls will test you and if you pass all will be well and you'll receive commission on sales. This will be paid weekly, on Monday, and wages will be paid every ten days. Do you understand?"

I said, "Yes, sir, I'll do my best."

"Good," he said, then gave me the code word, each letter to coincide with the number of pounds, shillings and pence and the cost of a pair of shoes.

Thus I learned the ways of West End trading and a week later I faced my first customer a trifle nervously. To my amazement she purchased two pairs of expensive shoes without being too difficult. Her bill was £7 16s 9d.

I served four customers that first day and did as well as the other girls. The manager explained to me to persuade the customers to buy stockings or fancy buckles for their shoes, decorated buckles being very much the vogue at that time. Commission for shoes was one per cent, but on accessories it was a penny in the shilling. At one per cent, a shilling in five pounds didn't seem much to me, but the shoes were expensive and the cash mounted, and I pushed accessories for all I was worth, and some weeks my commission topped my wages.

Mother and my brothers were interested in the ways of shoppers and listened intently to tales: how some women asked for sizes smaller than they really needed. Miss Bennet (later called Beno) sometimes whispered to me, "Take her the box," when a customer had large feet.

Evenings I was at the piano and Alf got a little fed up. We met each other three times a week. His shop closed Thursday half-day. All shops at this time had to close one half-day weekly – a Shop Act – if assistants worked Saturdays. I saw Alf Mondays, Thursdays and Sundays. Wednesdays I went out with my friend Louisa to the dance class, other times I was playing the piano, foot on the soft pedal. Constantly going over the scales, I didn't want to annoy our next door neighbours.

I was at the piano one night when Alf entered the room.

"Still at it?" he asked, I thought a little crossly.

I continued with the scales, not getting up to greet him.

"I sometimes ask myself if you think more of that piano than you do of me."

"I want to become a good player," I replied. "Surely you're not jealous."

"Well, are you coming to the cinema or not?" he demanded.

I went with him to the cinema, but we argued on and off all the evening.

I was really fed up with his carping mood, and saying goodnight I told him, "Until you're in a better mood, don't bother to see me. Goodnight."

When Jim came home from work next evening he said that Alf had been like a bear with a sore head all day, and had I upset him?

"According to him, I pay too much attention to the piano and not enough to him... I just told him to cool off a little."

"So, have you finished with him?" asked Jim.

"It's entirely up to him and you can tell him so."

Chapter Twenty

Coming home one evening, I touched the collar of a sailor as I passed him. He turned quickly. "Just for luck," I smiled, walking on.

He caught up with me. "My name is Edgar, and I have another two weeks before I return to my ship. How about it?"

"What a fast worker," I thought. Then I remembered Father was a sailor when Mum met him. "How about what?" I asked.

"We could see each other for the rest of my leave."

He was nice, medium build, very tanned and confident.

"Come to the pictures with me tonight?"

"Sorry, I've made other arrangements."

"Boyfriend, I suppose?"

"No, a dance class."

"Can't you miss it, surely you can?"

"I don't break promises, not to my old school friend."

"What about tomorrow night?" He was insistent.

"Thank you, yes. Where shall we meet and how do I know if you'll turn up? I promise you I'll wait just ten minutes, that's all."

"Seven-thirty. Where you touched my collar. Be there."

We shook hands as I repeated, "Remember, I'll give you just tern minutes."

On time, off we went to the cinema, to Hackney Pavilion. Afterwards we went to Paul's Fish Bar in Mare Street, where for

1s 6d one could get a fish supper. A middle cut of skate, chips, roll and butter and a cup of tea, served quickly as we sat at white marble-topped tables.

Telling Mum I was seeing a sailor and his leave was coming to an end, she said, "Bring him home and let's have a look at him, see what he's like."

So on Sunday he came to tea. His brother Victor was also a sailor. At this time Victor was sailing round the Cape of Good Hope, South Africa, and he would be joining his ship, *Dunedin*, at Portsmouth, on Tuesday, and would be on board for six months before they saw land again. Altogether we all spent a very pleasant evening and saying goodnight to him, we were in a very tight clinch when Harry let himself into the house. I introduced them and they began chatting. "Come in and have a drink, mate," said Harry, leading the way into Mrs Gee's sitting-room, where they both downed whisky. We never had strong drink in our house; we were all teetotal. When finally Edgar left he said, "I could get very fond of you, Belle. You're a nice kid. Promise you'll write to me. Promise."

I gave my word, saying, "A sailor has a girl in every port, I'm told. Is it true what they say?"

"They say too much for their own good... whoever *they* are." He laughed.

I felt a little sad when he left, but not too much and I did write many times and always received replies.

Jim bought a motorcycle, paying half the cash down, the rest by hire purchase. It was a BSA machine that looked quite large in our concrete yard and naturally Alf came round to teach Jim how to drive, and that is how Alf and I got back together. I compromised and didn't play the piano when he came. That pleased him and one Monday evening he arrived around 6.30 saying he had left Jim to lock up the shop as he had something special in mind.

We boarded a tram to Lower Clapton Road, then he looked

into a jeweller's window, asking, "Which ring would you like me to buy you?"

I stared at the splendid array of sparkling rings. "What you asking? Do you mean me to be engaged to you?"

"That was the idea I had in mind. We could save hard and maybe get married in a year or eighteen months. What do you think?"

Staring at the rings, it all sounded very romantic. "All right," I said, and we entered the shop.

The assistant smiled. "Can I help you?"

At Alf's request he laid a tray of rings on the counter. Alf pointed to a half-hoop. It looked too large on my slim finger. The assistant produced some metal rings and we found my finger size by slipping the metal ring onto a polished stick. Finally I chose a ruby surrounded by six diamonds. It looked just right on my hand. The price was £8 10s. Arriving home I was pleased to show Mum the ring. She laughed, "My goodness, Woolworth's make it look like the real thing." Alf was shocked.

"Mum, this *is* the real thing, we're engaged." I told her the cost.

"You're both crazy, and you, Belle, are far too young to commit yourself."

Alf said nothing. "But Mum, we have to save up for some time," I reminded her, "and I do have the piano to settle with first."

"I'll pay that for you, don't worry," Alf said quietly.

"No you don't," I snapped. "I'll pay that myself, thanks."

Jim came in and handed the shop keys to Alf. He looked at our glum faces. "Now what's up with you, Mum?"

"Ask him," Mum replied shortly, pointing to Alf.

After hearing the story, all Jim said was, "Well, it takes time to save money, and a lot can happen during that time."

Flashing the ring at work next day, Miss Bennet said during our elevenses together, "Do you love this bloke? How long have you known him?"

"Just over a year, Ben, why do you ask?" I hadn't thought too much about love.

"Would you use his toothbrush?"

"Why, is that a test of love?"

Since Miss Bennet had her elevenses with me, I had learned many facts of life from her. She lived in a bed-sit in a large house in Finchley with seven other boarders. There was a nice young man opposite her door on the same landing and they often shared a supper and sometimes spent the night together.

I was just a little shocked at the revelation but was careful not to show it. She told me about condoms and their use. It was then I understood Len Snowcill's action all those years ago. Speaking about the friend one day, I asked Ben if she was going to marry him. "Good Lord, no," she laughed.

"But if you are sleeping with him..." I finished lamely.

"We are both gaining experience, and that's essential."

So... did I love Alf? Would I sleep with him to gain experience? Most certainly not and some doubts crept into my thoughts about him.

Under Alf's tuition Jim's driving improved by leaps and bounds. Now Alf took Jim into the main-road traffic. (There were no driving tests as far as I can remember in those days.) While Alf rode with Jim, I practised.

I was now mastering an easy piece, *The Fairy Wedding*, and taking the skin off my middle finger of the right hand playing the treble gliss.

Payments for the piano were mounting. A good week's commission and I would pay ten shillings, and there were several times when I paid fifteen shillings. Until the piano was paid for I couldn't begin to start hairdressing sessions. Once a week I went to a dance class with Louisa. One week she said she would try for her silver medal. She had already got a bronze and now I was up to silver standard, would I like to try for medals? Quickly I told her to forget the idea. I had no interest in dancing to earn money and when the teacher started badgering me, I left, but kept up my friendship with Louisa.

Chapter Twenty-one

One day I met an old neighbour. It was late summer and I had bought myself a cream linen suit. As we stood talking, she told me her husband was in hospital over in South London. At that time there were shilling all-day Sunday tickets on trains and you could ride anywhere in the London area, and this was her husband's pastime – seeing London cheaply. He had been in hospital for three days and would be there for a while. "It's funny, Belle, a few weeks ago I had my fortune told. She said an accident would happen away from the home and there would be an addition to the family and later someone would walk on three legs. Who's going to be born with three legs, for heaven's sake?"

We both laughed and saying cheerio she promised to visit us. Some days later I repeated all this to Ben.

"Is she good, this fortune-teller?" she asked me.

I shrugged. "Well. Mr Painter's accident happened as she predicted."

"Where does she live, this lady?"

"Who, the fortune-teller or Mrs Painter?"

"The fortune-teller, stupid."

"No idea, but she calls herself Pollyanna." We both laughed. "When Mrs Painter visits us, I'll asked for the address." Then I forgot about the fortune-teller and Mr Painter, until Mrs Painter came about three weeks later and told us her husband would be home next week. He had been five weeks in hospital and still had an arm in plaster.

I asked about the fortune-teller's address. She didn't know it but her daughter Cissie would take me there. I said I would find out when Miss Bennet could arrange a meeting and would bring her along.

Ben and I met Cissie at Shoreditch Church one Wednesday evening and we walked down Kingsland Road until we arrived at an open door.

"It's the first door on the landing, said Cissie. "I won't wait, goodnight." She left us mounting the stairs.

There were two chairs outside a door on the dimly lit landing. A stout lady sat on one. I'm waiting for my friend," she told us smiling. "Have you been here before? She's very good, you know."

We shook our heads and Ben sat down. At that moment a young woman came out, smiling broadly. "I'm coming into money," she laughed. "Some hopes!"

"Shall I?" Ben queried. I nodded and she entered the room.

I sat quietly for some five minutes when two very young girls clattered up the stairs.

"What's she like?" one asked me.

"I haven't the foggiest idea. My first time here."

Ben came out looking thoughtful, but she smiled. "Your turn."

The room was lit by two candles at the end of the table. I stared at the dark-haired woman whose hair fell round her shoulders. Her dark piercing eyes looked over me. "You can take that off," she began, pointing to my ring. She shuffled the cards with dexterity. "Cut them in three, please." I cut the cards and she quickly began laying them out, speaking as she did so.

"You will be made an offer. There is a quarrel over coal and wheels. You will marry a little later. There is a blue-eyed boy out there who will be very very good to you. You will achieve by hard work. I see you covered in bricks and ruin, but I don't know why. The cards have finished. Three and sixpence, please."

She had placed the cards in three rows of thirteen and indeed as she had placed the last card so she had stopped speaking. I thanked her and left that dim room and felt a little creepy. How wrong she was. Alf and I were saving hard and I was paying as much as I could afford for the piano.

We talked as I walked with Ben to Liverpool Street Station. We said goodnight and I turned for home. Naturally this Pollyanna woman had got it all wrong. She had told Ben she would cross a lot of water and become a very rich woman. There would be two children and she would return to this country. We spoke about our fortunes next day and were so sure all of it was mumbo jumbo.

In July of 1927, Bill reached the age of fourteen and the weekly ten shillings stopped immediately. He left school when the school summer holidays began and landed a post in a shop selling all types of musical instruments, gramophones and records. He knew which band, classical or dance, played on which record and on the flip side too. He knew which singer sang on what record. His wage to begin was thirty shillings weekly. As we were now all contributing to the housekeeping, we persuaded Mum to give up shoe machining and have more leisure. Reluctantly she agreed and the factory was sorry to learn of her decision.

At Christmas we had a smashing time. All Harry's friends and our friends and cousins dropped in for drinks and a sing-song round the piano. The boys and girls were beginning to pair off, all getting a little serious about each other. Alf came on his motorcycle on Boxing Day. Flo and her husband came with little Florence, now four and a half, and Baby Leonard, now almost a year old, and another day was spent happily eating and chatting.

And so we drifted into 1928. In February I was twenty-one and we had a swell party. The house was filled with friends and relations. I received presents of flowers and chocolates, gloves, and my brothers bought me silk stockings; they ladder very easily.

Nylons had not yet come onto the market. They came, I think, with the US soldiers and World War II.

Occasionally one of us dropped in to see Gran. Since becoming the owner of her house she had put on an arrogant manner so our visits were few and far between. Bill had called in to see her and she told him Father wanted to see me. When Bill asked why, she replied, "Your father doesn't tell me his business. Ask your sister to come here next Thursday at two o'clock."

After repeating the message, I dashed round to see Gran.

If we worked on Saturday morning at the shop where I worked we were given a half-day off during the week, which we took in rotation. My half-day would be Wednesday of the next week. This I told Gran would be when I would see him. I didn't intend to lose time from work for him.

"Your father is a very busy man," she told me haughtily.

"And I too am busy. Who does he think he is, after all these years?" I was infuriated by her tone. "Has he just remembered I'm his daughter?"

I wore my new cream linen suit, and a tan satin-covered pill-box hat trimmed with two cream roses and a short tan eye veil. Tan court shoes with a matching bag completed the outfit. Mum said I looked quite smart. "Do be careful, Belle, and he may have a car. Please don't go riding in it with him."

"Don't worry, Mum, and as for a car ride, you must be joking."

It was a fairly warm sunny day towards the end of February as I set out.

Chapter Twenty-two

Gran opened the door to me, then turned to walk down the passage. I closed the street door thinking how rude her manner was. When I entered the room she was already seated. He stood, his back to the fireplace, straw hat pushed to the back of his head, his paunch bulging over his trousers.

"You asked to see me… well?"

"Where d'you get that bloody plummy accent?"

"It's laid on with a trowel where I work."

"You've grown quite a looker now, if you had your mother's green eyes you'd be really something."

I stared at him po-faced. "You remember her green eyes, you amaze me."

He snorted. "Sit down," he commanded.

"I prefer to stand, thank you. What do you want? I'm busy."

"I've come here to offer you a job."

"I have a job."

"Some tuppenny-ha'penny, pound-a-week lark, I suppose." He sneered.

"It's no lark, I assure you."

"I can offer you a decent job, where you can earn good money, wear good clothes, much better than that rag you're wearing, meet rich men – so?"

Rag indeed. I suppressed my rising anger with difficulty. I'd get back at him for that, I'd think of something. My nice suit that had cost me £4 10s and he had called it a rag.

"You could be the manageress of a pub, meet rich men. Think about it."

"I'd hate to work in a pub. If I came to work for you, I'd rob you right, left and centre."

"Yes? When I caught you with your hand in the till, I'd send you to clink. How would your mother like that, eh? I bet she wouldn't," he sneered. "I see you're engaged. What's he work at?"

"That is my business."

"Well, have you thought about this job?"

"I have said I would hate to work in a pub. I remember when I was five, I saw a man have a glass rammed into his face."

He looked at me shrewdly. "Your memory goes back a long way."

"It goes back farther than that. I remember you hitting Mother across her back with a chair."

"Belle," cried Gran, "how can you tell such wicked lies!"

"I'm not lying. I was there, you weren't. Ask him… ask him."

"You wouldn't do a thing like that, would you, Jim?" She smiled at him.

I waited for his reply but instead he changed the subject. "How much do you weigh? You could do with some more flesh on your bones."

"How much do *you* weigh?" I countered.

"Twenty stone," he boasted proudly.

"A little bit overweight, aren't you?"

He rubbed his paunch appreciatively; the action was obscene to me.

"Button your jacket, you look eight months pregnant."

He laughed derisively. Gran laughed too. "Now wouldn't I be the miracle man, just think," he slapped his thighs. "That deserves something." He took a roll of notes from a pocket and peeling off some, threw them onto the table, saying, "There's twenty quid, get yourself a decent suit, but if you give any of it to your mother, I hope it chokes her."

"What a gentleman," I said sarcastically.

When I made no effort to take it, he continued. "Pick it up. Do you think I can't afford it? Why, I could go to the races tomorrow and put that lot on a loser and I wouldn't bat an eyelid," he boasted.

I looked at Gran. The admiration on her face for her son sickened me. "You're so kind, Jim," she smirked.

I looked at the green pound notes as an idea began to form in my mind.

"Well, if you don't want the money...." He leaned forward to pick it up, but I was quicker. I snatched up the notes and stuffed them into my handbag.

"Your father is a generous man," said Gran. "I think you ought to thank him for that cash. Go on, Belle."

"Thank him! Thank him! For what? For the years of scrimping and scraping. For the measly ten shillings weekly sent to feed and clothe three growing kids. Thank him for never sending a birthday or Christmas card, for never sending a penny extra at Christmas-time when kids expect a present? Don't make me laugh – and you know all I'm saying is true. We had to come to you each week to collect the money. I hope you're proud of him. Honestly, he could teach Scrooge a lesson."

"Shut your trap," he bawled at me, "or I'll bloody well shut it for you."

Nothing could stop me, on and on I went. Lord knows what I did say.

"The many dinners of bread and marge, sometimes just dry bread. Did you think you could starve us to death? Did you wish a bomb would find us and you'd be rid of us that way...? No, we lived to torment you and I'll tell you something else...." I paused as Gran butted in.

"You're upset, Belle, and I know you don't mean all you're saying. Tell your father you're sorry, please."

I gazed at him incredulously, thinking of the years Mum had struggled to keep a roof over our heads. "I mean every word," I told her. "Say I'm sorry to him? What a hope! I'll tell you this." I turned to Father. "Your woman will never be Mrs Munday. Mum will never divorce you, never. You tell her that, and Mum will live to see you out. Now, you get back to your bastards, they need you, we don't."

"Why you saucy little cow, I'll knock your bloody head off for that."

He came quickly round the table. I hoped the momentary panic didn't show. "If you touch me, I'll kick you where it hurts most, and with your girth I wouldn't miss." I stood firm before him.

"Just like your bloody mother, you fight with your tongue."

"Better than using fists, like you," I replied.

He stood between me and the door. "I'll see you some time, Gran."

I turned to Father. "Out of my way, you." He moved slightly and I brushed against him on my way out. Knowing he watched me as I walked down the steps into the street, head up I walked past the railing of the house.

I felt upset by the encounter and sick. Intermittently biliousness still plagued me and I was breathing deeply as I made my way across Hackney Road. I looked at the white enamel plaque over the door. It read: "You may telephone from here." I would ring Jim at work to tell him of my idea. I looked at the long bell-shaped receiver, at the mouth-piece atop the short black column. Instead I bought a woman's magazine for two pence and through the shop window saw Father's car turn into Hackney Road at speed. "Goodbye, Father," I muttered. "Remember, there are no pockets in shrouds."

The doorbell jingled noisily as I entered the shop. A smart salesman greeted me. "Can I help you, madam?"

"I have had my eye on that dining suite for a time. How much is it?"

We stood by the mid-brown oak table, the polish bright in the weak February sunlight. "The complete suite is priced at £12 10s, and all furniture is made on the premises. Would you care to see our workshop?"

"I really haven't the time, thank you. Could the suite be delivered on Saturday afternoon to 23 Scawfell Street? It's just across the road from the shop. I'll pay cash."

"Certainly, Miss," he said smiling. "I'll show you the sideboard. It has spacious shelves, see." He opened the doors; the inside was deep and roomy. "And the chairs, they're covered in green rexine. Would you prefer another colour? It can easily be done for you."

"Thank you, green is fine. I like those big bulbous legs, strong-looking."

"In the trade they're called acorn-shaped."

I began counting out the cash when he said, "I'll knock five shillings off for the ready." I smiled. Looking round the shop I saw a dark oak wardrobe with a three-panelled front. The centre panel was a full-length mirror.

"The wardrobe, how much, please?"

"That's just ten pounds. Come, take a look." He opened the door to a roomy interior with a steel hanging rail. "There's a deep drawer at the bottom for linen and it's very well made."

I had £7 15s. I asked if I paid that much off the wardrobe would he hold it by for a couple of weeks or so until I could pay the rest.

So the docket was made out for the suite and wardrobe with £2 5s to pay and delivery would be Saturday afternoon. I left the shop on air.

I arrived home to find Mum crying. "Oh, Belle," she sobbed, hugging me close. "You've been so long and I've been very worried. I know the kind of man he is. I thought he would try to lure you away from me."

"How could you think that, Mum? Don't think like that. He offered me a job, in a pub, and I told him what to do with it. I launched off telling her what I could remember of all I had said. When I said he had better get back to his bastards, she was astounded at that.

"How could you lower yourself to use such language, Belle?"

"He said my suit was a rag. I had to get back at him and I can tell you, he didn't like the truth." I didn't tell her all that was said and I didn't say anything about the twenty pounds. I wanted to see the surprise on her face when the furniture arrived. She was careful and always saving for something that would brighten up our home. Just before the piano was delivered, Mum had bought some medium-coloured linoleum with a wood-block pattern and that had made a great difference to our existing bits of furniture. For me, Saturday could not come round quickly enough.

Chapter Twenty-three

When Jim came in he wanted to know how the interview went, and off I went, maybe into a little more detail, and I had to repeat it all again when Bill arrived home. When Mum began our evening meal, I beckoned my brothers into our sitting-room and told them about the twenty pounds and how I had spent it and to keep it secret until Saturday. They promised.

Over dinner that evening, we spoke about Father. "I hate him for all those years he has caused Mum to work and slave for us, and having to do without, no wonder we're all skinny. Don't you hate him too, Mum?"

"No, I don't hate him." We looked at her in amazement. "I have no feelings for him whatsoever. To me he died years ago. Now get on with your dinner and let's forget him."

"But Mum, he isn't dead," Bill said.

"I have something all his money can't buy and that is a name for his kids."

"Those children can't help being born any more than we could," said Jim. "Why don't you divorce him, Mum? He's no use to us."

"I made my vows before God's altar and I'm keeping them. 'Till death do us part.' Now, close the subject."

By three o'clock Saturday afternoon, I was biting my nails. Why hadn't the suite come as promised? Harry Gee came up and said, "Let's have a piano lesson." I answered, "You play and

I'll listen." Looking out of our sitting-room window, I saw it had been raining. Now it was four o'clock.

Mum entered the room. "Playing in the dark, Harry?"

"I have the eyes of a cat, Mrs Munday."

Mum switched on the light and I was reminded of Father's remark about Mum's green eyes. I looked at them now. In this light they looked clear green framed by black lashes. They were her best asset.

Then came a knock at the door. I couldn't get down the stairs fast enough. I opened the street door. A big man stood there, docket in hand.

"How do we get this lot over these railings?"

"I'll open the side gate for you," I said and quickly did so.

Soon the furniture was unloaded and was being manhandled up the stairs.

Mum stood gaping in wonderment and Harry stood beside her.

"I think I'm dreaming," Mum said. "Where has this come from?" She turned to me. "Is this something to do with you, Belle?"

"Yes, Mum. I wanted to surprise you. I never told you, Father gave me twenty pounds… at least, he threw it on Gran's table. I spent it this way to benefit all of us."

I thought she looked a little angry. I pleaded, "Please don't be cross, Mum, I wanted us to share the money and I thought this would be a very good idea."

The men were bringing up the sideboard and dumped it just inside the room. "Where's this going, madam?"

Harry suggested we move the couch diagonally across a corner near the window, and then the sideboard could stand against the space behind the door.

Soon all was in place. The men sat on the stairs wiping perspiration from their faces. Mum said to them, "Thank you both very much. I have just made some tea, how about a cup?"

she asked. "Do you take sugar?" They drank the hot tea quickly and thanked Mum profusely when she tipped them each a shilling. Harry suggested drying off the rain spots, which we did.

With the dining suite in place, we had tea. Harry thanked Mum then said he would get ready, as he had promised to take Lizzie dancing. When my brothers came in all was revealed and admired. "There's £2 5s to pay," I said, "and I have promised to settle in two or three weeks."

That's OK, Mum," said my brothers, and placing cash on the table Bill said, "Pay it into the shop on Monday and settle up."

I had to go into detail then as to how I had made the purchase, and when Mrs Gee came home from working at the police station the story was retold... no wonder I remember it all so vividly. Mum was so grateful to us and we helped the boys take down the rail Jim had fixed in the recess beside the chimney breast in the bedroom where we had hung our clothes, and the wardrobe was shifted into the space. We told her to play the piano while we filled the wardrobe with our clothes. Soon all was tidy, then we sat chatting.

Mrs Gee came up to join us. "What are you doing next Saturday, Belle?" she asked suddenly.

"Nothing at the moment, why?"

"Our vegetable cook has a wedding to go to, her daughter's, and I wondered if you'd care to fill in."

I never saw Alf on Saturdays. By the time the shop shut at nine o'clock, and he'd totted up the till, it was too late to do anything, so the idea of an afternoon at the nick rather appealed to me and I accepted.

The following Saturday afternoon I presented myself at Leman Street Police Station and asked for Mrs Gee and was duly shown to the kitchen. It was a huge room, all white tiles and clean worktops, with a double-sized oven on which stood large saucepans and steamers. A deep white sink was filled with peeled potatoes. The menu for the night was loin pork chops, stuffing, mashed potatoes and peas with apple sauce and tinned fruit with custard for sweet.

"Hang your coat in that cupboard, Belle," said Mrs Gee. I did so, then she dumped a string bag of peas beside me saying, "Get shelling."

"All this bagful?"

She laughed and placing a half-pint enamel mug on the table, told me, "Two of these mugs filled serves three men and there are twenty-eight coppers in for dinner tonight, so...." She laughed.

So I began, it seemed a never-ending task to fill twenty mugs of peas.

We worked quickly, and she was well organised. Thick loin pork chops were laid out in trays and peppered and placed in the oven ready for cooking; meantime the peas began to mount up in the large bowl. We broke off for tea then began again. My fingers were beginning to feel sore.

After filling the enamel mug nineteen times, cooking began. Potatoes were cooked in a huge boiler and with steamers added on top, and the vegetables were cooked on two gas burners while the chops and stuffing roasted in the oven. Just before seven the service hatch slid down and five dinners went up to the canteen. The dinners looked great, a succulent chop, stuffing, mashed potatoes and two-thirds of a mug of peas filled each plate. The sweet was served from a catering-sized fruit can and custard was made with three pints of milk. Mrs Gee rationed all the dinners and each policeman had an equal share. Two ladies came in to wash up and mop the floor. We left, arriving home at 8.30. I appreciated the experience, but had no desire to become a cook.

On an afternoon off, about three weeks later, I called on Gran. Opening the door to me she marched down the hallway without speaking. I followed her into her room; she sat stiff-backed, hands clasped over the silver handle of her ebony walking-stick. Secretly we kids called this her Queen Victoria pose. She had the same dumpy figure and did look a little like that lady.

"Sit down, young lady," she ordered, "I have something to say to you."

So she had had three weeks to simmer and now she had come to the boil.

"I am shocked and ashamed of you; to speak and shout at your father the way you did sickened me. You're going to apologise to him."

I opened my mouth to speak, but she wagged a finger at me.

"Be quiet and listen to me," she commanded, and then went on. "After he was so generous to you too, then telling him he was eight months pregnant, ladies don't mention words like that to me."

"Oh, I think he knew what I meant," I interrupted.

"And to swear at him too, calling your step-brother and -sisters names.

"They are no family of ours, and they are bas—"

"Don't you dare repeat that word, you're all children of the same father, don't you forget that, my girl."

"In your eyes, Gran, he can do no wrong. You amaze me."

"There's notepaper on the table. Sit down and write to your father telling him you're sorry and didn't mean all you said and apologise."

"Are you serious, have you taken leave of your senses?"

"I am perfectly serious, do as I say," she commanded haughtily.

"If he were here now, I'd tell the skinflint. When Jim reached the age of fourteen, he dropped the money to five shillings weekly and when I told you Mum would take him to court, he quickly coughed up with another five shillings and it remained at ten shillings weekly until Bill was fourteen. I think it gave him a fright, don't you? I think Mum should have got much more."

She glared at me. "What have you done with the money he gave you?"

"Like Father, I put it on a horse, a loser. Easy come, easy go," I lied.

"I made up the other five shillings from my pension," she said suddenly. "I knew your mother didn't threaten idly and I didn't want my son's name dragged through the court. I love all my sons." She tossed her head. "And the money stopped immediately Bill was fourteen, as your father wished."

"And you let him think that Mum meekly accepted five shillings?"

"Your father is a hard-working man. When your mother left him, he had nothing, now look at him." She smiled with pleasure.

"Neither did Mum, so they started even." I stood up. "And when I come to think about it, Gran, you're not short of a bob or two. You have the rents from the tenants of this house and I expect Father greases your palm whenever he visits you, so don't you ever cry wolf to me."

Arriving home that afternoon, I repeated most of the conversation to Mum. She could hardly believe what I told her Gran had done, knowing Mum didn't threaten idly.

"Your grandmother is a devious woman, and has been all the years I've known her. You have to be up early and abed late to beat her."

After dinner, we sat round the kitchen fire with a cup of tea. Mum asked, "Whatever gave you the idea, Belle, to buy furniture?"

"Not quite sure, Mum. When I snatched up the cash, I was thinking he has never given us a thing. I wanted something lasting that would give us pleasure and... here it is." Again she expressed her gratitude.

"Tell us, Mum," said Jim. "Why did you really leave the pub?"

She glanced at Bill, now almost sixteen.

"It was before you were born, Bill. I wasn't sure about you and I confided in Nanny – Mrs Renick – you never knew her – she was an angel. She said wait a few more weeks. I did. I thought your father would be pleased. He roared his disapproval. Get rid of it, the last thing we want in a pub is a squawking kid. I was so hurt. We spent an unhappy Christmas. He picked quarrels with me over the smallest thing. He punched me about my body… never in my face." She smiled. "You see, I had to serve in the pub."

Mum turned to me. "Then there was the incident when a glass was jammed into a man's face and because it made you ill, you stayed with Aunt Alice. Twice during the time you were away he tried to push me down the stairs. In spite of all the blows, you were born a healthy eight pounds. Two months before you were born, there was an outing from the church for the ladies who attended the mothers' meetings. It took place on Thursdays, that was your father's day off.

"The outing was to Westcliffe. There they saw your father strolling arm in arm with a woman, and gave him a ribbing. The next Thursday, when I was alone in the pub, they came in full of their outing and told me what they had seen. It appears they sang to him, "Who's your lady friend?" This woman flashed a wedding ring at them and said she was his wife and he gave them a half-crown to go away and they shocked me, telling me she was pregnant.

"I couldn't believe them. It was true, they insisted. I doubted your father had married her. He wouldn't do anything that might land him in prison."

She looked at each of us in turn and smiled a little sadly. "I made up my mind then to leave, even before you were born, Bill. Nanny advised me to stay until the birth. I had saved most of the five shillings weekly your father paid me for working behind the bar. I counted it and found I had nearly eleven pounds. I asked Nanny to take care of it for me. I told her I fully realised she would lose her work there when I left, but she said not to think of her, to worry about myself and you kids. Every Thursday while he was away, she took a few things to her home… a couple of sheets, pillow cases, some of your toys and some baby clothes. It all had to be done slowly. We didn't want him to miss things. I gave her my wages each week to buy some crockery, a kettle… that kind of stuff. My day off was Monday and I used to visit Aunt Lucy. When I told her what I intended to do she said if I went there, which I was quite at liberty to do, this would be the first place he'd come. I realised she was right. So I asked Nanny to find me a furnished room. Everyone who rented a house in those days let a furnished room, to help towards paying the rent. Landlords turned a blind eye as long as the rent was there when called for each Monday morning. Well, Bill, you arrived in July. Every Sunday if it was fine I used to take you kids to the park while he slept during the afternoon while the pub was closed. I left at two o'clock and had to be back by five. At such short notice, the best Nanny could do regarding finding a furnished room was at Number 7 in the same road as the pub, the rent was 3s 6d weekly. Nanny had brought groceries, bread and tins of milk and promised to visit every other day to do shopping.

"We were at Mrs Snowcill's for four days when he found us. I let him in quietly after he had thrown small stones at the window. I didn't know he had a gun. When I refused to return to the pub, he threatened to shoot me.

"I told him, do the kids first, then shoot me. He went to the bed, but you moved, Bill, so did Jim. He dropped the gun on the table and sat down, so quickly I rushed down to Snowcill's bedroom for help. Mr Snowcill was angry and turned your father out, then, I suppose naturally, he said I must leave, he couldn't have his children frightened. Aunt Minne took us in and suggested filling in a form to get rooms in the buildings. This I did, saying I was a widow and as you know we lived there for more than two years before he found out where we were living."

"And that was my fault, Mum. I'm so sorry," I said.

"Water under the bridge," replied Mum. "So now you all know the story." We had listened without interruption. She really was an amazing mum.

Chapter Twenty-four

Alf had been chatting a great deal about his elder brother and grass-track racing at Sewardstone, Essex. Truly I didn't pay too much attention until he said he would like to try his luck at it. One received three pounds in appearance money even if you didn't race, and his brother was good at the sport.

With Easter in the offing he thought he would get his name down to enter. He always came to take me out after dinner on Sundays. It was too late to see me after work on Saturdays and that was a permanent arrangement.

Jim was very busy making a wireless set. The kitchen table was strewn with valves and small coils of wire. He had made a very nice wooden case, and according to Jim all was going well. Recently he had quarrelled with his girlfriend Hilda. They were always having rows, then would come together again. Mother said that wasn't the way to happiness.

"She's all right, Mum, but she has the wants and the gimmies," he laughed. "I've told her to find a rich man if she isn't satisfied with me."

Easter Sunday, I had promised to meet Alf at Lea Bridge Station. I dolled myself up in my cream suit and tan accessories. He said he would be riding in two races on Easter Monday and would I watch? I promised.

He was waiting for me when I arrived a little after two o'clock. We entered the station yard, a huge area along the station siding where many trucks were filled with coal, with a huge mountain of coal at one end of this large space.

There were about a dozen men all tinkering with their motorcycles. There was an occasional burst of noise as they revved an engine. I was introduced to two girls, Daisy and Nan. I met Sprouts Elder and Billy Galloway. These two men I understood to be Australians who were looking for possible sites suitable for dirt-track riding, a sport I understood to be very popular in Australia at that time. I was speaking to the girls when Alf asked us to stand back as he was going to try a "grand prix" round the yard. He sat jauntily on the bike and revved the engine. The men clapped as he started off.

Twice he went round the yard gaining speed. Suddenly, as he slewed round, it skidded in the coal dust, the back wheel spinning madly as it lay in the dust. It sprayed all over my suit, down the left sleeve across the coat and down my skirt to the hem. I went berserk. The damp coal dust stuck tightly to the linen. I don't remember what I said. I tore off the ring and threw it into the coals. "It's all over," I screamed at him, "I never want to see you again. Stuff your bloody bike." I stormed into Lee Bridge Road and stood waiting for the tram that would take me home. Passers-by looked sympathetic, I stared back at them angrily. Boarding the tram the conductor quipped, "Been rubbing against the coalman, Love?"

"Very funny, ha ha," I snapped sarcastically.

The tram had long seats on either side. There was no way I could hide the mess made of my suit.

My mind was whirling. All I could see was that spinning wheel spraying coal dust over my suit. Coal... wheels.... Who said that? The fortune-teller... Pollyanna... about the ring... an offer... was that Father's offer of a pub...? and this ruined suit... coals and wheels? What else did she say? It was some time ago that Ben and I had visited that dingy room. I don't think either of us had paid a great deal of attention to what she had told us.

We thought she had been so wrong. Some blue-eyed boy would be good to me and something about some ruins.... Oh well, I suppose I'd go looking for a blue-eyed lad. There was plenty of time. At the moment I was fed up with the entire male population.

Mum said as I entered the room, "I didn't expect you...." She stopped open-mouthed. "My dear, what happened to you?"

I burst into tears. "That bloody bike, Mum," I sobbed, "and I've finished with Alf... it's all over between us." Between sobs I explained what happened. "He was showing off. Why couldn't he have skidded off at the far end of the yard? No... not him."

"Perhaps if I washed the suit it could be dyed black," Mum suggested.

I shook my head. "I wouldn't fancy wearing it again, so no, burn it."

I spent the rest of the holiday playing scales and having small weeps for my lovely suit... maybe I liked it too much.

Jim had fixed an outdoor aerial from a nail knocked high into the wall in our yard and boring a hole in the window frame threaded it into the house and wired it to the set he had made. Now we could all listen to the radio.

Chapter Twenty-five

In the summer of that year, 1928, our cousin Bert, Aunt Minne's son, who worked at the pawnbroker's, collapsed while at work and was rushed to hospital.

After a week of tests he was transferred to Homerton Isolation Hospital. After some months, showing no improvement, he was sent to Winchmore Hill Hospital, being diagnosed as having sleeping sickness, and was kept in strict isolation. We spoke between ourselves wondering how this could have happened to Bert. Finally Auntie came up with the idea that some kind of germ or virus could have been in some parcel or other that had been handed in for pawning, maybe something from abroad. He had said they handled all types of things and materials and he had told Auntie a few months previously that three very beautiful Indian saris had been pawned for two pounds. The customer wanted more cash, but Bert's boss had refused: two pounds was the limit.

This was the year Cousin Bill met Sadie. She asked him the way and they walked along together until they came to the street she wanted. Bill was a few months after his sixteenth birthday and said they had promised to meet again some time. She lived in Sydenham. Auntie wasn't too pleased, Bill told Jim. She said they were too far apart and too young. However, addresses had been exchanged and they corresponded. It was more than a year later before they met again, and Auntie wasn't too pleased about it.

I am not quite sure if it was later that year in the winter or the beginning of 1929 that Auntie and the boys hit the pools.

Cousin George and his brother Fred were football mad and whatever the weather they stood on the terraces of surrounding football grounds watching teams play, and they did the Littlewoods' football pools.

Aunt Minne came to see us with Harry and Bill one Friday evening to tell us they had won more than £1,600. Mum could hardly believe her ears. We were amazed, so much money. "You'll never live to spend all that, Minne," Mum said.

"I have to get someone to change the cheque first," said Auntie.

"Open a bank account," suggested Jim.

"No thanks, Jim. I want the money in the house where I can see it. I don't trust banks," she laughed.

"But, Minne, suppose you were burgled," said Mum.

"What, with four boys in the house and over a shop too?" She shook her head. "Not a chance. Anyhow, I'll get this changed tomorrow somewhere, maybe Bert's boss will do it for me. On Monday, Bella, will you come shopping with me? I've decided to buy a bedroom suite. The boys suggested this is a very good idea. Come round to me about two o'clock and we'll go shopping." Auntie laughed. "You know we couldn't believe our luck until the Littlewoods man came Thursday morning with the cheque. We'll have some tea out and I'll treat you, Bella. We'll enjoy an afternoon out."

Arriving home from work Monday evening, we all wanted to know how the shopping went. Mum told us that she went to Minne's and they set off immediately and rode to Hackney Station. They walked up Amhurst Road to Gibbons, a large furniture store, and Minne chose a bow-fronted suite, wardrobe, tallboy and dressing-table, and then chose a four-foot bed and mattress and pillows, the furniture in light oak. It will be delivered Tuesday afternoon. We had tea in Lyons' with cream cakes. I haven't been home long, we walked home through London Fields. It was cold, but not too cold, and she treated me," Mum laughed. "I was very surprised when Minne gave me a half-crown as a treat. When I did manage to thank her she said, 'Well, I did treat you to a tea.'"

"Well," laughed Bill, "it's going to take her a long time to spend the cash at that rate."

Me, I was disgusted. "How mean of her, Mum," I said.

Later Aunt Minne asked Jim to make them a wireless set like the one we had. "How much will it cost, Jim?" she asked.

"The valves are expensive, Auntie, so I'll let you know as I go along."

"Well, you know how much that one cost, don't you?"

"I bought and built it bit by bit, so I'm not entirely sure," Jim replied. "The loud-speaker is another expensive item," Jim told her, "but I'll get it finished for you as soon as possible. In the meantime, Auntie, get George to fix an aerial as high as possible. If he drops in he can see how I've fixed ours, so that won't be a problem."

The radio set was duly finished. I don't know what Jim charged Auntie, but I'm sure he never paid himself for his labour.

Chapter Twenty-six

In June, one evening at dinner, Mum said she had a surprise for us. This coming Sunday Aunt Minne was taking us all to Margate on the paddle steamer, *The Golden Eagle.* To say we were surprised is an understatement. It was her treat and she had tickets for us. George and Fred didn't want to go. We duly presented ourselves at Tower Pier after a very hectic rush and once on board found ourselves seats. We surveyed the murky Thames and the surrounding buildings while we waited for the departure moment. Finally with a loud blast of the ship's siren we slowly moved away from the pier… we were on our way. Soon we changed our seats as smuts from the funnel blew in our direction. As the boat got underway the paddles slapped as the boat gathered speed and the buildings on either side of the river slid past and we settled ourselves down to enjoy the trip. Never having been on a ship before we were surprised at its size. Bill and our cousin Bill stood by the rails.

"I could imagine I'm on a world cruise," said our cousin.

"Ocean liners must be of colossal size to this steamer. What made your mum dream up this idea?" my brother asked.

"Mum saw an advert in the newspaper and thought it a great idea if we all went to the seaside for a day."

As we had never been to the seaside, this was certainly a treat.

We disembarked (that was the word to use) at Margate to spend three hours ashore while the steamer chugged on to

Ramsgate. The sun blazed down on the pale sand and after the cooling breeze on the steamer the fine sand soon covered everything, and we could even taste it in our sandwiches that Mum had made for us. She had made cake too and we ate the thick slices with enjoyment. Auntie had brought Swiss-roll sponge and the jam was soon coated with the fine sand. We all took off our shoes and stockings and socks to paddle in the sea, only too late to realise our feet were thick with sand and we'd the problem of how to clean up our feet. We had deck chairs at two pence a time and sat and waved our feet in the sun until dry, then rubbed the sand from our toes with our handkerchiefs, but still with gritty feet we trooped down the pier to await the arrival of the steamer for the homeward trip. On the whole we all had a great day and thanked Auntie for the treat. That was our first boat trip and our first sight of the sea.... Marvellous.

In August, Uncle Charlie died. Mum had a letter asking her to come to the funeral, as she had written to Aunt Minne, and would Mum please go because Minne may turn up and Aunt Agnes didn't want any trouble.

"I don't want to go," said Mum. "He isn't worth it. I have never mentioned this to any of you, I thought the occasion would not arise. When Harry was about two years old, Uncle Charlie came to see me with a message from Aunt Agnes asking us to have tea with her on Sunday. Naturally, I said I'd make him a cup of tea and as I filled the kettle at the sink, he put his arms round me and said he'd always fancied me. I was shocked and told him to sod off, I wasn't the third sister on his list. I couldn't believe it. What a man for my sister to be married to."

We too were shocked. "So will you go to be with Aunt Agnes?" asked Jim.

"I think you should, Mum," I said. "Of course Aunt Minne will turn up, so you help support Aunt Agnes. She should shed no tears over him."

Mum decided to go to Uncle's funeral, taking a small posy.

That evening she told us, "Minne turned up with Harry carrying a large round wreath, and said to Aunt Agnes, 'It's only right Harry should attend his father's funeral to say goodbye.'" Mum said, "I could see Aggie's temper rising, but she said nothing." Later, after the service, Aunt Agnes said, "It's not the boy's fault, he didn't ask to be born, so I held my tongue. Aunt Minne left immediately afterwards." Aunt Agnes had taken a friend to live with her. The lady's name was Mabel. She had very piercing black eyes. For myself I didn't think her a very pleasant person, but if Agnes liked her, who was I to judge?

Chapter Twenty-seven

At the beginning of August I made enquiries at Revelle's Hairdressing Academy about their tuition and fees, and was told the new term began the second week in September and had my name added to their list.

The evening classes at the academy three evenings weekly, from six o'clock until eight o'clock, began. As the shop didn't close until six I was often the last one to arrive, but as I just had to cross the road, I was seldom more than a few minutes late. The tutor explained in our first lesson how all items in use must be scrupulously clean. Combs and brushes rinsed in a mild disinfectant and hairpins and clips rinsed in soapy water.

"None of us will want to pay any claims clients may make for damages, so we'll all be extremely careful. Now we will try shampooing, gather round and pay attention." There were seven students on this first Tuesday.

He turned on the spray. "Always test on the back of your hand until it is bearable. If the water's too hot for the back of your hand, it's too hot for your client's head." We all duly tested the water.

Attending classes at the academy, I had missed seeing my friend Louisa, and I arrived home one evening to find her waiting. I was pleased to see her, and apologising I began telling her what I had in mind... so for the time being I had to forgo dancing lessons. She said she now hoped to achieve her silver medal and the adjudicators would hold the class (there were six students trying for medals) the first Sunday in December, and wouldn't I like to try for a bronze medal? It was a tempting idea, but....

"My wages and commission are stretched to the limit," I said. "I have to pay for the piano, I contribute a pound weekly towards the housekeeping and now the weekly fee for the hairdressing lessons. Believe me, Louisa, I walk home most nights all the way from Bond Street to eke out my money."

"Well, I hope you haven't bitten off more than you can chew."

"I'm slogging away at getting commission and I'm hoping to finish paying for the piano by the coming April. Things will be easier for me then, I hope."

"How long does this hair course last, Belle?"

"About two and a half years, I think," I answered. "And I'm going to practise on my friends, you and my mum. What do you say to that?"

"My hair is straight. I like it that way."

"Your sister's is curly. When I get to the finger-setting stage maybe she'll become a model for me."

"Gracious, you're running before you can crawl." We laughed together.

I congratulated her at Christmas 1929 when she passed for her silver medal.

It was at the end of May 1930 I made the final payment on the piano and was given my signed agreement. I marched out of the shop feeling great. No one could take it from me now. It was mine... all mine. Farther along the road I entered a sheet-music shop. I bought Puccini's *Madame Butterfly* as a treat for my achievement. I couldn't get home fast enough. I rushed into Mrs Gee's room and asked Harry to play the song for me. He played it so beautifully. My mother was pleased I had got one rope from around my neck.

Since breaking up with Alf, my social life had been non-existent. There had been one or two evenings out with a few of the lads at the dance class, but recently I had been too absorbed in practising the lessons learned.

On a Friday evening a girl I worked with asked me to walk with her to her fiancé's shop in Charing Cross Road. It was early April and it was raining. We entered the shop, which sold pretty paste jewellery, watches and fancy trinkets. I was introduced to Mr Lockwood. He was tall, blue-eyed and blond... blue eyes? This was no blue-eyed boy. His manner was pleasant and waiting with my workmate until the shop closed, we sauntered along to Lyons' Corner House, Tottenham Court Road, for a light meal. His name was Harold and for our first meeting he was very attentive. Although he wanted to see me next day, I agreed to meet him Monday evening at seven.

My workmate, through her fiancé, told me that Harold thought I was a nice girl. She asked me what I thought about him. I realised whatever I said would be repeated so I was on my guard and replied that I didn't know him well enough to pass judgement and maybe time would tell.

I had an hour to waste before our meeting and spent it browsing in shop windows along Oxford Street and finally reached our meeting place, the Dominion Theatre. He was there. He asked had I eaten. Neither had he so we had a light meal in the Corner House and then we went to see the film at the Dominion. This was the first of many visits to films or theatres. I always insisted that he left me at the Bloomsbury tram terminus. Gradually I learned he had a bed-sitter in Great Russell Street and his parents lived in Slough.

One Sunday he took me to meet them. They were extremely courteous to me, asked me how old I was and did I realise their son was twenty-eight?

I told them I hadn't thought about it and age didn't bother me.

I discovered they were housekeeper and gardener in this very large house.

The house itself had impressed me greatly when I first entered. I thought it was owned by Harold's parents but I was sadly mistaken.

After I realised Harold's parents were working-class, I considered we were on level terms. I resented the supercilious way he spoke at me, instead of to me. During the short time we were together, he gave me small gifts… a chrome and green enamelled compact/cigarette/lipstick case and a green plush-covered three-inch teddy bear compact. In return, I bought him a wallet stamped "real leather in gold leaf".

He asked me why I didn't see him some nights during the week. I told him I was learning the hairdressing trade.

"Christ! Whatever for?" He thought that funny and so went down a few notches in my estimation.

One Friday evening, he asked me to have dinner with him in his bed-sitter. "Thank you but not likely," I replied. He asked me what I was afraid of; he was as tame as a domestic cat. "A cat has claws," I replied. He then asked if I was seeing someone else.

"You have nothing to be jealous about, so dry up." After that there was a subtle change in our relationship… sometimes he was late for our meetings. One day Miss Wardley told me Harold was seeing a girl who worked as a receptionist in Boots the Chemist. Was this a hint?

We had a blazing row. Enough was enough. That was the end of that.

Chapter Twenty-eight

By this time at the academy I had graduated to cutting and feathering hair. We usually practised on blocks and were now on to live models. These girls came regularly to the academy and our tutor expertly rectified our mistakes.

I practised hairdressing. I practised the piano. I wanted to excel in all I did. “Do try to practise the scales for half an hour daily,” said Harry. Mum agreed. “It will keep your fingers supple.” I thought I would never earn my living playing the piano, that was for pleasure. I concentrated on hairdressing and in May 1930 began learning Marcel waving, curling hair with heated tongs. I quickly mastered the art and practised every spare moment. I had to perfect it. I persuaded Mum to let me wave her hair, needless to say she was on pins all the time worrying about burnt hair.

I tried to persuade Louisa to have her hair waved but she liked straight hair. In July she asked me to make up a foursome. Her fiancé was taking her to Covent Garden to a dance and would meet his friend Trevor there and as he had broken off with his girlfriend he would be without a partner, so…?

“I don’t like blind dates,” I told her.

Trevor is a good dancer and is quite good looking and has the most gorgeous blue eyes, you would like him.”

Blue eyes, that rang a bell. “I’m not up to your standard of dancing.”

"Oh, come on, all you do is stick at home practising on hair and you know what they say about all work and no play...."

So off we went to Covent Garden and Trevor didn't turn up.

"Never mind," said Louisa, "you can share Andy with me."

The ballroom was large, all dark red plush, with a stairway leading to the many balconies. I wore a calf-length pink georgette beaded dress and prepared myself to play gooseberry. I had had two dances with strangers and one with Andy. Now I stood against a column surveying the talent.

"Please tell me your name?" said a voice behind me.

Without looking round, I asked, "Who wants to know?"

"Please, I do." I turned to look at an intelligent face, brown eyes peering at me through horn-rimmed spectacles. Brown eyes... not a hope.

He smiled, "Please shall we dance?"

It was an old-time waltz and he whirled me round and round until I felt giddy. "Don't you ever reverse?"

"Please, reverse?"

"Dance round anti-clockwise." Round and round we went again. With the dance ended he said, "Come to the restaurant for dinner."

"I've had dinner, before I came here."

"Please, you dine so early?" he queried. "So early," he repeated. "Please, I want to eat, so please eat with me."

"I must tell my friends," I said as Louisa and Andy sauntered towards me.

"He says he's hungry," I told them. "My friends," I turned to him, "Louisa and Andy."

He shook their hands and bowed his head. "Please to join me to eat." He pointed to the stairway.

"You go ahead," Andy said laughing, "I can't dance on a full stomach."

So I left them and with this foreigner reached the balcony and seated myself at one of the small tables. A waiter appeared from nowhere and handed me the menu. I handed it to my escort, and he quickly chose what sounded to me like sauerkraut and frankfurters and a bottle of wine: he named the wine.

"I don't drink," I butted in, "so you'll have to drink all the wine yourself, and I'll have egg on toast, please."

The waiter bowed and left. I stared at this man seated opposite and smiled. "What is your name?" I asked.

He rattled off something that was quite unintelligible to me.

"Please repeat it slowly."

"Please, Michael Angelo Heilperin," he smiled, "and you are?"

"Belle." The way he said it sounded like Bale. "No, *Belle.*"

"Oh, Beelie." So I settled for Billie.

Our order was placed before us; he eyed my egg on one piece of toast with dismay.

"That is not enough for you," he said, "you need more."

"I have told you, I have had dinner." I eyed the platter of sauerkraut with six thin brown frankfurters, which he proceeded to lace with mustard from the condiments on the table. He poured wine, took a sip and nodded appreciatively to the waiter. He raised his glass, I lifted my orange juice.

"Please, to our friendship." We touched glasses. He began forking up the cabbage. Truly this man lived to eat.

I slowly tackled my toast. "Your name is quite long," I began. "I shall call you Mickey."

"Like the mouse with the ears?" He laughed. "Please, I like that."

A thought hit me. Did he have the cash to pay the bill? Would I end up the evening washing dishes in the canteen? He looked up and saw my eyes fixed on him. "You are not eating?" He smiled.

"What European country are you from?"

"I am Polish and I am a student at the University of Geneva, in Switzerland, do you know it?"

"Switzerland, yes, the university, no. Where are you staying while you're in London?"

"The Imperial Hotel, Tottenham Court Road. You know it?"

I nodded. Now, more than ever, I thought he had me on a piece of string. How could a student afford to stay at the Imperial? I had even greater visions of washing up in the canteen.

"Are you telling me the truth, Mickey?"

"Please, I would not lie to my little friend."

I was still doubtful. Working in the West End, you soon lose any illusions you may have about the way of men.

"What subject are you reading at the Geneva University?"

"Please, economics of each country I visit."

"And which countries have you visited so far?"

"Austria and Denmark, now I am here, then I go to America. After I go home then I go to Russia."

"Quite a round trip."

He had finished the sauerkraut and was studying the menu.

"What will you have for dessert?"

"Just ice cream, please."

"I like a fruit salad," he smiled. "You like that too?"

I shook my head. "Just ice cream." I looked over the balcony and smiled down at my friends. Louisa gave me the thumbs-up sign. I smiled.

"How long have you been in London?"

"Please, two days. My friends told me to visit this place… so."

"You have friends here?"

"Yes, two students at the French Hospital, they are training to become doctors and have been here nearly three months."

Finishing our sweet, I sat silent. "Please be my friend for six weeks, I want you to show me your London… to see all the historical buildings, the Tower of London and the Royal Palace and other palaces and I am told there is a wonderful zoo. Please, Billie, I will pay you wages."

"I cannot leave my place of employment for six weeks… I would get the sack and with so many out of work, I may find it difficult to get work."

"Please, sack… what is this sack?"

"I would be dismissed from my employment."

"I will see your employer and explain."

"Forget it. Call the waiter and pay the bill, then we will join my friends and continue dancing."

The waiter came quickly to our table. "Please, the bill," said Mickey.

The waiter left and returned a few seconds later with a large piece of French bread on a tray. Mickey looked astonished.

I smiled. "He asked for the bill, I'm sorry."

The waiter quickly made out the bill as Mickey fumbled for his wallet.

When I saw the wallet packed with notes, I offered up a silent prayer.

He tipped the waiter a ten-shilling note.

I said as we entered the ballroom, "Two shillings and sixpence would have been a good tip for the waiter."

"Please, Billie, these men do not get many wages, so I help him, yes?"

We spent the rest of the evening with my friends, dancing alternately with each other and I told Louisa I'd get Mickey to take me to the tram terminus and she could go along with Andy.

"I don't like leaving you with a foreigner," whispered Andy.

"He's OK," I answered. "I have something to sort out with him." So we all said goodnight and went our separate ways.

Mickey and I strolled along and I began by saying he must remember to put the word "please" at the end of the sentence, otherwise he might often be given bread because waiters may mistake his first words. I had to go over this explanation a few times before it was clear to him.

We arrived at Tottenham Court Road and he said, "Come into the Corner House, I want to buy something."

"Surely you don't want to eat again," I said amazed.

I followed him into the teashop. An amazing array of fruit, tins of biscuits and boxes of chocolate met my eye.

He pointed out to the assistant two large pears, a tin of cheese straws and a large bunch of black grapes. The cost was £1 18s 9d. I had visions of him stuffing himself in his hotel room and was quite surprised when he handed the filled bag to me, saying, "For your mother."

I tried to express my gratitude and thanks for my mother's gift as we strolled along New Oxford Street. It was the first Saturday in July, and I honestly wondered if I knew London well enough. We reached the Bloomsbury tram terminus as midnight struck and waited for the tram to arrive.

"You will be safe, riding alone so late?" he asked and raising my hand to his lips gently kissed it. "Tomorrow we meet, please?" Brown eyes smiled at me, "And we will make some plans, yes?"

I nodded. "Meet me here after lunch about two o'clock, and thank you once again for a very lovely evening." I saw he stood watching as the tram began my journey home.

Mother eyed Mickey's gift. "Why did he send this for me?" she queried.

I repeated the events of the evening to her and that I was meeting him next day, but I didn't tell her he was Polish. I said he seemed to have plenty of money, but I think this made her a little suspicious. "Well," she ended, "I hope you have your head screwed on the right way, that's all."

Chapter Twenty-nine

Louisa came round Sunday morning and wanted to know how the evening had ended. I cautioned her quietly not to mention that Mickey was a foreigner.

Her news was that they were putting the banns up next week and would I be a bridesmaid for her? She and Andy had the choice of two flats and would marry the last Sunday in August. Her sister would be a bridesmaid with me, and her seven-year-old brother and Andy's cousin would be pages. She had made up her mind to hire the dresses and suits. "I think it will be cheaper than having the worry of getting dresses made by a needlewoman."

We all certainly thought it was a good idea and Louisa said she had been recommended to a good shop in Mile End Road.

I met Mickey as arranged and as we walked I suggested that wherever he wanted to go I would tell him what buses or tube to get and I would do this each day. He began again saying he would pay me wages until finally I told him, "If you keep saying that, you can find yourself another friend for six weeks, so shut up about wages. I cannot afford to be out of work after you have gone off to the States… now, do you agree?"

"My mother told me to find a nice girl to be my friend in each country I visited. She worries about me too much."

"And did you find nice girls in Austria and Denmark?"

"It was a little difficult in Denmark. This girl wanted me to buy her a flat, which she said we could share. It was very tempting."

I didn't ask any more questions about Denmark.

And so we met each evening and planned his next day's journey over dinner. He liked dining at the Trocodero, Shaftsbury Avenue. He waited for me outside the shoe shop and on Tuesdays, Wednesdays and Thursdays outside the academy.

On my half-day, Saturday, I dashed home, changed, then dashed to meet him and for six weeks I learned how the other half lived. One Saturday we visited the zoo at Regent's Park. He admired the care taken of the animals but thought it did not compensate for their loss of freedom.

Another Saturday we went to an art exhibition at the Burlington Galleries.

We stood admiring a painting of Aphrodite rising from the sea. It was a large picture roughly five feet long by three feet high. It was very beautiful. "I will buy that for you, Billie, you like it?"

"Gracious, no. It's massive, no."

"It would be a copy," he smiled, "and it would remind you of me."

I looked round at other paintings lining the walls. There was a small painting of a pretty lady in medieval dress. "I would like that to remind me of you, please, Mickey, that one." So we went to make the sale, he wrote in the corner, "A souvenir of our visit to Burlington House, July 1930, Michael." He had it framed and it hangs in my hall to this day so many years later.

There were three visits to theatres and twice we danced to Jack Hilton and his band at the Kit Kat Club in the Haymarket. Mickey could not get over Jack Hilton's fair curly hair. He had never seen a man with such curly hair.

One Sunday, after we had strolled around the West End talking about his thesis on economics, he hailed a cab.

"Where are we going?" I asked.

When he told the driver, "Savoy, please," I nearly had a fit.

"Mickey, please, I cannot go there, stop the driver."

He stared at me. "What is wrong?"

"It's evening and I'm not dressed for the evening."

When we arrived he would see what I meant.

I gazed down at my dark green calf-length dress, covered by a heavily embroidered Spanish shawl (a fashionable item in 1930) and entered the dining-room wishing the floor would open up to swallow me. The decor left me speechless; also the beautiful dresses of the ladies, wearing diamonds and golden jewellery. I fingered my one string of Ciro pearls and matching earrings that had cost just twenty-one shillings. Mickey? He fitted in like a glove. "I feel I'm sticking out like a sore thumb," I whispered to him.

"What is the matter with your thumb?" he smiled, looking concerned.

It was there I was first introduced to baked Alaska... a delicious sweet of ice-cold ice cream covered by a crisp warm meringue. We finished the meal with coffee, cheese and wafer biscuits. The bill was placed on a silver tray and Mickey tipped the waiter two pounds. He spent money like it was going out of fashion. When we left the Savoy Hotel it was ten o'clock and he called a taxi to take us to the Bloomsbury tram terminus where we stood talking. He said he was sorry his stay was drawing to a close and had he made me happy during the time we had spent together? I asked why he had picked me when there were so many other girls that night at Covent Garden.

"I shall remember you in that pink beaded dress... you sparkled, catching my eye and you looked so lovely."

"Thank you, Mickey, you say the nicest things. You're sweet."

"Please, will you wear that dress on the night when we will have a farewell dinner with my friends? There are just a few more days left for me in this country."

"Have you really enjoyed my country?"

"I wish I could stay much longer, but I have a timetable to keep."

"Tell me, how do you rate the economics of this country?"

"It is low, and will take time to recover, I think."

"We are in some kind of recession, but things will get better."

We stood talking and before we said goodnight, he asked if I had a photograph of myself to give him, he wanted to send it to his mother in Poland.

It was Wednesday in the first week of August and he would be leaving the following Monday. These past six weeks had passed too swiftly. I felt sad he was leaving; I had grown very fond of him.

Louisa came round on the Sunday morning to say she and Andy had found a flat and had put up the banns and would I be bridesmaid with her sister? She was excited and my mother and brothers congratulated her as she chatted.

On that Sunday after lunch, I donned the beaded dress and covered by the Spanish shawl set off to meet Mickey. I felt a little conspicuous but consoled myself it would get dark later. He was at the tram terminus and hugged me warmly when we met… the first time he had ever done that.

"We go to my hotel, Billie, I have something to show you," he smiled. Immediately I was on my guard. I didn't know him all that well and he had said we were dining with friends. I looked at my fairly long nails… natural weapons of defence.

I thought the receptionist eyed me as she gave Mickey the key to his room. It was on the first floor and overlooked a small green. Glancing out of the window, buses drove along Tottenham Court Road. The room was large, and the decor a rich dark red. I noticed large leather luggage cases strapped and labelled. He was standing by a large desk, he turned to me, "Pease sit on the bed and close you eyes, Billie."

"Why should I close my eyes?" I asked suspiciously.

"I want to surprise you." I bet you will, I thought.

So I sat on the bed and closed my eyes, ready to scream or run. He sat beside me and, taking my hand, I could feel him clasping something around my wrist. "Now, open your eyes," he said.

I looked at my wrist, at the three-stranded pearl bracelet with a diamond clasp. It was beautiful and I was sure it cost the earth.

"Mickey, I cannot accept this, it's too... too—"

"Don't you like it?"

"Yes, it's beautiful and... and... I don't know how to thank you, but I cannot accept such a costly gift."

"Well, I cannot wear that," he smiled. "And it is such a small reward for the happy hours we have spent together. Now we will have some coffee here, then we will go to meet my friends." He pressed a bell and he ordered coffee and biscuits and before we left the room I gave him a kiss of gratitude and thanks and as we hugged each other, he whispered, "I have grown so fond of you, Billie and... and... no... no...." He shook his head and changing the subject asked, "Will you come to Waterloo Station to see me leave?" And wondering what M'sieur at the shoe shop would say, recklessly I promised. Then we left to meet his friends, me wondering what they were like.

Outside the hotel he hailed a taxi and when I heard him say the Ritz Hotel I nearly fell over. As I climbed into the taxi and we began the journey, I said, "I cannot meet your friends in that place, it is too... too... my dress isn't suitable... is it...?"

"I am proud of you, you look lovely, please stop it."

I looked up at the façade of the Ritz... brilliant, privileged. I took a deep breath and with Mickey holding my arm, I entered the hotel, "to the manor born". His friends were in the foyer and as Mickey introduced me, each man kissed the tips of my fingers. There was a French surgeon and his two doctor friends... their names I have since forgotten, except one... an Austrian, Angelphi... I met him again later.

I followed Mickey as a waiter led us to a reserved table, his friends following; the waiter removed my shawl and draped it over the back of my seat. The real lovely diamonds of the ladies present made my beaded dress seem flashy as it sparkled in the light from the beautiful chandeliers. I whispered to Mickey, "I should have worn my black velvet dress." He just squeezed my hand.

The waiter arrived with a bottle of champagne and another waiter came to our table with the hors d'oeuvres trolley. I chose prawn cocktail, but I think Mickey and his friends chose each item from the trolley, their plates were filled. Mickey insisted I should eat more, but with a four-course dinner to come I told him to hush.

My glass of champagne lasted me throughout the dinner; these men sank two bottles... there were no drink-driving rules in those days.

I thought champagne grossly overrated, as I sipped the bubbles tickled my nose... I almost sneezed. Our dinner was noisette of lamb with all the trimmings; for dessert I had banana split and the men chose a variety of fruit salad topped with cream. Another bottle of champagne appeared and they tackled the cheese board as if beginning a meal... truly these foreigners lived to eat.

We toasted Mickey bon voyage a few times and finally left the Ritz at about 12.30. The doctors' car was called for and Mickey and I bade them goodnight, then called a taxi. Mickey and I arrived at the Bloomsbury tram terminus where we waited for the tram. I thanked him for a very enjoyable evening, he asked what I thought about his friends. We had all chatted, sometimes in English and sometimes in French and sometimes they had spoken in, I think, German, but on the whole they had always included me in the conversation. I told him I thought they were curious, meeting me for the first time. He nodded, smiling. The tram came into view and kissing me on the forehead, he reminded me, "At my hotel, nine o'clock tomorrow morning." I nodded and boarded the tram.

I watched him turn away as the tram bore me homewards.

When I related the evening's events to Mother, she said, "I think I'm glad he's leaving tomorrow. The Ritz, eh? I think you're getting ideas a little above yourself. Now you can come down to earth and forget your high life. I shall certainly miss his gifts of edibles, they have been very acceptable, so thank him for me tomorrow when you say farewell." I promised and continued to chat about his friends and the diamonds and the marvellous chandeliers.

His cases were bundled into the taxi and we arrived at Waterloo Station with about ten minutes for his train. I was near to tears.

"I shall miss you so much, Mickey. Will you write to me?" I handed him my address. "Yes, I will write, but in America I will be moving around, I will give you an address when I find a hotel."

The train rolled in, he bought me a platform ticket and we walked along until he entered a compartment. He pushed his luggage inside then came onto the platform to me and took my hands. "You go now, Billie, and don't look back. I... I... Please go now, please."

I turned, a lump in my throat and almost ran from him. At the barrier a porter yelled, "Ticket, please." The ticket exchanged hands and as I walked slowly from the station, I realised I would never see him again. His last words were *wyspomen menia* (I am not sure if the spelling is correct, but it means "remember me" in Polish). I walked all the way to Bond Street, arriving at the shop at 11.15. M'sieur was hopping mad and read the riot act to me. I said nothing. "Now, get up into the showroom and smile at the customers... or else...."

Chapter Thirty

The afternoon dragged on interminably. I longed to be on my way home. I thought of the things he said, of the places of interest he had wanted to see, of Buckingham Palace... I told him it was built by a Dutchman in 1703 for the first Duke of Buckingham and was purchased for £21,000 by George III in 1760. New wings had been added since and in 1913 the front was redesigned. Mickey thought it was a rectangular building with enough glass to keep window cleaners busy all year round. The Tower of London... it was built by the Norman invaders as a fortress and is the oldest building in the city. It houses the Crown Jewels and many famous prisoners were held there. It is open weekdays to visitors. He thought it an awesome and forbidding building and would not have liked to be a prisoner there a few centuries past. Tower Bridge amazed him. It spans the River Thames and took nearly eight years to build and was opened in 1894. There is a roadway 30 feet above high water and a foot bridge of over 130 feet between the two towers. The roadway is raised by an hydraulic mechanism to allow ships to pass. He said he had waited to watch the roadway raised and asked if the hydraulics were the same as used when the bridge was first built. I didn't know.

The whispering gallery in St Paul's Cathedral fascinated him. I said the cathedral was a unique building. Built from designs by Sir Christopher Wren, it was finished by 1710 and took over thirty years to build. The dome was unusual and from the ground to the top of the cross, the height was 365 feet. He told me there was nothing like the whispering gallery in Europe. So we did have something unique.

He found the chamber of horrors at Madame Tussaud's waxwork exhibition alarming and wondered how and where the torturers got their ideas. How could men be so inhuman? He liked the film-star effigies and I remember many of the statues and buildings I had told him to visit and what he said about my London. I was glad when time came to go home.

I cried a lot that evening. I realised I would never see him again. "He was so kind to me, Mum, and was always outside the shop or the academy when I finished work. I think I could have fallen for him. I'm heartbroken now he's left."

"Dry your eyes," said Mum sharply. "Hearts don't break nowadays, they only bend, so snap out of it."

I bought my favourite magazine and given away inside was a paper pattern of a long dance dress. On the model it looked stunning and I decided to have a try at making it. There was a Christmas social at Louisa's dance class. The following Saturday I marched into DH Evans and bought eight yards of old gold taffeta. It had a beautiful watermark and the colour was great. Making it would take my mind off Mickey.

Louisa came round that evening. She asked if I would go with her and her sister and the pageboys to sort out dresses to hire for her wedding, as she was being married the last Sunday in August. I agreed.

The next Saturday I hurried home, had a quick lunch, met Louisa and off we went to the dress hire shop in Whitechapel. As we entered the smell of mothballs greeted us.

There were racks and racks of dresses of all colours. Louisa chose a white satin straight dress with a full lace overskirt; no alterations were necessary. Next the pages were fitted with light brown velvet suits; the long trousers just had to be shortened for one of the boys. Next Louisa chose very pale green dresses for her bridesmaids. Her sister Doris's dress was pinned a little at the shoulders, my dress was a little too large at the bust. It was put on inside out and deftly pinned to fit, taking up material under the arms and a part of the upper arms, until it fitted. The pointed georgette overskirts of our dresses hung in long points almost to the ground. Louisa paid a deposit and the manager said they would be delivered next week when the rest of the cash would be collected. We left the shop and we all felt pleased with Louisa's choice.

On arriving home, I related to Mum the afternoon's shopping spree. I told Mum, when and if I got wed, I would never hire a wedding dress; it would be a memento of a special day in my life.

"There could be all kinds of memories, Belle."

Later I studied the instructions regarding the cutting out and sewing of the dance dress. As the model pattern was for a tall person, I folded the pattern to my body length. It was sleeveless, V-necked, a nipped in waist, with a full circular skirt flared from the hips. It all seemed fairly straightforward. Pulling out the extra flaps of the dining-table I spread out the material and carefully pinned the pattern into place. It took seven yards to make the dress; I had bought eight yards allowing for a mistake. Carefully I began cutting, keeping each piece pinned to the pattern and hoped for the best. I tacked the material together before beginning to machine, making sure of the fit.

Carefully, I machined in the waist darts, back and front. Then stitched the shoulder seams together. Next, using strips of material cut on the cross, I bound the neckline; so far so good. Fixing the twelve-inch side zip fastening caused me a problem and took me a long time and a few cussings, but finally I had had enough for one afternoon.

I practised some hairdressing on a wig and later washed and waved Mum's hair. Next day, Sunday, I washed and set a friend's hair. Then at home I did some tidying up of our bedroom and spent most of the afternoon at piano practice. My brother Jim had found a new girlfriend, and went to meet her after tea.

Two weeks later, Louisa was married. Our dresses fitted perfectly but no amount of Boots 4711 cologne could rid the clothes of the smell of moth balls, but everyone had a great time.

The dressmaking progressed and one Friday I was standing on the kitchen table while Mum was trimming the hem of the dress level when Harry came in. "Oh, golden girl," he grinned. "That's a gorgeous colour and suits you. May I have the next dance?"

"I'm making this for the social at Louisa's dance class."

"Listen, all the crowd are going to a dance at the Horns, Kennington. Why not come along, give the dress an airing?"

"The crowd is partnered off and I don't have a partner to take me, so thanks all the same."

"In that dress, Mrs Munday, she'll soon get a partner."

Mum laughed, "She has spent a lot of time making it, but I expect it will just hang up in the wardrobe."

"Do come along, Belle. I'll treat you to a ticket."

"I'll buy my own ticket if I come with you and the crowd."

"That's settled then. Last Saturday in September."

Mum finished trimming the hem level and I stepped down from the table and paid Harry the half-crown for the ticket.

"I came up to cadge some tea, Mum isn't home from the nick yet," explained Harry. "It smells like you've been cooking a cake, Mrs Munday." My brothers came in and we enjoyed our meal.

After tea I machined a waist slip with the extra material and I was pleased with the result of my labour.

Chapter Thirty-one

I received a letter from Mickey. It seemed he did not care much for New Yorkers. He said they were restless and brash; they wanted mostly success and achievement. As he was moving soon, he did not send an address for me to write an answer. I was pleased to hear from him.

During my lunch break a few days later, the young Austrian doctor stopped me in Oxford Street. "Remember me, Angelphi?" I smiled in recognition. "Have you heard from Michael?"

I told him I'd received a letter and he was not too thrilled with New York. "Will you have dinner with me tonight, then we can talk?"

I smiled, "There is no way to let my mother know I would be home late, and she would worry, maybe another night?"

"I am off to France tomorrow for a holiday, maybe we eat now?"

"I have to be back at work by 1.15 p.m."

"So, why are we waiting? I will join you." We had cheese and tomato sandwiches, coffee and buttered buns, and we talked.

"Michael was a small piece in love with you, he told us. We advised this was impossible for both of you. After meeting you for that farewell dinner, we thought… maybe…." He shrugged, "I'm sorry."

I stared at him. "I was fond of him too."

"Did he tell you his mother was a countess?"

I stared at this Austrian in utter disbelief, shaking my head.

"And his father?" I asked quietly.

"He died about ten years ago."

We sat silent and I thought, no wonder Mickey had appeared so much at home in all the high-class places he had taken me to. It was all too clear to me now... me a working-class girl and him....

We finished our lunch. "I must get back now, Angelphi." He paid the bill and outside the ABC I thanked him and wished him a pleasant holiday and held out my hand. He raised it to his lips and kissed my fingers, much to the amusement of some passers-by.

Was Michael Angelo Heilperin a count? And I treated him as just a student on holiday in my country. Arriving home, I told Mum about the meeting and the astonishment I felt at the time.

"Would you have gone to Poland, had things progressed, Belle?"

"No, Mum. No, I don't think I could leave England. No."

"That bracelet he gave you cost more than shillings, so treat that as a souvenir of his friendliness for you."

Chapter Thirty-two

On the night of the dance, off I went with Harry and Lizzie. At Shoreditch Church we met Charlie and his girl, Renee. Boarding a bus we eventually arrived at our destination and soon the rest of our crowd appeared. In the cloakroom we girls added more powder and lipstick, then we entered the ballroom and made towards the men.

Harry's friend, Joe Bendon, greeted me. "Hi, Belle," he waved a cursory hand. "Meet my brother," then turned to speak to Babs, his girlfriend.

I turned to Joe's brother as the rest of our crowd paired off to dance. Holding out my hand, I said in my best West End accent, "How do you do, Mr Bendon."

He glared at me. "Are you taking a… er… a mick?"

The ignorant oaf. I turned my back on him to meet the gaze of a tall chap standing near. I sent out the "come hither" signals, but evidently the signals were not strong enough, he turned away and resumed speaking with a friend. Mr Bendon and I stood alone.

He touched my arm. "Dancing?" he said casually.

"You asking?" I snapped without turning.

"Oh, come on." The slow foxtrot at that time was definitely not my best dance. He had a stride like a horse and stepped all over my shoes. He stopped dancing suddenly.

"Have you got two left feet?" he demanded angrily.

"I'm not sure, I haven't looked at them too closely."

"*Comic Cuts,* eh? Can you do this?"

I watched as he stepped and trebled up. "I can try," I replied sarcastically. So, facing the line of dance, we stepped and trebled up in rhythm to the music and when we came to the spot where we began he left me flat and danced off with a girl standing nearby. I sat down. If this was going to be the pattern of the evening, I would be off home when the next dance began. The music ended and our crowd came together. Lizzie sat beside me saying, "Come and join us." We heard the MC announce a waltz and the tall chap I had given out signals to was at my side. "May I?" he asked.

Now a waltz was something I could do… so could my partner. We were almost the first on the floor. We swayed and whirled, I showed off rotten. I hoped Mr Bendon was watching. Two left feet indeed!

"Is that tall chap your fellah?" asked my partner suddenly.

"Good gracious, no. Whatever gave you that idea?"

"I think the way he looked at you."

I shrugged, smiling, "You're quite mistaken."

"Perhaps we can have the next dance?"

"I'm not too good at other dances."

"Never mind. Will you have a drink with me during the interval?"

"Thank you, that will be nice." We finished the encore of the dance and he left me near our crowd.

"Who is that bloke?" questioned Mr Bendon.

"I don't know him from Adam. He's wearing clothes."

"You *are* a smart Alec," he said nastily.

"And I'm having a drink with him during the interval."

"You be careful he doesn't get you drunk."

"Fat chance he'll have, I don't drink," I retorted.

The MC announced a Paul Jones. "Form circles," he called. "Ladies on the outside, gents in the centre."

"Come on, Belle, let's go," said Renee. We circled and when the music stopped I faced Charlie Stevens. We danced to the veleta.

"These old-time dances are friendly and get you going," said Charlie, "and on an occasion like this we all mix."

We circled again and next I faced a man in shirtsleeves. We danced an old-time waltz to the music of *The Merry Widow.*

"My name is Thomas, my mates call me Tom," he informed me as we whirled round. "What's your moniker?"

"Belle."

"Oh, ting-aling-aling-aling-aling. Come here often?"

"First visit." I replied.

"You should come here Christmas Eve and the New Year, we really let our hair down then. Will you be here?"

"I'll give it some thought," I smiled.

After circling once more, I faced Harry for a quick-step. "You know I'm not too good at this, Harry."

"That's OK," he grinned. "How are you doing?"

"Better than I expected. I did think of going home earlier."

"This is a great ballroom for a pub, Lizzie and I like it."

The dance finished and after circling, I faced a tall stranger for a slow foxtrot. "I'm not good at this dance," I began.

"Neither am I. Not to worry, just shuffle round." So we shuffled round in a kind of two-step until the music stopped. Then round we went once again. The music stopped and I faced Mr Bendon.

The band struck the chords of *Jealousy*, a tango of all the dances. "I cannot do this," I said and turned away.

He grabbed my arm. "Don't you walk away from me. We will sit this one out." And as he led me to a seat, I almost reminded him that he had walked away from me, but I kept quiet. He sat right at the side of me. I watched the steps of the dozen or so dancers on the floor.

"The tango is an easy dance once you get the rhythm," he said.

"Looks very complicated to me."

"Sorry, what did you say?"

I turned to him. "Looks complicated." I resumed watching.

"You have a very good contrary body movement. You should learn to do other dances as well as you waltz."

So he *had* been watching me. I faced him. "I might do just that to get back at you." He laughed, it sounded so infectious. I noted the slicked-back blond hair, very blue eyes, a generous well shaped mouth... not good looking but a certain attractiveness. The dance over we walked to join our crowd and the MC announced the interval and my waltzing partner was at my side. Taking my arm, we walked away.

He said, "Brian, and you are?"

"Belle."

"Oh, two Bs together, so let's get busy and do some drinking." He smiled as we descended the stairs to the already crowded bar.

"What's your poison?" he queried.

"Tomato juice, please, and I'll stand over near the window."

I saw the rest of our crowd enter the bar. Harry gave me the thumbs-up sign and I nodded as Brian returned to my side.

We sipped our drinks as Brian asked, "You live local?"

Shaking my head, I told him. "The other side of the river."

"Long way to come," he remarked.

"As you can see, I'm here with friends."

"Yes. They look a nice lot." We chatted about the ballroom and he said it was a very popular meeting place and had dances once a month and on special occasions there were gala nights.

The rest of the evening passed quickly, some dances I sat out and some dances I had with strangers and eventually the dance ended.

We wrapped our dance shoes and together we walked to the bus stop and waited for a 38 bus that would take us to Shoreditch Church. The men mounted the stairs and we girls seated ourselves inside.

"Who's paying my fare?" I asked Lizzie as I sat beside her.

"Don't worry, Belle. One man pays and they share, so forget it."

Joe and Babs left the bus at Liverpool Street. Babs lived near Blackwall Tunnel and Joe hailed a taxi to see her home.

"Joe's brother is very hard of hearing," Lizzie said suddenly.

"He heard all I said to him," I told her.

"He's a very clever lip reader. He's been deaf for ages."

"How terrible for him. What caused it, do you know?"

"As far as Harry knows from Joe, it is a large bone structure pressing on the stapes of the ear, or something like that. Harry tells me that by reading people's lips, he doesn't miss much. He's quite a nice chap… we all like him."

Well I didn't think him nice, but I kept my thoughts to myself.

Leaving the bus at Shoreditch Church we crossed to Calverty Avenue, which led to Columbia Road. Except for Harry and myself, the rest of our friends lived in turnings off Columbia Road. I bade them all goodnight and walked away. Rounding the church, I crossed Hackney Road near the Boston garter factory when I heard rapid footsteps behind. Mr Bendon stood beside me. "I'll walk you home," he said bossily.

"I'll be OK, honestly."

"Oh, come along, it's late." He strode off. I slowed my pace.

He turned, waiting for me to join him. We walked in silence. I made up my mind he should do the talking.

"May I carry your shoes?"

"I'm not helpless," I snapped.

"Listen, I'm sorry if I was rude earlier this evening."

"I was being polite."

"I'm sorry. I apologise."

"I thought your brother's introduction very off-hand."

"I've never been called Mr Bendon before. Everyone calls me Sam." I looked at him, he was smiling. "I thought you were taking the mickey out of me. What would you have said had I called you Miss Munday?"

This man was hard of hearing; I raised my voice a little. "The manager where I work insists on being addressed as M'sieur, but always uses our surnames. Maybe it's because two of the girls are married and he doesn't like prefixes."

"Where do you work?"

"Bond Street."

"I work with my brother, Joe. We're upholsterers."

"I'm a shop assistant."

We walked for a while in silence, then: "Mind if I smoke?"

"Be my guest."

"Sorry. What did you say?"

"Smoke if you wish," I said turning to him.

He offered me the open packet. "Sorry, I don't smoke."

We stopped while he flicked the lighter; we stared at each other over the tiny flame as he drew hard on the cigarette. We resumed walking.

"You didn't drink and you don't smoke… your halo must be getting tight, don't you think?" He grinned.

"Yes, it does bother me. Sometimes I get headaches."

His infectious laughter fragmented into the night air. In spite of myself, I could not help smiling.

More silence. "How long have you known Harry Gee?"

"Since he was five and I was seven. Our mothers were next-door neighbours in Guinness's Buildings."

We reached Scawfell Street. I began fumbling in my bag for my key. I watched the tiny pink arc of light as he tossed his cigarette into the gutter. At my door I turned, "Thank you for walking me home."

"It was the least I could do. It's very late. He turned away. "Goodnight, Munday."

"Goodnight, Sam," I called loudly over my shoulder and without turning to see if he looked back, I quietly let myself into the house. Entering the bedroom I threw my coat onto my bed. “Are you still awake, Mum? Like a cup of tea?”

“That would be nice, thank you, and you know I can’t sleep until I know you’re safely home.”

I busied myself making tea, and then I heard Harry come and bolt up.

“Like a cup of tea, Harry?” I called quietly down the stairs.

“Wouldn’t I just.” He came into the room. “You bolted the door, so sure I was home.”

“We all knew you’d be OK with Sam.”

“Why, is he so harmless?”

“Being hard of hearing makes him very reserved.”

I took tea to Mum and Harry and I sat talking of the evening. Then, “You know we’re preparing to move soon, Belle?”

“Yes. Mum feels sad about it. Our mothers have been friends for so many years and I’ll miss your help with those horrid chromatic scales. Mum is thinking of asking the landlord if we can move downstairs, take over your mother’s rooms. I hope he’ll agree.”

“Mum has asked if this is possible,” replied Harry, “and she thinks it can be arranged.” He looked at the clock. “Heavens! Thank the Lord it’s Sunday and we can stay in bed. Goodnight, Belle. Sleep tight.”

Chapter Thirty-three

It was the first week in October and the days had been warm and sunny. Bill had been to see Gran (we took turns to pay periodic visits to make sure she was well). Bill rushed into the room. "Come and look at this airship. It's going along sideways."

"Is it the R101?" asked Mum as we rushed into the street, and in the evening light the airship was not flying straight. "Get the camera." This box camera was a gift from BVD in exchange for 200 coupons from packets of twenty cigarettes. My brothers had almost become kippers in their efforts to save that number of coupons, and we did get two very good snaps of the airship. We were horrified to read the newspaper headlines the next morning to learn that the airship had crashed at Beauvais in France with the loss of over forty lives; there were a few survivors.

The next week I received a letter from Mickey. He was in San Francisco. I read his letter through several times. He had found a guide, he wrote. A guide, not a friend. He wrote that the taxicab men chatted incessantly, chewing gum all the while. The places of interest seemed to be tall skyscraper buildings occupied mostly by insurance companies and commercial enterprises and the country was in deep depression.

His hotel address at the top of the page did not impress me much.

Should I answer this letter or not? I thought about Angelphi and what he had told me about Mickey's mother... what to say, if I answered? Was Mickey's mother a countess in her own right? Had she married a count? Was it a hereditary title? Angelphi had said Mickey was "a small piece in love with me". I had treated him as a student on a working holiday to my country. OK, he was at ease in the best hotels and had plenty of money. Now many things he had said and done fell into place. Many weeks later I wrote in my small diary: "Count Michael Angelo Heilperin. The end." I did not answer his letter and I never heard from him ever again. I was sorry, but thought it best.

Arriving home Thursday evening that week, Mrs Gee and Mum were chatting over tea.

Friday evening I visited friends' homes and did two Marcel waves and a trim. By this time I was charging shop prices for my work. I was saving the cash to buy a hand hair-drier, and then I would add shampoo and set for my clients. All homes by this time had a power switch for electric irons and that would hasten drying hair.

Saturday at the shop had been very hectic, we were so busy, we served one customer after another. I missed morning break, but M'sieur was very pleased. He had to serve too and I arrived home tired. Mrs Gee was packing, prior to moving, and Mum was helping her. We all had a sandwich lunch and by three o'clock Mrs Gee called it a day. I helped Mum do some dusting and then peeled some vegetables for dinner. Taking the peelings into the yard for the dustbin, Harry was in the yard towelling his hair. "Hi! How about setting my hair, Belle?"

"Oh, you big sissy," I laughed at him.

"Well, it's practice for you and I do have a little wave."

So I set his hair and pinned waves into place as he told me, "Joe's brother Sam is very ill in hospital. It's serious, his relatives can visit at any time, he has pneumonia, seems it's touch and go."

"I'm very sorry to learn this, please tell Joe, when next you see him. I wish his brother a speedy recovery, I do mean this."

I recalled to mind every word of our conversation as we walked along Hackney Road. I could not understand why. I never expected to meet this man ever again.

The next two weeks were hectic. When Mrs Gee arrived home from work, Mum helped her to pack goods in tea chests lent by the removals firm. Jim was seeing his girl, Queenie, Bill was cataloguing his records and some nights I was visiting friends and working on their hair. Mrs Gee had managed to persuade the landlord to agree to Mum moving downstairs, so in between I was packing small items prior to our move. The second week in November Mrs Gee moved to Beck Road, a turning off Mare Street, not too far away. She told us she had become friendly with a detective inspector and, in her words, "was going to shack up with him" as a trial before getting married. As Mum said, she was free, white and over twenty-one and should know what she was doing. Mrs Gee moved out on Friday. The removals men said it was a great idea having a side entrance, it would be fun and games lifting furniture over the railings and down the steps.

With Mum going on safari or fighting the Red Army or looking for mahogany flats, as she called her bug-hunting sessions, and with the help of the bug blinder from the nick, Mum and Mrs Gee had almost eradicated the pests, but Mum still sprinkled a little of the liquid around the skirting boards in the bedrooms. And so we moved downstairs and as the rooms were the same size there was no problem fitting the linoleum. Our cousins George and Bill came to help with heavy furniture. Getting the piano downstairs was the worst problem, but after much puffing and blowing, plus a few swear words, it was finally in place. Meanwhile I was preparing a meal, which we heartily enjoyed. The move had taken a weekend and now all Mum wanted was to put up clean curtains.

Arriving home from work on Monday evening, instead of going upstairs I went downstairs into the semi-basement. All was spick and span. The fire burned brightly in the range, Mum was singing as she prepared our meal.

"Had a good day, Mum?" I enquired.

"Yes, almost everything's in place, I hope the boys will not be long now." Even as she spoke we heard Jim enter and go down into the yard to haul his motorcycle through the side gate. He came in grinning, "Funny coming downstairs instead of going up… smells good." Almost immediately Bill came home. "I nearly trotted upstairs," he said.

The meal over I washed the dishes then went to practise some scales. I stood at the door of our best room and switched on the light. The wood-block patterned linoleum I kidded myself was parquet flooring. I cast my gaze over the high polish of the mahogany piano, the warm mid-brown of the dining suite, the two stuffed armchairs my brothers had bought standing one in each recess beside the fireplace. I closed the door behind me and admired the few ornaments on the sideboard against the right side of the room. The boys had a bedroom as did Mum and I and we each had a single bed. We had a wardrobe full of clothes. We had all worked hard for each other. Yes, we had come a long way from the wall-to-wall floorboards of Guinness's Buildings with the old brass bedstead where we had slept four in the bed. I sat at the piano and began to practise chromatic scales and was soon engrossed. Someone let themselves into the house. I quickly rushed to see who had entered, to meet Harry. He had come for some music he had left behind. "I've brought my key, it belongs to your mum now."

"Go down, Jim and Bill are home." I continued my playing.

He came up later to say goodnight. "Sounds like you're getting better at those scales." He sat down "You don't socialise much, do you?"

"I keep busy, one way or another."

"Don't you want to get married and have kids? You know what they say about 'all work and no play'?"

"I'm working to get my own salon, Harry. It's something I've always wanted, right from a small child, and until then...."

"You're daft, Belle. Go out more, find yourself a chap. There must be someone out there for you, he won't find you if you stay in here."

"Yes, I've been told there is a blue-eyed boy somewhere."

"That lets me out," he laughed.

"Shut up, you're engaged to Lizzie and you're not blue-eyed."

"You're coming to our place for tea Sunday, to meet Mum's new pain in the neck. Five o'clock sharp. Your mother has accepted."

We had a great time with Mrs Gee. Her new man was fun. My brother Bill had quite a good voice and with Harry at the piano, the inspector and Bill belted out the songs of the day and some old ones too. It was a fun evening, which we all enjoyed and we thought the new man a good sport.

The upper half of the house remained empty and with our friends and Aunt Minne we had a very noisy Christmas and New Year.

Chapter Thirty-four

The second week in 1935 a Mr and Mrs Beson moved into the top rooms. They had an eighteen-month-old baby boy. Mum explained the bathing arrangements and she confided to Mum that they didn't intend staying long, though she had not mentioned this to the landlord. They were saving for a deposit to buy a house with a garden. "When my little Frankie gets bigger he'll need a garden to play in, so for the time being, this place will do."

They were quiet and polite, always telling Mum when they would be down for a bath. Like us, they managed two baths each week and the baby was a good child. I always kept my foot on the soft pedal when I practised scales now. I didn't want to upset the baby.

By this time I had bought a hair drier. It cost £2 10s. It had three speeds and it became very useful as I began shampooing and setting friends' hair.

In those days workers had just a week's holiday for summer holidays. At the shoe shop, M'sieur let one assistant away at a time for the summer break. My turn was the last week in July.

In June an adjudicator came to the academy to examine our progress. I was tested over two evenings for Marcel waving, cutting and tinting and two weeks later for shampooing and setting. The permanent waving test was done with wigs on blocks. I had many feelings of butterflies in my tummy. You know the feeling when someone is watching you so closely.

There was also a beauty culture side to the academy and any spare moments I had while waiting for a set to dry or a tint to take, I always watched the students at work there. In this way I picked up quite a few useful tips on make-up and facial massage.

Mum decided she would redecorate our living-room. The landlord would supply paper. Mum chose an autumnal leafy paper and was supplied with six rolls and told not to paint over the grained and varnished woodwork.

Mum was great at paper hanging and during my week's holiday I helped, pasting while she stuck up the paper. The papering was finished by Tuesday afternoon and I began washing down the varnished woodwork. Next day, Wednesday, I was using furniture polish on the woodwork and suddenly felt very sick. Through the years I had coped with these attacks of biliousness, some lasting a day and some lasting three or four days. They left me drained and exhausted and I needed time to get back to normal.

Sometimes, M'sieur stormed at me to bring a doctor's certificate. He had seen me suddenly taken ill while at work and twice had to send me home and I always walked from Bond Street home, afraid to get into the tube or ride on a bus. People stared at me if I was sick in the street.

Everything was ship-shape and on this Saturday afternoon, I was quietly practising scales. It was about four o'clock when there was a knock at the street door. Mum was preparing tea, so I opened the door. Mr Bendon stood there, trilby hat a little raised. I was surprised. He looked taller, his cheek bones were prominent, he smiled.

"Mrs Gee has moved to Beck Road," I told him.

"Yes, I know. I have just had lunch with them."

"We have moved into Mrs Gee's rooms."

"She told me that too. How is your mother?"

"You'd better come in," I said standing aside, and off came his hat as he entered and I led the way down to the basement.

Jim was sitting at one end of our kitchen table drawing schematics.

"This is Joe Bendon's brother, my mother and my brother Jim."

He extended his hand to Mum, saying, "Pleased to meet you, Mrs Munday," and turned to Jim: "Glad to meet you."

"He has had lunch with Mrs Gee, Mum," I said.

"How is Lil, Mr Bendon?"

"She is fine, and please call me Sam… everyone does."

"Will you stay for a cup of tea?" asked Mum. He grinned and nodded.

Jim began clearing his drawing paper together and I put Sam's hat on the windowsill. I didn't know what to say, so I helped Mum while Jim chatted about his drawings. I heard Jim say, "It's a plan for a small talking picture screen. I don't know if it'll work, there are so many valves to work in sequence and then some type of speaker, but I'm working on it. At the moment it's a bit of a headache." Sam nodded as if he understood. "I have another brother," I interrupted, "but he's out 'junking', going round markets for old records."

"I've never heard it called that before," Sam answered. We laughed.

Tea was boiled eggs and wedges of homemade fruitcake. Introductions were made when Bill came in. He didn't like eggs and had cheese sandwiches. He was so excited. He had found a Tetrazzini record purchased for three pence. "It's in not too bad a condition and when I've cleaned it up it will be fine." He later sold that record to the BBC for eight pounds.

Over tea we talked generalities, then Sam asked me, "Would you like to come swimming with me tomorrow? The open-air pool at London Fields is large and great fun. I think you'd enjoy it."

"I can't swim and I haven't a swimsuit," I said shortly.

"I'll teach you if you buy a suit," he replied.

Mum gave me an old-fashioned look, but said nothing.

Tea over, he sat talking to my brothers while I washed the dishes.

"Like to come for a stroll, Belle?" asked Sam.

Mum said, "It will do you good, you've been in the house all the week helping me and perhaps you'll feel better."

As we set off he asked, "I thought you looked a little pale, haven't you been well?"

"Just a little sickness, it's nothing to worry about."

"Something you had eaten, I suppose."

I nodded. "Have you completely recovered from your bout of pneumonia?"

"I hope so. It began with a bad cold. I went to work as usual, but it became worse and I developed a cough. I went to the doctor, he told me to go home and get to bed. I did. He came next day, examined me, next I was in Bethnal Green Hospital. I think I was semi-conscious. I saw the ward was decorated and thought Christmas was coming. The nurse told me it was the 2nd of January 1931. I couldn't believe her."

"Harry Gee told me you were very ill. I was sorry to hear it." We strolled along Mare Street in silence for a while.

I decided to let him do the talking. I didn't fancy speaking loudly with so many people passing by.

"I came out of hospital and was home for a month, then went off to Eastbourne for convalescence for a month. The first two days there it rained, I was bored stiff. I read and chatted with other inmates. Next day the sun was warm. I sat on a seat watching a few stoics swimming, but I was forbidden to swim. A girl sat down and commented on the weather. We talked and then strolled along to Beachy Head. She mentioned it was a great choice for suicides... I told her to be more cheerful."

I remembered that he could lip read, I turned to him. "Recovering from an illness, I expect you felt a little low."

"A little, yes. As she lived there, we met each day; she kept me from being bored. I do not like my own company.

"Are you going to write to her?"

"We exchanged addresses, but I'm not a good letter writer."

Reaching Hackney Station arch we decided to retrace our steps. He asked if he could smoke. I shrugged. "Do you think you should after being so ill?"

"It's something to do with your hands." He grinned. "Otherwise you just swing them or stick them in your pockets." We laughed together.

After a while he asked, "Will you get a swimsuit for next Sunday? It's great fun in the water if you can swim and I think you'll learn quickly. It's very nice in London Fields."

"Perhaps I will, I'll think about it." We turned into Lamb Lane and he took me to see the pool. To me it looked enormous and was filled with people of all ages having a great time frolicking in the water.

Arriving home, we all had tea and some biscuits. He said a polite goodnight to my mother and brothers and I stood by the street door thanking him for the stroll. He said, "Be seeing you, goodnight."

Returning to work after the break I asked Miss Bennet during our morning coffee if she could swim. "Not likely, I hate too much water," she laughed. "Why ask, are you thinking of plunging in? It's perishing."

Nevertheless I bought a swimsuit for 5s 11d, I also bought my first bra for 2s 6d. The suit was red with white, yellow and green stripes running diagonally from right shoulder to left hip. I donned it and gazed at myself in the wardrobe mirror and thought how skinny I looked. Mum said as she eyed me, "You would certainly look better if you had a bit more up top."

I showed her the bra. Four hooks fastened it in front. Made

of white linen it covered my back. Mum said, "You don't need that contraption, but I suppose you could pad it out with cotton wool."

"Do you think I could wear it under the swimsuit?" She burst into laughter. "Don't be so idiotic, you cannot help being thin."

Sam came Sunday at eleven o'clock. I had donned the swimsuit under my clothes and after helping Mum prepare vegetables, we set off.

There were nice clean lockers in which to leave your clothes, all for the price of two pence and you were given a waterproof ticket to tie round your wrist. I marched out looking for Sam. He was standing at the edge of the pool; he turned and came over to me, and looking at the suit he said, "Red colour suits you."

"Thank you, kind sir." I gave a mock bow.

We were standing near the deep end, seven foot deep. "Ill go for a swim first," he said and dived in. He crawled swiftly along – to me it seemed on top of the water – and thought somewhere in bygone centuries he must have been a dolphin, his movements appeared effortless. I was preparing to put on my rubber hat, when suddenly I was given a hearty push and into the water I went. I screamed in fright and gulped a mouthful of water, struggling like mad. I was grabbed round the waist. "Stop struggling." I gasped and spluttered. "Stop struggling," Sam bawled in my ear. "You're all right." I relaxed as he swam to shallower water.

"Put your feet down now," but I hung on to him shaking my head.

"You're in four feet of water, so stand and hold that rail while I go and find your hat."

"Don't leave me." I held on to the rail as he swam away. Two lads near were splashing about in the water and one of them cupped his hand and swished water over me. When Sam came back with my hat, I thanked him and asked, "Did you see who pushed me in?"

"No, does it matter? It's all in fun."

"I don't think it funny, I can't swim."

"The bloke wasn't to know that." He took my hands from the rail. "Come on, first lesson. This is the hand movement. Push arms out straight, turn palms outwards and sweep them out and round to your sides – come on." I did as he said. "Now, hold on to the rail and shoot out your feet, bending you knees in the same circular movement." I did try, but somehow I couldn't get a coordinated movement. He was very patient, but telling him I felt cold he lifted me to the paving and hoisted himself beside me. We walked to where we had left our towels and we dried each other. My hair was still very wet so he towelled my hair, laughing, "What a curly wig you have. Coming with me again next Sunday?" he asked as we walked home.

And for the next three Sundays we went to the pool, but my swimming did not improve… in fact, I think that first encounter with the water, being pushed in, dented my enthusiasm for the pool.

He said as we walked home on the third Sunday, "I'm going to Eastbourne next Sunday, so we'll give the pool a miss."

"That's fine for you, have a nice time," I told him genuinely.

It was a month before he came to our house again and I was out on this Saturday hairdressing. Jim told me Sam had had some tea with them, had listened to some records with Bill, but had not said if he would call again. On Saturdays now when I arrived home from the shoe shop, I was getting more demands on my time hairdressing among friends.

Flo's two children were staying with us while she was in hospital for the birth of her third child. Pat, now ten years and Len, just over six, were happy to be with us. Their father came Monday evening, bringing the news of the arrival of a baby brother, Raymond. With him he brought chops and sausages, chocolates for Mum and sweets for the children. Pat slept with me and our old couch was turned front to the wall and that made a bed for Len. They were sorry to return home and when later Flo came to show off the new baby, she was so grateful to Mum for helping out.

Mrs Beason moved at the end of August. She told Mum they had paid a twenty-five pound deposit on a semi-detached three-bedroom villa in Rainham, Essex. It had a nice bathroom and a long garden and would cost £650. They would borrow the rest of the cash from a building society. This was the first time I had heard about a building society... Mum too, I think. The idea of Mrs Beason borrowing so much money shocked Mum rigid.

On Saturday mornings Mum still went bug hunting. The names she gave to this chore always raised a laugh. She was "on safari", "big game hunting", "fighting the Red Army" or "hunting mahogany flats", and although she had almost eradicated the pests, the bug blinder was always kept handy and regularly sprinkled around the bedroom skirting boards.

Chapter Thirty-five

In September the adjudicators came to the academy to issue the awards. The beauty culture students were awarded first and names were called in alphabetical order. My name was down the list. Two students were awarded certificates of merit and I had butterflies in my tummy when my name was called. I received a framed diploma, bound in passe-partout. My hand was shaken as I thanked the judge. I read the words through a mist. When I came to the word "excellent" I almost wept. When the final student had received her award, an adjudicator made a speech... about what I had no idea – I was on cloud nine. All I wanted to do was get home and tell Mum how happy I was... I was a good hairdresser. All my practising on Mum and friends had paid off. The hours I had spent practising on wigs, and all the mistakes I had made when I first began the course were forgotten in that moment. Like all the students, I dutifully applauded when the speeches ended. We said goodbye with a final warning from our tutor to remember always to sterilise our tools and to disinfect scissors and hairpins and rollers.

I couldn't get home fast enough. The tube train crawled along. I waited ages for a bus at Liverpool Street Station. I rushed in to tell Mum, showed her the diploma then burst into tears.

She laughed at me and ruffled my hair, "Don't be a baby," she said. "Why are you crying? You should be jumping for joy."

"I'm so happy, I just feel I can't believe I have passed."

"Well, now you'll have more money in your hand with no more fees to pay for, and another thing, you'll be getting home earlier."

I dried my eyes, smiled. "All I have to do now is find a small lock-up shop, then I'll really be happy." Mum shook her head. "It won't be for a while yet," I continued. "I'll have to save like mad to fit out the place with the necessary gear, and really I want a shop somewhere in this area... not too far away."

In my post office savings account I had saved £63 8s 4d, the odd figure caused by added interest. I would certainly need much more cash. I would need a drier on a stand, a permanent waving machine, and a basin, not to mention stock. I would need pounds and pounds more. I could continue working among friends, Friday evenings and Saturday afternoons and add to my savings.

The top part of the house remained empty and in November Sam turned up and asked me to a dance. "You know I'm not all that clever at dancing," I told him, "so that is out of the question." As Louisa did not now go to the dance class, I did not care to go alone.

"If you don't go to a dance occasionally, you'll never learn," he said, "so why not come along with me?"

"I don't want to spoil your evening."

"You won't do that, and that is no excuse."

I thought it a very good cxcuse. "Who else of your friends is going to be there, and where is this dance?" I enquired.

"Shoreditch Town Hall, and I don't know who we may meet there."

"I'll think about it, I may be busy Saturday afternoon."

"I'll be here at 7.30, so you be ready," he smiled, taking the bossiness out of his order.

I hurried home from work on Saturday. I had two iron wavings to do and wanted to help Mum with some dusting, though she said not to bother as I was going out. "I don't really want to go dancing, Mum."

"For goodness' sake go. You have no social life, go and enjoy yourself. You're only young once and life marches on. So go with Sam."

I had a quick bath and got ready with some reluctance and he came on the dot and watched me put on lipstick. I turned. "Do I suit?"

"You look smashing." I wore my old gold dress with pearls and for good measure Mickey's bracelet.

According to the teacher at the dance class I had reached silver medal standard and because she pestered me to try for the medal, bronze and silver, I had ceased to attend classes, so I hoped I had improved.

Dancing was in progress when we entered the hall. "Let's finish this," smiled Sam. It was a quickstep.

"Nothing fancy," I warned grinning. He was easy to follow. I concentrated and put my best effort into the dance. Once round the hall and that finished. "That wasn't too bad, was it?"

"No. I've been having some lessons with my friends."

"Good. Do I know the place?"

"It's a dancing school in Hackney."

We were dancing round in the gay Gordons when I saw Joe Bendon and Babs come into the hall. "Your brother has arrived," I said.

He saw Joe, who waved a hand and we continued dancing.

The dance over, we joined him at the back of the hall. I greeted Babs saying it was a long time since we had last met, then turned to Joe.

"Nice to see you again," I smiled.

He stared at me. "Meet Sam here?" he asked coldly.

"No, my invitation," said Sam quietly. I looked away, and wondered what I had done or said to account for his coolness. When the next dance began he whisked Babs onto the floor without a word.

"What's got into his pants?" I asked Sam.

"He's been in a mood all the afternoon. Take no notice. Come, forget him, let's dance." It was a waltz, but all the pleasure I had felt had gone. I wondered if it was something I had done, though I had not seen him since the dance at Kennington about a year ago. I did not want to make any upset between brothers. I decided to leave. At the end of the waltz, I said, "I'm going home, Sam. You stay. It seems I've upset Joe in some way."

"Please, Belle, don't spoil my evening. Don't go."

"What about him, spoiling *my* evening? He's rude and I've done nothing that I can remember to warrant it. So, I'm not staying. Thank you for asking me out." Dancers were around us as the dance ended.

"What's up with you two, quarrelling so early?" Joe sneered. I left, going to the cloakroom for my coat. Sam was waiting outside.

"Don't be silly, Belle, don't let him upset you, stay."

"I'm going home," I shouted at him, "and don't come for me again. It may upset your dear brother. I mean that. Goodnight and thanks."

I marched down the Town Hall steps into the heavy rain and stood sheltering under the railway arch. I had tucked my long dress into a belt I carried for such an occasion and waited for a bus or tram. A policeman stood nearby. I thought maybe Sam would come after me, but on second thoughts dismissed the idea. "Nasty night, Miss," the policeman said.

"Yes, has it been raining long?"

"Since nine o'clock. Where have you been not to know?"

"Dancing?" I said shortly.

"Bet you quarrelled with your bloke."

"Something like that," I replied.

"How about coming out with me, Wednesday evening?" I looked at his number, 319. "You're a fast worker."

"My name is Martin and I'm based over there," he jerked a thumb towards the police station opposite the Town Hall. "Where do you live?"

"Scawfell Street." It was out before I realised it.

"I'll call for you, what number?"

"I'll meet you at the top of the turning."

"Right. I'll be there at 7.30 sharp. You've missed a couple of buses speaking to me but thank you just the same."

I caught the next tram home and that is how I met Martin.

Martin Simpson looked much different in a belted raincoat and trilby hat; he appeared shorter. We greeted each other with a handshake.

"This month I begin night work," he began. "I have to be on duty at ten p.m. until six a.m., so what do you say to a ride up west, we can have a beer and chat? I'll get you back here at 9.30, that will give me time to get home and into uniform."

It was not my idea to spend an evening in a pub. "I don't drink," I informed him. "I would sooner have a coffee somewhere."

"That's fine. Let's catch a bus."

We rode to the Strand and walked along to Lyons' Corner House. We found a table for two. The band in the gallery was playing *What Will I Do?* This was where I had first brought Mickey. I thought about the bandsmen who had played and how amazed Mickey had been. Martin took off his raincoat and hat and hung them on a nearby stand as a nippy came to take our order. Martin smiled at her.

"You order," he nodded to me. "Coffee or tea?" So I ordered coffee and buttered scones.

"Now, tell me all about yourself, Belle," Martin said.

"To be taken down in evidence?" I asked.

"I like to know all about the girl I'm taking out."

"There's Mother and two brothers, the boys work at an electrical firm. I'm a shop assistant. I work in the West End."

"And your father, what does he do?"

"No father," I lied.

"Been dead long?"

"Many years." The nippy placed the order before us with a plate on which there were four buttered scones. Martin shovelled in the sugar, four spoonfuls... amazing. "Now it's your turn to talk," I reminded him. "I too like to know about the man taking me out."

"My father was a copper, he reached sergeant status. I have a married brother, also a copper, who lives in Poplar with his wife and little son, about two years old. He's based at Stepney nick. As Father was in the force, it was natural we should follow suit."

"Are you married?"

"Good Lord, no. I'm just twenty-four."

I looked at him. Light brown hair side parted, a wide brow, light blue eyes, straight nose and a firm chin, and slightly tanned complexion... a strong face. Was this the blue-eyed boy who would be good to me? He was pleasant enough to speak to.

"Like what you're looking at?" he grinned.

"Sorry, I was thinking."

"I think we'd better be moving." He stood up as the waitress came to our table, slid a sixpence under the plate and he paid the bill as we left. Walking to the bus stop he asked, "May I see you Friday evening? It'd be for a couple of hours."

"Sorry, I curl a friend's hair Fridays." I saw no reason at that time to tell him about hairdressing.

"On Saturdays off I go to football matches, like to come?"

"Thank you, no. I'm not keen on football." So we arranged to meet Thursday. Same place, same time. And Thursday was a repeat of the Tuesday evening except that we wandered along Regent Street.

We met sometimes Tuesday or Wednesday and sometimes Thursday evenings, and it was always a walk around the West End. A couple of times he fancied a beer, so I agreed to a lemonade or ginger beer. I didn't like the smoky atmosphere of pubs and told him so. He said coppers learned a lot overhearing conversations in pubs about the doings of crooks.

I think it was the second week in November when I came home from work for Mum to tell us the upper part of the house would shortly have a new tenant. The landlord's daughter had been round during the afternoon with a lady named Hughes, who had decided to take the rooms. She had been introduced to Mum and had been told and shown about the bathing arrangements and the new tenant, and Mum could sort out when and how bathing times would suit.

"You do have to remember, Mrs Hughes, that Mrs Munday has to use the cooker so I hope baths can be arranged amicably between you."

During the time the rooms had been empty, Mum had been having a ball playing the piano. Every spare moment she had she played.

"The lady has two boys, so I expect we shall have to use the soft pedal when playing."

On the last Saturday in November, Mrs Hughes moved in. It had rained all day and was very cold. As I had three friends' hair to do, I said I would help Mum on Sunday. I arrived home about seven. The front door was wide open as were the side gate and yard door. The removals van was still outside the house. As I walked into the house, I was almost knocked down by a boy, about ten, dashing out of the house. I went down into our semi-basement living-room. The house was like a morgue. There was no such thing as central heating in those days. Mum was wearing a coat. "This place has been wide open since about four o'clock, and I'm frozen. I don't know how much longer they'll be."

"Well, Mum," said Bill, "they can't move furniture through closed doors, can they?"

It was almost eight o'clock before the street door finally closed, then footsteps came clattering down our stairs and there was a loud knock on the door. It opened and a boy of about twelve years old stood there with a teapot in his hand. "Muvver said could she borrow free spoon of tea until she finds ours." Mum spooned in the required tea and without a word of thanks off he went only to be down again with a cup. "Muvver says can you lend 'er a cup of milk."

"There's a small grocery shop just across the road along Dunloe Street, he sells milk and if you hurry you can get milk there," I told him. "And tell your mother anything else she needs she may be able to buy there too, goodnight." A few moments later I heard the lad go out, leaving the street door open. I went up and closed it. I closed and bolted the side gate and shut the yard door. There were two loud knocks and I let the boy in. "Please close the street door whenever you go out. This is not wide-open Wednesday." He ran quickly up the stairs without a word and I heard him yell: "She shut me out."

The noise of them moving furniture about was horrendous. It went on until 1.30 a.m. It was impossible to sleep. We all thought it impossible to move furniture quietly, but surely they could have stopped a little earlier. I woke to thumping and the boys running up and down to the toilet in the yard. The time was just after 6.30. There was no more sleep for any of us that morning; consequently we were all a little irritable, especially Jim. He was always on a short fuse.

The shuttling and banging ended at last about eight o'clock Sunday evening. Mum was upset because she was too tired to go bug hunting.

"Never mind, Mum," Bill consoled her, "surely after all the hunting you've done, there can't be too many left."

"I hope not. They breed so quickly; you have to keep on hunting them. I really don't know how they can hide in daylight."

Home from work Monday evening, Mum amused us, relating the events of the day. Mrs Hughes had come down asking Mum where the copper was. "I had the small boiler on the cooker and was doing a first boil of washing. When I told her there was no copper she said, 'Had I known there was no copper I would not have moved in.'"

"You can imagine, Mrs Munday, the boiling I have to do with two boys. Do you think I could borrow that boiler?"

"I told her I had more washing to do and if she walked along the Hackney Road and turned down Goldsmith's Row, she would reach the Broadway where there were hardware shops and she would be able to buy a boiler."

We agreed that Mum had done the right thing and came to the conclusion that Mrs Hughes was a borrower.

I went out with Martin whenever his duty roster permitted. In December, his duty changed from ten p.m. to six a.m. We went to see films and by this time had reached the kissing stage outside the street door. He said, "One of these nights I'm taking a pot shot at that street light, then I'll really be able to kiss you."

It was nearing Christmas and this Thursday evening it began to rain. It was very cold too. I said suddenly, "Let's go back and you can come in to meet my brothers and Mum."

The light was on in the sitting-room and I thought maybe Mum would be playing the piano. When we entered the room I was surprised to see Sam there with Jim and Mum. I heard Bill playing the gramophone in the semi-basement. I introduced Martin and hands were shaken. Mum stood up, "Come on, you two, I'll make some tea," and they left the room.

I was surprised to see Sam. Martin said, "Do you think I've scared them or something?"

I shrugged, yet wondered. I pointed to the piano. "Can you play?"

"Yes, one finger, *Pop goes the Weasel.*" He laughed and continued. "We have a smashing police band at the nick and we hold police dances at the Town Hall on occasions. We get a good turnout. You must come along."

"I'll see if the tea is made… and you like plenty of sugar."

In the basement, it was warm and cosy. Mum was pouring tea.

"Where did you find him?" she demanded.

"Under the railway arch, Old Street." They all laughed. "He's a policeman," I ventured.

"That's what he's told you?"

"He was in uniform when we met and he's based at Old Street Police Station... so what's wrong with that?"

Mum watched as I spooned in four spoons of sugar. Putting some biscuits on a plate she asked, "Does he need all that sweetening?"

I picked up the tray and marched out of the room. He had taken off his coat and was seated at the piano.

"Like to hear my rendition?"

I thought how much Mum would laugh, as I nodded and he played. We both laughed as I clapped. We drank tea and chatted and after a while he left, calling down the stairs, "Goodnight, everyone." Someone answered, I don't know who, but it wasn't Mum.

Queenie, the girl Jim had been walking out with for two years, had moved. Her father, a sheet metal worker, had been offered a very good job by a Sheffield company and the offer had been too good to refuse, so the family had upped sticks and moved north. Jim was a little upset. He said he had grown very fond of Queenie, she was a nice girl, and we all liked her too and were sorry the family had moved. Jim had promised to write; a few letters were exchanged but it gradually ended as letters became fewer.

It was two weeks before Christmas and Martin suggested we ride to Victoria to book seats for a revue for the New Year. At Victoria Place we reserved bookings for the second Wednesday evening in January.

Leaving the booking office, we walked along the road and nearing a pub, Martin said he fancied a beer. After leaving the pub, we found a grocery shop and he bought a two-pound box of creams. "I always spend any leave time with my parents at

Christmas," he said as he gave me the box that the assistant had slipped into a Christmas bag with red string handles. "You do understand?"

"Of course I do, I too like to spend the time with my family."

"If we take the tube, we'll have time for a drink at Dirty Dick's, so let's hurry." This was not my ideal way to end an evening.

We crossed the road to the pub, after leaving Liverpool Street Station. There is some kind of legend about Dirty Dick's, about a room with a wedding reception table laid ages ago and for some reason left as it was. True or false... I don't know. The room is dirty and supposedly festooned with cobwebs... hence the pub's name.

He wanted me to try a "gin and it". I insisted on tomato juice. We sat chatting generalities and left at 10.30. We had been walking for about five minutes when Martin suddenly stopped, saying, "Good Lord."

A young girl barred our way. "So, is this your new fancy tart?" she demanded.

"Who are you calling a tart?" I snapped.

She waved her hand under my nose and clicked her fingers.

"You see this? That says we're engaged to be married."

I caught the sparkle of diamonds and stared at this angry girl.

"Oh, Martin!" I exclaimed. "How could you?"

"Martin," she screamed. "Who gave you that fancy name... her?"

"Here," I said, offering the bag of creams, and dropped it at her feet. I was appalled at the knot of people that had collected. I pushed my way through, to find myself confronted by a tall lady of ample proportions. "You ought to be ashamed of yourself," she hissed.

"You watch *your* man, he just might surprise you." I sidestepped past her and walked quickly, seizing the opportunity to cross the road when the traffic thinned and stood in a darkened doorway to wait for a bus. I watched the small crowd disperse, and then saw Martin and the girl walking arm in arm on the opposite side of the road and she carried the Christmassy bag.

In the bus I wondered what Martin's name really was… maybe it wasn't even Simpson either… Martin Simpson, why lie?

I stepped off the bus. A man passing looked my way.

"Holy mackerel, Belle! You haven't changed at all."

I eyed him in the light of the street lamp. High cheekbones, slightly sunken cheeks, a straight nose, and a wide smiling mouth showing good teeth. I took all this in at a glance, then shrugged.

"It's Jack… Jack Richards… remember?"

I laughed as we embraced and kissed. It seemed the most natural thing to do. My childhood playmate of Guinness's Buildings, when we lived at Number 79 and he lived at 73 with his parents and sister Violet. "After all these years, Jack, I cannot believe it."

"I'd know you anywhere, you haven't changed."

"Surely I've grown taller and look a little more intelligent."

"You still have the same pretty face."

"Come off it. Where are you going?"

"I've been visiting Mother and Dad. They're still in the buildings, but have moved lower down. Mum's rheumatism, couldn't take all the stairs." We were walking along as we chatted.

"How is your sister Violet?"

"She's been married for five years and has a year-old son."

"And you?" I asked.

"I have a small flat in a house in Nicholl Square, I was on my way home… Belle, it's great meeting you." As he spoke I studied him by the light of the street lamp. He had changed so much.

"Come home with me, Jack, Mum will be pleased to see you, so will Jim. I doubt Bill will know you; he was just two years when we moved. I live in the next street, it's not too late."

We entered the house to hear the Hugheses quarrelling. I led the way to our semi- basement living-room. Jim was reading, Bill was writing and Mum was stitching her embroidery. "Look who I found," I said.

They stared, no recognition in their eyes.

"It's Jack Richards."

He was greeted with words like "I would have passed you in the street, Jack," and "Gracious, how you've changed."

"Maybe it's because I worry too much," Jack grinned.

Tea and biscuits were soon on the table and Bill was told of the many pranks and games we played. Mum apologised for the din from the tenants above and told me they had quarrelled for almost two hours.

Asking Jack to drop in any time, we bade him goodnight.

Back once more in the living-room, Mum began. "What happened to Martin?"

"We had a row," I lied. "That's the end of him."

Mum made no comment and I began clearing the cups and washing up in the kitchen. I thought about Martin. Maybe Simpson was not his surname either. If I went to Old Street Police Station I could find out his real name. I knew his number. It wasn't worth the effort. For some reason known to himself, I had served his purpose. Damn!

Each day Mum was getting more and more disgruntled with Mrs Hughes and her boys. It wasn't too bad while the boys were at school, but as soon as they came home the side door was left open, the door to the yard too and they were chasing up and down the stairs, so Mum now locked the door at street level and the living-room door whenever she went shopping.

There were three lines for drying washing across the yard and two in the kitchen, and on fine days there was always something of Mrs Hughes's hanging in the yard, and on wet days her clothes hung in the kitchen. Mum washed and boiled white linens Mondays and did the coloureds Tuesday and finally we had a line in our living-room and this made us fed up.

Ten days before Christmas, Jack came and I went to the cinema. He bought a half-pound box of sugared almonds, which he remembered was my favourite sweet. He spoke of his feelings to me for his landlady's daughter, but she was just seventeen. "I think she looks upon me as an old man."

"Why not try the old-fashioned way, Jack? Ask the parents if you can take their daughter to the theatre and take it from there."

He grinned. "That's quite a thought."

Chapter Thirty-six

Christmas Day we spent with Aunt Minne and our cousins. We had a great time over-eating and roasting chestnuts on a shovel over the fire. We left at midnight and on Boxing Day we played host to Auntie and our cousins. Arriving home we found the light left on in the kitchen and singing and jumping from the tenants. Mum was furious as our meter supplied light to the kitchen. "Maybe someone had a bath," suggested Bill.

Mum decided to let the matter of the light pass, but with the boys being home from school for the Christmas holiday and the doors constantly being left open, the house became very cold and whenever we found doors open we closed them.

At the beginning of 1932 I seriously began to look for a lock-up shop to rent. I wanted something near; friends would not want to pay fares if my shop was too far. I studied the *Hackney and Kingsland Gazette*, but Saturday afternoons were the only time I had to find decent accommodation. A shop advertised, rented for 12s 6d weekly, appeared ideal. Securing the key, I inspected the shop. It was large but very dirty and in need of redecoration. There was a smaller room containing a sink and a gas ring on the hearth before a small dirty grate. A door led to a small concrete yard with an outside toilet. My heart sank as I inspected the loo. The pan was encrusted with a thick yellow scale; it would take ages to get rid of. I considered the time and money I would have to spend to get the place prettied up. I returned the key to the owner.

"It's so dirty," I told him, "I'm disgusted you offer the place in that condition. I wish you joy trying to let it."

"It only needs soap and water and plenty of elbow grease."

"Then you have a go and good luck," I replied. "Good day."

Maybe a shop with living accommodation would be more appropriate. But where we now lived the rooms were spacious and our furniture was shown off to the best advantage and the yard was so handy for Jim and our cousins to wheel their motorcycles in through the side door. Nothing would induce Mum to move... or so I thought. Meanwhile I had a few disappointments searching for a shop. Now I had my diploma, I was eager to open a salon.

Mum visited Mrs Gee and told us she had a jolly good moan about the conduct of Mrs Hughes and the boys, and Mrs Gee suggested Mum speak to the landlord. What could he do? It could make matters worse.

I saw in the paper a house to let in Treadway Street. This was the other side of Hackney Road and not too far. It gave a telephone number to ring for details. It was now towards the end of February and as the days grew brighter, Jim, Cousin Bill and Albert, who lived farther down our street, cleaned up their cycles in the yard and much to their annoyance were pestered for rides by the Hughes boys. One Sunday I got mad. I stormed into the yard. "Don't any of you give these kids a ride. They could fall off and break their necks, and you kids, get outside and stop worrying these men."

"Who do you think you are, telling us to go outside?" the eldest boy queried. "We ain't asking you for a ride."

"Do as the lady asks," said Albert.

"Er, a lady? Don't make me laugh, you make me pee my trousers."

In spite of ourselves we laughed. These cheeky kids.

Monday evening I rang the phone number given in the paper and asked if I could call on Saturday afternoon to inspect the house in Treadway Street, and where could I pick up the key? I was told to ask for a Mrs Jones at 58 Clarence Road, Hackney. Speaking about what I was thinking of doing, Mum said, "I think I'll be pleased to move but after making this place look nice, I'll be sorry to leave here. Let's hope it's a nice house and we can make it our home."

I duly presented myself in Clarence Road. To my surprise it was a shoe shop. Entering I asked for Mrs Jones and a tall lady greeted me, asking me to come into the shop parlour. It was comfortably furnished and she offered me tea, asking had I come far? I told her where we lived, saying it was not far, just a short distance from Treadway Street.

She was pleasant to speak to. "Now, about the rent. It's thirty shillings weekly, paid in advance, can you afford that?"

"If the house is suitable for us, the rent will be no problem," I informed her. She handed me four keys on a ring.

"The number of the house is 30 and it's a pub converted very nicely into a dwelling house. I think you'll like it." I took the keys. "Now we'll see Mr Jones. Have you a deposit for the keys?" Entering the shop, we waited while Mr Jones finished serving his customer. I offered a pound for the keys and he signed a receipt. "Will it be suitable if I return the keys tomorrow? Maybe my mother will want to think about the house."

I dashed home thinking how strange that shoes and a pub should come into our lives in this fashion. Was it an omen? Passing the street on the tram carrying me home, I had a quick glance… fairly wide it looked.

The time was almost 3.30 as I hustled Mum into her coat.

"It's an upheaval moving, Belle, more so now that we've a lot more furniture to shift."

"We don't know if it will suit us. Let's cross that bridge when we come to it, eh, Mum?"

We turned into Treadway Street. The spring sun cheered us as we entered the empty house. The street door was grained and varnished, a very short passage, then we opened another door. This was the entrance to a long passage ending at a cupboard under the stairs. There was an opening to a panelled good sized room with a quarry tiled floor. Mum assumed this was the bar parlour. In a recess to the left of a kitchen range was a deep butler sink, in the other recess three wide shelves. The very large room we entered we thought had been the skittle alley. There were three small windows on either side near the ceiling. Unlocking the door at the far end we saw a concrete yard and an outside toilet, beautifully clean, newly whitewashed. The toilet had a brown polished tip-up seat. We locked the back door and continued our inspection. We crossed the tiled room, opening a door to a room about sixteen feet square, no fire grate. There was a brass ring sunken into the floorboards and a large hook four feet up the wall. This was the cellar flap, Mum told me, and this room, she thought, had probably housed the bar. We walked into the large front room. There was a small grate with a pretty wood surround grained and polished… as was all the woodwork… and in these two rooms the walls were painted a delicate shade of pink. A very large window, roughly six feet square, let in plenty of light. Then we toured the bedrooms. The stairs were bright with light from a long narrow window. The master bedroom was large with two wide windows. Mum thought the wardrobe could stand between the windows. The back bedroom too was large. We thought my brothers would have plenty of room there. Back in the main bedroom, Mum said this would be our room and maybe both beds could face the windows. I began to think Mum was thinking seriously about taking the house. Downstairs again in the taproom, there was a nice grey enamelled cooker and a bath covered by a heavy wooden lid. There was a gas geyser, much like the one where we lived now. In those days gas cookers and electric lighting were always installed in rented accommodation. You notified the gas and electric companies when you were moving and men came to empty the meters as you moved. Your new dwelling was equipped with meters and when money was cranked into them lighting and heating was there ready to use, no problems.

"Well, what do you think, Belle, and you haven't yet said what the rent is… now how much?"

"Thirty shillings, Mum, in advance." I watched her face, as she walked slowly into the large front room. "Mum, you know I have long wanted a salon. If I could have this room, I'll pay you ten shillings a week for it, that will leave you paying the same rent, how about it?"

"If you have this room the furniture will be jumbled too close together, and we won't have room to move around."

"Let's have a try, Mum. The bedrooms… OK. Have the dining furniture in this tiled room, the piano and armchairs in there." I pointed to the room behind the front room that I wanted. "The living-room table and chairs in the skittle alley. What do you think?"

She thought for a while and looking round asked, "Where will I put the old couch and my machine?"

"Could it go against the wall by the door in the bedroom? And perhaps your machine would fit into that recess beside the range."

"Let's cross that bridge when we come to it. We'll come here tomorrow after dinner with Jim and Bill, and see what they say."

My brothers thought the place ideal. Jim could put his motorcycle in the long passage and they thought the street was wide and decent looking and the house looked clean and neat.

"I think you're getting snobbish," Mum laughed.

Jack came round on Monday evening and came with me to Clarence Road to return the keys. He told me he had tackled his landlady regarding her daughter and she had agreed, saying her daughter would be in safe hands.

"I took Susan to the theatre and do you know what the girl said?"

"You tell me," I laughed. "Sometimes we say stupid things."

Jack laughed too. "She said, 'Jack, I thought you'd never ask me out and I loved the theatre.' So I'm on velvet."

"My congratulations, Jack, I'm happy for you."

He waited outside while I paid Mrs Jones the rent in advance, telling her Mum had to give two weeks' notice to her landlord and we could move in the last week of March. This suited Mrs Jones and she gave me a rent book with the rent paid duly signed.

When Jack and I were nearly home he asked me about my social life. "Nothing much at the moment. I'm eager now to get a salon fixed and begin working for myself, but it will take time."

"Doesn't it worry you, not having a man friend?"

"Gracious, no. I'm told there's a blue-eyed bloke somewhere out there, so I'll wait for him to find me."

"The mountain didn't come to Mohammed, Belle,"

I shrugged. "Why should you worry about me?"

We all sat talking, putting the world right over cocoa and biscuits and Jack left at about 10.30.

Chapter Thirty-seven

The next two weeks were spent making arrangements for moving.

In telling Mrs Hughes we were moving, she remarked to Mum, "Now we'll be able to have a bath without asking permission." To that Mum retorted, "It has been just as difficult for us too, a shared kitchen becomes almost a battleground if you let it. I hope you get along with the next tenants and get your priorities right."

Mum arranged for the removals men for the last Saturday in March for two o'clock. By that time we were home from work for a quick sandwich lunch and a final collection of teapot, cups, plates, etc. Men had emptied the meters and with a final word to my brothers to make sure nothing was left behind, to lock all doors, but not the kitchen, and leave the keys at the landlord's office in Hackney Road. Mum's policy was to scrub out the new place before we moved in. I went for the keys on Thursday evening and Mum spent all Friday scrubbing out.

It usually took me an hour to get home from Bond Street. Jim was already home, Bill came in later. The removals men arrived on time and after a quick cup of tea began work. Finishing our lunch, Mum and I packed all the crockery into a shopping bag plus the teapot and sugar basin; the milk she left for the boys to drink.

The day was cold but sunny. After we arrived at the house,

Mum sent me shopping for meat and vegetables. "Get two pounds of sausages, we can have those for dinner tonight."

I now had seven regular clients. I did three waves each Friday evening and two waves and two shampoo-and-sets on Saturday afternoons. The sets usually took an hour and a half. Using the hand drier was tedious and took time and I was seldom home before nine o'clock, but I was earning money and was adding to my savings weekly. I now had £84 16s 9d in my savings account, but I knew I would need much more. After shopping for Mum, I set off to my clients. I spoke of getting a salon set up and they wished me good luck with the promise to become regular customers and asked how soon all this would materialise. Meantime I would continue to carry on as usual.

It was hectic, the removals men asking where we wanted this and that. The piano was left in the front room until the lino was fitted in the next room and curtains etc. When my brothers took up the stair-corded carpet Mrs Hughes complained long and loud. Mum told her we had once lived in the rooms and had provided stair covering, now she could do the same.

I arrived home about 9.30. My brothers and our cousin Bill had fitted the lino and the piano was in place, complete with two armchairs in the room next to the front room. Mum had kept my dinner hot and I thoroughly enjoyed the sausage and mash. We said goodnight and thanks to our cousins and sat back for a chat. Mum said, "Now I hope you'll put in a bit of scales practice, Belle, and I'll be able to play in peace."

Gradually everything fell into place. Mum used her long green bedroom curtains as a divider to the front room. They were pinned together with safety pins and looked great. I needed a toilet basin, a geyser and mirrors. Bill suggested I ask our old landlord if he could supply a basin and a plumber. He sold me a basin for £2 10s. The plumber connected it to the water mains, charging only three pounds. Next I tackled the gas company to hire a geyser. That was simple and I received a bill for a three-monthly hire. I bought a large mirror, three foot by four foot, from a picture framer's for six pounds, with some D-fittings and screws, and my brothers ordered a plank of wood planed from the wood yard in Tuilerie Street, plus a shelf to fit into a recess. All was falling into place. My savings were getting smaller, but I was pleased things were working out for me. Mum said the wood-patterned lino we had in the sitting-room would suit the room and there was enough over to fit the long passage.

"I don't think there are any bugs here," Mum stated one day. "I remember when we lived in the pub there were no bugs there, and as this place has been a public house, maybe bugs don't like the smell of beer."

"Perhaps as all the walls are painted, there isn't wallpaper for them to hide behind," Jim said.

"Nevertheless, when I scrubbed out, I sprinkled some bug blinder all round the bedroom skirting boards, just to make sure," Mum laughed.

All this work took time; it was now half-way through June. One Saturday afternoon, I went to a warehouse to eye out a permanent waving machine and a drier on a stand. A new type of model caught my attention. It was a cylinder, almost three feet tall topped by a deep disc on which were twenty-four light bulbs, to which were connected the same number of leads. I read the instructions on the accompanying leaflet. It seemed ideal and foolproof. The price was sixty-eight pounds. I didn't have that much in my savings account.

Next I looked at the driers. All were priced around sixteen pounds. I bought two pretty styled Tiffany lamp shades for the lights. They matched the pink painted walls, and at 2s 6d each I thought they were a bargain. Arriving home I found my brothers fixing the shelves they had grained and varnished. The graining effect had been achieved using an old comb. I really appreciated their help and thanked them. I told them of my browse around the warehouse. I said I had about forty-five pounds in savings and they immediately offered to lend me cash. I realised they would have to wait for repayment if I took up their offer, and they agreed to wait until the salon was paying its way. The next Saturday afternoon we went to the warehouse and looked over the goods once more. If that was what I wanted, my brothers were all for helping me. Cash duly changed hands and delivery would be Thursday the following week. All there was now for me to do was to give my notice at the shop. Wages being paid every ten days, M'sieur needed ten days' notice. This generally meant two weeks.

In those days, August holiday Monday was the first Monday in August. I had planned to open two weeks before the holiday. I had had a price list printed and, for the time being Mum had lent me two chairs. Later I would get two tub chairs.

I approached M'sieur this Monday morning requesting permission for an interview. In the stockroom I told him I was leaving. He glared at me asking for a reason.

"I wish to try something new, something I have always wanted to do."

"And what is that, may I ask?"

"I'm starting business on my own."

"It costs money to stock a shoe shop," he sneered.

"I'm not into shoes. I'm opening a hairdressing salon."

He burst into derisive laughter. "What in heaven's name do you know about hairdressing?"

"I've spent years being taught," I answered with spirit. "And I have a diploma of excellence to prove it."

"You must have taken leave of your senses. You want your brains tested. You have a decent job here and wages every week, so...."

"It is what I have dreamed about since I was small," I interrupted him, "and nothing is going to stop me, you or anyone else."

"If it all goes down the drain, don't come crawling to me to give you a job." He was shouting, I was sure he could be heard in the shop.

"Apart from the hairdressing, I have a good trade in my hands, and that is something I can always fall back on."

"Get upstairs and begin working and I'll be watching you for the next two weeks and I still think you're crazy."

"Thank you, M'sieur, you are most kind," I said sarcastically.

The following Sunday, I told Mum I was going to the Columbia flower market. I thought a plant with some trailing green leaves would look pretty. Before I left I put a notice in the window. The printed notice read, "Belle's Beauty Parlour", and beside it the times of opening hours. As at the time shops had to have an early closing day, I decided to close all day Mondays. I looked round with pride at my small salon, it all appeared squeaky clean and bright. I felt elated.

Columbia flower market has been trading for more than a hundred years. It is known far and wide. Everything to enhance the garden can be purchased there, from seeds of all kinds, plants and shrubs to fruit and flowering trees. All garden tools are on show and ornamental pots abound. There are many types of pesticides and, if asked, traders will tell you the way to get the best results from your plants. Cockney good humour can be heard on all sides, and whatever the weather, the market is open every Sunday from 8.30 until 12.30, and crowds flock there to snap up bargains for their gardens.

I walked along the stalls on the left side of the market from Barnet Grove to Virginia Road then down on the right side. On a stall by Columbia Road School I saw what I wanted. I picked up the small plant.

"Hallo, Belle, long time no see."

I spun round, "Good morning, Sam. How are you?"

The charcoal-grey trilby, slightly raised, he now settled back on his head.

"Fine, thank you. What are you doing in this neck of the woods?"

"Buying this." Briefly I showed it to him before handing it to the nurseryman. "Two shillings, Miss." I handed over the money. The plant was now in a brown paper bag and we looked at the small cream-edged leaves of ivy. "It's pretty, don't you think, Sam."

"It would do much better in a larger pot."

"The stall selling pots is near the Baxendale pub," I told him. We threaded our way through the crowds of people. He looked very smart in a light grey suit, blue shirt, diagonal grey and blue striped tie.

"Where are you off to, this sunny day?"

"I was going to see my sister, Edie." We reached the flowerpot stall. "Don't let me keep you," I smiled. "Nice seeing you."

"She doesn't expect me. I saw you from the window over the shop and then missed you in the crowd. I went to Scawfell Street a couple of months ago. Would you believe, two boys were playing football in the yard. When I said I had come to see your family, they told me you'd moved, I couldn't take it in. They told me they didn't know where you lived and they didn't care. I was disappointed. I went to see Harry Gee, Mrs Gee had forgotten the name of the road, something beginning with T."

We were passing the railings of Guinness's Buildings.

I said, "As a kid I was so happy racing around these grounds minus shoes and socks, until Father found out where we lived and caused a disturbance and had us turned out."

"You must tell me about that some time."

"I don't think it would interest you very much."

"Why not try me?"

I shook my head and for a while we walked on in silence. Suddenly he asked, "How's Martin?"

"Martin? Oh, Martin. I've forgotten about him... Full stop."

"And the current boyfriend?"

"Quite non-existent. I'll be too busy working to repay a debt."

He looked at me raising quizzical eyebrows. "You know what they say about all work and no play...?"

"Here we are." As we passed the window, he stopped. "'Belle's Beauty Parlour', eh. Bit upmarket for this area, don't you think?"

I ignored that and we entered the house. There was no door to the salon, and we walked in. My brothers had just finished fixing the long shelf. They were pleased to see Sam and as he looked around he told me it was a very good set up. He said his sister Emily had the downstairs front room of their house as a salon but only did waving. She had been doing this for two years and had quite a number of clients and when she was busy Joe and Sam helped her by curling up the ends of hair while she waved the next client. He looked at the permanent waving machine. I told him it was quite a new type of model and I was swotting up instructions like mad, saying I thought I would be having kittens when I used it for the very first time.

We then went down the passage into the tiled room. Mum was in the skittle alley preparing vegetables. She too was pleased to see Sam.

"I thought you went to buy a plant," she said. I showed it to her. "I'll ask the chap next door for some earth. Sam said it needs re-potting, then it will grow better."

"I'll re-pot it for you, Belle," said Sam quickly. "We have a garden and it will give me pleasure to do this." Mum gave him an odd look.

I made some tea and we spoke about moving. "Would you like to stay to dinner, Sam?" Mum asked suddenly. "It's lamb and stewed apples and custard for sweet. I can cook more potatoes, how about it?"

"Yes, Mrs Munday, if it isn't too much trouble."

The floor of the skittle alley had been painted and polished and Mum decided to keep it that way and now with a couple of rugs laid down it looked cosy. We sat at our large kitchen table and chatted as we ate.

I washed the dishes while Mum made Camp coffee. In those days it was a thick brown liquid out of a bottle. You could buy ground coffee but it was expensive. We sat talking. "When do you expect to open?"

"I hope to begin Tuesday of next week. My closing day will be Monday. I'll open at 9.30 a.m. and close at 7 p.m., and on Saturdays close at 8 p.m. I know hairdressers in the area close an hour later. I have my times of opening and closing in the window. I think that will suit me. I do have a few clients. I've been doing some Friday nights and Saturday afternoons for some time and now these people can come to the salon and use my gas and electricity."

Sam left a little later, saying he would bring the plant one evening during the week and we happily said cheerio.

Chapter Thirty-eight

Meantime I was working getting the salon ready and finally opened in September 1932. That morning I did Mum's hair and she was under the drier when a tall policeman walked in. My heart jumped off its hook and plunged into my shoes. What had I done wrong? In those days, if you wanted to open a shop and sell from your home, you went ahead and did your own thing.

"Can I help you, Officer?" I asked weakly.

"May I make an appointment for my wife? Shampoo and set, Thursday, 11.30?"

My heart fell into place, and looking business-like I entered his request in the appointments book. From that time, I never looked back.

Sam came and asked me to go swimming with him on Sunday. I agreed. "I've probably forgotten what you've taught me," I said.

"You'll never learn unless you get some practice," he replied.

I laughed, "I was never meant to be a fish." On Sunday the sun shone warmly and the pool was crowded. I slid into the shallow water. With Sam's encouragement, I waded into deeper water and swam towards him. As I did so he moved farther away. Finally, spluttering and gasping, he pulled me to shallower water. I waded to the bar. "I think I'll try to swim to the other side. Don't leave me." Ever so slowly I just did it.

"At this rate you'll soon be swimming the Channel," he grinned.

"You're joking, of course," I snorted.

"I am and I just can't stop laughing," he replied.

I reached up, grabbing his shoulders, and pushed him under the water. He pulled me under and was sitting on top of me. I struggled like mad against his weight, and seconds later we were above water. I was choking and he was thumping my back, saying, "Spit it out, spit it out."

"You tried to drown me," I stormed and slapped his face.

"Don't you ever do that again," he said furiously.

"You shouldn't try to drown me." I made my way out of the pool, and finding my towel proceeded to dry my hair. I looked round to see him speaking to a girl, who went in and out in all the right places, and they were both laughing. I turned my back on them and eyeing my slight bumps, I said, "Why don't you both grow a bit bigger, grow me breasts?"

"Speaking to yourself, Belle? That's the first sign of lunacy."

I didn't answer, and he went on, "That girl apologised for falling on top of us, she said she was pushed."

"I thought you were admiring her bust."

"Do I detect the yellow flag waving?"

"You should be so lucky," I snorted.

He spread his towel and lay down, stretching out his long length.

"Maybe I like thin girls. Lie on your towel and get dry."

I sat beside him, knees drawn up to my chin and swathed my towel around me. I eyed his long legs, the slight covering of fair hairs and his big feet. His head rested in his hands clasped behind his head. I looked at the hairs covering his chest and thought viciously, if I grabbed a handful of those hairs and tugged, he would jump out of his skin.

"You look so angry, Belle," he said suddenly. "What are you thinking about? Take that scowl off your face. It doesn't suit you."

We were silent for quite a while and walking home did not speak very much. He stayed to tea and later played chess with Bill.

In October came the first booking for a perm. Any spare time I had I spent swotting up the instructions regarding the machine. The client said she had washed her hair. Thinning and winding were no problem. That finished, I plugged in the first lead after setting the clock for hair type. The small orange coloured bulb shone brightly. I quickly plugged in the rest of the leads and as the clocked time passed the light went out. I applied the re-agent. Finally as I unwound the rollers, the hair was springy and soft. I set the hair in the style the client required and supplied tea while she was under the drier. The price of a perm in those days was 12s 6d. She gave me a two-shilling tip and made a booking for a set the next week. She became a regular weekly customer.

Sometimes I went to a dancing class, and if a fellow there asked me out I went along. I was in no hurry to marry.

I did perms Tuesday, Wednesday and Thursday. I was too busy weekends with sets and iron waves.

One afternoon in November a young girl came in and asked if I could give her a Saturday job. She was well spoken and looked bright. I had modified my own speech, realising my West End accent would not go down too well with the East End clientele.

I could certainly do with some kind of dog's body to help around. It was Friday, a customer was under the drier and soon I expected an iron wave. She told me she had come in straight from school and had wanted to learn hairdressing for ages and ages. I had seen her in the street at different times. "Do you live near?" I asked her.

"At Number 36." As the salon was Number 30, distance would not be a problem. "What about your parents?"

"Mum agrees, she told me to ask you about a Saturday job."

"Can I come to see your parents this evening, around 7.30?" I asked as my next customer turned up.

"Thank you, yes." She went out, a beaming smile on her face. I settled down with my customer and soon we were chatting away. She was a regular and had sent me some customers.

At 7.30 I knocked at Number 36. The girl was delighted to see me. Her name was Ivy and she was fifteen and would be leaving school at Easter. I explained to her parents it would be impossible to pay their daughter a wage. I was busy and had commitments to meet, but if they were willing I would teach her the trade for free. It was hard work and tiring and there was a lot to learn. It was a personal service and there was no room for mistakes, and if that was understood and their daughter was still willing, as time went by she could keep any tips she may get.

"I want you all to understand this thoroughly," I finished.

The father said it was something his daughter had wanted to learn and since I had moved into the street he had had no peace until he had agreed to let her see me. "Can I begin tomorrow?" Ivy pleaded. What could I say? I looked at the mother. "If that's all right with you." At 9.30 the next morning, Ivy was on the doorstep.

My mother's opinion was, was I doing the right thing? She thought I ought to pay the girl something, however small. "When I think of how much it cost me to learn... she'll be getting tuition for nothing," I said.

Sam stayed away. Ivy was eager and attentive. I impressed the need for cleanliness and hygiene, and she became adept in this. I taught her to shampoo, taking particular care to scratch lightly round the hairline to remove make-up, and how to test the water heat. She used her mother as her model. As Christmas drew near my appointments book began to fill. The salon was an open one, clients could see me working and hear any tuition I gave Ivy as I worked.

I had bought a dozen white towels and a dozen striped ones. The striped ones I used for tinting and permanent waving. All used towels I washed each night after closing. Mum had fixed two lines for drying in the skittle alley and they dried overnight.

During the Christmas school holiday, Ivy came in every day. I was more than glad of her help. She now knew how to give a good shampoo, take clients from under the drier and remove pins ready for me to comb out.

I sent a Christmas card to Sam, signing it, "To Sam and family, Belle". We received one from him, "To Mrs Munday and family, Best Wishes, Sam".

Ivy and I worked like mad Christmas Eve, finally closing the door at nine o'clock, the last client leaving at ten o'clock. Ivy said her tips amounted to 10s 3d. I gave her a pound; she argued about taking it but thanked me.

She said, "I leave school at Easter and will have to find work. I realise you cannot pay me wages and I really would like to continue in the hairdressing trade. Do you think I could get a job as a shampoo girl?"

"I don't see why not. If you need a reference I'll give you one."

I was really tired Christmas Day but cleaned up the salon. It was very untidy and took me some time. I washed the dirty towels, and then helped Mum prepare vegetables. And through Christmas we had a happy family time. Jim was now picking up songs on the piano, much to Mum's amusement.

After moving in and getting the house cleaned and everything in place, Mum had had three or four goes at bug hunting; not finding bugs. I think she felt deprived and disappointed, but from that time on these pests vanished from our lives. My piano practice at scales improved and this pleased Mum. Any spare time she had, she too would play.

I had two clients for tinting. One lady, a mousy coloured blonde, liked a shade of warm light brown. The other lady, middle-aged, grey hair showing early, chose to have her own colour matched. I used Inecto colourants as these had been used at the academy, and these clients both needed a re-touch every five or six weeks. I shopped at the warehouse each Monday to re-stock items I needed and soon after Christmas began appointments for perms. In between I started Ivy iron waving, paying particular attention to how to test the heat of the irons. I tried her first on newspaper, then how to smell the irons for the heat. I lent her a wig I had tried and practised on myself... it took her quite a while to get a natural-looking wave. She was determined to get it perfect and watched me when I was working on a client. We were busy during the Easter week and after closing Ivy told me she would have to look for work. I wished her lots of luck and privately wondered if I could manage without her. I would certainly have to juggle my appointments differently.

Easter Sunday afternoon Sam turned up. Mum was playing the piano and I was listening to her. Jim was out, Bill was writing and he let Sam in.

Coming into the room, I said, "Hello, stranger, where have you sprung from?" Handing Mum a boxed Easter egg, he said, "With my compliments."

"Lovely surprise," said Mum. "Thank you, Sam."

Handing me the smaller one, he grinned, saying, "Remember, you mustn't get too fat, say ta nicely."

I took the decorated box. The egg was chocolate-filled. I said, "Ta, kind sir. Is this a peace offering?"

"If that is what you would like it to be," he replied.

"How about tea and a buttered bun?" said Mum standing. "I'll leave you two to argue if that's what you both want."

"What are you doing tomorrow?" Sam asked after a long silence.

"Who wants to know?"

"Will you come with me to see my sister?"

"Why spring me upon her suddenly? She doesn't know me."

"She lives in Streatham. It's quite a journey and I need someone to chat to on the way."

"You could read a newspaper."

"I've read the newspaper this morning. So you won't come with me?"

I didn't answer. Right on cue Mum entered with tea and buns on a tray. We didn't have a small table in this room. I put the tray on the piano stool and sat in the other armchair. We drank the tea and ate the buns in silence. "Would you like another cup?" I asked. He handed his cup to me with a smile, as I took it, he pleaded, "Please come with me tomorrow, Belle?" I went to get more tea without answering and after handing him more tea, I asked, "Why pick me, isn't there another girl you know to take to Streatham?"

"Why do you think I've asked you?"

I shrugged. "Give me a clue." I searched for an excuse. "Besides, how does your sister know you'll be taking a girl?

"She doesn't. I'll phone her later."

When I finally agreed he was so relieved I almost laughed. I was ready when he called for me at ten o'clock on the holiday Monday. We caught two buses to London Bridge and boarded a 133 bus. It was crowded and we had to go up to the top deck. There were just two empty seats. I sat in one at the back of the bus and Sam sat in a seat two from the front. I sat next to a man in a conductor's uniform. Up came our conductor and going to the front of the bus he began collecting fares.

I heard Sam ask for two to Streatham Library and hand up a ten-shilling note. The conductor clipped the tickets and did a double-take as Sam held out a hand for the change. The conductor counted out the change then came slowly along collecting fares. He came to my seat and speaking to the man seated next to me said, "Blimey, Charlie," jerking his thumb over his shoulder, "yer oughta see the size o' that bloke's mitt, it enough ter 'old dahn the national debt." He looked at me. "Fares, Miss."

“The bloke with the big mitt paid for me,” I smiled.

“Sorry, Miss, I meant no offence.”

“Don’t worry, none taken.” Again I smiled. It was a long ride and leaving the bus we walked along Pendennis Avenue and turning at the end of this road we stood outside his sister’s house. Sam introduced me as a friend to “my sister, Edith, Mrs Neal and her husband, Ted”. Edith was about five foot seven, light red hair and brown eyes, her face slightly long and smiling, showing good teeth. Mr Neal had a fair complexion and light brown hair and shook hands cordially.

“Take off your coat and make yourself at home,” he said.

“Where are the boys, Edie?” Sam asked.

“Rushing around in the garden… as usual,” she replied. “I’ll make some coffee. You take sugar, Belle?” I shook my head.

“So, you’re sweet enough,” laughed Mr Neal. Seconds later two boys dashed into the room, one aged about seven and the other about two years younger. Both wore large horn-rimmed spectacles and gazed at me owlishly.

“Hello,” said the eldest. “What’s your name?”

I didn’t know whether to say Miss Munday, but settled for Belle.

“Oh, ding dong. Ha ha ha,” laughed the boy whose name I was told was Teddy. The youngest one was Leslie and they grabbed a handful each of biscuits from a plate and rushed out into the garden. They raced around inside the house; I thought they were hyperactive. Amazed, I asked Edie wasn’t she worried their spectacles might break and maybe hurt their eyes as they played. “They’re always fighting and romping but the lenses would probably fall out. You can’t stop them running round.”

She made a nice tea. I spoke when spoken to; Sam did the talking with Mr Neal mostly. Later in the kitchenette, Edie asked, “Have you known Sam long? He hasn’t spoken of you to me.”

“On and off for roughly three years.”

“What do you mean on and off?”

"Oh, we just meet up occasionally, sometimes he comes to our house."

"Do you know he is hard of hearing, like me?"

"He hasn't said you're afflicted in the same way."

"So, what is your opinion about that?"

"I don't think about it. We get along. He hears all I have to say and he can lip read easily."

"What do your parents think about him?"

"My mother treats him like my brothers." I ignored the reference to Father and she didn't seem to notice.

"Have you met other members of my family?"

"Just your brother, Joe... at a dance."

Mr Neal came into the kitchenette and demanded to know how much longer we were going to be and asked if I played cards.

"Whist, cribbage and rummy," and added that I wasn't all that good.

So we played whist as the boys raced round the rooms and in the garden. They were so noisy they distracted me a little and really I was pleased when Sam said we should be leaving.

I thanked Edith for a pleasant time and Ted too and they both said, "Hope to see you again soon."

"What do you think of my sister?" Sam asked as we walked along.

Personally I thought she was brusque, but did not say. I said the boys were noisy and a little of them went a long way and I wondered Ted didn't discipline them more.

I thought they reminded me of the Hughes boys, our overhead tenants in Scawfell Street. "Your sister told me she is hard of hearing, just like you. I'm sorry for her."

"Are you sorry for me too?"

"Of course I am. I think it's a terrible affliction."

He made no comment and we chatted generalities on the way home.

We said goodnight with our usual handshake and saying he would be round one night in the week, he left in good spirits.

I told Mum and my brothers about the conductor's comments about the size of Sam's hands. "His speech was real cockney when he spoke to his mate beside me but I never told Sam." I spoke of the Neal family and the noisy children. Mum said, "It's better the kids are lively and not laying about grizzling because they don't feel well. Maybe that's how Mrs Neal feels about her kids. I know I would."

Chapter Thirty-nine

Sam came round Thursday evening about eight o'clock. I was washing towels as I did every evening after closing. Jim and Bill were out and Mum was doing some mending. He sat talking to Mum until I had finished my washing. I made tea, then he asked, "Can I show Belle a couple of new dance steps in the skittle alley, Mrs Munday?"

Mum laughed, "You're dance mad, Sam."

We went through the routine of a quick-step, brushing against the hanging wet towels. I watched his steps as he demonstrated to me. After a number of errors I finally managed to get the steps right to his satisfaction. I flopped into a chair saying, "I've been on my feet all day and he expects me to perform dance steps. You're a slave-driver."

Mum said she was going to do some playing. We sat in the dining-room and he began smoking. "Bill has managed to stop smoking, Sam. He says he's saving money. Why don't you try?"

"Perhaps I will one day. When that will be… " he shrugged. "Come out with me to a dance on Saturday?" he asked quietly.

"Oh, Sam, I'm not up to your standard, besides, I have a heavy day Saturday and now Ivy has found work I do feel a little rushed."

"I'll come round to help. I do help my sister Emily sometimes."

"She may want your help this Saturday, so…."

"She's asked Joe to help her, I would like to help you."

"Customers may not like a man working on their hair."

"If they see me around, they'll get used to me."

I stared at him. What was he saying? Was I reading too much into his suggestions? I shook my head.

"I'd like to take you out sometimes, Belle. It would give me pleasure… please don't say no. Give it some thought."

"Why don't you ask girls of your age? I'm older than you."

"I know that. So who's complaining?"

"The answer is no. Find a younger girl."

"What the hell do you think I've been doing if I haven't been round to see you, eh? I've been out with a few girls. They talk about film stars, or talk about what a horrible woman their forewoman is… as if I want to hear that chat. One girl I took dancing a couple of times asked me if I had my brains in my feet. Am I such an idiot?" I smiled as he continued. "When I told another girl I liked a little that I was hard of hearing she said she thought there was something funny about me and told me to forget about her."

"And did you?" I asked.

"I want us to be friends, Belle. What do you think about that?"

"Friends share, if I agree, we go Dutch."

"If I take you out, I pay," he said stubbornly.

The argument went on and on getting nowhere. I cannot definitely remember all that I said, but I realised that when he dug his heels in, he could be positively mulish. He spoke of being embarrassed taking money and I knew I had to concede. I sat silent, listening to Mum's playing.

"If you find a girl you like, that will be OK by me," I said. "And if I meet a man and want things to deepen, so be it. If we are friends we are free spirits… no strings on either side. Agree?"

Lighting another cigarette, he stared at me over the flame. "If that's your terms, I suppose I must go along with that."

"You don't have to, the choice is yours."

He stood up. "That's settled. I'll be off." We were standing by the street door. "Goodnight." He raised his hat. "See you around." I watched as he walked swiftly down the street and thoughtfully closed the door.

I made tea for Mum and myself and Mum was surprised that Sam had not wished her goodnight. "He didn't want to interrupt your playing."

It was two weeks before he appeared once again. He then asked if I would like to go skating with him. I turned that down flat.

"You must think I can skate, just like that? I'd fall flat on my face." I laughed at the thought of me skating around.

"You could learn with my help," he told me.

"Yes, just like the swimming lark. You can't teach an old dog new tricks... no thanks."

"Why do you keep on about your age?"

"I like to remind you... you seem to forget it."

"My dad's brother lives at Stepney near the skating rink... we could drop in to see him and the family."

"Just like that? Whatever would they think about meeting me?"

"There are four children, all girls. They would like you."

A little reluctantly I agreed to visit his uncle and family the following Sunday, wondering what this Bendon family were like.

Chapter Forty

Every Monday morning I paid Mum the rent for the room plus five shillings for gas. The electric meter was quarterly and we shared the cost when the bill arrived. I kept up contributions to the National Health and unemployment stamps as a self-employed person. I paid cash into the post office savings account and very soon there would be enough money to repay my brothers the money they had lent me to purchase the hair drier and permanent waving machine. I had sent off and received my registration certificate from the Hairdresser Guild, had it framed in passe-partout and now that hung on the wall. The salon was an open one. All clients could see how I worked and the conversation was about all things topical. Many of my clients lived in the street and knew each other. As Mum remarked, "It was like a friendly society."

Sunday came for the visit to Sam's Uncle Joe and family.

We changed buses twice. A girl, about eighteen, opened the door and greeted Sam with a wide childish smile. To me she said hello, then marched down the passage leaving Sam to close the door. "That's Ivy," he said as we followed the girl into a bright room with the table laid ready for tea. As we had not arrived until about 3.30, I thought tea would be early. Sam pushed me into the room before him. A thin pretty woman rose quickly as Sam introduced me. "Aunt Lil, this is Belle, a friend."

As we shook hands she leaned towards me and lightly kissed

my cheek. "Welcome, let me take your coat and hat." The girl, Ivy, jumped up. "Me… me take." She snatched my hat and coat from her mother and rushed from the room, and was back immediately. I looked at the other girls. "This is Lily." I thought Lily was about twenty. "This is Joan and this is Edna." Edna looked about seven or eight and Joan about twelve. I thought Ivy a little peculiar, but learned later she was an epileptic. She began knitting on two steel needles, a narrow strip quickly and not looking as she knitted. "Belle," she called to me suddenly, "I'm knitting you a scarf." I smiled, first at Aunt Lil and secondly at Ivy.

There was something in the aunt's eyes… a warning…?

"That's very sweet of you, Ivy, thank you." After that we all chatted easily. They asked Sam about his parents, I spoke when I was spoken to and I must say I was made to feel welcome and at home.

Tea at five o'clock was a cheerful meal. Winkles, toasted muffin, bread and jam and homemade cake. They knew Sam's taste. They supplied him with an eggcup of vinegar and he proceeded to fill the eggcup with winkles from which he ate with enjoyment. Mr Bendon sat next to Ivy and attended to her wants. She called to me telling me she had new bloomers. I smiled at her, but her mother told her not to speak of these things at the tea table. "Please excuse her, Belle. She doesn't mean to be rude to you."

"I think it's lovely, Ivy, when you a share a secret with me. Don't you, Joan?" I asked the sister who sat next to me.

Joan grinned. "She does get a little outrageous sometimes, but we don't take much notice of it. She's the big sister, she tells us."

Tea over, Lil and Joan washed the dishes. It was a pleasant evening and Uncle Joe and Aunt Lil, as they asked me to call them, made me feel one of the family and asked me to come again soon.

Going home, Sam told me the story about Ivy. It seemed she was quite a bright child up to the age of nine, when she was pushed down a flight of steps at school. She complained constantly of headaches until Aunt Lil took her to a doctor who immediately sent Ivy to hospital where she was given a lumbar puncture and sent home to rest in bed for two days. She slept most of the time and a week later at school had a terrible fit and was sent home. Her left eye remained slightly out of focus ever since. "She's nineteen now and has the mentality of a nine-year-old in a woman's body. I feel so very sorry for such a lovely family," Sam finished sadly. "Will you come with me to visit them again, Belle, or are you…?"

"Naturally I'll go with you again. It's a very heavy burden for your aunt to bear… for the other girls too. Your aunt has to neglect her other children most of the time to attend to the demands Ivy makes."

We sat in silence for a while with our own thoughts.

"How old are the other girls, do you know, Sam?"

"I think Lil is seventeen, Joan about twelve and Edna seven. Uncle Joe works on the railway; he's a guard. Dad has a sister Lou. She helps Aunt Lil, does some shopping for her, things like that because Ivy can't be left alone as sometimes she has a fit and may hurt herself."

It was all so tragic for such a nice family. Each family, I thought, has a story to tell, each one different. Sam thanked me once more.

"Try to have an easy day next Saturday and I'll take you dancing."

We said goodnight and shook hands. I spoke to Mum about Sam's aunt and Mum said, "Time and time again I have thanked God for the good health of you kids, that I have not had to spend money on doctors for medication when money was so scarce and for my own health, being able to work and keep a roof over our heads." She paused. "Tell me honestly, Belle, what do you think about Sam?"

"How do you mean, Mum? We're just good friends."

"I seem to have heard that expression somewhere before. Do you know the meaning of the word proximity?"

"So. What are you getting at, Mum?"

"He's younger than you. You should be looking for a man about your age. At the moment you're wasting your time."

"We have argued this out, Mum. If he finds a girl he likes and I meet a man I could fall for, that's it, and on this point we have both agreed, so for the time being…."

"You're both wasting time. You tell him that from me."

"Please, Mum, drop the subject. I'm busy working. When I'm ready to marry, you'll be the first to know."

She argued with me for a long time along the same lines.

Chapter Forty-one

I think it was about August in that year of 1933 when Sam hadn't been round for about a month. He breezed in one Thursday evening asking if I would like to accompany him to visit his sister May, who with her husband, Stan, was buying a house in Welling, Kent. They had managed to get the house straight to their satisfaction and now needed some help to clear the garden. "You'll like May and they have a little girl, Joan."

"Why don't you take your new girl with you?"

"I don't think May would like me taking someone I hadn't known for very long. You seem to fit in wherever I take you to visit my family."

So I agreed and we caught the train at London Bridge Station to Welling. There was a long walk from the station and no bus service.

May was tall, dark haired and slim. She greeted me warmly as Sam introduced me: "My friend Belle."

There was much laughter and noise coming from the garden and as she took my coat and hat, she said, "All the Fitzes are here, Sam."

I looked at him questioningly. "That's Stan's family. There's a crowd of the Fitzpatricks, I'll introduce you."

Sam was greeted like a long-lost brother. Introduced as a friend, I duly shook hands with brothers, their wives and some children and immediately forgot names. They were packing rubble left by the builders into sacks and large brown paper bags. Truly I had not come all this way to help clear rubble. I found my way to the small kitchen. It was roughly ten feet square, with a glass-fronted cupboard on one wall and a deep butler sink beside a low cupboard. May entered carrying a tray of crockery. "I must make coffee for them, they must be thirsty."

"I'll help if you tell me where the gear is. May I call you May?"

"Of course. 'Mrs Fitzpatrick' is a bit of a mouthful."

I set cups and mugs on the table and soon coffee was ready.

"Call them in, please, while I get some biscuits."

I went to the garden door and bawled out, "Come and get it."

Everyone trooped in and helping themselves to sugar and biscuits returned to the garden, sitting on steps or anywhere they could find a seat.

Little Joan, drinking her milk, eyed me shyly. She stood close to her mother. "Auntie Belle," she said suddenly holding out her beaker to me, "take me to Auntie Pam."

May laughed. "Be careful, Joan."

"Auntie Belle" for heaven's sake! The child led me to Pam, a large lady with a shock of dark brown hair and a wide smile. "Little Joan wants to see you," I informed her and left the child with her. I looked round for Sam. He wore an old boiler overall and was busy racking up the small stones at the end of the garden, which was quite large.

I returned to the kitchen to find May peeling potatoes.

"Can I help you, May? If you're feeding all these people you'll need some help. So… it seems I cannot do much in the garden." So I set to work.

"I can sit ten with a squeeze round the dining-table, some can sit at the bench in the garden, we'll manage, you'll see."

"How many of us are there?"

She thought for a moment, counting. "Seventeen, counting three children, quite a party," she laughed. "And I do thank you for your help." She left the kitchen to return with a pile of plates. They went into the oven to warm. “I made some apple tarts yesterday, they can reheat while we’re having dinner.” Then she asked, “Have you known my brother long?”

“About three years. It’s an on and off friendship.” As she didn’t speak, I continued, “I am a little older than Sam.” Still she didn’t speak so I let the matter drop.

Dinner over… it was roast beef and Yorkshire pudding with the usual trimmings and the apple pie with custard was a dream. I tucked into the washing up, which seemed endless. Finally a cup of tea all round as everyone rested after the dinner. We sat chatting mostly about how Stan would lay out the garden, what fruit trees he had ordered. I just listened.

May made a set tea that was, like the dinner, thoroughly enjoyed, after which we said cheerio and left. “What do you think of Stan’s crowd?”

“They’re a big family. I can’t remember all the names.”

“And there are a few more who didn’t turn up.”

“Why didn’t your brothers turn up?” I enquired.

“They had other arrangements,” he answered.

“Why do you always ask me to fill in for you?”

“I don’t think you get out enough. Have you been anywhere since I last saw you?” I had to admit no. “So coming with me does get you away from that damned salon.”

“It’s something I’ve worked for, so don’t you knock it.”

“What do you think of my sister?”

“I think she’s an amazing person. She took on all that cooking without batting an eyelid, made very light of it, in fact.”

“Will you come with me to see her again some time?”

“If I’m not otherwise engaged. You may be taking another girl to see her, so don’t make plans.” Arriving home, the house was empty. I thought Mum might have gone to see Aunt Minne. I made tea and we sat chatting. He finally left at about eleven o’clock and was concerned leaving me alone so late. “Mum will be home soon, so don’t worry.” As he said goodnight, he bent to kiss me, I turned my cheek, and then said, "Thank you for an enjoyable day… see you some time."

In the few weeks that followed I went to the cinema with a client's brother. I had been out with this man before a few times. Robert worked in a shop in Theobald's Road, a men's outfitter's. He was pleasant and always presented me with a small box of chocolates, most of which he ate himself. He told me this night, "We may always be friends, nothing more, I don't want a long-term commitment. In a couple of years I hope to emigrate either to Canada or Australia. I'm just biding my time… that is unless you could think about coming with me."

"I would never think about leaving my family to emigrate. So you find someone who will go with you and don't ask me out again."

I queried his remarks to his sister when next she came in for a wave. "Robby is always going on about emigration. My dad gets furious."

Sam took me dancing, telling me I was really getting good. We didn't stay together for every dance, we circulated around. He eyed out the girls who were "nippy on their feet" (his expression) and I did the same, but we always had the last dance together and I always asked had he found himself a new partner and his answer was always noncommittal.

As Christmas drew near my appointments book filled. I missed Ivy dreadfully. She had adapted so quickly to my way of working and was a very good shampoo girl. I hoped she was appreciated where she worked.

Sam's birthday I had found out was the 8th of November. On the off chance that he would put in an appearance I had purchased a box of 200 of his favourite cigarettes. Sure enough, he turned up smiling as I was studying my appointments. "I simply cannot take on more clients and I really hate turning them away. I'll probably be working until nearly ten o'clock and if anyone is late on Christmas Eve… I don't know…."

"I'm willing to help you, you know that. I'll come each evening after work if you'll let me." I handed him the cigarettes. He was so surprised; he embraced me, lifting me off my feet. "Thanks a million, you're a little darling," he laughed, "among other things." He opened the box and selected a cigarette. "And when is your birthday?"

"Not until next year… forget it."

"Now what about this Christmas rush, will you let me help?"

"Your sister may want you to hclp hcr."

"I'll tell her to ask Joe. I've made other plans."

Half-heartedly I agreed.

"That's settled then. Now let's go and chat to your mum. What's she doing?"

"You go through, Bill is in. I'll clear up here." Instead he helped me tidy the salon ready for the next day's work. We spent the rest of the evening listening to Bill playing his records and what we could dance to, practising some dance steps in the skittle alley.

With a nightcap of a cup of tea, Mum had made a large jam tart. As she cut Sam a wedge he told us, "You should see my mother's jam tarts. They're like bloody battle fields, the dough pokes up amongst the jam."

We all laughed. "Well, Sam, you don't look bad for all you say about your mother's cooking and with six of you to cook for she couldn't be too fussy about presentation. Be grateful to her."

"I am really, Mrs Munday. Goodnight and thanks for the tea."

I went to the door and as Sam left, Jim came in. I left them chatting at the street door.

The two weeks preceding Christmas were really hectic. Each evening I worked late and Sam was a great help. After closing he tidied the salon, disinfected brushes, combs and pins while I washed towels and hung them to dry in the skittle alley. I was too tired to go for walks with him or go to a dance. We sometimes did a few steps in the skittle alley, but sometimes played cards or simply listened to the radio. Mum often played the piano and between times prepared for Christmas.

On my closing day, Monday, I dashed to the warehouse to stock up with goods I needed and hunt for presents. I settled on slippers for my brothers. At Hensler's, the jeweller in Hackney Road, I bought Mum a pair of pear-shaped pearl earrings for 17s 6d. A woman in the shop was buying cuff links, which gave me the idea of getting Sam cuff links too. I had to get something to repay him for all the help he had given me and I simply could not offer him money, so I bought cuff links for 18s 6d. In those days there was no fancy wrapping paper so presents were wrapped in coloured crêpe paper.

As Sam finished work early Christmas Eve, he turned up at 2.30 and we really slogged, closing the door at 9 o'clock. The last customer left at ten. It had been a very happy time, with everyone in a happy mood and after the usual clear-up I left the washing of towels until Christmas Day. Mum bought a bottle of sherry and we all drank a toast, Sam saying he would be round Boxing Day early, and could he spend the day with us? Mum agreed. He kissed me, thanking me for his present and slipped a small box into my hand saying, "I hope you like it."

We opened our gifts next morning to find Sam had given Mum chocolates and to Jim and Bill good ties. The box he had given me contained a pearl drop on a silver chain. It was a beautiful gift and I wore it constantly, which pleased Sam. He said, "Now I know you like my gift."

Boxing Day we ate ourselves to the full, we sang, we played cards, we did all the things people do when feeling happy together.

Sam wanted me to go to a New Year's Eve dance with him and was a little upset when I told him we always spent that time waiting to welcome in the New Year. "It's something we've always done together, Sam. Please understand. Mum would be upset if I weren't there."

He sighed. "If that's what you want, OK."

It was Easter-time when next I saw him. The salon was closed for Good Friday and Bill opened the door. I heard him say, "Hi, Sam. Go through."

That Easter of 1934 I was feeling really chuffed. I had repaid my brothers the cash they had lent me to buy the permanent waving machine and the hair drier. The salon was stocked with the commodities I needed, I had cash in my post office savings account and now I was looking around for two salon chairs, then Mum could have her kitchen chairs back. I was washing my hair when Sam entered the salon. Giving my hair a final rinse, I grabbed the towel he held out to me.

"Thought I'd seen the last of you," I grinned at him.

"Like a bad penny, I always turn up. Can I help?"

Together we towelled my hair roughly dry, then I combed it through, pushing waves into place, donning a net as he pushed the drier over my head. He pulled up the other chair and sat down beside me and began speaking.

"You know I cannot hear you while this is going," I told him. About half an hour later, hair dry, we talked while he smoked.

"After Easter," I said, "I'm going to buy two salon chairs, can you recommend a shop?"

"Why can't I make them for you? My brother George will make the frames and I can upholster them, no problem at all."

"Only if I pay for all materials and your labour."

"That's settled then. What colour cover were you thinking of?"

"Green, I think, in rexine, it will match those green curtains."

"Will your mother's machine stitch rexine?"

"It's stitched leather for many years." I combed though my hair again, then we went through to speak to Mum.

"Hello, stranger," said Mum. "What kept you away?"

"I found myself a girl, it was going all right until we quarrelled. Being hard of hearing, I don't always make the right reply and so get the worst of any quarrel." He grinned. "There's something I want to ask. I've agreed to make two salon chairs, it's a messy job, may I work in the yard here, would you mind?"

"I have insisted I'll pay Sam for the work, Mum."

"Suppose he makes up the quarrel with this girl?" Mum asked.

"Let me worry about that, Mrs Munday."

We had muffins and cake for tea, our cousin Bill went out with Jim. They were taking two sisters, who lived in the next street to the cinema, but these girls did not come to the salon.

We spent a pleasant evening playing cards with Bill and Mum.

True to his word, Sam's brother made the frames, one tub chair and the other a straight-backed one with arms. I did the machining and Sam worked in the yard stuffing them. It really was a messy job. I did not realise he worked in such dusty surroundings. He worked quickly throwing handfuls of tin tacks into his mouth after blowing off the dirt and dust.

I asked him if he ever swallowed a tack.

He laughed. "When I was first apprenticed I swallowed a few. When I told Mum, she made a boiled suet pudding and believe me, no tack would argue with my mother's suet puddings. It left my body naturally." We laughed heartily.

At last the chairs were finished and he said all I owed him was six pounds. He told me when I argued his brother had charged two pounds for the frames, and so I paid and was so excited. When the chairs were in place I felt at last the salon was complete. It was five weeks before I saw Sam again.

Chapter Forty-two

He turned up one Monday evening. I was surprised to see him.

"Made it up with your girl?" I asked in greeting.

"No. Had a bit of a cold." It was a warm May evening. "Like to come for a walk?"

I don't know why, but I always seemed to fall in with his plans. He said his brother George had married his Edie and how much everyone had had a wonderful time. I had met Edie once some time ago. She was a pretty girl with a ready smile and later I found she had a dry sense of humour. "I know she will make my brother very happy. They are very much in love and have known each other for some time. Brother Joe will be the next one to leave and get married. That will leave just me at home."

"Then you had better find yourself a girl quickly." We laughed.

"How about coming skating next Monday?"

"That's a laugh," I replied. "Skating is not one of my assets."

"I could teach you. There's a rink behind The Princess Alice public house in Stepney. Please say you'll come with me."

Reluctantly I agreed. Entering the rink reception we borrowed skates for sixpence a pair. Sam strapped them tightly to my shoes. Taking my arm he said, "Keep your nose over your toes and you won't fall."

I looked at him and laughed, took one step and sat down hard on my bottom. My spine jarred badly and my head throbbed. I sat in the learners' area for the rest of the evening, while he enjoyed himself skating. The brass band blared and with many skaters whirling round, the din was terrific. We argued all the way home. Next day I had a splitting headache.

We went skating again and I made myself a short red velvet dress, sleeveless with a circular skirt lined with white silk and a pair of red tight-fitting knickers. Needless to say, my mother eyed the outfit with some misgivings. "It's too short," she sniffed.

"The girls there are wearing dresses much shorter," I answered.

With Sam holding me tightly and guiding me round, I was now skating backwards, and with his help I could now execute a slow waltz.

I think it was August, his sister Emily had a baby son. She named him David. She moved to Edmonton and gave up hairdressing and some of her customers found their way to my salon.

I think we reached the stage where we took each other for granted. If I was busy and he didn't turn up to help me, I felt a little narked. Sometimes we danced, sometimes we skated. The MC at the rink was Sammy Samuels and what he could do on skates was out of this world.

And so we drifted into 1935. I took Sam a few times to see Flo and her children, who lived in Walthamstow, and a few times to visit Aunt Minne. She didn't live too far from us. I don't think Sam liked my aunt very much. He said she was too outspoken. "Somewhat like your sister Edith," I reminded him. He shrugged.

Sometimes we made a foursome with his brother Joe and his girl Babs. She was a dark haired, brown eyed girl, slightly reserved, but was fun when one got to know her. She lived near Blackwall Tunnel.

One Sunday we all paid the sister May a visit. I was surprised to see our butcher's assistant there. She was walking out with May's husband's brother Bob. That is what she told me next time I went to the butcher's to buy meat. Mabel was left-handed and she amazed me by the way she could chop the pork or lamb chops apart, and after that meeting at May's she picked out the nicest chops or joints for me. She lived, I think, in Lambeth. She was extremely fond of Bob and eventually married him.

Christmas-time in 1935 we exchanged small gifts and we spent the holiday period with our families. That year, 1935, there were many events happening. The Prince of Wales was often in the news. He visited the poorer areas of the country and most of the people thought he would make a good king when he eventually came to the throne. We learned King George was ill and bulletins were gloomy regarding his health. When he died people were sad. He had been a good king and during the war years had visited troops in France. Later there were rumours that the Prince of Wales was squiring a US divorcee around. Mother, reading the papers, said, "I cannot see the people of this country accepting a divorced woman as queen." As time went on papers were full of Mrs Simpson, still married to her second husband, yet still going around with our future king.

Stanley Baldwin, the prime minister, had conferences at Buckingham Palace and the headlines in the papers came in very large print.

Christmas came and Sam spent the evening with us. It was a quiet but pleasant time and I promised to spend the Boxing Day evening with him and his family. Said Mum when I told her of the arrangements: "All the while he hangs around here, he's keeping other chaps away. You'll never get a man to marry you that way."

"I don't ask him to take me out, he just turns up."

"But I notice you don't tell him to stay away."

"Mum, we like dancing together and it's a nice way to spend an evening. There are no strings and we are both at liberty to dance with other partners, and this we do, we don't stick with each other all night."

"Well, all I can say is, something should have materialised from this friendship after all this time."

"I'm grateful for his help in the salon, so let's drop it, eh?"

My brother Bill was taking out two girls who were my clients. He took them out alternately, but only one was interested in his records. They were both nice girls and he said they were funny. Whether they were jealous of each other, I never knew, but one, Ethel, stopped having her hair waved each week, but I made no comment about it.

The Prince of Wales, the uncrowned king, that summer of 1936 made his historic abdication speech, saying: "I cannot do my duty to my country without the help of the woman I love."

A short time later they slipped quietly out of the country to live in France, and the Duke and Duchess of York finally came to the throne. They had two children, Princess Elizabeth and Princess Margaret Rose. Their father was crowned King George VI.

Mum went to visit Mrs Gee, to be confronted by a stranger, being told Mrs Gee had moved six weeks ago and he didn't know where. I asked Sam if his brother Joe had seen Harry recently and was told Joe was seeing Babs more often and in this way the Gees dropped out of their lives. Mum was sorry, she had known Mrs Gee since before they were both married, and consoled herself that Mrs Gee might write. Life went on in the same pattern, and we drifted into 1937. After Easter of that year, Sam came more often. Sometimes we stayed in, played cards, or he played chess with Bill while Mum or I played the piano. It was all very amicable. Always after Christmas the furniture trade slackened, picked up a little towards Easter then slackened off once more then became busy around June until Christmas again.

When Sam was on short time, he turned up early to help if he could. We did some swimming most Sundays, visited his sisters, sometimes we visited Flo, her youngest child, Maureen, who always said "Uncle Sam and Auntie Belle". This amused us and Sam never corrected her.

Once he said after leaving Flo's house, "It would be nice if Maureen's words were for real." We just laughed together.

On the 1st of April, George Bendon became a dad, and named the little girl Sylvia. Mrs Bendon was very pleased. Sylvia was the first girl grandchild and when Sam told me the news, I said, "What a lovely Easter egg."

June and July were very warm months. Several Sundays we spent swimming. About this time I began to notice a subtle change in Sam's attitude towards me and the clients. He was not his usual cheery self and was quiet.

I asked him if I had upset him. He told me Joe was marrying Babs in September, then he would be the one left at home.

"Then you'd better find yourself a mate, maybe you'll become more amicable. I don't like sulky people, Sam, and if you can't be more pleasant to clients, stay away until you're in a better mood."

He stared at me then said, "Your swimming doesn't improve."

I laughed. "I don't intend to swim the Channel."

He turned away. "I'll be pleased when York Hall opens, then we can dance."

In August most firms closed down for the bank holiday, which was always the first Monday in August. Works had a week's holiday, I don't know if they received wages. Sam, being a piece worker, received no pay.

Jim, with our cousin Bill King, was having a motorcycling tour of the south coast. Sam said he was spending the holiday with his sister May, and would help her husband in the garden. Just saying, "I'll be seeing you," he left.

I worked in the salon and at the end of August Sam surprised me with an invitation to his brother's wedding. "I thought maybe we could get a joint wedding present for them. What do you think about that?"

I shrugged, "If that is what you want, go ahead, you choose and we can go Dutch." He gave a little smile of thanks. Whatever was wrong?

Babs made a beautiful bride. The bridesmaids wore tangerine

coloured dresses and a great time was had at the reception. I asked Sam what present he had bought. He said he had given Joe cash and then refused to take my money… so it was my turn to be upset.

One evening Bill said, "Has Sam been asking you to do anything?"

I looked at my brother. "Why? Have you discovered why he's been behaving like a camel recently?"

"No, I just wondered… you know he's upset."

"Well, if you won't tell me and I can get nothing out of him, I wish he would stay away, or find himself a girl."

Bill laughed, "Who would play chess with me, if he stopped coming?"

Chapter Forty-three

The second week in October, Sam came during the week and said, "Try to finish early Saturday and come to a dance." He appeared more cheerful than of late. Saturday came. I managed to finish work by seven o'clock. I had had a long day Friday and felt more like putting my feet up than dancing and told him so. "You get dolled up, I'll tidy up here, and please hurry, you'll feel brighter when we're dancing."

I just had a quick wash, donned my red dress, my diamanté necklace and matching long earrings, picked up my silver leather court shoes and matching evening bag. He helped me into my coat and we set off. It was a pleasant evening, warm considering the time of the year. As I came out of the cloakroom he said, "Belle, you look lovely."

I smiled, "Thank you, but you've seen me in this gear before."

We walked round to find an empty chair on which to leave my bag.

We joined the dance, and that finished we had the next dance, after which the MC announced the interval.

York Hall did not boast a bar; so collecting our coats and passing out tickets we crossed Cambridge Heath Road to The Reindeer pub. Sam had his lager and lime drink, I had a tomato juice. We chatted to other dancers there then returned to the hall. An excuse-me dance, the MC announced, was called a smoochy waltz. As the band began, their singer stepped centre-stage. The lights dimmed, the spotlight shone on the mirrored globe hanging from the ceiling and tiny facets of light whirled around us as the globe spun. Sam took me in his arms grinning and the singer began:

"Everything went wrong, and the whole day long, I'd
feel blue.
For a longest while, I forgot to smile, then I met you.
Now that my blue days have passed, now that I've found
you at last.

All the dancers were singing softly, we were too as we danced.

I'll be loving you always, with a love that's true always.
When the things you've planned, need a helping hand,
I will understand, always… always.
Days may not be fair always,
That's when I'll be there always.
Not for just a year, but always."

"Please marry me, Belle. I'm so in love with you."

He had raised his voice a little above the band. I stopped dancing, astounded. A couple brushed against us.

"Put the poor sod out of his misery," called the young man as they whirled past. My knees jellied.

"I must sit down," I murmured. Seated, his arm across my shoulder, I was shaking my head negatively, looking at the many colourful long dresses gliding past and stupidly thought of confetti.

"Give me one good reason why not," Sam asked.

"There is the age gap. It's almost seven…."

"I never think about it. We argued this out three or four years ago."

"That was for friendship, this is vastly different."

"I wouldn't care if it were twenty years."

"Don't talk so bloody stupid." The band stopped playing, we sat silent. The band began for the next dance.

"Haven't you noticed a change in my attitude towards you these past few months? I'm told women sense these things."

So this was the reason for his quietness.

"What about those girls you met? Couldn't you have fallen for one of them? I'm sure they were all nice girls."

"Every time I kissed them, I thought of you, Belle."

"That was a little idiotic."

"I might ask you the same question. What about the blokes who took you out? What about them, tell me?"

"A few kisses as a thank you for a very pleasant evening."

"So, you were flirting?"

"I was man hunting." Again we sat silent.

"So, it appears we're to be just dancing partners until… until… until we're old and decrepit. That being so, let's make a clean break now… tonight." There was a long silence between us.

"Is that what you really want, Belle?" He spoke quietly.

The lump in my throat was like a rock. I couldn't speak.

"Look at me." I gave him a quick sidelong glance, then looked away. "Face me and be honest, tell me you have no feelings for me."

I looked at those blue eyes so full of pleading. Here was the blue-eyed boy who would be so good to me. I slid an arm round his neck. "Oh, Sam, of course I love you. I have been so blind."

My search had ended. I was hauled to my feet and we were kissing passionately, oblivious that the music had ceased, oblivious of dancers crowding about us. "Stop snogging, you two," someone called. We broke apart and I was crying… crying… crying. I grabbed at the handkerchief fluttering before me and sat down, dabbing at my eyes. I looked at the dark smudge on the clean linen. "My mascara is ruined," I wailed.

"You look better without it."

"You would say that, just like a man. I'm sorry, Sam. I'll wash this hanky for you. I'm so happy."

"No. I'll have it." He was fumbling in his pocket and handed me a small red velvet-covered box saying, "I've been carrying this around for a few weeks, waiting for the right moment to give it to you."

"And was tonight the right moment?"

"When you looked at me and we were singing together, 'not for just a year but always', that was exactly the right moment."

I opened the box, the solitaire diamond sparkled a myriad of coloured facets in a claw setting on a platinum hoop.

"Sam, it's beautiful… lovely, thank you." I spread the fingers of my left hand. "If it fits, I'll marry you." I think even at that moment I was half-hoping it would be too large for my skinny finger. The fit was perfect.

"I'll spend the rest of my life, be it long or short, trying to make you happy. Darling, you won't regret saying yes tonight."

"If you get dramatic, Sam, I'll start crying. Shall we join in this dance?"

"Why not?" and we whirled into a quick-step.

"My friend is old St Vitusi," he laughed, "I'm dancing on air and I'm the happiest man alive." He hugged me tightly.

He was so happy. Me? I wondered what my mother would say.

The dance ended at midnight. As we strolled homeward the night sky was peppered with stars and filmy clouds floating across a bright half-moon. He held me tightly beneath the railway arch. "Let's get married at Christmas."

"Heavens, what's the rush?"

"We have wasted so much time, so why not?"

"We have to find somewhere to live. We need a shop with living accommodation… somewhere not too distant."

"There's a large flat over the shop, my mum would love that."

"Out of the question, Sam. Living with relatives spells disaster."

"Get the *Hackney and Kingsland Gazette.* You can look around on Mondays and we can vet what you may find together on Sundays."

"There's furniture to choose and cooking gear, there's much to do."

"Brother George is a cabinet maker, Dad's a polisher, me, I'm an upholsterer… furniture… no problem." As we walked along Hackney Road, he airily dismissed all problems. "I want us to be together soon," he said as we kissed goodnight. He held me in a bear-like embrace; I thought my ribs would crack. "We'll make plans tomorrow."

I put the ring in the box. Mum was still awake and as I quietly undressed she asked if I had had a nice evening. I simply replied that I had and wondered what she would say when I told her of my intention to marry Sam.

At breakfast Sunday morning I showed her the ring. At first, she looked intently at me. "It's a very expensive ring, Belle, and I hope you know what you're doing, marrying is a very serious business. Are you going to continue with the salon after you marry? Have you thought how you're going to cope, working and looking after a man?"

"Mum, be happy for me. You've brought us up to stand on our own two feet. I'll cope somehow, I'll find a way to arrange appointments to fit in with being a wife, I hope." I spoke the last words in a whisper.

In 1936 there were rumours of an anti-Jewish cult steadily forming in London's East End. I think at first people didn't take a great deal of this seriously. However, from 1936 onwards the Brown Shirt Brigade was getting stronger, holding more parades and demonstrations, which by 1937 were rife.

Jewish houses and shops were targeted and bricks were hurled through their windows and Jewish people were afraid. The Brown Shirts and the Fascist Black Shirts were led by a man named Mosley. Mother said he should be imprisoned for causing a disturbance of the peace.

One Friday evening early in January 1938, our cousin George King came with the news that his brother had had an accident near Crystal Palace. His injuries were very serious. Mum and Jim went with George to see Aunt Minne. I was washing towels and Sam was tidying the salon for me.

"Shall we leave this?" asked Sam, "and go along to your aunt's?"

I decided against that and we waited until Mum returned. Jim was devastated. My brother and Bill King were great mates.

Bill died four days later from his injuries. All Aunt Minne said when told the news was, "That girl Sadie lived somewhere over that way; Sydenham, I think. I suppose he was secretly seeing her."

Jim had a wreath made like a pillow with the words "My Pal" in silver lettering across one corner.

At the inquest it was discovered Bill had an ulcer and it was suggested he may have felt ill and that may have contributed to the accident.

Sam came to the funeral and as we rode along Hackney Road, these brown-shirted men did not raise their hats.

For a while we were a little saddened, but life has to go on and Mother said her sister did not appear too upset about her son's death.

Sam and I were searching the local rag, almost in vain.

Finding a shop with living accommodation was not so easy. Some were so dirty, needing cash spent to decorate and some the rent was prohibitive. I needed a place not too far from where I was now living, I wanted to keep my clients if possible and not have to build up a new clientele. At Christmas Sam gave me a gold wristwatch. I bought him a gold expanding strap for *his* wristwatch. I sent my post office book off for the interest to be brought up to date and was pleased when it returned to see I had £184 9s 10d. I withdrew forty pounds, went to the warehouse and had a spending spree. I bought a pretty Marsela quilt for thirteen shillings, two pairs of sheets and four pairs of pillow cases and two Whitney blankets and a dozen assorted tea towels. That lot came to nearly ten pounds. The warehouse delivered the goods next day. Curtains I considered I would wait until I knew the windows I might have. Mum said she would get a complete set of crockery. Jim said would I like a crystal dressing table set. Bill said he would get two large rugs if I gave him an idea as to colourings. I told him, something with autumnal shading.

A few weeks after Christmas I bought my wedding dress. A simple heavy white satin model with decorated shoulders and sleeves, it cost £4 10s. The long veil, heavily embroidered with true lover's bows, cost £1 10s. An orange blossom headdress was just ten shillings. I decided I would like shocking pink for my bridesmaid's dresses and although I searched for this colour in dress shops it was to no avail. I wanted three bridesmaids, a page boy and two small girls. So, Flo's daughter Pat was one and two school friends, Grace Morrel and Dolly Brown, were my choice. Speaking to Sam, we thought his sister Emily's David, now four years old, for the page and his sister May's daughter Joan from his side of the family, and he asked his brother George to be his best man. I asked George's wife Edie if, when we decided on a date, Sylvia could be included, but she thought her a little too young. Buying twenty yards of deep pink taffeta I began making the dresses after finding a pattern for the style I had in mind. I wanted floor-length circular skirts with a fitted top and with Mum's help cut out the dresses after getting measurements from my friends. Flo's daughter was a bigger girl, so we visited Flo one Sunday early in March. Pat was delighted; we had been friends for so long. Now every spare moment I had I was machining. Mum was a great help, tacking and pinning seams together and at every stage as we went along Sam was kept in the picture.

One evening he asked, "What type of flowers had you in mind, Belle?"

"Something yellow… tea roses, I think."

"What about little David? You can't dress him in pink."

"How about a lemon silk?" suggested Mum. We thought it an idea.

"How about some kind of gold leaf headdress for the girls?" Sam suggested, and we agreed and that was another item settled.

I withdrew thirty pounds more from my post office account. I gave this to Mum, telling her to spend ten pounds on an outfit and put the rest towards the eats for the wedding. I considered she had done enough for me and now it was my turn to help her. She thanked me and shed a few tears.

After a fruitless trail around seeking somewhere to live I worked my way to see Aunt Minne. When she opened the door I could see she had been crying. After asking, she said she had been thinking about Bill.

"I know he was seeing that Sadie secretly, has your brother said anything about it? I sit here and wonder." I was shaking my head negatively as she went on. "And why do you want to get married? It's a messy business when all is said and done."

"You were married, Auntie, so what's the problem?"

"I was twenty-three when I married, girls at that time were being married in their teens… what fools they were."

As Auntie had a fit of the miseries, I quickly left. Deciding to buy my wedding shoes, I entered Mr Sigging's shop. I bought most of my footwear there and knew the owner well. He greeted me cordially. I asked for white satin court shoes. "I'm getting married as soon as I can find somewhere to live," I told him as he showed me some shoes.

"The flat over the shop is vacant, but you wouldn't want four rooms to begin with, would you?"

I caught my breath, then said, "What would you think about having a hairdressing sign over the side door? I might consider it if the rent wasn't too high. May I see it while I'm here, please?"

Handing me some keys, he said: "All doors are locked; just lock them again when you've had a look at the rooms."

Unlocking the heavy street door I entered. A fairly long passage led to a flight of stone stairs. Turning left and up four stairs I surveyed a large landing about fourteen feet square. Against one wall stood a large freestanding wardrobe about six feet wide. There was a large window and four doors. I unlocked the one on the left, it was a very light room, and two large windows overlooked the street. There was a small fire grate with a tile surround at one end. Relocking the door I entered the room facing the short stairway. It was a box-room about fourteen feet square, no fireplace. I relocked the door and looking out of the window I saw a large flat roof. This evidently was a roof over part of the double shop. I walked out, counting twelve steps to the outside toilet. Inside again and into the next room, large, well lit by a window. This room was probably a living-room. A black cooker was in a recess beside a kitchen range and a larder cupboard was built into the right recess. A door led from this room to another room, this too was large and light and overlooked Moye Street. There was no bathroom. Locking up, I saw in the living-room near this door a deep sink and a geyser fixed over it. I stood there wondering how this place could be fixed to suit my needs. Perhaps Sam would have an idea, perhaps my brothers. I returned the keys, asked Mr Sigging if I could talk things over with my family and asked about the renting. He said it was a weekly rental of £1 10s. I made my way to the Bendons' shop and asked Sam's mother to tell Sam to come round to me straight from work. As Mr Sigging did not close shop until eight o'clock we would have time to look over the place again before he closed.

Sam arrived soon after six o'clock and we dashed off to view. We wandered from room to room… no bathroom, I remarked, and laughed.

"Then it's back to the tin tub," Sam grinned. "What do you

think the old boy will say to you hanging your board over the street door?"

We strolled along in silence homeward bound. He stopped suddenly, clapping his hands. "I've just had a brain wave. Do you think your mum would move over the shoe shop? If she was agreeable it would be great. She likes large rooms; I've heard her say so many times. I'll buy the lino for the two biggest rooms for her," he offered.

"That would put her back up. I'll buy the lino. Maybe we're jumping the gun, maybe she won't want to move. I'll take things slowly, take her to look at the place first and ask her opinion on how I can alter the place to suit us and maybe I can suggest a move. Leave it to me."

"Although everywhere is clean and nicely decorated, Belle, it will be costly getting it how you want it, and have you asked Mr Sigging about the work you intend to do here? Would he like that?"

Returning the keys, I asked for a week to think things over.

Next day, I told Mum, "I think we could make a go of those rooms, the rent is so cheap, and all the places I have looked at so far have been dirty or too costly. You wouldn't like to live there, would you, Mum? I'm joking, of course, but Aunt Minne is only a few doors along the road."

"It's a thought, Belle, but could you manage to pay thirty shillings rent? It's a bit different from the ten shillings you pay me now."

"Well, Sam will be with me, remember, that'll be no problem. I'll finish early Tuesday, come and have a look at the rooms, maybe you could suggest some alterations for me… which would be the best room to use for the salon. Mum, will you help me?"

By seven Tuesday evening we were looking again at the rooms. Mum liked the space. "The landing is like a room," she remarked. "I think it would cost you the earth to convert any one of these rooms to suit your working needs; and do you think Sigging would agree to having a sign over the street door? At this moment I think you should have second thoughts."

"If I do take it, there isn't a bathroom – could we come a couple of times a week for a bath?"

We returned the keys and to my surprise Mum told Mr Sigging we would take the flat. I paid him the two weeks' rent in advance and he said we could move in any time and then gave Mum the keys. On the way home, Mum told me she would move as soon as possible and then I could make my plans.

I insisted I would pay for lino for two rooms. She thanked me saying, "None of the floor covering would be of use for those large rooms."

Chapter Forty-four

Things now moved swiftly. Sam was ecstatic. He hugged Mum and gave his brother George the go-ahead to make our furniture, which I chose from illustrations. We all helped Mum pack, ready to move. With the thirty pounds I had given her, she chose a pretty floral two-piece in cream, a brown pill-box hat with matching shoes and bag. At the end of May she moved over the shoe shop and Sam helped my brothers get the flat in order.

The bridesmaids' dresses were finished. I asked Sam's sister Emily what size little David's trousers were and matched them to the colour of little Joan's dress. Every Monday the salon was closed and I raced around.

On the first Wednesday evening in June I went with Sam to see the vicar of St John's Church and the day for the wedding was fixed for Sunday the 10th of July at twelve o'clock. Now I had a definite date, I ordered two cars and the flowers. Sam insisted on buying my bouquet, "and I'll keep it secret from you until it arrives with the other flowers", and he sent me out of the florist's while he ordered. The bridesmaids agreed to buy their own gold leather shoes. Meanwhile the hairdressing kept going.

Mum came round with her wedding present and told me my brothers would bring the rest of the presents; we unwrapped a really beautiful tea set.

A silver and green futuristic design decorated the edges of the cream background. "It's so beautiful, Mum. I'll treasure it forever." I hugged her and thanked her.

"There's a full dinner set to match, a breakfast set and a set of soup dishes, so you will have plenty of crockery."

I saw tears in her eyes. "Please don't cry for me, Mum, be happy."

"I sometimes worry about you marrying a younger man... What if later on he finds someone his own age, what then?"

"You make it sound as if I'm decades older, it's only a few years." She dried her eyes. "Look at Aunt Edith and Uncle Fred. They seemed happy enough when we stayed with them years ago and Aunt Edith is twelve years older than Uncle Fred... that you have told me so...."

"My eldest sister Edie has a vastly different temperament from you, she's so much more placid."

"Mum, I wouldn't put up with a fraction of what you did, if he puts a foot wrong, I'm off to the divorce court."

"There's no divorce in this family," she replied sharply.

"There's always a first time for everything," I reminded her.

The rest of the crockery arrived, Jim gave me a lovely crystal dressing-table set and as Sam decided to cover the floor of the skittle alley with lino, Bill gave me two large autumnal patterned rugs. I felt a little choked as I thanked them both. They had been so good to me.

I decided to visit Aunt Agnes. I would like her to be at my wedding. Knowing how bitter she felt towards Aunt Minne, I knew I would have a hard job persuading her to come to my special day. On this sunny June Monday, I walked through Hackney churchyard. I stopped in amazement and listened to Blind Fred in his usual place, looking a little older, his thick brown moustache now white, his hair showing white beneath... was it the same old bowler hat? I scanned the treetops for a glimpse of the birds, but the foliage was too thick. I had stopped some ten feet from where Fred sat. "Is something wrong? Are you all right?" His sightless eyes were turned in my direction. I walked towards him and gripped his hand.

"I used to speak to you when I was a kid, Fred, on my way to school in Plough Lane... it must be eighteen years ago and here you are."

"I speak to so many children, they sound more grown up these days."

"I'm visiting an aunt in Homerton High Street, I want her to come to my wedding, I'm marrying a man who is hard of hearing, Fred."

"Oh, my dear, how terrible for him, never to hear a bird trill or hear a dog bark or even to hear the inflection of your voice, if you are pleased or angry, what a terrible affliction."

I stared at the opaque skin covering his sight. "What in the world could be worse than being unable to see?"

"I'm going to give you a bit of advice, young lady."

"Advice is easy to give, but hard to take, Fred," I replied.

"Nevertheless, I want you to promise me you will remember my words when things are not always going right. Never let the sun go down on a quarrel. Promise me and remember my words."

"OK, Fred, I promise. And now I must fly, bye."

Mabel opened the door to my knock, turned, and then left me to close the door. Auntie greeted me brightly saying, "Must have known someone was coming, I made a cake yesterday. Put the kettle on, please, Mabel." She smiled. "So what brings you here?"

"I'm getting married next month and thought I'd ask you personally instead of sending you an invitation." She looked hard at me and I was remembering how bitter she must still feel at Uncle Charlie's betrayal.

In silence Mabel poured tea and cut the cake.

"Is Minne... will she be there, and the boys?"

"I have sent them an invitation." A stony look came over Auntie's face. "Please, Aunt Agnes, could you forget your differences just for one day. Try to be there for me and my future husband."

"You will never know how it feels to learn a sister you trusted would sleep with your husband and eventually produce a child."

I did not press her to turn up; if she did I did not want an upset on my special day. Every family has a story to tell or hide, I would never tell Sam the origin of Harry's birth. Now eighteen, Harry had grown into a nice polite lad and Sam liked all my cousins. I placed the invitation on the table and sat chatting on everyday happenings and left much later.

Blind Fred had gone, his seat covered by tarpaulin. I arrived home to find Sam having a sandwich with my family. He looked very unhappy.

"Bad news, Belle." He hugged me. "I don't know how to tell you. The firm is closing down, today we received our cards. Joe is worried, Babs expects their baby in September. Do you think we should call off the wedding until I get another job?"

"If we put it off, we'll never marry, so we will go ahead."

"I think you should consider a postponement, Belle," Mum said.

"We'll get married then his luck will change." I was so sure.

Mum and Aunt Minne went to church to hear the banns read out.

George delivered the furniture and all was going smoothly. Sam was covering two armchairs, one was almost finished. When the salon closed one evening a few days before the wedding, I was quietly tidying the salon ready for the next day. I went to speak to Sam and found him asleep in the armchair. Time to have a really good look at this man. Brushed back blond hair, centre parted over a wide brow, eyes slightly deep-set, high cheekbones, slight lantern jaw, straight nose over well shaped mouth, a firm chin. Not handsome, just nice-looking. He had an attractive smile showing good white teeth. From the cool indifference at our first meeting, of the long periods apart, his girlfriends, my boyfriends, our friendliness that between us had steadily turned to love… for better or worse.

Quietly I made tea and gently woke him. His ready smile and greeting: "Oh, darling, you're the sweetest girl in the boys' class. I really needed this. What's the time?" He drank the tea quickly as I said it was 9.30. I'll help you tidy the salon.

"It's cleaned. We've both done enough for one day." Tea finished we went to our separate homes. "Just a few more days and we'll be climbing up those stairs to bed." He laughed as we walked to my mother's flat after a goodnight kiss, and I watched as he walked off to his parent's shop.

Chapter Forty-five

The Saturday before the wedding I slogged in the salon. Sam helped all afternoon. Grace and Dolly arrived as Sam left. I did their hair, and as we were all sleeping in my bedroom that night there was much to do. The girls slept together and I slept in my single bed Mum had given me. We rolled into bed about 12.30. I could hear the girls laughing and gradually I slept. I woke later. It was four o'clock. Birds were chirping and the sun was beginning to shine. I would have a bath.

I looked round the skittle alley as I soaked in the bath. My brothers and cousins had done a good job. Stacked against the wall were boxes of china and trestle tables lent by the church and boxes of glasses, lent by the off-licence, where spirits, beer and soft drinks were bought. From the warehouse I had bought paper plates and serviettes. Who would arrange tables and forms in time for the reception? After the bath I went back to bed and slept to be awakened by laughter. In the swing already.

By 7.30 my brothers and cousins were fixing up tables and forms. Paper tablecloths hid the dull tabletops. Cutlery, also borrowed, was in place. The tables, one across the top and two tables down each side, formed a large U-shape, then the boys rushed off to get ready.

Pat arrived with her mother and youngest sister Maureen. Little Joan and David came with their parents and soon our bedroom was a sea of pink and lemon as we dressed. They fixed each other's headdresses of gold leaves and ribbon. The flowers arrived. Sam's bouquet for me was two dozen long-stemmed red roses, they were lovely. The girls carried bouquets of tea roses and for little Joan there was a posy of tea roses and pink statice.

Something borrowed, I was lent a short head veil, something blue, a garter, something old, I wore an old pair of knickers, something new, well everything else I wore was new and I had a sixpence in my left shoe.

We instructed David how to walk slowly behind me and we walked round the room, he was perfect... at four years old, how would he act in church?

"You're not to take any notice of your mum and dad, David, OK?"

The place was quiet, just my brother Jim and me waiting for the car. Twelve o'clock. "I should be in church now, Jim."

"Perhaps there's a traffic hold-up," he replied cheerfully.

Twelve-fifteen... the car was at the door and off we went.

A few butterflies, "Do you think Father will turn up, Jim?"

"Christ almighty! Why think about him on this day of days?"

"I left telling Gran till late last night, then when I got home I realised she could get someone to phone The Baker's Arms pub."

At the top of the steps leading to the entrance stood my bridesmaids. Someone called, "It isn't Trinity Church, Belle."

I turned to the voice, wrinkling my nose just as the photographer snapped. I turned as they were arranging my veil. The dresses and flowers were perfect. We entered the church as the organ played *Here Comes the Bride.* I quickly gazed at the assembled congregation... no Father.

Walking slowly, I reached Sam's side.

"Thank you for the roses, darling," I whispered.

"You're late, I thought you'd got cold feet."

The marriage service began. I repeated my vows, my voice a whisper. Sam sounded firm and strong. "With all my worldly goods I thee endow," he repeated. I smiled up at him. My new husband was unemployed.

We stood listening to the vicar reading the riot act. "You will not always see each other as you look at this moment. There will be trials and tribulations; marriage is a very rough sea. If you ride the waves, happiness will be your reward."

I breathed a sigh of relief as we followed the vicar to the vestry to sign the register. We stood in the church porch posing for photographs. I looked across to The Salmon and Ball public house. There at the traffic lights in a grey car sat a man in a straw boater. Did he draw back quickly as the lights changed or did I imagine it? I shivered in the warm sunshine. Sam gripped my arm. "Say cheese," grinned the photographer. Many more photos were taken and at last amid a shower of confetti we were entering the car when a strange woman dashed towards me. "From your gran," she said handing me a silver card horseshoe.

I had arranged for Ivy's mother to let us into the house and as she opened the door Sam lifted me in his arms over the threshold. He embraced me in the salon. "At last, my wife." He laughed happily.

The photographer came and more photos were taken. It must have been half an hour later before we sat down to eat. During that time the tables had been laid. Bowls of mixed salad and platters of cold beef were in place and the bouquets adorned the tables. We were all chatting as sixty-eight guests sat down to eat. Sam had made a present of a bracelet for each bridesmaid. That was so thoughtful of him. A photo of us cutting the cake had already been taken, but now we cut the cake for real. After that the tables were cleared and stacked in the yard, the piano was manhandled to the end of the skittle alley and the enjoyment began, with short breaks for buffet eats and cups of tea. As the evening wore on guests began to leave. I had already changed my bridal gear for a green silk dress with floral yoke and sleeves. At twelve o'clock, Mum and my brothers left. Mum told me to leave everything; she would clear the place after we had left next morning. I was so grateful to her.

Sam sprawled in an armchair. "Think I'll have a bath," he said.

While he was in the bath, I tidied our bedroom. Tissue paper and odds and ends were everywhere. As it was hot, I rolled down the quilt and blanket to the end of the bed and put Sam's pyjamas on his pillow. I took his dressing-gown and, going downstairs, called to him loudly that it was on a chair. I too would have a bath. I took my nightie and dressing-gown into the spare bedroom and waited for him. "I'm having a bath too," I said when he appeared, "and no smoking in bed, it's not nice."

"OK, darling, don't be too long."

I entered the bedroom and hung my dressing-gown behind the door. He was sitting in bed bare-topped. I eyed his pyjamas at the end of the bed. "Do you always sleep starkers?" I enquired.

"Yes, in the summer, and on hot days like this the sheets are cool against your skin. Take it off," he smiled.

"Pardon."

"Take your nightie off."

"Switch off the light."

"Oh come, we were married this morning, remember?"

"Switch off the light," I repeated. As the room was plunged into darkness I dragged my lovely pink cream-lace-trimmed nightie off and slid into bed holding the sheet tightly under my chin. He was eager and I was apprehensive. Gently he pulled at the sheet.

"I've seen a lot of you in a swimsuit, but I haven't seen all of you. You're not ashamed of your body, are you?"

Slowly my grip on the sheet loosened. "I have never been in this situation before," I informed him.

"Neither have I, so we'll learn together."

All Miss Bennet's sex lessons during our short tea breaks at the shoe shop had not prepared me for the hurt. His whispered

"Relax, darling" did nothing for me. Gradually the hurt eased, he shuddered, hugged me and cradling me in his arms was soon asleep. Eventually I slept. I was awakened, something was scratching my nose.

"Wake up, I've made some tea." He put the tray on the bedside table, hung his dressing-gown behind the door and slid into bed naked. Pulling the sheet over his legs, he reached for the tray. I eyed the plate of biscuits as he handed me a cup. "Do you suffer from night starvation?"

"You must have something to soak up the tea," he grinned, and proceeded to dunk biscuits in the tea. As I sipped my tea, I watched in amazement as six biscuits quickly disappeared.

"What's the time, please?"

He looked. "Ten minutes past four."

Crockery back on the tray, he slid down onto the pillows and I am sure in ten seconds flat he was asleep. In a few hours' time we would be on our way to Eastbourne for four days' honeymoon. I fell asleep.

Arriving at Victoria Station we caught the train without trouble and arrived at the hotel in time for lunch, after which we unpacked and changed into some holiday gear. Our room was average size, nicely furnished and the bathroom was along the corridor. There were three other rooms on our landing. I presumed we shared the bathroom with them.

Sam said he discovered this small hotel while he recovered from his illness. It was open to non-residents and made a nice cup of tea.

Along the esplanade I saw many bath chairs, light brown cane, high-backed, curving to a low point, two large wheels at the back, one small one in front, pushed by relatives or carers. I was surprised at the number.

Seated and looking out over the calm sea, I felt content. Sam lit a cigarette. "Happy, darling? No regrets?"

I laughed, “Married five minutes, what a question!” He looked so serious. “Tell me, why so long after our first meeting did you decide to visit? I did think you were very rude.”

“You kid yourself. I came to see Harry Gee, and you were playing the piano with him. You left immediately when I entered the room.” He pointed. “How about a dip in the briny ocean?”

“No fear,” I grinned. “Too much water.” We sat silent. “You tell me why you turned up at intervals, even after the Gees moved.”

“Your family ignored my deafness and didn’t treat me as a freak. Your brother Bill played a good game of chess and although I did not really understand all Jim’s schematic squiggles, he went to great lengths explaining them to me and your mother always made me feel welcome. My sisters, May and Edie, were married, Emily was getting married and George was busy making her furniture and Joe was walking out with Babs. I was just wandering around the house on my own. The night you walked in with that bloke in the bowler hat, I felt trying to talk to you was hopeless, so I stayed away.” He lit another cigarette. “I felt I had lost my friends when I was told you’d moved. I went to dances, picked up a few girls, but I wasn’t happy and I didn’t know why. Then I saw you in the flower market. Well, you know the rest. That’s my story, what’s yours?”

“I think I liked having you around. I think I took it for granted and maybe I was half in love with you, but it took your declaration to make me realise how much I cared for you.”

“And, here we are, on our honeymoon. Tonight I’m going to make wonderful love to you,” he grinned roguishly. And with this gentle caring man, we gradually got it right.

Chapter Forty-six

We arrived home Thursday evening about five o'clock. Mum had bought fresh bread and milk and other goodies. For dinner we had eggs and bacon and a sweet of tinned pineapple. About 7.30 Sam's brother Joe turned up. He was working at a firm in the Wood Green area of North London and had spoken to his boss. The result was that Sam was to go for an interview the next day. Joe said the work was first class. Next day Sam left at ten o'clock, and I wished him luck. Clients arrived and I was soon back in business. When Sam returned, he poked his head round the door and gave me the thumbs-up sign. After that we were too busy working together to talk much. I was thrilled for him. I quickly learned to juggle my appointments to fit into my new mode of living. I prepared vegetables for dinner before I began working. I did a little housework each night. Washing I did Mondays, rubbing clothes up and down the washboard and, like my mother, boiled the whites in a bucket on a gas burner over the cooker. Washing machines were unheard of in those days of 1938.

Newspapers reported events in Berlin. Chamberlain went to Germany and interviewed Hitler. He came back, waving a paper saying brightly, "Peace in our time." My brother Bill said quickly, "I wonder how long Hitler has given us to prepare for war?" How we laughed at the idea.

Sam's brother Joe and his wife Babs became parents in September. They named the baby John.

Christmas 1938 was a very happy time. Food was plentiful and not too costly, there were parties everywhere. So into 1939.

Babs's baby became ill after Christmas and was admitted into Bethnal Green Hospital. Throughout the wintry days, Babs went daily to feed her baby. Unfortunately he died in February.

In July we gave a party to celebrate one year of happiness.

As I coped with household chores I felt grateful to Mum for renting the flat over the shoe shop, thus saving me the hassle of finding other accommodation. Everything was right. Summertime we both liked salads, quick and easy to prepare. In winter, casseroles too were an easy dinner. Sam would tidy the salon while I did some housework. We had some musical evenings together and if he wanted to dance, I'd quickly get ready and off we would go. I always agreed to do what he wished.

Mum came often, helped me or played the piano, which she said she missed. "Do keep your fingers flexible, Belle."

Hitler marched his armies into Poland and war was declared on the 3rd of September 1939. I remembered my brother's words.

Until that time Sam's job was doing well and his wages were good. His employer, Mr Keith, had left Germany four or five years previously because of the unrest there. He had found this factory in Wood Green, North London, and being a furniture designer the orders had gradually increased. Now, being a German, he had the choice of being interned or joining the Pioneer Corps. This he did and the factory closed and Sam and his brother Joe were unemployed.

My cousin Harry, just nineteen, was called up and age groups were called to the colours. Sam found work in a factory making cases for ammunitions. Christmas 1939, and rationing. We registered with Mrs Bendon and so did Mum.

Christmas-time was quiet; food was in short supply and people lined up for a long time hoping for just that small extra for their diet.

Harry had four days' embarkation leave. He had been learning to drive heavy lorries and liked driving. Naturally we all wanted to know when he was leaving for France. "I don't know. We're not told, maybe tomorrow, maybe next week or month." Aunt Minne cried a lot when he left.

Replacement items I needed for the salon were getting scarce and daily we saw long lines of children being evacuated. It was sad to see them with gas masks in boxes carried over their small shoulders.

When first I heard German armies had marched into Poland I thought about Mickey. Where was he when war was declared?

Sam was called up in his age group. "I'll try to get into the Air Force," he said smiling. "I'll lip read then they won't know I'm deaf."

I smiled with him and for him. These doctors would soon discover his affliction and I nearly said so.

Later he came home dispirited. All was going well, he said, until he came to a sergeant with a moustache and Sam could not see the movement of the man's lips. The sergeant told him. "A very good try, Son. Men's lives depend upon hearing an officer's commands, we cannot take that risk." So Sam continued making ammunition cases and helping to build bomb shelters.

I managed to cope with my Christmas appointments and for a present Sam gave me a Singer sewing machine in an oak case. It was a fine piece of furniture and a very useful gift. I couldn't thank him enough. His brother Joe was called up and joined an artillery regiment. My two brothers were exempt because of their electrical engineering knowledge. Jim was transferred to Rediffusion, a factory near the Kingston by-pass. Bill stayed with the Lea Bridge Road factory complex. Air raids began nightly and Sam and I would spend the nights with Mum, sleeping, if permitted, beneath the wide heavy wardrobe for protection, always staying dressed. The news from France was not good. Our armies were retreating from the German onslaught and finally came the miracle of Dunkirk. Harry arrived on a week's leave in July. He said, "It was an unforgettable sight. There were ships of all shapes and sizes stretched out at intervals as far as the eye could see. Small boats rowing as near as possible to the beaches to pick up soldiers. Scrambling nets were hung over the sides of ships and everyone helped each other. Dogfights were going on overhead and soldiers who had kept their rifles were shooting at the German planes. In the distance I saw the *Golden Eagle* pleasure boat full of men. Suddenly whether the pilot was suicidal or whether he was shot, his plane dived onto the steamer and it turned sideways and sank into the water. Aunt Bella, I thought of the many journeys I'd had on that boat when I was a kid and I cried, I couldn't help it. A sergeant saw me and said, 'Ain't there enough water round here, mate, without you adding to it!' So many men were rescued, over 300,000, but so much equipment was left on the beaches."

Jim was going to work by train and tube, now he decided to travel on his motorcycle. If he was late, Mum worried knowing he had to cross London. There were some daylight raids and I was a little scared to be in the salon on my own.

The shoe shop was next to Kimber's, the undertaker, and next to that was the Harbour Lights Mission Hall. Dealing at the greengrocer's farther along we got to know Elsie Dummit, who was carrying on the business after her brother was called for service. Aunt Minne was often at Mum's living roughly 200 yards farther along Goldsmith's Row. My brother Bill was put on two weeks' day work and two weeks' nights. It played havoc with his digestion. He said that during raids the workers lay in the fields and watched the dog fights, but couldn't tell which planes were shot down.

Meantime I coped with clients who made and kept appointments.

I saw Gran. She was upset and frightened, she told me she sat in the passage of her house with her lodger. I pleaded with the sisters at the Dunloe Street Priory to take Gran into their shelter and I was pleased when they agreed. At six o'clock I borrowed their wheelchair and Gran was settled into the priory for the night and then collected at nine o'clock next morning. Mum fumed. "It's your father who should be caring for his mother, not you. Have you thought should she die, have you thought about that?"

At the priory next morning I was in for a shock. The sisters were furious. Did I know my grandmother was incontinent? "She needs medical care twenty-four hours daily, we're sorry but we cannot be responsible for her, you must see her doctor. We are very sorry." What could I say but apologise to them. I saw her doctor immediately, explaining the situation to him. He said, "Your grandmother is old, younger people have a preference for evacuation." I kept pleading and finally he agreed to get something done… "otherwise they will have to pay". She was finally sent to Ryhope in Sunderland. I couldn't visit, only write.

I tried to make my letters to her sound cheerful. I did not dwell on the nightly air raids. Her replies were always short, always telling me to collect rent from her tenants and save it for her. This I did not bother about. Mother asked one evening had I thought what might happen should Gran die. Truly I had never thought about this.

"I'll send a letter to The Baker's Arms pub, jolly quick, and there my responsibility will end," I replied to Mum's question.

"And if anything happens to your father?"

"Heavens, Mum, you *are* in a morbid mood."

"These days we are all in danger, one day from another."

There was a slight respite over Christmas if I remember. Food was short, there were queues for anything eatable and potatoes were scarce.

So came 1941. It was icy cold as I made my way to the salon after spending the night at Mum's flat. I was in for a shock. The night's air raid had not lasted too long. Bill had returned from night work and was ready for bed as I left.

The salon was severely damaged by blast, plaster from the ceiling had smashed the toilet basin and mirrors were broken. The silk lampshades were in ribbons. Luckily the permanent waving machine was undamaged. I had pushed it into the recess and piled clean towels on top thus protecting the light bulbs. The drier had received a small dent.

In the small room next to the salon, the piano and the two armchairs had not come off too badly. Plaster had not done much damage. I walked through into the dining-room, where all my matching crockery lay shattered on the tiled floor. I picked up the milk jug that was intact. A few items were still in the cabinet. The table was badly marked, maybe that could be re-polished. The skittle alley came off best, beyond one broken window all was well. It would now be impossible for me to carry on working there. Perhaps I could become mobile, going to clients' houses. I had to inform Mrs Jones, it was her property and for her to claim.

I returned to Mum's and telling her I was going to see Mrs Jones, set off for Clarence Road. She was nice about the damage and told me not to worry, Mr Jones knew how to deal with this. "I shall have to move, I have to find somewhere to live." She said she understood.

In the bedroom, the heavy velvet curtains had protected the furniture from too much damage; my nice marsella quilt was soiled by dirty plaster. All we had worked for gone. I cussed Hitler right, left and centre.

Sam helped me clear up. When we finished he said, "It cannot last much longer." I felt angry and yelled, "We have come out of France without guns or tanks, if we're to stop this bombing and get back into France it'll take ages." I was crying and I didn't know why.

Joe had a week's leave and soon found a house in Totteridge, and Mrs Bendon moved in with Babs when Joe's leave was over. Walking through Kaye Street on the way to Mum, I saw a house to let. I dashed round to the agent, got the keys. It was a small two up and two down, small concrete yard, outside toilet, no bath, rent one pound weekly and moved in three days later. Mum lived just five minutes round the corner.

At the widest end of the concrete yard was a brick-built shed with a large window. In a deep recess beneath the stairs was a deep butler sink. In the recess opposite stood a black cooker. "It's not Buckingham Palace, darling, and it's back to the tin tub to bath. It's a great life if you don't weaken, so cheer up." He held me close for quite a while.

A few yards from Mum's flat was the greengrocer's. It was kept open by Elsie Dummit after her brother was called for military service. Every other morning about five o'clock Elsie was off to market to purchase what vegetables were available.

At this time potatoes were in short supply. If Elsie managed to get fifty-six pounds of potatoes she rationed her customers to one pound each. Elsie was a real East End cockney. She was about five feet in height, slim, oval-faced with mid-brown hair and brown eyes. She hauled around sacks of vegetables like a man. She introduced us to her sister Nell, her husband Jack and their teenage son George. We became firm friends and the friendship lasted years.

Late in 1942 Elsie shut up shop and joined the Women's Land Army, and we kept up a correspondence. After the war, about two years later, Nell opened a bed and breakfast boarding house in Littlehampton and was very successful. On leaving the Land Army, Elsie rented a one-room flat in Guinness's Buildings. She made friends with Mum's friend Flo and they visited each other regularly and we all met frequently after the war.

The rooms were small. Forty square yards of oilcloth were cut to fit the two rooms downstairs, with enough left to cover the six-by-four-feet entrance passage and the same sized landing. The salon oilcloth covered the bedroom. The spare room contained all the gear that was salvaged from the salon. My brothers helped Sam get our furniture in place and the furniture made the room appear even smaller. From the window we looked down the length of Teale Street to Pritchard's Road with a view of the gasometer.

I had to buy blackout material for the windows, I could not spare clothing coupons for curtaining. For some privacy when bathing I pinned a dark tablecloth across the recess under the stairs where the sink was. We heated a pail of water over the gas burner on the cooker, then added cold water. How Sam folded his six-foot length into the tin galvanised bath, in which I did the washing, I'll never know. It was most awkward for me and I was almost a foot shorter. This performance occurred twice weekly for each of us... somehow we managed.

Sam bought a cycle and journeyed to work this way and the cycle was kept out of the way in the shed in the yard.

Sam's brother George came round in May with four chickens – three hens and a small cockerel – saying eggs were scarce and these hens would come into lay about August. He had bought some maize and a bag of straw, arguing that they could roost in the shed and all we needed was a broom handle for a perch. The birds were fed and put into their new roost. Sam's cycle was brought into the living-room, then saying he would knock up two nest boxes for the birds, George left for his fire service. Laughing, Sam told me that looking after the birds would keep me busy doing a war effort.

A week later Sam walked in with a large Alsatian dog. He had been speaking to a chap in Elsie Dummit's shop and had bought the dog from him for three pounds. It had a pedigree as long as Piccadilly, was registered at the Kennel Club, and would be shown there after the war ended. Sam had bought a tin of Chum for this animal. He said it was three months old and was named Rajah of Goldsmith. I eyed the dog with some apprehension as he sniffed around the room. He had a good sniff at me as I gingerly patted his head, then he went to Sam who ruffled the dog's neck and body and the animal clearly liked this, he jumped up, barked loudly and really was ready for a romp. With the dog dashing around there was hardly room to move.

"You realise he will need long walks. A dog his size needs lots of room. Whatever were you thinking about to buy him? More so now there's a war. Food for him may be hard to get if this conflict goes on very much longer. Oh, Sam, why didn't you think?"

"I've always wanted a dog, Belle. Be pleased for me."

"Have you thought how, when he sees the chickens, he might kill them? I'll bet that idea never entered your head."

"No, I didn't think about that. Keep the chickens in the shed when he's in the yard. He'll get used to the sound of them. It'll be all right, Belle, you'll see."

What was the use of arguing? The dog was here, so be it. So I walked the dog over London Fields. He was obedient, came when called, but when Sam came home from work each evening, the dog had no time for me.

When I took him to Mum's she was amazed that Sam should give me the worry of taking care of Rajah while he was at work, and we took the dog with us to Mum's each evening. He was quiet during raids, when bombs dropped he growled deeply and bared his teeth. Strangely enough he warned us even before the siren blared. He would run around whining with his tail curled under his body and he would bare his teeth. At these times he looked vicious and dangerous. The birds came into lay in August. One morning while I was cleaning the shelf under the roosting perch, I looked into the nest boxes George had made and there were two eggs. I was thrilled, I couldn't believe our luck. Fresh eggs… Golly.

Sam came home with a small kitten a few weeks later. He said it was sitting on the ledge near a broken window mewing pitifully. "I just couldn't leave it there. It's a lucky black one."

"The dog will eat it. Where were your thoughts, Sam?" The kitten saw the dog and hissed trying to wriggle from Sam. The dog growled.

"Rajah, you hurt this kitten and I'll slap you." Sam's tone was sharp, but the dog's tail was waving. "It'll be all right, Belle, they'll get along fine, just need a little watching at first." And it was. The dog seemed to sense the kitten was harmless.

"We have to give this kitten a name. Is it a tomcat, Sam?"

"Give it a shake. If it rattles, yes, it's a tomcat." It was sitting beside a dirty pickle jar when I picked it up.

"That's it, Pickles. That name will suit either male or female." And the name stuck, though Mum thought Pixie was better.

A man, nicknamed Lord Haw-Haw, frequently broadcast over the German radio. He always began deriding the miracle of Dunkirk. He boasted non-stop about the victorious German armies, insisting Hitler would rule the world. The confident way he threatened we thought we were soon to be invaded and overrun by the German armies.

Winston Churchill broadcast to the nation giving a pep talk.

Among other things, he concluded, "We will fight them on our beaches. We will fight them on our land, we will never surrender."

"It's fine for him to talk. I expect he's a bomb-proof shelter somewhere in the country," said Mum. "Where can we go?"

Our cousin Harry had a week's leave. He had written in July 1940, saying he was safe in England. He wouldn't say where he was stationed, just telling us square-bashing went on daily.

During the week I went to a few clients' houses. I was never out after five o'clock. Twice daily I took the dog for walks.

The summer of 1941 was warm. The raids, not so frequent, came later, lasting maybe two or three hours. We didn't get much sleep but everyone appeared fairly cheerful. We always took the dog with us to Mum's and he liked the fuss she made of him.

One Saturday afternoon Grace came to have her hair waved. She was quiet, I asked was she well. She said, "You know I'm in love with your cousin George."

I nodded asking, "Are you both spending nights in the shelter?"

"That is the only way we can be together," she replied.

We wondered what Aunt Minne would say it she knew. I remembered how she quarrelled with our cousin Bill over Sadie.

"Carry on as you are. Does Fred know?"

"No, George thinks it best. That way we can be together even for a short while. Sometimes we sleep together in the shelter among other people. When the raid is over, he takes me home, it's all so difficult."

Poor Grace, she said they were so much in love.

There was a heavy raid a few nights later and Sam was fire watching at his firm. The dog lay next to Jim and the kitten was sleeping on Mum's lap. I was sitting near Bill. The dog snarled as there came a loud knocking at the street door. I pulled the dog into Bill's bedroom, and then pushed in the kitten. Jim opened the street door to Elsie Dummit.

"Come out, you lot, and help," she screamed.

A few months earlier, Elsie and I had joined the Volunteer Fire Service. We had been lent a stirrup pump and told how to use it. Now the occasion had arisen. Louie Lapsky, a Jewish crippled man, was already using the stirrup pump. Mum said, "I can't run up and down stairs, I'll fill buckets." Incendiary bombs were everywhere. Bill was up and down stairs carrying the buckets from which Louie was pumping. I was directing the hose at the flaring bomb nearest to me. An elderly man and wife were dragging a settee, which was well alight, through their doorway. The man doused it with a sandbag. Elsie was pumping away a short distance along the road. It is strange how doing this we seemed to forget the bombs dropping all round us. The warning from the fire service was, "Don't let a fire take hold,

Jerry will drop a bomb there." Incendiaries were everywhere, all gradually dying out, water was everywhere too. From somewhere came a ladder. An incendiary had gone through a window of the undertaker's next door to us. Jim and a man were climbing the ladder with a small sandbag between them. They walked along the shop's fascia and pushed the sandbag through the broken window onto a flaming armchair. A warden came along. "Where's the undertaker?" We told him Mr Kimber used the brick shelter near London Fields. The warden quickly cycled off.

Mr Kimber stood surveying the broken upstairs window. He said, "And there's a couple of stiffs in the chapel of rest." Mother thought him callous to speak of the departed that way. Next morning, Mrs Kimber moaned, "My carpet is ruined, covered in glass and sand and the armchair is burnt beyond repair. I wish we'd been here. It would have been different." Ever after a shower of incendiary bombs were named "Molotov cocktails".

An air raid at the beginning of December lasted about two hours. A slight mist rose. We were standing at our door in Kaye Street, speaking to a warden and looking down Teale Street at the flaming gas holder behind Pritchard's Road. The holder was low down, but the flames were higher than the iron casing. The warden said, "The bomb fell slanting, pierced the top of the holder then went out through the side. It won't explode, gas is run off, what's burning there is just residue." The flames lit up the street. He continued, "Maybe there's fog over the Channel and raiders have been recalled."

Mum appeared suddenly. "Belle, I'm worried for you both, if you stay in this house you'll be killed. Think if it came down on top of you. Please try to find a better place where you'll be protected."

"Ma, we are all at risk, all in the same boat," Sam replied.

London was burning in very many places when the "all clear" siren blared. We wondered why the raiders had left. We learned later that fog had come thickly over the Channel.

Chapter Forty-seven

An announcement later told us the Channel Islands had been overrun and occupied by victorious German armies. Lord Haw-Haw gleefully informed us that the islanders had welcomed the armies as friends.

Then Hitler sent his armies east towards Russia.

Mum thought Hitler mad. Didn't he know his history, how the Russian winters had defeated Napoleon?

On the 7th of December, the Japs bombed Pearl Harbor; the loss of men and ships was heavy. The USA immediately entered the war to join with us.

Said Mum, "They've been sitting on the fence too long. I'm sure they were waiting to see which side would win this war."

The USA began a "lease lend", and supplies crossed the Atlantic. Our merchant service paid a very heavy price in men and ships as they neared these shores to be met by and run the gauntlet of the German U-boats waiting below the sea.

Taking Rajah for his morning run over London Fields, I decided to take a back way home. I walked into Albion Drive. There in the front garden of the second house a "to let" notice caught my eye. I noted the phone number and at the first call box rang the agent. He asked me to meet him at the house at ten o'clock next morning. This I did. We went into the house. The rooms were large. The semi-basement consisted of two large rooms and a long passage leading to stairs to the long garden.

The two rooms just above street level opened from a long passage and stairs to upper rooms.

I said we didn't want to rent the whole house and could we rent the four lower rooms? He was agreeable saying the rent was a pound weekly with two weeks' in advance. I paid the cash; he produced a rent book, telling me to move in whenever I pleased. "There are so many properties empty," he said.

We all viewed the house that evening. Mum was pleased. So we moved on the 13th of December, just two weeks before Christmas. We unpacked just the bare items needed to make the place liveable for the holiday. Much was left in tea chests and stuffed into the machine space with the door handles securely tied. There were no raids Christmas and Boxing Day nights and we had good nights' sleep. On the 27th of December, two weeks after we had moved, Sam and I sat talking. Bombs were exploding in the distance. Sam had made Rajah a bed. It was three feet long and two feet wide, on sturdy legs with a soft padded top. The cat was curled asleep in front of a dying fire. The time was about eleven o'clock. We felt safe being slightly below ground. An iron bar held sturdy shutters over the windows. The dog growled softly as bombs exploded. Sam was saying, "Let's go up west to see Charlie Chaplin in *The Great Dictator*, it should be a laugh." I turned as the dog barked. His ears lay flat, his eyes staring, his teeth bared. For a moment I felt scared of him. Suddenly came a very loud clap.

"Incendiaries in the garden, Sam," I yelled. He was out of the room in a flash followed by the dog. As I reached the doorway to the passageway and stairs something crashed on my shoulder, knocking me to the ground. Bricks and rubble fell over me and the tearing sound seemed to go on for ages, yet it could have been but a short time. I remember screaming, "We're being buried alive." The screaming went on. I shouted, "Stop that woman screaming," then realised I was the screamer. The vibration of exploding bombs shook loose plaster around me.

Suddenly I felt wetness round my bottom and legs and assumed I had wet myself in fright. Burst water pipes were spreading water, and then I smelt gas. If we were not found soon, we'd be drowned or gassed.

I called again for Sam. Then came a voice: "Is anyone in there?"

I answered loudly: "Yes, two people and an Alsatian dog."

"Keep talking, is the dog friendly?"

"I'm not too sure, he doesn't bark or whine." Came the sound of shovelling and dust fell. "Keep talking, please."

With my left hand I tried to shift the rubble from my right shoulder. It had become so painful and as I pushed hard, more rubble fell, but some of the weight had eased. My left hand as I felt the flooring touched fur. The dog's tail? I called and pushed only to discover it was my soft-haired broom. I tugged at the broom as more plaster fell. Something flapped against my face, it was my handbag. At least now I had some money. Then I felt the dog's lead. A thin beam of light filtered through the rubble. I heard: "Someone here, Jack, I think he's a gonna." Had they found Sam? "We can get him through here, this passage is fairly clear." I heard more shovelling and moving of rubble, then the "all clear" siren blared. "I'm in the basement passage," I called to them as I heard footsteps overhead. "Be back soon," they called. Then I thought I heard the cat mewing. Water still trickled through the ruins. I reached out and realised the sleeve of the knitted jumper I wore was ripped and loose threads of wool snagged on all the roughness. I felt the woodwork of the stairs that led to the garden. My movements were slow, and my shoulder hurt with each move I made. I dragged the broom from the rubble. It was impossible to stand. I heard the wardens return.

"Still around, lady?" they called. As I answered they began shovelling. Soon there was a hole more than large enough for me to crawl through.

"Please can you help me to find our cat and dog," I pleaded after thanking them. "Lady, people come before animals, and is that man your husband?" They pointed to a man lying stretched out in the roadway.

And there was Sam. A quick flash from a torch shone on a blood-covered face. I thought his face was half blown away. I knelt beside him, "Sam, Sam, I'm here, darling." I felt choked.

"I thought you'd bought it, Belle." I was afraid to touch him, I might hurt him. "Please find the animals." Then he passed out.

He was gently lifted into an ambulance with others and I was told to get over to the first-aid tent to get my scratches painted.

In the first-aid tent my cuts and grazes were dabbed with iodine. This made my wounds feel worse. The skin over my left eyebrow was torn and it was trimmed off and plenty of iodine dabbed over it. A little later I stood before the ruins of the house wondering how to get back in to find the animals. I held on to the broom, my handbag and the dog's lead. Now I threaded the bag on the lead and buckled the lead round my neck. I had two hands free. A young lad stood beside me. "Is that your house, Miss?"

I nodded, "And my cat and dog are in there, apart from the chickens." It was the first time I had thought about them, I supposed they'd been killed as they were in the garden. "It was quite a large bomb, Gayhurst Road is flattened, you can see right through your passage."

"Maybe I could get through the passage and try to find the animals?" I asked hesitatingly. "Will you stay here while I go in there?"

He looked at me. "I'll come with you, I might be of some help." Together we walked gingerly through the passage. I called the dog.

"Be careful, there's a large gap here." He took my hand. "That's where the warden rescued me. That's near the garden stairs. The dog may be somewhere near here." I was still dragging the broom along. Slowly we neared the stairs. "There's a puddle here."

He shifted some debris and more plaster fell. I looked through the doorway into the garden, the stars shone brilliantly on this frosty night. I became suddenly aware of my wet skirt flapping round my legs. Putting out my hand I touched fur. "I've found the dog," I told the lad. I felt a leg, Rajah's back leg, then the next one. I ran my hand along the legs, they didn't feel broken. I asked the lad to try to lift the door that the dog appeared to be under. "That broom might help," he replied. He wedged the broom on a stair and slowly we both lifted the rubble-strewn door enough for me to get my hand along the dog's body. As my hand neared his head, he whined. "Come, Rajah, it's all right, come on." I tried to drag him from under the door. He growled. "Help me drag him clear, please."

Somehow together we managed. The dog stood shivering, head lowered. We descended the stairs and again I heard the kitten mew. The lad crawled under the slanted doorway. "The window is completely blown out," he called. A few moments later he called, "I've found the cat, it's OK."

He came through the gap between us. "Now we have to get back to the street." Very slowly we made it and my prayers thanked the Lord.

It was chaotic. Soldiers and wardens were shovelling bricks and rubble to clear a space for ambulances to collect wounded. I stood outside the house; along the road it was a strange sight. The wide columns of the porches held up parts of roofs while the rooms had fallen into semi-basements giving an undulating appearance. A warden spoke: "You look as if you need some first aid. I'll take you."

With the cat clinging over my shoulder, I buckled the dog's lead round his neck. At the tent as the blanket lifted, I put the now almost half-grown kitten down and told the dog to stay.

He was always obedient. I entered the tent. Inside the nurse was binding a splint to a lady's arm. Another nurse turned to me. "No broken bones?" she asked me.

"No, my shoulder is very painful," I answered.

"Let's have a look see." She pulled the sleeve of my jumper from my arm. She really rough-handled me, pumping my arm up and down and drawing it round to my neck. "Good, just very bad bruising." She dabbed iodine over my shoulder, then as I lifted my left hand she saw a sliver of glass in the palm. She drew it out with tweezers and then jabbed and probed making sure all splinters were cleared. To this day all I have to show for that dreadful night is a small scar in the palm of my left hand.

Again I stood outside the house. Where had they taken Sam?

A soldier spoke to me. "Have you somewhere to go, lady?"

"I'm thinking of going to my mother in Goldsmith's Row."

"That's not too far, I'll walk with you. We can't go through The Broadway, there's too much glass around, you must think of the dog's paws. We can go through the back street, much clearer there."

I thanked him and we started off. I asked him, "Would you please carry the broom." He laughed. "I'll carry the cat, you hold the broom." Soon we came to the end of The Broadway and the Regent's Canal Bridge came into view.

The sirens blared once again and almost immediately guns and searchlights lit up the sky. "I think we'd better take cover, Lady." Something fell in the canal as a jet of water splashed up.

"I have to get across the bridge now." The dog growled as I began running across the bridge, the soldier followed. The soldier knocked loudly on the door. It was opened immediately by my brother Jim.

"Christ, Belle! What's happened, where's Sam?"

"I think he's dead," I replied and burst into tears.

"Thanks a lot, soldier. Coming in for a while?" The soldier stood in the passage for a while then sat on the stone stairs.

Mum was asking all sorts of questions, I was too upset to reply.

The animals settled themselves near Mum. The "all clear" siren sounded about an hour later. Then I began trying to tell what happened.

"Have you some undies I could borrow, Mum? What I have on are so wet. It doesn't matter if they're a little larger." She soon found undies and a skirt and warm blouse. It was great to feel warm.

"My God, Belle, your shoulder, it's bruised down to your waist."

"It does hurt, Mum. They gave it a good going over in the first-aid tent and dabbed all my cuts and grazes with iodine. That hurt more than my cuts and scratches." She was busy making tea as I continued my story. Jim was listening too. "All we have now is what I stand up in. Our home gone and all we have worked for. I could murder Hitler if he was here."

"You put your hands together, my girl, and go down on your knees. You have your life. Possessions, you can always work to get possessions, but you cannot get another life, so you thank the Lord."

She was right of course, but....

If Sam died I felt I would not want to live without him. We were so happy together. Too happy? "I'll take the dog to the vet tomorrow and have him put to sleep. He seems so cowed. He hangs his head and his tail is curled under his tummy. That's not like our Rajah."

There came a knock at the door. Rajah went berserk. We had to shut him in a room before opening the street door. It was Dave Shooter, a man Sam had worked with. Dave was now in the fire service. "Sam was taken to St Joseph's Hospice for the terminally ill, Belle."

Tearfully I thanked Dave. Quickly Mum made tea, which we drank thirstily. Dave said as he left, "Don't worry too much, Belle. There are so many people hurt, they're taken anywhere for first aid."

I thoroughly combed through my hair over a newspaper, the dirt and muck surprised me, yet my dark brown hair still was streaked with greyish dirt. Mum made me cosy to sleep on her old couch.

"In the morning, we'll take down Bill's bed and put it in Jim's room and you can have my bed in Bill's room. When Sam comes home, if pushed against the wall, and you lie close to the wall, maybe he'll have enough room for his long length." She went on, "I'm sorry we only have single beds. I'll manage quite comfortably on the couch, so, for the time being that's all fixed." I hugged her tightly.

I lay awake. I heard Mum call the animals, she had shut them out for a sniff round the flat roof over the shop, the house was so quiet. I slept to be awakened by Bill home from night shift.

I dressed in Mum's lent clothes after giving myself a gentle wash. The iodine still showed round my cuts and scratches, it was the best I could manage. I related to Bill what I thought had happened.

Next morning, putting on the dog's lead, there was no frisky tail wagging. Jim asked, "Are you sure you're doing the right thing? You know how fond of the dog Sam is."

"Look at him. He seems cowed. He may go berserk next time the sirens blare. He might attack us, so what else can I do?"

With my brothers, I walked slowly along, the dog between us. He walked, head lowered, tail tucked under his tummy.

Nearing The Broadway we saw men shovelling glass into dustcarts.

"See you at the house. I'll go the canal way, I'm thinking about the dog's paws and glass splinters."

Entering the vet's, he smiled, then looked shocked. He patted the dog. "The house came down on us last night, I don't know if Rajah is hurt. I want him put to sleep, please." He nodded and spoke softly to Rajah.

"This dog is in a strong state of shock. He's so lovely."

The vet pulled forward a long narrow box and opening a door led Rajah into it and then shut down a glass-covered top. The dog went meekly enough. I turned away as the vet pressed a switch. Seconds later he said, "It's all over. He's at peace now."

"Take a look." He spoke kindly.

There was no charge, you made a donation. I fumbled in my bag, slipped half-a-crown into the slotted box, thanked the vet and stumbled into the street, blinded by tears. I was crying for Sam, for our home, for our dog and the pain in my shoulder. I stared across Mare Street to the entrance of St Joseph's Hospice. Should I enquire about Sam? If the news was bad.... At that moment I felt I had had just about as much as I could take. Slowly I walked round to Albion Drive.

My brothers stood outside the house. The roadway had been fairly cleared along one side. A large removals van stood near.

"They've managed to get the piano into the van and now they're trying to find whatever else there is." I looked through the semi-basement hole where once there was a window. A man pushed the broken half of the piano lid. That was packed into the van. The man working in the basement wore a tin hat. He pulled at a chair top and a tea chest appeared. Another man dropped in to help and together the chest was put into the van. Next they hauled out my machine. "You the lady that lived here?"

I nodded.

"What's your name?" He eyed my iodine-streaked face. "Not improved your looks, have they?" He sounded sympathetic.

"This lot is docket fifty-seven. It'll be stored until you find a place to live. Meantime, take care of this or you'll lose the goods."

"Where will it be stored?"

"London Lane warehouse, under the railway arches."

"But the raiders are bombing railways."

"If you're lucky these bits will be there when you need them."

A large cover was thrown over my few items; the van drove further along the road. Jim walked slowly along the passage of the house, Bill followed. They came out into the street. "There's a crater about twenty foot wide at the end of your garden. I don't know how deep. The next road is flattened. Belle, you're so lucky to have come out of this alive." Bill said, "A warden told us he heard it was a 500-pounder, let down on a parachute, said he didn't know if that was true." I listened in amazement. Whatever next?

Standing beside my brothers I thought about the chickens. They must have died in the blast. They had been laying two or three eggs daily. I had given Elsie four eggs weekly in exchange for outer cabbage leaves, which I put into a wide meshed net, the leaves helped with their feed. The eggs would be missed; they had helped eke out rations.

"You go home, Bill, get some sleep, you have to work tonight."

"There doesn't seem much we can do now the piano is in the van, I'll see you later." I looked towards the removals van, then turned to Jim.

"Was it difficult?"

Jim shook his head. "It came out through the front porch easily. It was getting it over the rubble that was tricky." Jim touched my arm. "The fall over the keys split the lid along its length, I think it could be repaired later."

Elsie met us as we neared home. "You look a sight, Belle, what happened to you?" Briefly I explained, ending with Sam in St Joseph's, that I thought he was badly hurt. She was very sympathetic.

Arriving home we found Aunt Minne and Cousin Fred and they wanted to know what happened. Each time I related the bombing it seemed more unreal.

"Try to look on the bright side," said Auntie. "Injured are taken anywhere for help in air raids, I'm sure Sam will be all right. But I'm truly sorry to learn you've lost your home."

Fred said he would try to join a motorised regiment in the hope of meeting up somewhere with Harry. I was glad when they left.

With Mum's help I washed my hair and hoped the plaster dust would be washed clear. It appeared OK when dry.

Next day I saw Maggie Rowe. I went to school with her.

"I've just seen your Sam, Belle. He looks awful, he was with a policeman." I thanked her and turned to go home.

"Listen a minute. You say you've lost everything and Sam is injured. There is this Lord Mayor's air raid fund to help us. I've been blasted and I've received twenty pounds. So you go to Hackney Town Hall and state your case and my very good wishes go with you."

Thanking her again, I said, "We have a few savings that will get us over this bad patch, Maggie, so I think we can manage."

She laughed, "Don't be such a bloody fool all your life, give it a go. There are people there with just laundry bills."

I told her I would try. I was eager to see my darling.

He sat, looking a little grey-faced, bandages round his head and under his chin, stitched along one eyebrow, down the side of his nose and down the top lip, his right arm in a sling. I went to him and gave him a gentle hug. He wore an old brown jacket, given to him at the hospice, he said.

"We're alive to tell the tale, darling, and what a tale!"

Mum said, "I've told Sam you haven't seen his mother yet."

I then spoke about Maggie and the air raid fund. "I thought we might try, Sam. What do you think?"

Mum started. "Belle, Maggie has two kids, her husband is in the forces. It makes a great difference in this case." She went on, "Sam, I know you cannot work for a while. You're quite welcome to stay here. I've moved Bill's bed into Jim's room and you can both have Bill's room. If you can manage with my single bed, I can sleep on the old couch."

"I can sleep on the couch, Ma," protested Sam.

"You… with your long legs, your feet would freeze…. No, do as I'm asking. I know there isn't much room in a single bed, but pushed against the wall Belle can't fall off, that will give you room enough." And so it was agreed and we coped.

Chapter Forty-eight

The 1st of January 1942. Mum had washed and ironed my clothes and lent me a warm blouse and a coat. Like me Sam had been wearing slippers when the bomb dropped. We both entered Mr Sigging's shop. I had already told him of the event and now asked him, please could he fit us with shoes and when we got new ration books we would let him have clothing coupons.

My court shoes cost 6s 6d, Sam's shoes cost 10s 6d and Mr Sigging said forget about the coupons.

We could not thank him enough. Then telling Mum we were off to the hospital, then to the shop to stay a while to ask George, Sam's brother, if he had spare clothes to lend Sam as nothing of my brother's would fit, as Sam was that much bigger. Mum gave me a ration book, asking Mrs Bendon for tea, sugar and margarine. (All the family were rationed at the shop.)

We arrived at the hospital about ten o'clock.

We waited our turn, the nurses were very busy, there were so many casualties in the area. Sam spoke quietly. "I just cannot believe what we've been through. I thought it could never happen to us. When I heard you stop screaming I thought you'd bought it. I think I passed out then."

"I thought the same about you when you didn't answer my call."

"Ma told me about our dog. I hope it was for the best."

"Mr Bendon," a nurse beckoned. "You too." We followed her into a cubicle. She took off Sam's bandages and examined his stitches. "That hand has to be x-rayed." She left and a few moments later returned and another nurse took Sam away. "I'll dress that graze over your eye, it looks nasty." She gently dabbed the graze, it felt very sore. "Looks like you've lost half an eyebrow. The hair may grow, but you can always use a brow pencil." She smoothed on some cream and then a plaster. "That's better. Now wait outside for your husband." This after she had taken names, present address and from where we had been injured. I waited about an hour before Sam came to me. His right hand was in plaster from fingertips to four inches or so past the wrist and in a sling. With the small coat, arm in the sleeve and the rest round his shoulder and some plaster patches covering scratches, no wonder people stared as we passed them. Babs was serving a customer as we entered the shop. I smiled as we walked into the shop parlour.

Mrs Bendon sat down heavily at the sight of Sam. George's wife, Edie, said, "I'll put the kettle on." The questions began. We both replied in turn. "And it happened on the 27th, you say, why didn't you let us know sooner?"

"There was nothing you could do, we thought this way best, Mother." Then she wanted to know how my mum was for sleeping us. We told her.

"As you and Babs were travelling to Totteridge from the shop each night, we knew George and Edie opened the shop early, we thought it best to wait until Sam came out of St Joseph's."

George kitted Sam out in some clothes and he looked much better in gear that fitted. Mrs Bendon gave us rations for two books and packed them in a bag. She said forget the coupons for some goods. Gratefully we thanked her. It was nearly five o'clock and was beginning to rain. Hopefully, we thought, we might get some sleep. Grace came and walked with us, she told us she was spending as much time as possible with George in shelters. We would often see her as she came along Goldsmith's Row, meeting George on his way home from work to make evening arrangements. When Fred joined the forces, George said, he'd spend two nights weekly with his mother.

"If your aunt was more amicable we could spend time with her as it is.... She told us when George does have to fire-watch at his firm she spends the time there with him. 'It's not the easiest way to do our courting, but what else can we do?' She was married, so what has she against marriage?"

To that neither Sam nor I could answer.

It rained continually and that night I had a nightmare dream. Came this blinding glare, I woke screaming. Sam's head was lying in sawdust.

He was holding me tightly with his good arm and I was struggling to get away. Mum stood in the doorway as I began to calm down. I was crying. "Try not to wake the boys, Belle. They have to work tomorrow."

"I have had bad dreams too, darling, and we must talk about them." Sam said quietly that in St Joseph's the sisters and nurses said that way was best and would help one to forget slowly. "So in the morning we'll talk."

Sam had lost his hearing aid as wardens dragged him from under the rubble. He asked me to go with him to the London Hospital, Whitechapel, to get it renewed. This I did. A nurse took a mould of his ear, gave him batteries, saying the mould would be in the post in two days' time. Saying he could fix it together himself and thanking her we left. The new mould arrived two days later and Sam was back in the hearing world.

Chapter Forty-nine

I decided to take Maggie's advice. Mum was furious. "I have always taught you to be independent. Don't beg, please."

"The air raid fund is to help people like us, so come along, Sam."

"Maybe your mother has a point."

Arriving at Hackney Town Hall, we waited while three other persons were attended to. We were ushered into a large room, our feet sinking into the thick pile of the carpet. Heavy red velvet curtained the windows. Behind a wide mahogany desk sat the mayor, a chain of office round his neck.

He waved a hand for us to be seated. He eyed us, his face stern.

"In what way can I help you?" His voice was like gravel.

"We need some clothes, sir," I began. His glance of amazement stopped further speech. He shuffled papers on the desk.

"We lost all we had on the 27th of December." I spoke firmly.

He eyed Sam's arm in the sling. "You were hurt?"

"I think it looks like it, don't you?" Sam answered.

"My husband is a little hard of hearing," I informed him.

"Where did you live, when the bomb fell?"

Sam gave the address and the mayor turned some pages of the papers and put a small tick against some writing. He looked at me. "What do you do for a living?"

"I belong to the Voluntary Fire Service."

His supercilious glance implied I couldn't blow out a match, never mind a fire. He turned again to Sam. "How long is that hand going to be in plaster?"

"Six weeks at least, then I'll be given finger exercises."

Opening a drawer, the mayor said sternly, "I've decided to give you a lump sum. You're to make it last you for the time you're incapable of work, so don't spend it all at once." From the drawer he laid three one-pound notes on the table. I stared astounded. Three pounds!

"Where are you living now?" the mayor asked Sam abruptly.

"We're staying with Mrs Munday," replied Sam.

"At the moment we're entirely dependent on the generosity of my mother," I put in and immediately realised the stupidity of my words. If you were with relations, in the opinion of the authorities, you were housed; you had a roof over your head. That was it. Full stop.

"The church hall is just along the road. They will fit you out with a coat each." He said good-day. I picked up the notes and we left.

In a lower corridor a porter directed us to the food office. We were given ration books with coupons neatly cut to date, plus ten extra clothing coupons each. We entered the church hall, many people were there on the same mission as we were... gents to the right, ladies left. My turn came; I stated my needs, saying the coat I wore was loaned. Did I need undies? Nodding, I was given a dark green pair of fleece-lined bloomers elasticised at the knee and waist (real passion stoppers), a bra of sorts, a slip and a brown skirt and a knitted jumper. The coat was dark grey tweed. I was given a paper carrier bag and bundling the clothes in the bag I waited for Sam to join me near the doorway. A while later he came to me grinning. "Just wait until you see what I have. Come, let's get home to show Ma our treasures." Back home, we related to Mum the mayor's words and cash. To say she hit the roof is to put it mildly. She raved.

"It's an insult. Why did you take the money? Why didn't you ask him if he could afford it? Why didn't you ask how he expected two people could live on ten measly shillings a week? Where was your guts, Sam, to let her take the money? I pleaded with you not to go there, but no, you knew better. I could spit." It was no use interrupting, Mum in a rage was something to see. You just had to let her come to a full stop.

"Well, it's little enough, heaven knows," I said when she had calmed down. We showed the contents of our paper bags and had a good laugh.

Sam had tried on the suit he had been given, it was a tight fit. The turn-ups on the trousers were turned down but were still a trifle short on his thirty-three-inch legs. A striped blue and white shirt, a little short on sleeve length, but shorts and singlet were fine. I gave Mum the passion stoppers amid much laughter. There was a bad raid that night and I felt really scared. I couldn't stop shaking. I think Sam was scared too as the bombs dropped nearer. Next day we went shopping for some decent underclothes. Sam had been given a warm overcoat, so far, so good. We gave Mr Sigging coupons for our shoes and also we returned the ration coupons to Mrs Bendon and bought supplies for that week.

Babs told us she thought Joe was in the East and she was worried about the Japanese advances in that area. Our cousin Fred was passed "A1" and Auntie cried a lot when he left for an army unit.

The allied forces were suffering heavy losses in the desert and the Russian army was also falling back against fierce German advances. Altogether the German army appeared invincible. Over the radio, Lord Haw-Haw was having a field day. The raids over our cities were not quite so frequent. The enemy bombed ports, wrecking docking facilities for ships.

Occasionally we wrote to Gran, always making light of events. I briefly wrote we had lost our home during a raid.

"No good upsetting her as she isn't well," Mum said.

Gran wrote back about two weeks later to say that German battleships had bombarded the Sunderland coast. As we had heard nothing about this over the radio, we assumed maybe she had dreamt this. Bill remarked, it may be true and the authorities were keeping quiet about it, not to scare people.

I had another bad dream and woke frightened. Next day, I related to Sam the nightmares of my childhood, of Father's treatment, how I spent time with Aunt Alice and Cousin Florrie at their home in West Ham.

"Now I can really understand why you dislike the colour blue."

Mum began, "I feel so guilty, Sam. I persuaded you to move from Kaye Street. I felt that small house offered no protection, I'm so sorry you've lost your nice home. Please forgive me."

"Of course I do. Forget it, Ma, it was to be. It was on the cards." Immediately my mind went back years, to the fortune-teller's dingy room. What had she said? "I see you surrounded in ruins… I don't know why. Now I've run out of cards."

"I wanted to make that house look nice. I wanted pretty floral curtains with plain swags for the windows. I wanted cream-painted walls and wood-patterned lino resembling parquet flooring. In the bedroom, I wanted pale pink walls and a pink carpet to show off the walnut-veneered furniture, and in the front semi-basement I wanted to make everything so comfortable."

Mum interrupted me. "I've told you time and time again, Belle, the Lord will always attend to your needs, but not your wants. Remember that."

Sam said, "I know maybe I'm reminding you about the old life, but I think Ma was a very brave lady to walk away with you three kids." Sam was sympathetic. "Your father was a real bastard."

I shrugged. "You don't know, nor do I, how much Mum suffered before she left the pub with us kids. Thinking back, had she stayed, she may have done something drastic. She once spoke of taking us to heaven with her."

"And you have all grown up a credit to her." He held me tightly.

I was steadily making withdrawals from the post office savings book, and without that we would have been flat broke. I seriously thought about trying for a job. I suppose I could serve in any kind of shop.

Bill had asked his boss to put him on day work, he felt two weeks on nights then two weeks' day work was upsetting his digestion. He was sleeping badly during the day and didn't want to make mistakes with his work when feeling tired during the night shift. A month later his request was granted… much to Mum's relief. She worried herself sick during a raid, wondering if the factory complex escaped being hit.

After another bad raid, Mum burst into tears. "I can't stand much more of this. I want to get out of London before we're all killed."

We tried to pacify her, each of us putting forward our doubts. Where could we go? What about the distance of getting to work? But no, she had many excuses. Jim came up with a possible solution.

"It's a few miles from London where I work, but it would be a fair way for Bill and Sam to travel." After seven weeks Sam had had the plaster removed and was now back at work, but doing finger exercises during spare moments. "Perhaps we could get work in Surrey, how about it, Bill?"

We turned in for a few hours' sleep; with the weekend ahead maybe we could discuss the situation more thoroughly.

We all managed to get two baths a week. The old zinc bath was curtained off in one corner of the room, which gave a little privacy.

A bucket of water was heated over a gas burner on the cooker, and when it reached boiling point the bucket was lifted from the cooker… a tricky business… the water was emptied into the bath and jugs of cold water added and so we washed up and down in roughly three inches of water. Thus we kept ourselves clean after a fashion. When Sam's right hand was in plaster, he fumed and swore. I used to wash up and down his back while he cussed Hitler right, left and centre.

We all considered the move. How could we find a place in Surrey? Jim said there was an estate agent in Rayne's Park. He would make enquiries during a lunch break. No joy there at all.

We needed batteries for two torches and two 60-watt light bulbs. I took the old batteries for size and went to the large electrical shop in Cambridge Heath Road, then I went into the newsagent's and bought *Dalton's Weekly.* That paper advertised property all over the country.

Someone called my name.... A big man hurried across the road. My heart jumped.... Father. Then I recognised his brother. I smiled a little.

"Uncle Bill," I exclaimed in surprise, "how are you?"

"Fine, and you and all the family?" We were shaking hands as he spoke. "It's ages since I last saw you. How's the old girl?"

"I assume you mean your mother. She's in hospital in Ryhope. Didn't you know? We couldn't care for her in war time, could we?"

"Ryhope? Where for Christ's sake is that?"

"Sunderland... and she's not too well."

"Look, let's go home to see your mother. I parked my car in Bishop's Road when I saw you come out of the shop." He took my arm and we crossed to his car. "How's your daughter Pat, Uncle?"

"She'll be fifteen in a few weeks' time. Christ, if she grows up to be anything like you, I'll be a very happy man." He laughed. "Your father doesn't know what he's missing."

"If you're going to talk about him, stop the car, I'll walk. I disassociated myself from him long ago... we all did... so?"

"You can't deny he's your father."

"Maybe if he could he would wish us off the face of this earth."

He laughed, "Goldsmith's Row, you said?" We arrived and I inserted the key, we climbed the stairs. In the living-room Mum started as we entered. Like me I am sure her first impression was that it was Father.

"Hello, Bella," Uncle Bill said cordially, "you look blooming. You haven't changed much. The years have treated you kindly."

"Flattery will get you everywhere, but I'm pleased to see you. How is Barbara and your little girl? Well, I hope." Mum picked up the kettle. "You'll stay for a cup, Bill. Coffee or tea?"

"Let's have tea, Bella. I was on my way to visit my brother George, but seeing young Belle, I just had to speak to her." Mum nodded.

Over tea Mum asked, "How much longer do you think the war will last, Bill? These raids are beginning to get me down."

"Christ, Bella, I hope it goes on for ages."

"You wicked bugger," Mum said crossly. "With all these people being killed, men fighting, how can you say that?"

"I've got a damned good job in the Tottenham food office. I have three girls working for me. When I first started there, the eldest one brought me in some papers to sign, asking if she was doing things the way I liked it. I didn't know what the hell she was talking about. I just told her to carry on the way things were, so far I was satisfied." He grinned. "I begin work at nine o'clock, leave at half-past four and finish the week Friday at two… so… on with the war."

"How did you get the job in the first place?" Mum asked.

"Handwriting. You know, me being ambidextrous, no matter which hand picks up the pen, it's all in neat copperplate style."

He left about five o'clock with best wishes for the boys. Turning to me at the street door he said, "I'd like to meet your husband some day, Belle."

"Who knows how or when. We're thinking of moving from

London." I shrugged. "How do you like being called Mr Munday, by your staff?"

"I prefer it when they call me sir," he laughed.

"You're a bit of a snob, Uncle Bill."

He shook my hand warmly saying, "Be seeing you soon."

Mum said as I entered the room, "Belle, that gave me quite a start when I saw him. I thought it was your father."

"Father is the last person I'd bring here, Mum."

That weekend I withdrew more from our savings and went shopping with Sam for a mattress and bed linen. Reaching Gibson's furniture shop in Amhurst Road, we chose an interior-sprung four-foot mattress, price £5 10s and two feather-filled pillows at five shillings each, and they were delivered that same afternoon, no charge. Next we bought two pairs of Irish linen sheets at 12s 6d a pair, two pairs of pillowcases at 4s 11d a pair and a thick cream and green Whitney blanket at a linen draper's. The shopkeeper tied our purchases into two neat parcels and we made our way home. Sam said suddenly, smiling, "You know what I really miss these days, Belle? Our short dances and steps round that skittle alley. I always liked that."

I laughed with him. "And I miss my piano playing." We walked along in silence, and I decided to speak of my secret fear.

"Sam, I'm scared of getting pregnant. I'm afraid when the siren blares. I could scream. I don't want to bring an idiot into this world. Please do try to understand how I feel. Can you buy something?"

He was silent. I was asking too much of him, I thought.

"I know how you feel, darling, I'm a little scared myself. Anyone who says they're not frightened is, in my opinion, a liar. Don't worry, I'll buy some protection and you'll be safe from pregnancy."

I murmured a grateful thanks. My Sam was a darling.

During that week George delivered our new wide bed. It was the same style as our original one, walnut veneer over mahogany.

He charged us ten pounds and that was the first night we had slept in a large bed for over two months... it was really marvellous because there was no raid that night either.

Chapter Fifty

For the next month we scoured *Dalton's Weekly*. An estate agent near Rayne's Park Station advertised lettings in the area. Jim phoned. Yes, they were open on Sundays and with me riding pillion we set off early. We found the agent, stated our needs. There were three properties we could see. Standing Jim's motorcycle outside where the agent said it would be safe, we set off in the agent's car. It appeared some distance until we stopped outside a semi-detached chalet-type house. There was a wide front garden with a low lavender hedge dividing the front lawns. The entrance was through a wide gate down a drive leading to a green painted garage.

The door opened into a wide L-shaped hall, stairs immediately to the right as one entered. The agent opened a door to the left. The room, some fourteen feet square, had a large leaded diamond-patterned window, but no fire grate. The room facing the street door was large with a high ceiling, with the window also diamond-patterned, as with all the rooms. The next room was a large one looking out onto a garden through French doors. The fire grate was across a corner. Next we entered the kitchen. "It's all electric," said the agent. "There are no gas fixtures here." The large white enamel cooker stood beside a low squat fire. "That will give you all the hot water you need in winter, always providing you feed it coal." The agent smiled. Up the stairs were two large bedrooms. In the front bedroom a door led to a small annex, which had a round bull's eye leaded light window. The toilet was separate from the white tiled bathroom, which also contained an airing cupboard. The rent was two pounds weekly, two weeks in advance.

We were in the upstairs back bedroom when a train passed, we could see it clearly. "Oh yes," the agent indicated the train. "New Maiden Station is just along the road round past the school, eight minutes' walk. Twenty-five minutes on the train to Waterloo... very handy, don't you think?"

"What do you think, Belle?" Jim asked.

"It's a very nice house. I like the domed recesses in the rooms."

"There are two more houses for you to see," the agent said.

"I think the station has settled it for us, we've decided this is the place we like." The agent took us back to the office.

We paid the necessary cash, telling him we had to make arrangements for removals and had to give notice to our present landlord.

"I understand, call for the keys when you move in." He gave us a receipt for cash paid and we rode home in high glee. The address of our new home would be 119 Lawrence Avenue, New Malden, Surrey.

There was much to do, letters to write. I wrote a short note to Gran. Mum wrote to Flo. Aunt Minne was not too pleased at the news.

"If a bomb has your name on it, it will find you wherever you go," she said sourly. "We'll stay put, no matter what."

Flo came two days later, asking, when we were settled in the new house, would we have Maureen stay with us for a while? "She is so frightened when the sirens blare. Her teacher says her schoolwork is affected." Mum agreed. Flo was so thankful.

We moved in May. Removals cost four pounds, a lot of money in those days. Mum always scrubbed rooms out whenever we moved, so now she was very busy. We all helped get furniture into place.

Sam insisted on paying Mum a pound as weekly rent. "We are using the rest of your furniture and we have the use of the bathroom, so please, Ma, I'll be happy if you are." So we settled to life in Surrey. We arranged that I would go to Mrs Bendon's shop each Friday to collect rations and help serve customers. I learned to bone out and cut up a side of bacon expertly and skin a cheese of its protected linen cover and use the cheese wire. I also used the cheese wire to cut up a fifty-six-pound box of cooking fat into half-pound sections and wrap ready for sale, then help in the shop. Sam would pick me up and with the rations and we would travel home together. Occasionally Mum would travel to London to visit Aunt Minne or Aunt Agnes. Bill would then travel home with Mum.

Raids were not so frequent. Our planes were targeting the Ruhr arms complex with heavy bombing.

We had the large front room and the annex for a bedroom.

I helped Mum with the household chores. I joined the Women's Institute (WI) two mornings weekly and I joined the Volunteer Fire Service.

Sam planted vegetable seeds and suggested ordering six twelve-day-old chickens. "The eggs will help." I ordered Rhode Island Reds and three days later they arrived. Meantime Sam knocked together a roosting shed. I bought a bale of hay and some corn and bran and warning the cat, the birds quickly settled in. I spoke to two neighbours about the birds and asked for all their peelings and their ration books, thus enabling me to get corn and maize. The birds came into lay four weeks later and I was able to give the neighbours two eggs each weekly.

Flo wrote she was coming to see us next weekend and with her was Maureen. Flo asked if we would mind if she stayed with us for the time being.

"She will miss her schooling, Flo," said Mum.

"Well if she's staying for any length of time, I'll try to get her into the school at the end of the road." I turned to the girl, "Would you like that, Maureen?"

She looked serious. "Is it a nice school, not rough?"

"Some very nice children pass here, so… why not try it?"

Maureen cried a little when her mother left. I took her down the garden to look at the chickens and she dried her eyes.

Monday morning I managed to get her a place in the school. I explained her stay was indefinite. The headmistress was pleasant and assured me Maureen would be fine. She came home for lunch full of beans and had already found a friend. I was pleased. "Her name is Linda, and we are both just seven years old," she stated. During air raids she wondered about her family. She wrote regularly. With relatives and friends in London we kept in touch by letter.

About six weeks after we had moved to Surrey, we received a letter from the Ryhope Hospital saying Mrs Munday was in a very low state of health and would we visit as quickly as possible.

Mum exploded. "If she dies they'll expect us to pay all funeral expenses. No doubt she has said you are her only relative, Belle, she always was a devious woman. So now what?"

"I know what to do, Mum. Don't worry." I dashed off a short note to The Baker's Arms, enclosing the hospital letter. I heard nothing more. We don't know when Gran died, if she is buried in Sunderland, or if she is buried in London near Grandfather.

Soon after Maureen arrived we discovered she couldn't tell the time. The boys made a cardboard clock face, explaining the numbers from twelve to six meant past the hour and six to twelve meant to the hour. She quickly began to learn. I promised to buy her a signet ring if she became proficient in a month. Three weeks later she was choosing her ring. Nine-carat gold, priced at 4s 6d (22.5p in today's money).

During September we had fire drill and exercises… with my neighbour at Number 113, a Mrs Grant (we called her Bart), on this Saturday afternoon we were instructed how to tackle an incendiary bomb. After the actual happening in London, I was amazed. Taken to a school playground we were told to stay at least ten feet away from the bomb, a bucket was placed under a tap, thus supplying continual water. We were shown how to work the stirrup pump and stoop low, playing the hose on the object. The bomb was duly lit, there were seven of us and we all had a go squirting at the bomb.

"Never stand over the object, and never pour water straight onto the bomb. It could explode," warned the instructor. I thought he meant well.

Next we were led to a shed where we donned oil boiler suits. A fire was burning in a small bath in the centre of the shed. There were no windows. The place was filled with smoke. The instructor told us to crawl round the floor, heads well down. Bart was a tall thin lady and as I crawled behind her, I looked at her crawling legs and backside. I was reminded of a small elephant and burst out laughing, only to end in a fit of coughing and streaming eyes. The instructor was not amused, though I never said what I was laughing at. He then told us to stand, almost immediately we were all coughing. "That's it, in a smoke-filled room always crawl along the floor," the instructor bawled above our choking.

At Rediffusion, my brother Jim was a supervisor over a number of engineers making components for the navy. He had mentioned some time past that he had a new secretary, her name was Miss Webb, he called her Spider and she didn't seem to mind and he'd just got her into his way of working.

About September an allied contingent made a raid on the French coastal town of Dieppe. It was a disaster. The enemy captured many prisoners along with much ammunition and heavy guns. Meanwhile the allied armies were making successful landings in Morocco and Algiers. A General Montgomery was massing an army at El Alamein and successfully relieved allied forces besieged at Tobruk. Churchill, while speaking on the radio, told of the surrender of Singapore and the sinking of an aircraft carrier and a battleship by the Japanese. This was a terrible blow for Britain.

The allied armies were slowly driving the Germans from the desert, but the Japanese armies had overrun Malaya and the Philippine Islands.

Regularly every Friday, I journeyed to the shop for our rations. The fare to Waterloo then was 1s 9d return. I went down the City and Waterloo tube (at that time nicknamed the drain), changed at the Bank for Liverpool Street Station and then took a bus to the road that led to the shop. Once there, I helped wherever I could.

A girl at the WI asked me one morning did I like dancing. I wanted to know why. "I go to classes at the Victoria," but now her father didn't like her going out alone at night. She asked would I go with her for company. I said I would ask my husband, if he said yes, OK.

I spoke to Mum about the classes; she would agree only if Sam would go with me. Very reluctantly he agreed saying, "I don't think I should be enjoying myself while my brother Joe is fighting in the East. I'll think about it."

"It would be an evening out, instead of sitting here waiting for the sirens to sound and I don't want Belle going out alone," said Mum.

"It's only one evening a week," Sam agreed, "so why not!"

Joyce was delighted, and on Monday evening off we went.

Situated on the Epsom Road, the hall was quite large. A dozen or so middle-aged couples were already there and a few young girls. The yearly fee for membership was 2s 6d. Classes were 1s 6d, lasting from eight o'clock until ten. We were duly enrolled. We danced to Victor Sylvester's strict tempo records.

The tutor started us off with a warming-up quickstep. The dance over she came to us asking, "Do you have medals?" I said no, Sam said yes. I was so surprised. "You've never told me you had medals, and I've never seen them, so why the secret?"

"Unless you get your machine back, you'll never see them. I put them in the drawer with some cuff links, so...." He shrugged.

After that, the teacher pestered me to try for medals and in November I danced before the adjudicator for the bronze and silver at the same time and was pleased to learn I had passed with commendations.

Early in December I achieved my gold medal, then the teacher suggested I try for the associate medal. I had no wish to teach dancing. All I wanted was the war to end, to rent a shop and begin hairdressing once again. Was it asking too much?

Corn and maize for chicken feed was becoming scarce, so I decided to get the butcher to kill some of them for me. A week before Christmas he did. I gave him one for his trouble, kept one for ourselves and sold ten to neighbours as boiling fowls for a pound each.

Maureen's elder sister, Pat, came a week before Christmas, the sisters were delighted to see each other and we spent a pleasant time together. When Pat was leaving she began asking Maureen to go home with her. The weather was bad. It had snowed all day and was extremely frosty. I suppose it was a natural thing that Pat wanted her sister to spend the holiday with her family. I was a little annoyed. I had enrolled Maureen into a nearby school and the teacher had said she was doing very well for her age.

"Maureen, if you go home now with Pat, you cannot return here. I mean what I say. You're doing well at school, so if you go, I shall tell the teacher you've returned home for good."

"I can come back after Christmas, can't I, Auntie Bella?" She turned to Mum. "Please make Aunt Belle change her mind."

"You must be crazy, Pat, to take her back. It's a terrible night".

"I know you've been kind to her and she's been happy here, but we miss her and my mother will be pleased to see her."

So we said, "Take care on the journey. It's a long way to Walthamstow," and they left.

We had a letter from Flo, she was furious we'd let Pat travel with Maureen in such bad weather.

She had slept in a folding bed chair in Mum's bedroom, now it reverted back to an armchair. We spent a quiet Christmas and we really missed Maureen.

The Merchant Navy, crossing the Atlantic, paid a heavy price in men and ships, sailing only as fast as the slowest ship, bringing supplies of food and guns and ammunition to these shores, while German U-boats lay in wait as ships entered coastal waters. So many lives and ships were lost as well as munitions for our troops, which were needed so badly.

Montgomery was slowly hounding the enemy from North Africa.

Bombing raids continued over Germany, targeting the industrial Ruhr.

Between times, our fire exercises continued. On this Saturday afternoon, we had been told to wear low-heeled shoes. Taken to an empty house, our instructor explained we were to drag an unconscious man down a staircase to safety. The model, a burly fifteen-stone man, lay on the floor and we were shown just how easy it was to get the man to safety. You dragged him to the top of the stairway, then getting his head onto your shoulder and your right arm under his and holding tightly your arm round his chest, with your back against the wall, the man's own weight would help you get him down the stairs. The instructor suiting the action of words as he spoke quickly had the man out into the road. It took him two minutes. Now he wanted us to do the action in three minutes. Needless to say he was very dissatisfied with our efforts. I took five minutes to do this, so was made to haul this man downstairs again. The man, named Pete, lay on the floor. I waited for the whistle, then began to drag Pete along the floor. He was a big man; I could barely get my fingers round his wrist. Hoisting his head onto my shoulder, he said, "For Christ's sake get it right this time, my arse is getting sore bumping down these stairs."

I laughed, "You're supposed to be unconscious. If you make me laugh, I'm hopeless." I wrestled with my victim and emerged on the street still nearly four minutes later. The instructor glared at me.

"What do you expect, he's twice my weight, isn't he?"

"You'd do it in bloody quick time if it was your father in there." Everyone wondered why I laughed. I told them all it was a long story.

Aunt Minne wrote saying she had received a letter from Fred, who was hoping to meet Harry. We then knew Fred too was in North Africa.

There happened on the 3rd of March the worst civilian tragedy of World War II. People had taken to sleeping down the many London tube stations. The government had fixed up metal bunks and people took blankets to keep warm these cold nights. This night sirens sounded about eight o'clock. People in the area of the Bethnal Green tube hurried there for shelter. The Museum Cinema turned out and the rush for the shelter began. As bombs dropped and guns fired, did someone stumble? Was there blind panic? No one will truly know the answer. Bodies piled on top of each other completely blocking the steps. There was no centre grab-rail. Sam's brother George, on his way home, helped doctors and nurses from the nearby Bethnal Green Hospital drag out bodies of men, women and children. The death toll on that March night was 173. George had his shoulder injured and it always stuck out a little despite treatment. There is a commemorative plaque let into the wall of the station entrance.

At the shop on the following Friday, many theories we discussed, to which there was no answer.

Singapore had surrendered and Japanese armies marched through Malaya and the Philippine islands, but in the desert under Montgomery our armies were beating back the Germans and slowly the enemy was leaving Africa for Italy and France to continue the war in those countries.

Everyone carried on with their lives. Sam and I went to dance classes on Monday nights, and he said again one evening as we walked home, "I sometimes think I ought not to be dancing while Joe is out East fighting, but I was getting so rusty without exercise."

"Me too," I assured him, "but you're doing war work and I'm trying to help at the WI and the fire service, so...."

In the adjoining semi lived Mr and Mrs Ley, with their small son Brian, just four years old. When we had chickens he would stand on a stepladder and watch with interest. Sam asked if he would like to come into our garden, but he said he had to ask his mummy. It was two days later before he knocked at our door.

We had discovered Pickles was a she-cat and at this time was beginning to look very pregnant. Mum had prepared and lined a large carton and placed it in the cupboard under the stairs. The cat was not too much in evidence, just showing up to be fed. I was in the kitchen with Mum and had let Brian into the house. As Mum was making some tea she asked him if he would like a cup.

"Yes, please, Mrs Munday, and I'm not to have your sugar, my mummy tells me it's rationed, so we each just have a little."

Pickles wandered in, her tummy rounded like a balloon.

"I see Pickles is going to have kittens," observed Brian.

Mother was aghast, positively speechless.

Brian looked at Mum. "Didn't you know?" he enquired.

Mum placed a cup in front of him, not answering. She looked at me, shaking her head. "Have a biscuit, Brian," she said as Pickles waddled off into the garden. Each day after that Brian asked if Pickles had had her kittens yet.

Mother went on and on about a four-year-old saying such things.

"Children are brought up differently these days from the time when you were small," I answered her.

"Me, I was as daft as a brush," Mum said. "What the world is coming to, I don't know. It's all wrong for such a small child to speak about pregnant cats," she finished in disgust.

Our next fire exercise was escaping from an upstairs room that was supposedly on fire, and we had come prepared in flat shoes.

The instructor demonstrated with the help of a colleague. So, one by one we followed the instructions. He asked each of us how tall we were. There were seven ladies this day, all differing heights. Bart thought she was five feet seven, and stretching up her arms as bidden, how much over six feet did she think she was? She thought about six feet four.

"Don't skimp," bawled the instructor. "When you hang from that window, it's roughly thirteen feet. Off you go." We were using the same empty house we used to drag the man down the stairs; maybe it was on loan to the fire service for exercises. He bawled each move at us as we had first been shown. Then it was my turn. "And how tall are you?" he demanded.

"Five feet two and a half." I replied.

He grinned. I should forget the half. "Arms stretch, now how tall?"

I stared up at my fingers. "Six feet, sir."

"So, six feet from thirteen, how many left?"

"Seven?" I questioned hesitantly.

"Get along with you and listen to me, do as I say."

I hurried up the stairs to the window, and looking out it seemed a long way to drop. "Ready?" he yelled. I nodded. "Right, sit on the windowsill." I followed his instructions. "Turn slowly, holding the frame with your right hand, swing legs over sill and face me, turn over onto your stomach, now wriggle back, resting on your arms until you can grip the sill with your fingers." So far, so good, I thought. "Now, come right to the edge of the sill, slightly bend knees, now turn your body sideways and drop." As soon as my body turned sideways there was no way I could hold my weight with my left hand and down I went. I landed on my knees and grazed them badly, my stockings in holes and ladders, the palms of my hands felt sore... a seven-foot drop, it felt like thirty feet. I gazed at my holed stockings in dismay, meanwhile he was bawling at the next lady. I was trying to wipe the dirt from my grazes. Despite the fact we had dropped to grass, it hurt. Now he was telling us to prepare for next week when we would practise hauling the man downstairs and dropping out of the window.

"I'll be among the missing next week," I informed Bart.

Tuesday morning, washing up at the WI, Mrs Jeffries informed us next Sunday we had a date to wash up at the headquarters of the Home Guard, and were to assemble at Worcester Park Station by eleven a.m. Six ladies were already there when I arrived. Minutes later up rolls a jeep, and me thinking we were going by train. We rode for miles and miles into the Surrey countryside. Eventually we came to some low camouflaged buildings. I stumbled from that jeep, feeling bones in my backside I never knew I had.

"Fall in, the awkward squad," a voice yelled.

I turned towards the sound. A stiff-backed sergeant stamped to attention enough to dig holes in the grass. "Is he speaking to us?" I enquired.

He strode towards us. "Follow me," he ordered, striding out at a fast pace, though we could hardly walk after bumping along in that jeep.

Entering the low building, we were shown where to hang our coats, hats and bags. Given striped blue aprons to protect our clothing, we then were shown the privates' mess, then the officers' mess. There was one trestle table in the officers' mess and in the privates' there were three tables. We were shown where the cutlery lived and were told to lay tables for thirty men, ten and a sergeant at each table in the privates' mess and just six places in the officers' mess.

Rationing. What a laugh, here it appeared unknown. In the cook-house there were three large legs of lamb from which the chef was carving thick slices, a large cauldron in which a cook was mashing potatoes with a wooden-type dolly. In another cauldron with a low tap, a cook was pressing water from greens and it all smelled very appetising. An enamel jug of gravy was simmering over a low gas jet. Mrs Jeffries was mixing custard powder with milk in a large bowl. The man mashing potatoes was smoking a cigarette, it had a long ash. I watched for a moment fascinated, waiting for the ash to drop into the potatoes. He looked at me, shook his head and the ash fell to the floor.

There were two trolleys, each with two shelves, which carried eight dinners. The chef began dishing up as plates were passed in front of him. Next the potatoes. This man amazed me. He scooped up the mashed spuds with his bare hands and as each plate passed him, he deftly flicked a neatly rounded heap of mash onto the plates; he must have had asbestos fingers. Next cabbage, this was picked up by wide tongs and was liberally doused with thick gravy. Off went two ladies pushing a trolley and told, "Officer's first." With a lady named Jenny, I pushed the trolley to the privates' mess and was told, "Sergeants first." We hurriedly placed dinners and went back for more. "Hello, darling, what do they call you?" a soldier asked me grinning. "However did you guess?" I replied. I suppose there were about forty privates. Meanwhile, Mrs Jeffries had made tapioca pudding. "This will stop your ribs from chapping," the men chorused as we placed dishes before them. Dinner finished they filed out onto the parade ground. We could hear the sergeants bawling orders as we washed up.

Then we were told to set out mugs, some without sugar, some without milk, and we put a tin of biscuits on each table, then we were taken back to Worcester Park Station.

All in all, it was a marvellous experience.

Meantime, Pickles had produced three kittens. One she brought into the kitchen, Mum said she dumped one by the kitchen door. Next day that kitten died leaving the other two, one tabby, the other a long-haired black. Mum loved cats, the tabby she named Tommy and the black one Fluffy.

Tuesday mornings and Thursday I queued at the Continental butcher in Epsom Road for horsemeat for the cats. Fridays I left early for the Bendons' shop to help and collect our rations. It was all very organised and between raids we listened on the radio to the songs of Vera Lynn and Anne Shelton. The excellent comedy series *It's That Man Again* and *Much Binding in the Marsh* helped to keep our spirits up. We wrote continually to Sam's brother Joe and to our cousins Fred and Harry King and waited eagerly for replies.

The enemy was slowly but surely being driven from North Africa, Stalin was demanding we begin a second front to take pressure from his troops. Meanwhile the enemy was massing troops to continue the war in Europe.

Chapter Fifty-one

About this time, mid-August, Flo's daughter Pat quietly married a Patrick Coyle at a registry office in Walthamstow.

In the autumn our clocks were put back two hours. It made no difference: if the weather was good, sporadic raids were made on coastal towns. There was a great comradeship among the population as life went on.

As her sister, Nellie, had recently died, George's wife Edie returned home with her two small children. We were all delighted to see her. Customers at the shop welcomed her return. Not living far from the shop George and Edie were able to let Mrs Bendon and Babs arrive a little later at the shop. It was a real family business.

I was beginning to feel a little restless. I felt the need for a home of our own. I was grateful to Mum and to my brothers for all they had done and the help they had given us. Before being bombed, I had lived for three years making my own decisions. Now we said where we were going and at what time we'd be home. After all, it was Mum's house. Although Sam said nothing, I knew he felt the same.

Going home the next Friday, I bought a paper from the station kiosk and with Sam scanned it in the train. Flats seemed to be the places to rent. "Could we buy?" I asked hesitantly.

"I have saved about £200," Sam told me, "but we need about a quarter of the house price as an initial deposit, so we have to find something in the £800 price range, and there's nothing in the Surrey area in that bracket. What made you pick a Romford paper?"

"It was the first one that came to hand." I pointed to a column.

"Perhaps we could find something down the line, Seven Kings or Chadwell Heath." We sat both scanning the paper.

"I don't think Ma is going to like the idea," Sam said.

Getting near Christmas, my brothers bought a second-hand piano for Mum. It had been neglected, but Mum polished it until it shone, then had it tuned for five pounds and really enjoyed playing again. I did too and we spent a really happy Christmas together. Our Christmas dinner was chops, Brussels sprouts from our garden and potatoes. We had apple pie for sweet. Boxing Day we had Spam fried in batter with the same two veg. I had made a seed cake for our tea.

So we entered the eventful year of 1944.

The first Friday in that year, I took the train to Romford.

Immediately opposite the station was an estate agent, Hillberry Chaplan. I studied the house sales for a while, then marched inside.

"I'm looking for a house in the price region of £800," I told the smiling assistant. "As near to a station as possible, please." She leafed through some files. "There are two here in your price range, and both are near Gidea Park Station, would you like to view them?"

I sat silent in the car; it seemed quite a distance before she stopped.

"This one is nice and the station is just up the road." I gazed at the pebble-dashed house on a corner. Bay windows upstairs and down. I eyed a swiftly flowing shallow stream running alongside. Five stone steps led to the front door. The hall and a flight of stairs to the right were narrow. Three bedrooms, two reception rooms, the usual offices, it appeared tiny after the large rooms in the Surrey house, a pocket-handkerchief garden and the price £895. "What do you think about this?"

I shook my head. "May I see the other house?" I queried.

A short while and we arrived at 81 Cranham Road. I liked the look of this house. A deep front garden, red brick half-way up then pale cream-painted plaster to the roof. Bay windows top and bottom with leaded transoms, a wide domed porch to a green-painted street door again with a large leaded window, also a side entrance. Opening the street door, it swung to the right to a wide L-shaped hall, doors opening to the left. The front room, bright with the January sun, looked inviting, and had a low grate with a tiled cream surround. I smiled at the assistant. Next a door opened to a large living-room. An oak surround framed the fire grate. French doors led onto a concrete terrace and then down three steps to a sixty-foot garden. At the end was a large shed. There was a back entrance, said the girl, and the shed was large enough for a garage. A door led from this room to a small kitchen. Under a large window was a deep white butler sink. Stairs, which curved at the top, were lit by a large casement window. The master bedroom, fairly large also, had a tiled surround round a low grate, the back bedroom overlooked the garden and from this window I could see the length of the road as this semi-detached house was next to the corner house. The bathroom was tiled white and had a white bath and toilet basin and the loo was separate. A small room about ten feet by nine completed my tour of inspection. I thought the price, compared with the first house, would be out of our reach. "How much?"

"It's priced at £758 and there's no chain, what do you think?"

No chain? I wondered what she was talking about. I had never heard that expression before, but then I had never thought of buying a house before. "Have you a house to sell?" she enquired.

"We're first-time buyers. I like this house, but my husband must see it before we agree to buy. Is it possible for him to view the house tomorrow?" She nodded and she took me back to Romford Station.

The day at the shop passed quickly. I gave no excuse for my late arrival. In the train home, I told Sam about the house.

"What will your mother say? You'll have to tell her if we're both going out to view this house tomorrow."

"Leave it to me, Sam, I'll choose the moment."

Dinner over, I washed the dishes. In the living-room we sat listening to the radio. The enemy was leaving Malta and fierce fighting was continuing in southern Italy, but mopping-up operations continued in northern Africa to repel small pockets of resistance. Since the pilot-less rockets exploded over our cities (people called them "buzz bombs") the country was on constant alert. Explosions could be heard at any time.

In a quiet moment, I said, "I went to look at a house today."

Came the questions "Why?" and "What for?" from my brothers. Mum said nothing. I continued: "We have encroached upon your generosity long enough, Mum. We want a place of our own. I want to work with Sam to get a home together. When the war ends I want to start a salon and return to hairdressing again. Maybe I'll want to start a family." For the moment there was silence.

"I have said this to you before, Belle," Mum began. "The Lord will attend to your needs, but not your wants. Why leave here? Time and time again I've blamed myself, asking you to move from that small house and losing your home and being injured in Albion Drive. I have tried my hardest in my way to make it up to both of you. You don't have to go, stay here as long as you please, this home is yours too."

"We're happy here, Mum. Please try to understand. I lived away for three years, got used to being my own housewife, and... and..." I took the plunge, "I want Sam to view the house tomorrow afternoon."

Sam had sat silent, and he turned to Mum. "Please don't be upset, Ma. We're more than grateful to you, for heaven's sake, don't feel guilty about the bombing. It happened. It was on the cards." Sam was still speaking. "I haven't seen this house yet. I may not like it. I may not like the area and there'll be much to consider."

"If she says it's a nice place, you'll like it, I know," Mum said, shaking her head dismally. My brother Bill shrugged, Jim said nothing.

Sam worked Saturday mornings and I met him at Liverpool Street at two o'clock. We arrived at the Romford estate agent's. Given the key, the clerk told us, "Take as long as you wish to decide. We're busy at this moment. Catch the number 7 bus at the end of the road. Cranham Road is the first turning along the Brentwood Road, on the right over the narrow railway bridge. It's the last house on the left. Good luck."

We followed his instructions and were soon standing outside the house. It was not a bright day. Sam eyed the privet hedge as we entered.

"I like this wide porchway and the leaded light panels each side of the street door," he said as we stepped inside the wide hall. All the walls were distempered cream. "All the plaster looks in great condition and I think, when this war ends, we could make it look good. We could get some good wallpaper later and paint over all this brown woodwork." We took our time browsing around. In the garden next door we saw an Anderson shelter, buried deep and covered with earth and tree branches.

"I suppose we'll have to apply for one of those," Sam said, grinning.

I thought of Albion Drive, of the lady living next door, losing her children; they had been sleeping in such a shelter and had died.

"You won't get me sleeping in one of those, so forget it."

Back at the agent's, Sam told them we would get a surveyor and we would have to arrange a mortgage. We were told to take our time, not many people were buying houses in wartime.

This sounded a little ominous to me. Sam talked enthusiastically all the way home. "I'm a little worried, Belle, you'll have to do so much running round arranging appointments. I can't get time off during the week, so try for Saturday afternoons for any form-filling."

"You spoke about getting a surveyor. I'll find another estate agent and get their surveyor to do the work. Building societies lend cash, so where do I look for one? In Romford or near where we are now?"

"Romford for sure. Now, first we have to face Ma," he laughed.

Immediately we entered home, Mum began: "I can tell by the look on your faces you both like this house. How far away is it?"

"Gidea Park, and Sam likes it very much."

"Gidea Park! Where's that? I've never heard of it."

"Hornchurch," I replied.

"Christ! You going to meet the bloody enemy? Where's your sense, Sam, going all that way? Couldn't you find something in Surrey?"

"House prices in Surrey are beyond our price range, Ma."

As the words sank in she exploded. "Don't tell me you're thinking of buying? You could lose everything if these bloody rockets explode near the house, then what, your money is lost. Don't do it, Sam. All that way, I'll never see you both. Really get some sense."

"You visit Aunt Minne sometimes. Make it Fridays then come round the shop, my mother will be pleased to see you and Bill can call there and take you home. We'll see you that way and we can visit you here sometimes."

Sam was trying his best to placate her. Suddenly she asked: "What about rations? If you move I think it would be best if we get registered around here. Definitely it'll save a journey. Under the circumstances I don't think your mother will mind."

"If that is what you want to do, Mum, that's OK," I told her.

I travelled back and forth, doing my best to make all appointments for Saturday afternoons to keep Sam in the picture, but had to find a surveyor to see the house myself. With me he eyed the roof. "Belgian tiles, very good," he scribbled on a pad. Opening the side gate, "The walls pebble-dashed all round to the back of the house." He did more scribbling. We walked the length of the garden, looking at the large brick-built shed and peered over the fencing into the back entrance: more scribbling.

Walking back we entered the house. The leaded light panels each side of the street door threw coloured rays into the L-shaped hall, stairs to the right led to three bedrooms. He had a good look round the front room, testing casement windows. He thoroughly scrutinised round the floorboards and followed the same procedure in the large back room. The cupboard under the stairs was in this room. It had been used as a larder; in it were shelves, a small window and a trap flap in the floor. The surveyor pulled at a sunken ring and getting down on his knees lifted the flap and peered down. In the kitchen he eyed the tiled walls, window and sink.

"The walls are sound and in good condition, this cream distemper is nothing to worry about when you decide on your own decor. The house was built in 1934, is very dry, has good air vents and is four feet off the footings. Now for the bedrooms." I was certainly learning house-buying jargon. He did a thorough inspection of the bedrooms, bathroom and toilet. "Well, Mrs Bendon, you have a bargain here. I'll admit the fittings are poor, but for a few shillings these can be changed. Give me your address and I'll send a full report on each room along with my fee."

"We need to borrow cash from a building society, also we need a solicitor. Can you recommend one, someone reliable?"

"We don't recommend. There are three or four of them in Western Road. Choose your own. Western Road is the next road past our office." He drove me back to Romford Station.

I found Western Road and picked the first solicitor I came to and made an appointment for a Saturday afternoon in two weeks' time. I searched the telephone directory for the nearest Co-op building society in Surrey.

Facing an understanding clerk, Sam made the request to borrow £550.

By this time we had received the surveyor's report, which Sam showed the clerk. "We make our own survey, Mr Bendon, and if that is satisfactory cash will be lent to you. How long for repayments had you in mind... fifteen years... twenty?"

We looked at each other. "I think fifteen years," Sam answered.

And so the conveyance went along slowly. Telling Mum we were borrowing £550, she hit the ceiling. "Where's your sense?" she stormed. "It's a rope round your neck for the rest of your lives. Fifteen years! You'll never repay it. What if you're bombed again, you'll lose all."

"Don't put the mockers on us, Ma, please," Sam pleaded.

She turned to me. "Talk to him, how do you propose to repay all this money? You must both be out of your bloody minds." We let her rant on. It was best to keep silent. Finally she began playing and bashed her temper out on the piano.

A letter from the building society agreed to the loan, repayable at the rate of £4 12s 6d monthly. We gave a sigh of relief, it was settled.

On the 4th of April I was helping Mum with the housework. I was dusting in her bedroom when I heard her cry out. I found her in the garden. She said she had stepped on a stone and fallen. She had twisted her ankle badly and in helping her to her feet, the ankle swelled up quickly. I made a cold water compress with wadding and wrapped it tightly round her ankle. The swelling scared me and I suggested a doctor. She dismissed the idea immediately. "It'll be all right tomorrow," she insisted. "Meantime if you can manage, I'll rest for a while." I was a little worried and wondered if she had broken a bone.... The boys were worried too.

On the radio we learned a thousand bomber raids had bombed German cities, Berlin, Essen, Cologne and Krupps, the armaments factory in the industrial Ruhr complex. Frequently came the sound of exploding buzz bombs.

On the 6th of April I answered the door and stared at the telegram boy in his navy blue uniform with red piping. "Munday?" He handed me the pale orange envelope. Munday. Which of my brothers? Slowly I faced Mum. She smiled. "I've been reading the report on your house. Seems solidly built. Have you paid the twenty-seven pound fee?" I held the telegram behind my back. "Yes. I sent the cash registered post last week. This has just...." I handed her the telegram. Slowly she opened it. "Good Lord, no."

Silently she handed the slip of paper to me. I stared in utter disbelief at the four printed words, "HARRY KILLED STOP. MINNE."

"My poor sister," Mum said, "and I can't get to help her."

"I'll go, Mum, and explain to her, I have a black skirt. Will you lend me your black jacket?" Hurriedly I changed and was soon on my way. Arriving at 139 Goldsmith's Row, I was surprised when Aunt Agnes opened the street door. "Auntie!" I exclaimed, "How are you? What a time to meet. How is Aunt Minne taking the terrible news?"

"I've now seen it come home to her," she replied sourly as I followed her up the stairs. Aunt Minne was crying when I entered the room. My cousin George, an arm round her shoulder, was trying to comfort her. She looked up. "Where's your mother?" she demanded roughly.

"She had a fall and twisted her ankle two days ago, it is badly swollen and she cannot wear a shoe. She sends her love and condolences."

"I suppose it's too far for her to make the journey," she snapped.

"I'm speaking the truth, Auntie. May I ask when Harry...."

"It happened on the 4th of April 1944 and he was twenty-four."

"All the fours," Cousin George informed me. "We had a letter from his sergeant."

"Somewhere on the continent, or Africa?" I asked quietly.

"The army was mopping up at Gabes Gap... in Algiers, I think."

We listened in silence as Aunt Minne recalled details of events in Harry's short life. I made tea at intervals; no one wanted to eat. I said my adieus about five o'clock and arrived home to find Mum hobbling about in the kitchen, with the boys' help, getting dinner. I had to state all that had occurred. Sam could not understand Aunt Agnes's bitterness. I had never mentioned Harry's father was Aunt Agnes's husband. Mum came to the rescue, saying there had been a feud between the sisters, it happened a long time ago and should have been forgotten about. They were stubborn.

We heard about the "bouncing bombs" that had cracked the wall of the largest dam in Germany, causing havoc. At last the war appeared to be going our way. At the shop on the next Friday, I asked George if he knew of someone with a small van who would move our bed to Hornchurch. It was pointless to hire a removals van for a bed and a few things. Happily a friend of his could oblige. I had been gradually buying things I would need, a bucket, floor cloths, a scrubbing brush, kettle, teapot and cutlery, a washboard and a few pieces of china. I packed these and after a quick lunch this Saturday afternoon journeyed to Hornchurch and awaited the arrival of our few possessions. In between I had contacted the war damage claims department in Hackney and was promised a cheque would arrive shortly.

We had paid two monthly repayments for the mortgage. Eventually the van was emptied of our gear, Sam gave him five pounds for his trouble and we were left alone together. We hugged each other and I cried. We spent the weekend scrubbing out the rooms, putting up the bed, making tea and cooking our frugal rations. We slept like logs; if buzz bombs exploded we were too tired to hear them. "Next week I'll contact the address for locker fifty-seven to find out what has been salvaged from Albion Street."

"I'm sorry you have to do all this alone, Belle, but I cannot ask for time off, we're working flat out, perhaps the war will end soon. I do hope so. Then we can get cracking together."

Before moving, I had written to friends and relations giving our new address. I raced around for necessities. I applied for an indoor air raid shelter and being asked my husband's earnings, I answered, "I think £5 10s weekly, paying rail fares to work of about £1 18s weekly." I wondered what Sam's wages had to do with wanting a shelter. It was delivered the next week. The deliveryman fixed it together. A thick metal top was erected on three-foot angled iron legs, the sides fitted with thick wire mesh. "Lady, when you get under that to sleep, you hook this mesh here." He pointed to two heavy-looking hooks at the end. I thanked them and they left.

The shelter was three and a half feet wide and six feet long. There was no way our four-and-a-half foot interior-sprung mattress could be used. It would not bend and could not be pressed into the shelter. Sam had an idea. He bought three long sacks and flock. He told me this stuff would be used when he made our three-piece suite. He stuffed the sacks then stitched them together with a fine twine and with sheets and blankets over them we snuggled down together. "Now I know what a wild animal feels like in his cage," Sam said as we crawled into the shelter the first time.

I found locker fifty-seven in a large furniture warehouse near a railway arch in Hackney. I waited a while after answering questions put to me.

"We did the best we could, there was not too much to salvage from the ruins, but sign this form and we'll deliver tomorrow. Be in."

They delivered my piano, the full lid split along its length, my machine, a tea chest and my four kitchen chairs, two with seats split, and a wooden stool. "That stool isn't ours," I said pointing to it.

Then you've got a bit extra," they laughed. Enquiring how much for delivering the furniture, they laughingly said, "No charge." I gave them ten shillings and smiling they wished me luck.

The buzz bombs, V2s, exploded at intervals. The radio told us the air force had bombed Peenamunde and the pads from which the V2s were launched. Towards the end of May, my friend Grace, who had been a bridesmaid at my wedding, asked if she could visit and stay over the weekend.

It would be nice for her and we quickly made arrangements. Her firm, making parachute silk, closed Fridays at three o'clock and I would meet her at Romford Station. Our meeting was arranged for about four o'clock if the train ran on time. I entered the Romford Station hall at roughly fifteen minutes to four. It is not a large hall, at least it wasn't at that time. I found it full of US soldiers all standing around in small groups, some chatting to girls. I sat at one end of a bench. The other end was occupied by a US soldier kissing a girl, he was all over her. A few moments later a soldier touched my arm and said, "You waiting for me, honey?" I shook my head. He sat down close beside me. "Have some gum." He offered a Wrigley's Spearmint packet to me.

"Thank you, I don't chew," I replied. I eyed these soldiers, all chewing, their jaws going up and down, like cows chewing the cud.

"You know, we've come over here to win this little old war for you." The soldier nudged me. "Did you know that?"

I stared at him. "For me?" I asked sarcastically.

"Well you an' a few thousand others."

How brash could they get, I asked myself. I was sure if the Japs hadn't bombed Pearl Harbor, they'd still be sitting on the fence.

I remembered Mother saying they didn't enter World War I until 1917, and then boasted they'd won that war. If this soldier ever made it to France, he would probably boast how they'd won this great big war. He nudged me again, jerking a thumb over his shoulder. "I bet she'll have her legs wide open for him tonight." I gave a cursory glance at the couple at the other end of the bench, he seemed to have six pairs of hands, they were everywhere, and the poor girl was smothered by him.

"Shall I tell you something?" he whispered. I stared at the stairway. Please let the train be on time, I prayed. He continued, "Do you know, you're sitting on a gold mine."

Two seconds. The penny dropped. I clenched my hands to stop myself slapping his face. I would be laughed at by his mates if I made a scene. It was true what was being said about them, they were "over-paid, over-sexed and over here". Why should I walk out into the street? This was my country. A train rumbled into the station overhead. Seconds later a few people descended the stairs. "You heard what I said?" he asked.

"Shall I tell you something?" I whispered conspiratorially. He edged closer, putting an arm round my shoulder. "Years ago, my husband staked a claim on the mine, and he's the only one who's allowed there to dig for gold. Understood?" He scowled, his arm slid from my shoulder.

"Your old man wouldn't miss a slice off a cut loaf."

I swore, in the only language I thought he would understand. "Piss off," I said angrily, staring at him as he stood up.

"You go sod yourself," he snarled and walked over to a group of soldiers. They looked my way and laughed. A train rumbled into the station and seconds later the stairway was filled with more Yankee soldiers.

I spied Grace coming down the stairs speaking to a US soldier. I stood and waved. She came towards me, the soldier in tow.

We kissed. "This is my friend, Belle." She introduced me.

He held a hand towards me, "Hi," he said as I took the limp, damp hand, no grip. "We'll get a car, Grace," I said turning away.

"Hey, ain't yer going ter invite me home fer coffee?" the Yank called after us. "My big husband wouldn't like that," I answered. We crossed the cab rank. "Where did you find him, Grace?"

"He boarded the train at Stratford and chatted me up the rest of the journey. I learned he was married and would divorce his wife when the war ended. I didn't ask why. He just talked and talked."

I related to her the US soldier's chat to me.

"Don't say a word to Sam, he'd be furious." She laughed.

We did a guided tour round my empty house. "At least you have a bed, Belle. What can be done about the piano?" She eyed the damaged lid.

"Sam said he can fix it with some dowelling. It needs the keys removed and cleaning from the dust and rubble; all I hope is I'll be able to play it again. I'll get it re-polished and hope for the best."

In the small kitchen she laughed at the midget cooker. I related to her the running back and forth, getting things done. I had borrowed twenty pounds from Bill with the intention of paying hire purchase for a cooker. In the gas showrooms I saw this reconditioned cooker for eighteen pounds, and asked for delivery now while I was in Romford, pleading the distance from Surrey. I pleaded the same tale to the electricity company, then I asked the estate agent for the water board phone number. They kindly contacted them for me and I roamed around this empty house, cold and hungry awaiting the arrival of these people. First came the water man. The cooker and electricity came together. The cooker was fixed, and all burners lit and the lighting tested I arrived back in Surrey at 7.30, happy with my day's work.

Grace had brought some rations with her and we shared our food and had an enjoyable weekend. Sam insisted he would sleep upstairs in the bed, while we girls shared the shelter. Grace told me she and George were still spending nights together in various shelters. It was better than nothing, spending just three nights a week together. George said he felt a little guilty leaving his mother alone in the house. We could not understand why she was against Grace meeting George. "It was unnatural the way Mum ranted at Bill when he was seeing Sadie, George told me," said Grace. "This is why we meet in secret." Grace finished. We slept. It was a quiet weekend, no raid and no buzz bombs. I showed Grace a letter I had received from Flo. In the summer of 1943 Pat had a quiet wedding and on the 11th of May she had produced a daughter and named her Anne-Marie. "Just a few days before I came here," said Grace smiling. "I think we should send Flo a card, congratulating her on becoming a grandmother."

We both saw Grace safely on her train and there appeared to be more and more US soldiers in Romford.

Chapter Fifty-two

Monday morning, the day after Grace left, the post brought a cheque from the war damage claims department for £360. I was hopping mad. That was the assessment of our nice home, and with that money we had to get a home together from scratch. Whatever would Sam say? He said plenty, with a few swear words to emphasise his feelings. I did as he told me, opening a bank account next day, banking £300 and drawing out £60 cash. I posted registered mail the cash I owed Bill. That done I chose twenty-seven square yards of oilcloth for our living-room at 2s 6d a square yard and it was laid free next day. I had chosen a deep green background with an autumnal design and that pleased Sam. We unpacked the tea chest, stowing china in the cabinet and other odds and ends we discovered. The china, all that was left of our wedding present, was six dinner plates, a tureen and a cup. There was a fancy clock and two tea towels and plenty of bits of plaster. Over the weekend I scrubbed out the airing cupboard and with the immersion heater going it dried quickly.

Next we tackled my machine. So much had been packed into the space that enclosed the treadle. In the drawer I found some hairdressing gear, curling irons, clippers, combs and scissors, and six towels, a table cloth, a large biscuit box containing insurance policies, our marriage certificate and the small tin box I used in which to keep my rings and odds and ends of paste jewellery. Underneath the treadle I pulled out a large envelope; it contained ten proof pictures of our wedding. I burst into tears. "Stop it," said Sam. "You're upsetting me too. We'll get a couple of these framed, just to remind me I have a little wife." He shook me and picking up a Player's cigarette box exclaimed, "And here are my medals!" The medals were dated 1935, still in small cellophane envelopes.

On Saturday afternoon we went to the bank and had our cash put into a joint account. We gave specimen signatures and received a cheque book. We drew out twenty pounds and treated ourselves to some undies. I wrote a letter to Jim asking him to find time to make us a radio set. Fridays I regularly helped at the shop. Mum visited Aunt Minne occasionally and when she did, she always made it Fridays and dropped into the shop. It was always nice to see her. Bill always came to take Mum home at these times.

After Grace left we were having some very quiet nights and into June, Sam suggested we sleep in our bed. This was great. I was awakened one early dawn to heavy droning. I immediately thought about a raid. I looked out of a side bay window. The sky was filled with planes flying high towards the southeast. I watched as they flew into a bright red early dawn sky. Good luck, boys, I murmured as I thought of another thousand bomber raid on Germany, "Red morning, shepherd's warning." I dismissed the thought and watched again from the window. So this was what a thousand-bomber raid looked like. The German people must dread it.

The next day in the papers we read that a bridgehead had been made at a place named Caen in France and our naval guns were pounding enemy strongholds and our troops were making progress on the ground. Was this the opening of the second front? A big battle was being fought in Italy for Monte Casino by British and Canadian forces and the fighting was continuing right up the leg of Italy. It made exciting reading, and sadly of course there were many casualties as the war progressed.

I attended an auction sale in Romford and bought a table and a dumb waiter for six pounds. I didn't know what they were like, not seeing the lot before the bidding began. I heard the man say "table" and we needed one. When it was sent home, I was surprised. It was square and large, with a thick mahogany top with grooved edges and thick bulbous legs and very heavy. The three-shelved dumb waiter was highly polished. When Sam saw what I had bought he grinned saying, "The three-tier bunk will be useful later," and congratulated me on the buy. That evening we sat at the table and ate our meal, instead of off a plate on our knees.

"We are gradually getting there, darling," Sam remarked. "When the war ends, I'll get George to make a decent bedroom suite for us and then we can slowly get a home that you'll be proud of. This weekend I'll tackle that piano lid for you, and then we can find a polisher. Will that make you happy?" Thankfully I hugged him. Next day I took all the notes from the piano and thoroughly cleaned them, brushing as much of the dirt from the felts, now wishing I hadn't given Mum my small Goblin vac.

Now my machine was cleaned I was able to stitch the blackout curtaining together firmly. We prowled Romford market Saturday afternoons for any bargains. Sam was looking for material ready for when the war ended to make a three-piece suite. Now I had curling irons, I mentioned to the lady next door (a Mrs Campbell, a Scot) that I was a hairdresser and did she know anyone who would like a home visit? At this moment, no, but she would ask her friends. The word soon spread and I became fairly busy. Then I was taking bus rides to the various clients and by the time I'd totted up my earnings and deducted bus fares I was almost out of pocket.

I applied at a saloon for a weekend post. The proprietor told me the lady he had, had worked for him a number of years, and at the present time business was not too good, probably owing to the war.

I continued going to the shop and took the many nearest clients I had made. Having no drier, I could do only waving and cutting.

Sam drilled small holes in the piano lid and dowled it together. He mixed a little brown paint with wood filler to smooth into the splintered crack and two days later gently sandpapered off any roughness. He did a great job and we began trying to find a piano polisher.

The bombing had eased since we made landings in France and we were now sleeping in our bed upstairs. We were making slow progress in France, but the enemy was being pushed back. Getting supplies to the Russian port of Murmansk caused heavy losses in the icy Arctic seas. Once a month, I made the journey to Surrey.

I took care of Mum's hair and three neighbours there. I sent a letter to Mum to warn the neighbours of my arrival to wash their hair. It more than paid my fare and I learned my family were keeping well and the boys were busy working on naval components.

With the Yanks came nylon stockings and rock 'n' roll.

Rocket raids stepped up in August and we were back sleeping under our metal shelter. We were roused one night to a loud explosion, the ceiling plaster clattered down on the top of our shelter. The din was awful. "Bloody hell! Not again!" Sam held me protectively close, as he spoke. "Have you written to Hitler giving him this address?" I laughed then choked from dust rising from the falling plaster. Three times I cussed, as every ceiling was damaged. Strangely enough this time the piano escaped falling plaster, but was covered in thick dust. We surveyed our ruined ceilings, Sam swearing like a trooper.

Broken glass from blasted windows was everywhere. We learned the houses opposite to ours had very long gardens and at the end of these gardens ran the Upminster to Romford railway and a buzz bomb had exploded in the field beyond. Mrs Campbell had taken her two girls to relatives in Scotland and stayed there with them. Mr Campbell had slept through the explosion. I called to him through their broken French windows. It was some time before he answered, but he was fine, he told me.

"Now you have to do more running around, Belle, just when I thought we were getting settled. Maybe I'll stay home to be with you."

"Go to work, Sam. I'll find out what's what, then maybe I'll need your help. Meantime, I'll do what I can." Reluctantly he left for work.

From the post office, I was directed to the Town Hall. There I waited until called. There were four tables in the room, each with an attendant questioner. I sat facing a middle-aged man. His brusque manner put my back up immediately. "Name and address" he said sharply.

I answered politely. "What are you asking for?" he enquired.

Briefly I explained the situation, my needs… electric light bulbs, windows, ceilings repaired and blackout curtaining. He stared at me.

"You're not the only one, you know."

"I fully realise that and this is our third case of damage from bombing, maybe we're unlucky." I smiled.

"I should count *myself* lucky to come through that unscathed."

"Unscathed? You don't know the half of it. We're Londoners."

He sniffed. "Well, what do you need?" He began writing as I spoke. "Eight light bulbs." He wrote quickly. "That's twelve shillings."

"Tell me," I said sharply, "where in Romford can I buy bulbs for 1s 6d?"

"Wear and tear," he snapped.

"Wear and tear? Wear and tear?" I raised my voice. "We moved into this house in April, and owing to having to blackout have had lights in just two rooms. Wear and tear? You must be joking." I was furious. "I want the full price of those bulbs, I've been before your sort before." I stood up, bending towards him. "Do you know, the war damage people sent a cheque for £360 for our lovely home. If we'd known what we know now, we would have had veneered kipper boxes instead of veneered mahogany, I assure you."

"Calm down, Mrs Bendon, you're upsetting yourself."

"Don't patronise me, just be fair."

"About clothes, any damage to those?"

"We're using the cupboard under the stairs as a wardrobe at the moment. As I have said, we moved in at the end of April."

"This £360 cheque you've received?"

"Three hundred is banked and there's a standing order for the bank to repay the monthly mortgage. Sixty pounds has been used to buy a cooker, kitchen utensils, china and cutlery and the blackout curtaining. There isn't much left." He was busy writing as I spoke. "The curtaining was ripped by shattered glass… that's also wear and tear, I suppose?"

"How many yards of blackout material are you requesting?"

"Sixteen. That did two rooms and that was 2s 6d a yard. You probably know the price of that." As he stood up, he smiled. "Oh yes, I forgot. Our bed quilt is quite a mess, full of holes… glass doing the damage."

He sat down. "How much are bed quilts?"

"The price here for those, I have no idea, sorry."

He glanced down at his notes. "I'll make you an immediate relief allowance of £3 15s 6d. Do the best you can with it. If you go to the office along the corridor, you'll receive the money."

I thanked him and in the next office duly signed for the amount.

In the departmental store, I bought the curtaining and a quilt for 19s 11d and the electric light bulbs. The two pence change I had paid my fare home. There were many elderly men working in the road replacing broken windows and by four o'clock three men arrived and about three hours later all our broken windows had been replaced. It was not perfectly clear glass, very slightly misted, and I was told the proper glass would be replaced when the war ended. At least we were draught-proof. I machined the curtains and Sam fixed them when he came in from work.

It was some time in mid-July that there had been a plot to kill Hitler, but had failed. An allied airman on patrol had machine-gunned a fast-moving car on a French road. We learned later, reading the papers, that this car was carrying Field Marshall Rommel and some aides; they were all killed. I'm sure Churchill gave a whoop of joy. Rommel had had many victories over the allied forces in the desert.

One day I decided I would try my fingers with a few chromatic scales on the piano. It sounded dim and a little tinny. I removed the front panel; the felts round the hammers were in a dreadful condition. During the two and a half years it had been stored the moths had had a field day… several field days. Some of the felts were completely eaten away. It would be a costly repair job, and then it would need tuning.

Counting the savings from my hairdressing rounds came to £8 9s.

I continued travelling to the shop to help on Friday and three weeks later entered a large furniture shop on the corner of Victoria Road near Romford Station. I explained my needs to an assistant. He called a workman from the back of the shop. On inspecting the damage he said he could do a good job for six pounds. I was delighted and told him to go ahead.

He came next day and worked really hard. Finishing his work, he told me not to play and wait two days for the glue to dry thoroughly.

I asked if he knew a good tuner, he scribbled an address and told me to phone the number. I thanked him and at the shop the next Friday, made an appointment. A week later the tuner came. He was great. I heard him testing note after note and when he was finished he rattled off some of Grieg's composition of Ibsen's *Peer Gynt.* He sat with eyes closed, head back, lost in a world of his own. It sounded marvellous. He charged me five pounds. I gave him a tip and he thanked me profusely.

About this time we read in the papers that the enemy had broken through our lines in the Ardennes and heavy fighting was causing heavy casualties on both sides. To help, hundreds of allied soldiers were parachuted into Arnhem, a town in Holland, with the idea of attacking the enemy from the rear. We were betrayed by a Dutch collaborator and our soldiers were shot to pieces as they floated to the ground, and the battle of the Bulge raged on. Meanwhile, a team of four men came to repair our ceilings. Believe me, I was amazed when they began knocking down plaster right to the edge of all walls. When I protested, they told me they were going to fix plasterboards to rafters and this needed to be squared off.

I folded the old torn quilt over the piano; it was kept in place by lumps of plaster. The plasterboards were roughly eight feet by four feet and the joins were covered with thin strips of bandage. Finishing the large living-room, I was told, "We'll be here tomorrow at eight a.m."

Early September we had a letter from Jim. He had a small radio set ready and would bring it along with a surprise at the weekend. I could hardly wait. I made a seed cake as he wrote it would be Sunday after lunch. I heard Sam laugh when he opened the door. In walked Mum and Bill, I was so pleased to see them. "Go outside and have a look," said Bill, and there were Jim and Sam admiring a red car. It was second-hand, Jim told me, had had just one owner previously and had been well maintained.

After purchase, Jim had stripped down the engine and here they were and he was delighted with the result. The radio set, in a neat green plastic case, was duly fixed up and we spent a pleasant few hours together.

As Christmas and the winter drew near, Mum had small grumbles about our ceilings. I cannot repeat what she said when first she saw the damage. She really went to town. It was decided we would spend Christmas with her in Surrey and that made her feel better. We had a very happy Christmas. Elsie Dummit had brought three small chickens from the farm where she did war work and came with her sister Nell, her husband Jack and their son and his girlfriend. We asked our neighbours Bart, her husband Maurice and little son Peter, to tea. We were happy together. How we slept didn't matter… on the floor, covered with coats, in armchairs, it was all part of Christmas.

Chapter Fifty-three

In the January sales of 1945, Sam and I went hunting for a kitchen cabinet. Sam saw a red and yellow metal cabinet he liked. As our kitchen walls (or the upper half) were painted yellow, he thought it ideal. It was six feet high and four feet wide. The top half consisted of three deep shelves covered by two doors. Below this was a worktop over two drawers, and beneath the drawers were shelves for pots and pans and other kitchen gear. It was marked down to £3 15s and delivery was free. We were very pleased with our bargain. It would fit the space as one entered and as time went by it proved a very useful buy.

Everyone was praying for the war to end. It would be the end of rationing. People had barely enough to eat, but strangely enough the population stayed fairly healthy. Without exception we all tried to get extra, buying on the black market.

We listened intently each evening to the BBC nine o'clock news. The Russians were swiftly advancing to Berlin and it was said were taking no prisoners. They had been driven to the gates of Stalingrad, from that point the German armies had retreated, the terrible Russian winter adding to the victories. Hitler had retreated to his bunker, still raving orders, it was said, of "no surrender". We listened to comic programmes, to the current singers of the latest songs. Life went on, everyone hoped the carnage would soon cease. The weather was no help to our fighting men, but having the enemy retreating cheered them.

Mrs Bendon and Babs were still travelling from Totteridge to the shop, though George was opening the shop early and Edie, his wife, served early customers. Mrs Bendon was a sucker for hard-luck stories. One Friday, a pleasant lady came into the shop asking to see Mrs Bendon. As Edie, Babs and myself were all in the shop, all married to the Bendon boys, we wanted to know which one of us she wanted. She said the elderly lady.

Mrs Bendon was having her usual afternoon nap. Babs woke her.

The woman greeted her, saying, "I hope you can help me. I've just returned from evacuation with my three children, so until I can get rations for them could you please let me have some rations for them?"

Edie asked, "Where are your ration books, surely you have them with you? We cannot serve you without them, you know that."

"It's just until I get unpacked. I'll bring the books later."

"We'll get your rations ready, you go and get your books," I said.

"That's all right," Mrs Bendon said, "you can't deny children. What do you need for them?" So, over the counter went a week's ration of sugar, tea, margarine, bacon and cheese. Bread at that time was not on ration. The woman was profuse with her thanks. None of us knew this person, neither did Mrs Bendon. "Well, she knew my name," Mother said.

An hour later, the woman returned with a man. We thought she'd returned with her ration books, but no, the gentleman was from the Food Office. The woman laid the rations on the counter. There was quite an argument and for the sake of 6s 8d, Mrs Bendon was fined twenty-six pounds. A colossal sum in those days, and a black mark was placed against her name at the Bethnal Green Food Office. Poor Mum!

In the meantime we had bought a few things for our home. We bought yards of curtaining, which I machined to fit our windows. Slowly we began to look civilised. Sam's sister Emily paid us a visit and although we were now sleeping upstairs in our bed, Emily grinned when she saw our Morrison shelter. Emily was a big lady, tall, weighing about sixteen stone and her husband matched her in height and weight. She laughed, "Can you imagine me and Arthur having fun and games under there?"

Whoever came to visit brought some rations too. It became the thing to do and no one was offended.

Spring followed a long winter and although we did not know it, the war was nearing its end. On the 8th of May 1945 the German army surrendered and peace in Europe was declared, but, in the Far East, Japanese armies were still waging war. The stories of the torturing of prisoners and the inhuman treatment of men building the Burma railway were beyond belief. At the cinema films of men looking like living skeletons were shown of those freed from concentration camps, the skin of their bodies hanging in folds. There were stories of many Jewish people gassed in huge chambers. It was appalling, the sadism and torture that went on year after year.

After the war ended some German scientists went to the USA, some to Russia, their knowledge later helping in the space race.

On the evening of the 8th of May Sam and I went to Piccadilly Circus to see the lights switched on. Crowds thronged the pavements and the roaring cheers that greeted the burst of light could be heard for miles.

We were swept along with the cheering crowds; sometimes it was a little frightening. If someone should stumble, others would fall too, and I thought of the Bethnal Green tube disaster and decided to get into Haymarket, where I thought it would be less crowded. It took time but finally we made it, the time now a quarter past two a.m. We sat for a while in a shop doorway, happy but tired. It was long past our bedtime.

"What about your work tomorrow, Sam?"

"Work?" he laughed. "I'm not working tomorrow, no fear. I'll be celebrating like the rest of the people. First we have to get home, and the tube doesn't begin running until around four o'clock, so let's begin walking, that way we'll stay awake." He pulled me to my feet.

We walked for an hour. A large lorry stopped beside us. "Am I going right for Hackney?" the driver enquired.

"Give us a lift and we'll show you the way," Sam replied.

He wanted King Edward's Road. We asked him to drop us at Bethnal Green tube station, which he did, and we pointed out the right way for him, then caught the tube train to Stratford where we waited for a train to Gidea Park. We arrived home at nearly five o'clock.

"I think I'll have a quick bath, Sam. I feel dirty."

"Me too," he said. We were asked by the water board not to use more than five inches of water for a bath and I sometimes thought Sam used more, as he always moaned it wasn't enough to warm up the bath.

"I think if you use your five inches and I use my five inches and if we bath together the water will rise a little," Sam grinned at me. "How about it?"

"I'm too tired for fun and games."

"So am I. I'm out on my feet." So without more argument, we hopped into the bath together and after fell into bed. We woke next day at eleven o'clock to brilliant sunshine, and to find our road decorated with bunting of every description. The war had ended, rationing would soon end, and we could live without fear of bombs or rockets.

"We'll go to see Mum at the weekend, you'll like that."

"That's great, Sam. We'll take some rations."

I went to the shop on Friday as usual, but called first to see Aunt Minne. I found her in a good mood. We both said Fred would soon be demobbed and she would be happy. She mentioned Harry, "He was so young." I told her we were going to see Mum that weekend and would she come along? She answered we would probably be rejoicing, but she would be sad, so, no.

Leaving Auntie's I met a Mr Middleton who was a regular at the pub when we were small. After chatting for a while he said, "Did you know your father has left The Baker's Arms pub?"

"You amaze me, I didn't think he'd ever leave that gold mine."

"He had a very bad stroke. He can't speak properly and is in a wheelchair. Happened some time last year. I think he now lives somewhere near the coast. Clifford is living in the house in Epping with his wife.

I enquired after his family then said cheerio and made my way to the shop. What would Mum say to this news?

We arrived in Surrey early Saturday and although Mum and my brothers were pleased to see us, they said they were disappointed we did not celebrate the war ending with them. We described the events and the crowds in Piccadilly Circus and I then related the news Mr Middleton had given me. "I still cannot credit it, Mum."

"God pays debts without money," she said quietly. "Maybe he'll have time to reflect on his treatment of you kids."

"I never even knew him, so…" Bill shrugged.

"You're a free woman now, Mum, and the war has ended, let's be cheerful," I said.

Sam put an arm round her. "Smile, Ma, you came up trumps."

While chatting I mentioned next Friday would be my last day at the shop. George and his wife Edie were taking over the running of the shop; Mrs Bendon had had enough and would continue to live with Babs.

I told Mum to get registered for rations locally, that would save journeys to the shop, she agreed.

Chapter Fifty-four

Meanwhile the war in the Far East continued unabated. The Japs refused to surrender. As nylon stockings came onto the market, a shop in Romford Arcade offered to mend ladders in stockings at sixpence an inch, thus saving precious clothing coupons. A girl sitting in the window worked under an angle-poise lamp and with a very fine hook picked up the loops. I had a two-inch ladder repaired for a shilling and it was quite invisible. That shop did a roaring trade in repairs.

Through an advert in the Romford paper I found a piano polisher.

"I'll strip it down, make a good job and it will take three days and my fee will be six pounds. I'll come at ten a.m. and leave at five. I'll bring a Thermos, not to worry about making me tea." I agreed.

He did a marvellous job; I was delighted, my piano looked new. Any spare moment I had I played scales and it sounded great.

Early in August an atomic bomb was dropped on Hiroshima. The Japanese town was in ruins and casualties were enormous. Still the Japs continued the war. A few days later a second atomic bomb was dropped on Nagasaki, with the same devastating results. Only then did the Japanese emperor sign the Articles of Surrender and ended the war in the Far East.

As hundreds of soldiers were demobbed, rationing became more stringent. When Mum visited Aunt Minne she was told

Fred would be home early in 1946. In asking if Aunt would have a welcome-home party, she asked what for if Harry would not be there with her.

Sam saw an advert for an upholsterer and landed a job at Harrison and Gibson's, a furniture shop in Ilford. There he met George Culmer and they became firm friends.

Three elderly workmen came to repair the plasterwork to damaged walls and ceilings, their work was first class and we were pleased with the result. "Now we can get on with some redecoration," Sam said. "I'll get some pebble-type paper to line the ceilings, that will hide the joins in the plaster boards and all the brown varnish we will paint white. It'll take time, but that doesn't matter. It'll take cash too."

Two nights later I had a bad nightmare. They had occurred at intervals through the years since we were buried beneath the house. I woke, perspiring and crying, Sam's arms were round me, he was saying, "Stop struggling, what's the matter with you?"

"It's these nightmares, Sam, they're terrible."

"Let's go down and make some tea, then tell me about it."

Still sobbing, I followed him, and then we sat talking over the teacups. I told him all, right from my childhood, then in the ruins of the house in Albion Drive they had returned.

"I too have bad dreams at times, Belle. My dream is when I heard you stop screaming when we were bombed. I thought you were dead. That is when I wake; I always feel your heart to make sure you're alive. Whenever we have these bad dreams we must talk them through together, that way we'll slowly forget them. Promise me?" I nodded and we returned to our bed.

This we did and as the years passed, so did the nightmares.

With the pinky apple blossom patterned paper on the bedroom walls and a light wood-block pattern on the floor, we awaited the arrival of the bedroom suite. In May 1946 it arrived and at last I felt we were getting our home together. We used gallons of undercoat and gallons of high gloss white paint, covering the drab brown varnish.

"Now maybe we can start a family, Sam. How about it?"

He didn't answer, so I repeated the question.

"Let's sit down and talk about that. You won't like what I have to say, I know, so listen to me." He began very quietly. "When I was about thirteen, I had a very bad attack of mumps and was later told I may be sterile, so, had I told you this, would you still have married me?"

I sat quiet, a little stunned I think.

"There, I knew, that's why I never mentioned this to you."

"I would, Sam, truly I would, I love you, so forget about your mumps, we can adopt. We can give an orphan a good home and love."

"Not bloody likely, you never know from what background it came from, how it would grow up."

"Well, you can never tell how your own kids will grow up."

"I'd make sure my kids would grow up good citizens, don't you remember how your mother corrected you and your brothers? Spare the rod and spoil the child, that saying is a rule to live by, Belle."

I was disappointed, I talked round adoption, but he was adamant. I hoped a miracle might happen, but as time went by, I devoted my life to him, trying to make up for his disappointment and my own.

Babs gave a party when Joe was demobbed towards the end of 1946. All the family turned up, Babs's family too, we all spared something from our rations and all had a happy time.

In mid-December snow fell heavily, it was bitterly cold and as it continued I wrote to Mum telling her we would stay home for Christmas as the weather was so bad. With difficulty we journeyed to Surrey to spend New Year with Mum, the snow there wasn't quite so deep. Jim introduced us to his "Spider", a dark-haired, bright eyed girl. She mixed in well and helped make things ready, then helped with the dishes.

Jim said they had thought about getting engaged in the summer and would try to find somewhere to live, then would marry, but with so many soldiers still being demobbed finding somewhere suitable may be difficult.

For Christmas we had treated ourselves to a light oak dining suite. Made by Beautility to government standards, over the years it has darkened to a pale golden oak and has stood the test of time. It cost £48 10s.

The snow continued throughout January and down side roads was almost six inches deep. As householders swept pavements mounds of snow appeared in gutters and froze, which took time to melt away.

As the winter passed, Sam suggested getting a form from the post office to apply for a telephone. We were all living far apart and a phone would keep us in touch. The form, duly filled in and signed, was sent and a month later we were fixed up with a phone. Our number was Hornchurch 3963, so much easier to remember than the eleven numbers we have to dial today. We were told not to make outside calls until we were notified. When informed we went raving mad, phoning everyone we knew... you know how it is with a new toy. The quarterly rental was fifteen shillings and calls cost a penny. I don't remember being charged for distance at the time, and when the phone rang we both rushed to answer it.

Jim and Myrtle were busy flat hunting in their spare time.

Bill suggested to Mum that if he had the small room downstairs for his bedroom, perhaps the furniture could be rearranged for Mum's bed in the front room upstairs, then Jim could have the two large rooms and annex upstairs.

As far as I could gather from letters Mum sent and phone calls from Jim, much talk and suggestions had taken place. Myrtle wanted her own cooker and as the house was all-electric, Jim fixed cabling from the annex through the floorboards and ceiling to the meter under the stairs. It all took time, but slowly the annex was turned into a small kitchen.

Gradually Jim and Myrtle assembled quite a nice home together and began making arrangements to marry. I agreed to make the dresses and tammy-type hats and agreed to be a matron of honour with Myrtle's sister Olive: 1947 was passing.

In the autumn of 1947, India had been granted independence, and a few months into 1948 various factions were at loggerheads, causing trouble, and Ghandi appealed for calm and prayer.

Chapter Fifty-five

I think it was towards the end of March, Sam complained of pain. When I asked where, he told me he was passing blood in his urine. I phoned the doctor and Sam's mum. The doctor's verdict was hospital at once.

"Please, Doctor, what is wrong?"

"Epidermitis," he replied shortly. "And he's very ill, you should have called me earlier."

I tried to explain, Sam had only mentioned being in pain that morning, but the doctor was phoning for an ambulance. Mrs Bendon arrived as the doctor was leaving. I explained to her what was happening.

"He's my baby, Doctor," she said. "He is going to be all right?"

"He's been standing around in the cold weather and has caught a thorough chill to his kidneys and bladder. He'll be in hospital for some time, I'm afraid." He left. When the ambulance arrived I went with Sam. He was admitted to a ward in F Block in Oldchurch Hospital, Romford, and was there for seven weeks.

Mrs Bendon stayed with me for two weeks and we visited Sam each evening. He told us he was having hot kaolin poultices placed on his naughty bits twice a day plus penicillin injections. His mother said jokingly, "I bet that makes your eyes water, Sam."

"It's not that bloody funny, Mum," he snapped. "And that nurse isn't too gentle when it comes to putting on the poultice."

Mrs Bendon left. I had already written to Mum, she came and saw Sam in hospital, and she thought he looked drawn. He certainly looked very ill and I longed to have him home. I went with Mum to Liverpool Street Station and saw her safely on the train. Waiting for a bus, I met my old neighbour, Mrs Painter, and her daughter Dora. I was amazed to see Dora on crutches. We were pleased to meet again. I enquired if Dora's injury was due to bombing. Dora said she had slipped down a kerb one wet night and badly grazed her ankle bone, and the doctor had given her various creams but the wound didn't heal and became ulcerated, so much the hospital had advised amputation below the knee, and now Dora was waiting to be fitted with an artificial limb. "And this is my little girl."

I turned to the pretty child. "Hello, darling, what's your name?" I asked

"Kitty Painter," she replied smiling. I congratulated Dora and we said cheerio.

I thought over all that had been said. What had Sissie told me about the fortune-teller…?

Mr Painter would have an accident away from home… that had happened. There would be an addition to the family and someone would walk on three legs… Dora, minus a leg on crutches… and Dora's little girl…? I really do believe there are a few rare people who can foresee the future and this Pollyanna person was one of them.

I was pleased to have Sam home. He was very weak and was told to do no heavy lifting on a full bladder and had to wear a surgical support. The one supplied by the hospital was a small bag on a wide tape… not much support really. In a surgical supplier's we bought two Y-shaped fronts on a three-inch-wide elastic band, which Sam said was very comfortable. He wore these supports for almost three years.

In July 1948, I went to see my cousin Fred Munday's wife, Doris. She told me Father had died recently. Sam picked me up at her house in Buckhurst Hill that evening and we made a great fuss of the new baby, Bobby.

I wrote Mum a letter telling her the news, saying I would try to get a copy of Father's will and death certificate. Next day she phoned, telling me not to bother, as she wasn't interested.

"You're a free woman now, Mum, and we're shot of him."

"I've been a free woman for years, Belle," she laughed.

By trial and effort, I got a copy of the will and when I read the death certificate I saw the words, "present at death, Mrs Munday"! I saw red. I dashed over to Surrey telling Mum that the woman could be prosecuted. Mum and I saw a solicitor in Romford, who said, "This will has been drawn up by a very astute businessman, and to contest it would be throwing good money after bad, and let's face it, you've shown yourself to be independent of him for years." He smiled at Mum and she grinned as if she'd been given an accolade.

I went to Buckhurst Hill asking Doris Munday if she knew the address of this Mary Bransgrove (Father's woman). All she knew was the son's address. So off I went to Hill Top, Epping. The door, numbered 19, was opened by a heavily pregnant young woman. Saying who I was, I demanded to know where Miss Bransgrove lived. All I could get out of her was that the woman was down at the coast. I told her to get the death certificate altered as my mother, Mrs Munday, was thinking of going to court.

Two evenings later, I opened the door to a young man who informed me he was Clifford Munday. As Sam was out I asked a neighbour in. If anything came of this visit it would be his word against mine so I needed a witness. He began in a blustering manner.

"Who do you think you are, coming to my house and upsetting my wife? And my mother can call herself whatever she likes."

"I didn't bawl or shout at your wife, I was positively ladylike."

"She's ten months pregnant and is very upset."

"Then she'd misquoted her dates," I smiled "Or maybe she'll be entered in the *Guinness Book of Records*… longest pregnancy."

"You trying to be funny?"

"No, it comes naturally… Munday humour."

"You'll never get your hands on the coaches," he yelled suddenly.

"Stuff the coaches. What would I want with them?" I opened the street door. "On your way, Bransgrove, and don't come here again."

He marched out. "Mr Munday to you," he answered furiously.

"And please shut the gate," I called after his retreating back.

Mrs Field, my neighbour, said, "He looks a nasty piece of work, I should be careful if I were you." I thanked her, saying goodnight and when Sam came in later I decided to say nothing about the visit.

In June of 1949, Joe and Sam decided they would take a holiday. Joe decided Cornwall would be a grand place to visit. We sent away for brochures and picked a hotel in Falmouth. Writing away for a reservation, we were informed there were two double rooms vacant for that period in the annex. Twelve pounds per person for the week and please bring ration books. We duly accepted and sent off the initial deposit.

We stayed the night with Babs, Totteridge tube station being at the top of their road, and caught the first train to Paddington Station, then the ten past five train from Paddington to Truro. We had catnaps on the train and had sandwiches we brought with us for the long journey. We arrived at Truro and learned we had an hour's wait. It was then just after one o'clock. We bought tea and ate a sandwich then had a freshen-up in the waiting room. Our train duly arrived and we were deposited by taxi outside the hotel at 4.15 all ready for tea.

The register duly signed we were shown to the annex. Amazingly we followed the hotel porter out of the hotel to a private house roughly 200 yards along the road. He opened the door and we followed him upstairs. Our rooms were bright and clean. The porter pointed out the bathroom, saying, "Dinner is served at the hotel at 6.30 sharp, if you need anything, come along." He left.

Joe said they would have the room overlooking the road, so Sam and I had the back room. Wearily I sat on the bed, only to jump up quickly to the sound of squeaks. "Good heavens, mice!" I exclaimed.

Sam laughed. "I think it's a straw-filled mattress."

We went into Joe's room complaining and we sat waiting for some tea; none came. Eventually we found a nearby café. Over tea we discussed the situation. "I didn't think an annex could be 200 yards away from the hotel, should we complain?" asked Babs.

Had we known then what is known now, maybe we could have claimed compensation for misrepresentation. Dinner that evening was, I think, cottage pie. A thin two-inch square of pastry covered some minced beef, carrots and mashed potatoes, followed by a peach half and some thin custard, and a cup of coffee with a biscuit. Needless to say we were none too pleased. "We won't put on weight on that fare," Joe said moodily.

"Maybe it's the end of the week and it's a cook-up," said Babs.

I remembered that first meal, all the rest are hazy, but breakfast always came up with one slice of bread, a streaky rasher with beans, fried tomatoes or dried egg scrambled. All right, rationing was stringent, but I'm sure there could have been a little extra for the men.

We travelled all day the following Sunday arriving home at midnight and so pleased to be home. Falmouth... never again!

Now we were all set for Jim's wedding. The pink taffeta dresses I made looked great and I had trimmed the tammy hats with pink artificial roses to match the bouquets Olive and I carried. Albert Remon's little son was the page boy. The reception was held in a pub at Earlsfield, who put on a swell buffet and never asked for ration books.

Before the wedding, Jim had taken Myrtle to see Aunt Minne and insisted that he wanted Aunt Agnes to be at the wedding. "She missed Belle's wedding because you were there, so if you, George and Fred, come along, I want no upset on my day." Jim said Auntie made no comment. He journeyed on to Aunt Agnes's, insisting she was invited with Mum's offer for her to stay for a while after the wedding and she accepted. Jim never told Myrtle the cause of the enmity between the sisters.

I was pleased to see Aunt Agnes looking so happy and told her so. "I'm having the time of my life," she answered. "I've never been to a party like this in my whole life. It's great."

Chapter Fifty-six

Mid-summer, 1949, Sam complained of raging earache. His doctor prescribed drops. While dripping drops into his ear, he said the doctor mentioned a surgeon at King's College Hospital, Denmark Hill, was having some success operating to help defective hearing and would Sam care to see this surgeon? We discussed this idea at length. Sam got a letter from the doctor who made an appointment. Explaining to his boss, Sam went off the next week to see a Mr Dagget at King's College. The appointment was for 11.30; he refused my company. The day seemed endless to me. Sam arrived home about 4.30. His first words were, "All I've had all day is a sandwich and a cup of tea. What's for dinner?"

Over dinner I heard that the cause of Sam's hearing loss was a large bone formation. Bone it seems was pressing on the stapes that vibrate to sound, but all the surgeon promised was a fifty-fifty chance of complete success.

The operation entailed making a deep incision behind the ear, then drilling a hole in a bone down to the mastoid area then packing the hole with skin to stop the bone knitting together. Mr Dagget told Sam to go home and think about it for a week before making any decision. So we talked and talked. I would not persuade him either way. This was a thing he had to decide for himself. I felt that if I said "Go for it" and it went wrong, I would never forgive myself, neither would he. I put up with his moodiness, trying to understand his feelings. Finally he said, "Belle, I feel I ought to take this offer, if I don't, I think when I'm an old man and maybe completely deaf, I will have missed a good opportunity for a better sense of hearing. What do you think?"

"Whatever you decide, I'll agree to.... Best of British."

A week later, the operation was performed at Horley Mental Hospital, Surrey. I went to stay with Mum and gave my friend's phone number in the event of a crisis, which I hoped would not come.

Bart came at 7.30. The hospital told her the operation had been successful and I was allowed to visit. Bart came with me, leaving her husband, Maurice, to take care of their little son. Walking through the darkened corridors was an eerie experience. An orderly took us to a dimly lit room, where we were unprepared for the sight of Sam, head bandaged twice the size, lolling back without pillows and a young nurse sitting beside him. "He's in a strait jacket!" I exclaimed, shocked.

"Please go along to the end of this corridor and you'll see a doctor, who'll give you details," replied the nurse.

"Why is my husband in a strait jacket?" I demanded as soon as I saw the doctor. "This has upset me."

"Please try to understand, Mrs Bendon, with these major head operations, we never can tell how the patient will rally from the anaesthetic. Mr Bendon is a big man, his nurse could not cope if he became violent."

There was a lot in what he said and I felt a little scared.

"You can bring clothes and his toiletries next time you visit, we get patients on their feet as quickly as possible after head ops."

We sat in the room talking quietly for almost half an hour, but there was no movement from Sam. "Do you know, Nurse, how long the operation took, he shows no sign of returning to consciousness?"

"These fenestration ops usually take about seven hours. I think now he may be sleeping." She felt the pulse in his throat, while looking at her watch. "His pulse is regular." We thanked her and left.

The following Sunday, Sam's cousins turned up to visit and with Mum, my brothers and Myrtle there was quite a crowd, but we walked round speaking to other patients so as not to draw attention to the many visitors Sam had. He walked a little sideways and when I mentioned this, he grinned, "You should have been here to see me when I first stood up." He could not hear us speaking with the thick bandaging, he was as usual lip reading, a skill I am happy to say he never lost. He stayed in hospital for three weeks and at home for some four or five months and his hearing was good. However it slowly deteriorated and going for check-ups at the hospital, he was finally given a small pocket attached to a thin cable leading to a mould in his ear powered by a small battery and he was in business and happy.

I made small pockets for his shirts for the microphone when he was at home. He said he was glad all went fairly well.

A few weeks later, Bill paid a surprise visit. He had found a record of Caruso and one of Gigli on a stall in Romford market. "I'll make a few bob on these when I've cleaned them. The BBC are very interested in Italian tenors," he grinned.

"How have you been keeping yourself, Bill?" I asked.

He sat quiet for a while, then, "I've met a very nice lady. She was in a music shop buying a record and I suggested she buy the HMV records, which I thought were better. For two years she's been a widow and has a four-year-old girl, Hetty. The child is quiet and well mannered and the lady's name is Connie. She's very interested in records and music. We first got talking outside the music shop, I asked her to have a coffee and it went on from there. You would like her, I know."

"So what are you going to do?"

"That's the point. With you and Jim married, I feel I ought to help Mum more. At the moment I feel a little trapped."

"Why not talk it over with Mum, test the water?" I suggested.

"I think I'll wait a while, discover Jim's plans."

"We all know they're saving, hoping to buy something, so...."

Sam came in; he'd been out buying some hessian and was pleased to see Bill. They chatted while I made more tea and Bill stayed to play some chess, a game for which they were both enthusiastic.

In 1952 people learned that King George VI was ill and later died. His daughter Elizabeth, away on holiday in Africa, returned home. After the funeral, preparations went on for her coronation, and 1952 was a busy year. There were rumours of spies and double agents. In June it was Mum's seventieth birthday and we decided she should have a slap-up party. For weeks we saved what we could of our rations and on the 4th of June the relatives and friends descended on Lawrence Avenue, and Mum also believed in inviting the nearest neighbours. She said then they couldn't complain about noise, so a great time was had by all.

Saturday the 6th of December dawned as just another day. There was a slight haze and it was bitterly cold. After shopping I was glad to be home in the warm. At ten o'clock at night the phone rang, and it was Jim, asking was Bill at our place. I was amazed.

"It was foggy here when he left at two o'clock to meet some chap at the BBC. He said he'd be home about seven. I'm phoning from Bart's and here the fog is really black. Do you know, it took me minutes to grope my way to Bart's and that's just four houses along the pavement, so as you can guess we're worried sick."

"Have trains and buses stopped running?" I asked.

"They stopped running about three o'clock," Jim replied.

"He could get to South Wimbledon by tube, Jim... maybe he's walking from there. He could find his way by street lamps."

"You just cannot see the street lighting, it's that black."

"Do you think you could let us know when he arrives home? I'm sure Bart won't mind you phoning. Thank her for me."

I related our talk to Sam. "Do you realise, Belle, that's about seven miles to walk? I wouldn't like to do that journey in thick fog."

Ten minutes later the phone rang and we rushed to answer it.

"Bill is home," Jim said. "He just collapsed when I answered a knock. All he said as he fell, was that twice someone had tried to run him down."

We thanked Jim and discussed what kind of man would try to run down a lone walker in fog. "Bill must have been very frightened, Belle."

I wrote to Mum, asking her to tell me details and what Bill had told her. I waited a week for her reply. She wrote Bill had arrived at South Wimbledon about 6.30 and realised he had to walk. He had groped his way through Merton and after passing the Nelson Hospital he was then on the Kingston by-pass. He thought if he kept close to the buildings and gates it would be fine. The going was slow and he was not sure if he was walking straight. Some cars were crawling along and he concluded he was still on the bypass. Suddenly a car brushed against him, he stepped aside and the car passed. "'Walking quickly and suddenly that same car was behind me. I was wearing my light raincoat and he could see me in his headlights, Mum – he almost ran me down. I was near the fencing of the Canadian camp and held on to that for almost half an hour. I then walked and came to the traffic lights of South Lane. Lawrence Avenue was the next road, walking straight home, I hoped. I hesitated before knocking on the door, not sure if that was where he lived.' Those were his words, Belle, and he's not well. He wakes in the night. Twice I've found him sitting by my bed. When I ask what's wrong, he shakes his head saying, 'I'm so glad to be home.'"

Sam thought I ought to go to Mum. "Get Bill to see a doctor."

Next weekend when I saw Bill, I was shocked at the change in his appearance. With a week to go to Christmas, Bill looked in no mood to celebrate. "I'll get the doc home to see you, Bill. You're ill."

He said nothing. I dashed to the doctor explaining the situation. He told me he would be round later that afternoon.

He gave Bill a cursory examination, said he was in a very nervous state and gave me a prescription for medicine. After the first dose, Bill sat quietly. He asked Mum to play the piano and said he was feeling better. Later I left for home. Telling Sam what had occurred he said, "I don't like the sound of things, it's not like Bill."

On the 21st of December Jim phoned me in the evening.

"Can you come over? Mum says Bill is dying."

With Sam we dashed over to Surrey. The doctor had been and said there was nothing wrong with Bill. "Just take the medicine; all he needs is a good sleep. If you'll come to the surgery, I'll give you a couple of sleeping pills for him. Give him one tonight and one tomorrow and he'll be fine."

Myrtle prepared some eats for all of us, but Mum didn't like the idea of sleeping pills as she said Bill was sleeping normally; she had sat up two nights beside him. Sam went off to work and said he would go home to see all was well there while I stayed with Mum. On the day of the 23rd Bill was a little light-headed so we gave him one sleeping pill. Five minutes later he was asleep. "I'll sit beside him, Mum, you go to bed. You're all in. He'll be OK. Now go to bed."

"I haven't been out of my clothes for three days. I'll have a bath, then I'll have a nap, its nearly ten o'clock. Wake me about lunch-time." She had another look at Bill, then went to bed.

The day was bright but very cold. I poked at the fire, tidied the grate and made tea. I shook Bill asking if he would like tea. He muttered something. He was sleeping soundly, I felt his pulse, it was beating regularly, all appeared normal. A little later I prepared some dried scrambled egg on toast and roused Mum. Placing the tray beside her I told her I thought Bill was all right and after eating lunch she was soon asleep. Busying myself round the house, I had the occasional peep at Bill. He had not moved. He was so still.

Myrtle came down once and said did I think she should put up a few decorations? I didn't think that too wise. Jim came home from work and Sam came a little later. Their first thoughts were for Bill.

I managed sausage and mash for dinner. Mum wanted to get up but was persuaded to stay in bed to be fresh for Christmas. Sam was sleeping in a bed-chair in the living-room. All were sleeping while I kept vigil beside my brother. I put a spoonful of powdered glucose into some warm milk. I raised Bill, saying, "Drink this, Bill," as I spooned the warm liquid into his mouth, which he swallowed. I plumped the pillows and covered him. The time was 11.30. I poked at the fire then sat beside his bed. At five minutes past twelve midnight, he suddenly stopped breathing. I shook him, called him. I rushed upstairs to Jim. He was in his dressing gown and pyjamas. "I'll go for the doctor, you tell Mum, be gentle. "Oh, Jim, what shall we do?" I grabbed my coat and dashed out. I hardly remember crossing South Lane.

The doctor was still up. I don't know what I said to him.

"Wait, I'll get my car." Arriving home he felt Bill's pulse at wrist, throat and heart. "He's been out of bed," the doctor said tersely. "What are you saying?" demanded Mum. "My son hasn't moved from that bed for two days and nights. I gave him one sleeping pill as you said, here is the other one. That pill has killed him."

"That's nonsense, Mrs Munday," the doctor replied shortly. "I'm sorry, there will have to be an inquest to find the cause, I'll make the necessary arrangements for the body to be removed tomorrow. I'm sorry."

We were all too shocked. Sam stared in disbelief. Mum was crying and calling that doctor terrible names, "bloody murderer" uppermost.

Christmas Eve Myrtle and I went shopping. People everywhere were very jolly. I picked up what rations were due on Bill's and Mum's books. I managed to get half a chicken, three small chops and half a pound of sausage meat.

Christmas Day 1952. No decorations or holly. The house was bare. Undertakers removed Bill's body early Christmas Eve. Mum walked round the house like a zombie, she didn't eat, all she drank was tea, cups and cups of tea and cursing the doctor, no matter what we said.

And so Christmas passed into New Year.

Chapter Fifty-seven

The first Friday of January 1953 we attended the inquest of my brother. Dr Zoa was called first. He gave a description of how he was called, saying he found Bill in a highly nervous state and gave a prescription for a calming medicine and later was again called and gave two sleeping pills. He was asked what ingredients were in the medicine and what pills were given. He went into details, Latin I presumed. Next, Jim was called. He was asked what the time was when I said Bill had died. Then came Mum's turn to stand in the witness box. Taking the oath, she was already in tears. She was questioned closely about the night of the 6th of December. "Please give his exact words when your son arrived home."

"As I opened the door, he stumbled into the hall, saying, 'Some silly sod twice tried to run me down on the by-pass.' He seemed very agitated, saying he had never been so frightened in his life."

"Do you know where he had spent the earlier part of the day?"

"He said he was meeting a man who worked in the gramophone record department at the BBC and would be home about six o'clock."

Then I was called. I answered the questions and my story was much the same as Jim's and Mum's. "There was a quantity of white powder in the stomach. How do you account for that? What did your brother ask you to give him? Remember you're on oath."

"He never spoke to me. I made a little powdered glucose mixed with warm milk; he swallowed two spoonfuls, that was all."

"And you say he never spoke. Did he ever contemplate suicide?"

I stared aghast. "Such a thought would never enter his head. He was a caring man, he thought the world of his family."

"And you swear this glucose was all you gave him?"

"That sleeping pill killed my son," Mum screamed before I could reply. Immediately Jim pulled her to her seat as order was called.

Sam and Jim half-carried Mum out to Jim's car. We had all had a very shocking experience. The coroner returned an open verdict, saying this man should never have died. I asked a policeman standing near, the meaning of the open verdict. "Who was with this man when he died?"

"I'm his sister, I was with him," I answered

"It means the body can be exhumed any time, so watch your step next time a person dies and you're with them."

The funeral over, I said I would have to go home with Sam. Would Mum like to come and stay with us for a while? "Jim and Myrtle have to go to work and you'll be alone in the house, so?" But Mum said she would be all right, she would get over it all somehow.

We said a tearful cheerio and arrived home to find a burst pipe and the kitchen flooded. Thanking the heavens for a tiled floor and a step down into the kitchen, we set to work clearing up and finding a plumber… it was an anti-climax to all that had gone before.

With three weeks' rations due on two books, I went shopping, first stop the butcher's. I was amazed when I was told that as I had not come for meat over Christmas it had been assumed that I didn't need it. I could have a week's ration on each book. Needless to say some furious words were exchanged and I stormed out of the shop, taking myself to the next butcher's. I re-registered and received the full ration due to me. Bread was now off ration, and at the grocer's I collected full rations and with vegetables I went home loaded. It was great to have a Sunday roast and I loaded Sam's plate with slices cut from the shoulder of lamb.

We received a letter from Grace. She was still meeting George and with Fred was going to football matches each Saturday and Fred was keeping quiet about it. She sometimes met George on the way home from work to spend a precious few minutes together. "I do not understand your aunt," Grace wrote, "after all, she got married and who does she think will take care of her sons when she dies? Maybe that is something she hasn't thought about."

Rationing ended in 1953. Jim brought Myrtle and Mum to spend Easter Monday with us. Somehow conversation turned to Bill.

Said Mum, "When I had that lovely seventieth birthday party in June and listened to Bill singing in harmony with my old brother, I never dreamed my son had just six months to live." We were very quiet.

"I wonder what really did happen on the Kingston by-pass on that foggy night of the 6th of December. Unfortunately, we will never know," said Sam. "Bill must have been scared to death." We all felt very sad.

My next-door neighbour, Mrs Field, asked me if I would go with her to watch the procession of the coronation of Elizabeth II. She said she had studied the route to be taken and had decided St James Street would be the best spot. "The street is narrow, the pavement's not too wide so maybe not too many people will be in front. How about it?"

"Is Mr Field going with you?"

"No. He thinks I'm daft to want to stand for ages to watch some carriages ride past. He doesn't suppose I'll see too much… so?"

"I won't promise, I'll see what Sam has to say."

As you can guess, Sam ridiculed the idea. "You'll have to get up very early to get there or you won't see a thing."

However, I managed to persuade him and on the morning Mrs Field and I set off at five o'clock. The early morning wasn't too warm.

We found a spot and were able to see plenty. Many people had camped out all night. There was much laughter and gaiety among the crowds and many patriotic songs were sung. As time drew near for the procession, excitement rose. People cheered anything that moved.

The queen, glittering with diamonds, rode slowly past, a hand gently waving, acknowledging the cheering crowds... she was not smiling.

Every carriage received a rousing cheer and despite a drizzling rain, Churchill, head out the window of his car, doing the V-sign, had the crowd cheering madly, and the queen of Tonga Islands rode in an open carriage smiling and waving enthusiastically.

It took ages for us to leave the crowds to get to our tube station. We arrived home late afternoon and Sam greeted me saying, "I watched television and I bet saw more than you did."

"Maybe you did," I replied, "but we had the atmosphere. I'm very pleased I saw what I did."

With rationing ended, I asked Sam if there was any way I could start a salon in the house. I thought about the spare room.

"There's no way to get water to the spare room, also I think the cost now of fixtures and fittings would be very high. Why not be contented with what you're doing, surely that's sufficient?"

"I want to help you, add my share to expenses."

"You have enough to do with household chores, so forget it."

I think more than anything I wanted cash of my own, to get something without asking Sam for money. Buying eggs, I noticed the assistant was rushed off her feet. "You could do with some help," I said.

"You're telling me, I certainly could!" she replied.

"Would you consider me?"

"If you mean that, come here Friday about three o'clock, the boss will be here then. See what he thinks of the idea."

At the appointed time, I met Mr Chrickmore and suggested part-time work. We arranged that I worked Thursdays from nine until one o'clock, Fridays from nine until five and Saturday from nine until four, with the usual breaks for lunch. My wages were £2 10s. I agreed and began the work the next week. I learned a lot about eggs, the customers were many and varied. Fridays they lined up for cracked eggs at 2s 6d per dozen and disappointment was shown when they were all sold.

Going to see Mum a few weeks later, Sam said he had an idea. "Tell me about it, Sam," I questioned but he said wait until we saw Mum.

She was so pleased to see us and cups of tea were soon prepared.

"What do you think about this, Ma? How about coming on holiday with us... say, to the Isle of Wight? You need a break."

"You don't want a miserable old girl like me with you."

"Ye gods and little fishes, listen to her!" Sam laughed. "If we didn't want you, we would not have asked you. Come on, Ma, the holiday's on us. We'll make the arrangements, you pack your glad rags."

Mum still protested but finally agreed. Sam bought *Dalton's Weekly* and I wrote away for accommodation and settled on a hotel in Sandown, sending a deposit reserving a single and a double room, for one week at the end of July. At that time, one week's holiday was all bosses allowed and all wages were cut by half. I informed Mr Chrickmore of the date of the holiday and got paid my full wages.

The holiday time soon came. Jim brought Mum over on the

Friday night and we started away early. Mum loved the ferry crossing and we arrived in Sandown, meeting Captain Annis and his wife, the proprietors of the hotel. Our room was nicely furnished and Mum's room was a little farther along the landing. We had a verandah with French windows overlooking the road across to the beach. The meals were varied and plentiful and the cost per person was ten guineas weekly. There were three young men staying there and they were great fun, making Mum laugh quite a lot. I think for a while she forgot her sad loss of Bill.

Chapter Fifty-eight

In 1954, Aunt Minne, while on holiday with her sons, had a massive heart attack and died. George and Fred with Grace came to tell me the sad news. They had been to Mum before coming to me. After the funeral, we all had a family discussion and came to the conclusion that Grace's suggestion was sensible. She and George would marry quietly and they would live in Auntie's flat and she would take care of Fred too. The flat was convenient for her getting to work and we all thought it the best possible solution.

Grace looked lovely in a pale green suit with cream accessories.

Just a few days after the wedding I had a strange dream. It was so clear; I was standing beside Auntie, looking into a mirror, I had no reflection. Auntie was standing beside me, her reflection strong in the mirror. She spoke loudly. "Not for her. I'll have him from the grave." I woke disturbed; the dream worried me for days.

A week or so later, Sam surprised me. He said grinning, "With your brains and my money, we'll go places and do things."

"What's brought on this sudden rush of blood?" I enquired.

"A man at work went to Jersey last year and he hasn't stopped raving about it, so I thought, why don't we have a go?"

"It's a long boat ride to Jersey," I said shaking my head.

"Who mentioned boats? Let's try flying." I stared at him. An aeroplane trip was a thing I had never ever thought about.

"I'll get a brochure from a London travel agent and we'll take it from there. This year bosses must give you two weeks' paid holiday. It will probably be a little later in the year, but don't worry."

We studied the colourful brochure to find a hotel within our limits. There were two, one in St Helier and one in Beaumont. I wrote to both. The one in St Helier was fully booked, the one in Beaumont could reserve a double room for two weeks at the end of August. The price was thirteen guineas per person per week, full board plus two nights' dancing weekly. Sam was in high glee, telling me to send ten pounds to secure the room. I sent a cheque the next day. Where to apply for air tickets? I wondered. Asking Sam about this, he said the travel agent in London could reserve plane seats, no problem, and we could fly from Southend Airport. It was now late June.

I informed my boss; he agreed, but I don't think he was too pleased and said he would have to make arrangements. However, three weeks later, he agreed, but I would have to forfeit one week's pay.

Sam came home with the air tickets... twelve pounds each return flight. Be at the airport at ten a.m., take-off one hour later. We arrived at Rochester for Southend Airport a little early. We presented our tickets and were given boarding cards; we were very green air travellers.

We sat in the departure lounge awaiting our flight call. It came at last and following other travellers, I caught sight of the plane. It looked to me like a great white whale with wings. "Channel Airways" was printed on the side in large black letters. Sam gripped my arm.

"Looks like it's held together with sealing wax and safety pins," he laughed, I thought a little nervously. Inside the plane were double seats on either side. It was far larger inside than I anticipated. We were warned to fasten seat belts, and then the propellers whirled. The plane shook madly then it slowly rolled along the runway. A young smiling stewardess appeared saying, "Good morning, ladies and gents. I will now demonstrate the use of the life jacket. It is put on this way." She draped it round her shoulders: "It is tied like this. When the cord is pulled, the jacket will quickly inflate." We all watched as the jacket ballooned round her slim figure. "Used this way it could save your life. In case of emergencies there is a life jacket under each seat. Thank you, ladies and gents. Happy landings." In the momentary silence that followed Sam said loudly, "She's so bloody cheerful about it." There was a burst of laughter and the tension eased. We landed safely at Jersey Airport an hour later and picking up our cases we waited outside for a taxi. We had no idea where Beaumont was, but after about fifteen minutes' ride, we arrived at the Cambrai Hotel. Greeted by a smiling porter we were shown to a large airy room, nicely furnished. Along the corridor we were shown a shared bathroom and toilet. On this floor were two single rooms. We were told that breakfast was at 8.30, lunch at 12.30 and dinner at 6.30, and ours was table eight. We thanked the porter and Sam gave him a tip. "We'll just have time to change and be ready for lunch," I said as we began unpacking. "How much was the cab fare?"

"Just 2s 6d." I saw as we passed a garage that petrol was 1s 9d a gallon. Back home it cost 3s 6d.

We were served a salad lunch, rolls, coffee and biscuits and cheese. The proprietor informed us there would be dancing this evening to get to know each other, and the hotel was licensed. "I hope you all enjoy your holiday in Jersey. There will be trips, which I'll tell you about each day at breakfast, but you don't have to take them." We were asked what papers we would like placed on our table and Sam gave his order.

The dinner was superb as were all meals, and drinks were served if wanted. The dance would begin at eight sharp and end at twelve.

The dining-room was cleared for action. It was a large hotel and there were many guests. The proprietor played the saxophone or the accordion, there was also a pianist and a violin player and the timing was excellent. Our first day was thoroughly enjoyable. The bar closed at midnight and re-opened five minutes later. In bed that night, tired but content, Sam said, "Darling, I think we're going to like Jersey."

Beaumont is midway between St Helier and St Aubin's. We crossed a narrow road and walked down a slipway to the beach. The wide sweep of St Aubin's Bay was two miles of fine white sand. Our first day we spent lazily soaking up the sun. As Sam had been forbidden to swim after his ear operation, he moaned about it continually. We made friends with a French lady serving in the beach tea kiosk. Telling us her name was Madeleine, she asked why we were not swimming. Sam mentioned the doctor's warning. She told us she had been a nurse and suggested we go to a chemist's in town where they sold earplugs.

Sam was delighted with these wax plugs and almost lived in the water. I just pranced about and really tried to swim. I did a little better with Sam's help; I was never meant to be a fish. Sam fell in love with Jersey. "Let's come here again next year," so we booked in provisionally for the next year for the two middle weeks in June. Like his fellow-worker, Sam talked about the holiday for ages.

We were amazed by the German fortifications they had built while occupying the island. From the weighbridge in St Helier, an eight-foot-high concrete wall stretched along the beach of St Aubin's almost half a mile past Beaumont. The wall, eighteen inches wide at the top, would be impossible for soldiers to climb. A large gun emplacement had been turned into a café, with many tables inside and a service counter with kitchen facilities; it was large and was named the Gun Site Café. The proprietor of our hotel organised a ride to the German Hospital at St Lawrence… it had to be seen to be believed. Built deep into the hillside, the concrete wards were large and wide; lit by electricity, it was a dim and cold building. We were told, true or not, the prisoners of war were made to dig and build the hospital and fortifications and if any died, their bodies were buried in those walls. It could be true but....

In 1955, while visiting Sam's sister May, she informed us that her daughter, Joan, would be marrying Bill Hobbs in July 1956, so make sure we were not on holiday at that time.

Also in 1955 there was much tribal unrest in Africa. Would there ever be peace in the world? Conflicts seemed to flare up for no apparent reason.

Way back in about 1950, Sam discovered Bren's School of Dancing in Brentwood Road, and suggested we try it. I always agreed with him, and I wanted him to be happy and contented. So we joined this school of dancing and spent two evenings a week there. We learned jiving, the samba and rumba, also the up-to-date steps in ballroom dances. It was fun and we made many friends. The school closed during the summer months and re-opened in September. We spent time there as the years passed.

Gradually we furnished the back bedroom, buying a bedroom suite and bunk beds. Everything was falling into place for us.

Our next-door neighbours were a Mr and Mrs Campbell, real Scots. Mr Campbell played the bagpipes in the Romford Scottish band.

One weekday afternoon, Mrs Campbell was looking very sad. I enquired if anything was wrong. She said sadly, "It's Mr Campbell, he's hurt his pinkie." I tried hard to suppress a grin.

"However did he do that?" I asked, my mind running gutterwise.

"He shut it in the door this morning, it's so painful."

I wondered what his pinkie was doing to get shut in a door.

"I don't think he'll be able to play the bagpipes this Sunday. The little finger, the pinkie, does much pressure work."

I expressed my sympathy and wished the finger well. That, I thought, would teach me. Oh well, you live and learn!

Chapter Fifty-nine

Early in 1956, Jim and Myrtle finally found a house they liked. The mortgage repayments would suit their income without too much strain on their pockets. Property had risen since the war ended. It would need some cash spent on it, but like Sam, Jim could take his time.

Now I had to plan fast. I had to try to get Mum settled before our holiday in June and Joan's wedding in July.

There was some kind of argument over Suez between Egypt and Israel. Anthony Eden was travelling to and fro between those countries. The papers said he was an ill man. I didn't take too much notice, I was too busy between working in the egg shop and racing around trying to find somewhere for Mum to live. We wanted her to be near to us and at the moment I wasn't too successful. Time was getting short. Jim would shortly be signing contracts and then would soon be moving.

I was getting worried. I didn't want Mum to stay much longer alone in that house and Sam suggested I ask round if there was a flat to let in the vicinity. I was told a Mrs Blackwall had an empty flat at Number 21 in Cranham Road. As we lived at 81 in the same road, if I could get this flat for Mum, it would be ideal. A rather formidable tall lady answered my knock. I explained that I was asking on behalf of my mother and could I see the flat? Leading me upstairs she said, "I let only to one person, is your mother a widow?"

Assuring her, I was shown a large front room with a square bay, a sizeable back room and a small off room, which I thought would make a kitchen. "Your mother can have the bathroom to herself, I can't get into the bath myself, but we must share the toilet. The rent is two pounds weekly."

"I'll take it," I replied eagerly. "I'll pay two weeks' rent in advance to secure it. May I have a receipt?" She took the cash. "If you buy a rent book, I'll sign it," she answered.

Relating this to Sam he was very pleased Mum was so near. I phoned my friend, Bart, to tell Mum to start packing and said that Sam and I would be in Surrey on Sunday. When told all the news, Jim and Myrtle were happy because they had made arrangements to move in two weeks.

Jim said he would go to the agent to tell them the house would be empty in three weeks. Jim found Mum a removals man and a week later Mum was installed in Number 21, and Sam and I had a hectic time getting her straight. As there was no cooker, we contacted the gas people, with Mrs Blackwall's permission to get gas laid on in the off room for Mum to use as a kitchen. Finally all was in order and we were happy.

The Suez crisis had been resolved and all breathed freely again. Africa, it seemed, was a continent of tribal unrest. The name Nelson Mandela cropped up in the news, but I think it went over my head. Africa was so far away. I was busy with my part-time work, showing Mum around Romford and keeping the household chores up to date.

Time went by. The manageress at the egg shop left to have a baby, so Mr Chrickmore asked me if I could do full time. I would work an extra day, I told him. He took on a Mrs Stokes and between us we worked out times that would suit us and our wages rose to five pounds each week. Very nice.

I hired a television for Mum, costing £2 10s monthly, payments lessening every six months. It gave Mum pleasure and she sat glued to the screen and became very clued up with the latest news.

In February 1958 several Manchester United footballers were killed in an air crash, which stunned fans. The plane leaving Germany crashed soon after take-off, caused, it was said, by ice on the wings. Matt Busby himself was in hospital for some time.

We flew off to Jersey for our 1958 holiday. Arriving at the Cambrai Hotel, we found a new proprietor and many changes. No more twice-weekly dances, meal times changed and the bar closed at eleven o'clock.

Since our first visit to the island, I had corresponded with Madeleine and telling her about the new proprietor, she said her husband knew a Mrs Williams. Later introductions took place and for 1959 we reserved a room with that lady. We had a lovely time there, though there was no dancing, but we made friends there with some nice German people. Their son, Rolf, then thirteen, acted as interpreter and we had a great time correcting Rolf's English where sometimes he put the cart before the horse. We exchanged addresses on leaving and have kept letters flowing between our countries since that time.

Jim and Myrtle went to Jersey too in 1959, spending their holiday in September. They too fell in love with the island.

Christmas was looming ahead and arrangements were made to spend time together. Mum came along and we welcomed them and to our great surprise, Myrtle looked very pregnant. Mum was delighted when told to expect to become a grandmother some time in May. Sam and I slept in the bunk beds, letting Jim and Myrtle have our bed. Sam said, "You can't expect Myrtle to go mountaineering in her condition."

Sam and Jim saw Mum to her flat on Christmas night telling her to arrive early Boxing Day, and so we passed into the year 1960.

On the 11th of May a son was born to Myrtle, and Jim said a boy to carry on the name of Munday. A month later he was christened Anthony James. Mum was thrilled with her grandson. She studied the small face then declared, "He's certainly not like any of the Munday babies." Sam laughed, saying, "Don't look at me, Ma!"

Many events occurred in the years that followed.

In June 1961, Sam's brother George's daughter, Sylvia, married Ronald Herbert. Sylvia made a lovely bride and the large families on both sides and a large circle of friends were there. A great time was had by all.

Towards the end of 1961, the Cuban crisis blew up and by 1962, President J F Kennedy of the USA and President Khruschev of Russia brought their countries to the brink of war.

After some time had passed since Mum had moved into Mrs Blackwall's flat, we finally persuaded her to donate her piano to a church hall. This was gratefully accepted and collected. I gave Mum a key to our house and whenever she felt like it she could play our piano.

We kept in touch with relatives and friends by letter and phone. A letter from Grace informed us that George was very ill. Not feeling good for some time, his GP had sent him to hospital for tests. The result came as a shock; George had cancer in both lungs and would soon be accepted into St Joseph's Hospice for the terminally ill. My cousin George was a chain-smoker of Woodbine cigarettes. He called them coffin nails. We were devastated when he died less than three months later. I recalled the dream I had soon after Grace married George. After the funeral, Grace said, "I cannot stay here now. I will find a couple of rooms and move out my things. I'll let you know when I find a place."

We have never heard from her since. Cousin Fred let the lower half of Aunt Minne's house furnished to a newly married couple.

It began snowing in December 1962, continuing through that month. Householders swept pavements clear outside their houses and the snow began piling up in the gutters. There were heavy falls of snow in January too. It froze hard into 1963. I fell down twice on my way to work, luckily only getting bruised.

Newspapers told of spies Burgess, Maclean and Philby defecting to Russia and UK intelligence was hunting for a fourth man.

That year we took our holiday in the last week in June and the first in July. We spent a pre-celebration of our silver anniversary with Madeleine, her husband and their godchild, Marie-Claire, dancing at the Somerville Hotel, St Aubin's, and we enjoyed a salad supper.

We arrived home two days later and next evening we invited Mum, Jim and Myrtle out to an anniversary dinner, that day being the 10th of July, the actual date of our wedding.

On a visit to Dallas, Texas, President JF Kennedy was assassinated, shot by a man named Lee Harvey Oswald... that was America.

Early in 1964, February time, Sam told me rail fares would again rise, and the fare to work would then be £3 14s 9d weekly. His journey to work took almost two hours each way. "Let's move back to London," I said. "We're not getting younger, the journey's so long for you. I can look around for something suitable. Somewhere nearer your work and near a station. I don't want to live in Wood Green, and it'll have to be a larger house, with room for Mum. I can't have you rushing back here if she gets ill. How about the Lea Bridge area, where there's a station?"

The first thing I did was to get a surveyor to value our house.

After a very good look round he gave an estimated value of £4,500. I was amazed.

The agent went on, "This house is around thirty years old and has been beautifully maintained. The decor is very nice and the garden is well laid out. You can always drop a hundred or so for a quick sale. Any questions?" Shaking my head, I asked his fee.

"All valuations at our office are free."

I asked if he knew an estate agent in the Lea Bridge Road area.

"Try Donaldson's, they're in the phone book." I thanked him profusely: £4,500… phew! True, we had spent cash on the house and in the time we'd been there, almost twenty years, we'd tarted it up well.

The newspapers were full of the "Cold War". Britain was flying food and medical aid to Germany while the Russians were building a wall across Berlin with huge blocks of concrete, and in 1964 Germany became a divided country… West and East Germany.

When we mentioned to Mum that we had decided to move back to London, she was shocked. "He's made that place a palace, he's stupid to move."

"Mum, we're getting older. Sam's journey to work takes two hours each way. You don't have to worry, we're not leaving you here. I have to look for a larger house and you will be with us."

"Belle, I don't want to live in one room. I put up with enough of that when you were small. I've got used to space in rooms."

I had to find answers to all her queries, sometimes a little difficult, more so as I hadn't a clue where to look for a house.

I phoned Donaldson's for a list of houses about the £4,000 price.

Three days later I received a list of six houses, only one at our price. There were phone numbers with each one for an appointment.

The first house I phoned had four bedrooms but at £4,250 had an expectant buyer. Then I phoned a four-bed house in the Wanstead area.

I asked to view on Thursday afternoon, if that was possible, and the reply was yes. I told Mum to prepare a light lunch as I was taking her with me to view a house. I had asked directions of the vendor and a 66 bus to The Green Man, Leytonstone, would take us most of the way.

The walk along the side of the forest was quite pleasant. We found the road easily. Walking along past stone cream painted houses, with porchways and large windows, it came as a shock to find Number 41, the stonework painted battleship grey, and all woodwork round the windows painted black. A tall dark haired lady answered our knock, and we entered a long passage that seemed endless, covered with twelve-inch squares of black and white lino tiling. One wall was colour washed pale pink, the opposite wall a deeper pink. The front room was large and light despite the dull day. The window was large and the pretty decorated ceiling high. We followed the lady into a large breakfast room, which had a Rayburn room heater. This room led to a small kitchen from which a door opened to the garden. Opening a door from the breakfast room she showed us a roomy cellar, for coal etc. Another opened to a walk-in larder. From there we were shown a spacious lounge, again with a very decorated ceiling. Wide French doors led to a lean-to across the width of the house, hence to the garden. At the end was a large shed and a side entrance, situated next to the corner house. There was a large back room upstairs overlooking fields, which the lady informed us were called Wanstead Flats. At the top of the stairs was the bathroom. I immediately pointed out that this was a painted bath and I didn't like that. The room next to the bathroom, although small, was about twelve feet square. The main bedroom was huge, with a large bay and another side window, which overlooked the tree-lined road. There was also a large back bedroom. The lady's furniture was small, thus the rooms appeared much larger. In my mind, I was placing our furniture in the rooms, adding Mum's too. In all there were eight rooms, of which Mum could have three with more space than she now had. "Would it be possible for my husband to view the house tomorrow afternoon?" I asked. "I cannot decide on my own."

She agreed, smiling.

Going home, Mum said, "It wants so much doing to it and it's so dirty, every room wants decorating. I don't think Sam will buy that, so don't make your mind up." She sounded so pessimistic.

"Soap and water can make a big difference, Mum, and I definitely won't travel the distance to work, also, I'm good at paper hanging, even Sam tells me that, so if he paints the ceilings I can carry on."

"Listening to you, you're already moving in." She eyed me thoughtfully. "Don't count your chickens, Belle."

Arriving home, Mum chatted a little dismally about the upheaval the move would cause, finishing up saying, "Well, wherever you move to you know I like my own rooms. I don't want to live in with you two."

Chapter Sixty

Sam always finished the week Friday afternoons and we met about two o'clock. As we walked along Bushwood I pointed across the road. "That's the beginning of Epping Forest."

"I'm not a bloody monkey. I don't live in a forest," he snorted.

So, he wasn't in a very good mood, I thought. Perhaps he didn't want to move. I'll admit I'd been pressurising him. However.

He surveyed the outside of the house with a face like a kite.

The elderly lady greeted us with a bright smile and the day was sunny. Sam eyed the long hallway grimly. He looked round the front room and walking to the fireplace asked, "Whatever made you paint this beautiful marble mantelpiece? Whoever did it must be crazy." I glared at him.

The lady asked me if I'd like to show my husband around adding, "If you need me, just call." I thanked her and we prowled around the house.

"What's the asking price, Belle?"

I turned to him, saying "Cheer up, for heaven's sake. What's bugging you?"

"The outside was enough, the inside's a bloody sight worse."

"So, it's no go?" I really was disappointed.

"I didn't say that," he snapped. "I'm just thinking how much it will cost to bring this place up to scratch."

We took our time going round the rooms, and finally we met

the lady in the breakfast room and Sam asked about stations. She said it was roughly fifteen minutes to Leytonstone Station across the fields and the same time to the Underground across the High Street, and buses ran to most places. The house was very central. Next came the price. Her husband, Gerry, was asking £4,500. What did we think?

"If, and it's a big if, we buy it, it needs redecorating throughout and I've noticed all the marble fireplaces have been painted over. It will be costly to redecorate a large house and I will want a surveyor to look it over, so my offer is £4,000. Take it or leave it."

"I must tell my husband of your offer, I can do nothing myself. He's an architect, he knows the value of a house this size."

We exchanged phone numbers and left.

Going home we talked all the pros and cons. She had told us to make the appointment for the surveyor to call next Friday as she was a nurse at Whipp's Cross Hospital and was sleeping during the day. She was doing night shift at this time. Somewhere I remembered I'd been told, "Never buy a house from a teacher or a nurse, it would be dirty." Well, this house was certainly in that category. Naturally our conversation for the next few days was about nothing else. Two days later the phone rang to tell us her husband had accepted our offer. The survey of our house cost twenty-seven pounds. I put our house on the market, hoping the sale would be quick. That was on Friday. Monday I was doing the washing, the day was dull and wet. About ten o'clock, I answered the door to a very pretty coffee-coloured lady, hair black as midnight, brown smiling eyes. "This house is for sale?" she queried. I nodded asking her in. "May I see it?"

I showed her round the house. In the small off room (it was roughly ten feet square) she said, "Yes, I could get a four-foot bed in here with a couple of chairs. Yes, I'll buy it. I have the money here." She opened a large bag she carried. It was packed with notes.

She offered me her bag saying all the money was there and I could count it, and how soon could she move in? I was so surprised.

"I can't sell you this house just like that. It has to be done through a solicitor, the deeds are legal documents." I tried to explain, "Go to the estate agent who gave you the details, I'm sure he'll explain more fully about buying a house." She left looking very disappointed, still insisting she had the money with her.

Relating this later to Sam, he said, "Maybe that's the way they sell houses where she comes from." And Mum said much the same thing when I told her the story.

I rustled up a surveyor to look over the house the following Friday and phoned the approximate time of his arrival to the seller.

We awaited his report a little apprehensively and our conversation was about the house and what we thought were its good and bad points.

Saturday afternoon of that week, Sam answered the door and a middle-aged couple came to look over the house. He said he was in insurance. They thought our house was just what they were looking for, and Sam dropped the price to £4,250. They said they would get a surveyor. They said our decorating was to their liking and for the time being would save them money and hoped all would go well for them.

Receiving our surveyor's report came as a shock. There was woodworm in the cellar and the front room and floorboards under the window in the lounge were spongy, probably owing to water seeping through, perhaps from a leaking pipe. Sam read through the report. I asked him, "Shall we forget this house and look for something else?"

"Tomorrow you see this surveyor and get his opinion. I like the layout of the place and the nearness of stations to my work. Pick his brains, he may know much more than we do. It's worth a try."

As the next day was Thursday, I had half a day off from the egg shop; I went straight off to see the surveyor.

He greeted me warmly and I explained our worries.

"It will be a cash sale, and we're wondering if it's wise to sink our cash into a house in bad condition. What do you think?"

"All houses near a forest tend to get infested with woodworm. The water seepage may be from a small pipe leak and do remember the house was built in 1906 and that Edwardian houses were solidly built. The leakage may be of short duration and can be found."

"About the woodworm, is that bad?"

"There is a wood preservative and woodworm eradicator on the market, Rentokil. You can order it from hardware stores here, it comes in five-gallon drums and will be delivered. It's great stuff."

"I still feel in doubt, so is my husband. Please tell me truly is the condition bad? Can it be rectified?"

"You phone the District Council, it won't cost you a penny. Their men will go round the house and tear it apart until the cause of the spongy floorboards is found. These men are very helpful."

"Is the condition bad?" I asked once more.

"Good Lord, no! I've surveyed houses in five times a worse condition that have been made perfect. Mind, if you do decide to go ahead and buy, you'll need plenty of elbow grease." I thanked him.

I related to Sam all that had been said, leaving out the bit about "tearing the house apart".

Sam decided the house was what he wanted. The rooms were large, the ceilings high and it was miles nearer his work and above all there was enough room for Mum to be with us. So I paid the initial deposit of £600, subject to contract, all with some misgivings.

When I told Mr Chrickmore I was thinking of moving to

London he wanted me to continue working for him. The long bus journey would be fine in the summer, but dark winter evenings were out of the question.

The sale of our house and the house we intended to buy went ahead smoothly. In between we borrowed tea chests from a removals firm and packed. We would move two weeks later, after we had cleaned the rooms, and Mum could move in too. We left curtains and lino, but took our carpet squares. The removals cost £240. Closing the street door we went on a tour through the rooms. Sam was in high spirits. We were back near friends and relatives. A little later the gasman came to fix the cooker, then came tea and eats. Between us we fixed up the bed and amidst all the tea chests and jumble of furniture we sat watching television. We had moved on Saturday, the High Street was a short walk. On Sunday Sam prowled around the neglected garden and in the deep cellar he found many half-empty tins of paint, half a dozen railway sleepers and a luggage rack. Between the long passage and the lounge a railway luggage rack was used for hanging clothes. Sam said, "I think the bloke who had this house must have worked on the railway. Everything points to that."

I watched Sam hurrying across the fields on his way to work. There were many animals grazing and quite a number of people were walking in the field too, taking no notice of the animals. We learned later there were grazing rights dating from the time of Elizabeth I and in many of the roads the notices read "beware cattle".

After Sam left that first morning I phoned the District Council and was promised they would see the trouble on Wednesday. Meanwhile, I washed down paint and scrubbed up the rooms Mum would have. I bought yards of curtaining at Bearman's departmental store, making curtains first for the bedrooms. I unpacked just the things I needed, leaving furniture where the removals men had dumped it. Leaving work at 5.30, Sam was home forty-five minutes later and naturally the fares to work were much less costly.

We decided Mum would have the large room overlooking the fields, the smaller room could be her kitchen and the room I had already cleaned would be her bedroom. "These are the rooms we will decorate first. Get Mum fixed, then we can then take our time. Nothing we can do down here until the men from the council have given the place the once over," Sam said.

By the time Wednesday came I had scrubbed clean the rooms we had ready for Mum. I was hanging curtains when, about ten o'clock, I answered the door. A large burly man said, "District Council. What's your trouble?" he asked shortly and marched past me.

"Quite a lot, I think." I handed him the surveyor's report.

When moving we had brought with us two five-gallon drums of Rentokil and three quart cans of emulsion paint. These now stood in the fireplace in the lounge. The man finished reading the report.

"Let's have a look at the cellar first." I led the way. I hadn't yet been down the cellar; I had switched on the light and taken a cursory look down the steps. Now I followed the man down the ten steps. It was really filthy. "Where did you get those sleepers?" he asked.

"They were here already."

"You can get rid of them as soon as you like. They're all infested and naturally coal from mines bring these creatures into houses too. Looks like the place needs a thorough going over." He turned, going up the steps, saying, "Where's the spongy flooring and the leak?" We entered the lounge. I pointed under the window. As he trod, the boards bent beneath his weight. He took a small book from a pocket and began writing quickly.

"Would you like a coffee or tea?"

"That would be nice. I'm a tea man. Two sugars, please."

We sat down to tea and biscuits. "That Rentokil is excellent stuff, it'll do the trick," he grinned at me. "Don't look so worried, it'll all come out in the wash." He stood up. "My men will be here a little after two. They'll bring some gear, and tell them to burn those bloody sleepers, pronto. Thanks for the tea and don't worry."

Shortly after two o'clock three tatty men arrived on the doorstep, two carrying a large iron incinerator. "Come to find the leak, Lady," one said brightly as they marched in. I looked at the incinerator.

"That won't hold water," I laughed. They put down a large piece of material that looked like cardboard on the grass and dumped the incinerator on that. I stared at them wonderingly.

"You leave us, Lady. We'll call you when we want your help."

I had been scraping old wallpaper off in Mum's bedroom when they came. Now I continued with my work. The day was warm and windows were open. Suddenly I heard the sound of sawing that went on and on. Soon the fire was blazing in the garden. I wondered what the neighbours would think.

I left my wallpaper scraping; I had to know what was happening.

The lounge was large, about twenty-two feet by fifteen. The sight that met my eyes shocked me rigid. The flooring beneath the window had been sawn away from the window to the door, right back to the fire hearth. There was a large gaping hole eight feet square and the men were scraping from the footings large scoops of wet slimy earth. My God, I thought, the money we've paid for this house, £4,000, and to be confronted with this.

I stammered, "Er… would you like some tea?"

They grinned. "Why ask a silly question?" one said.

I made tea, tears welling into my eyes, wondering where they were dumping the slimy earth. I composed myself then called them for tea and biscuits. They made themselves cosy and, seated around, I asked how they were doing. "We're burning up all the rotten wood and we're hoping to find the water seepage tomorrow. Your old man will just need to get some new flooring fixed after we've finished, that's all."

I nodded. That's all? What would Sam say when he came home?

Suddenly came the call, "Please flush the toilet, Lady." This I did and went downstairs into the lounge. They went round the house, putting a brown thick powder into the plug hole in the toilet basin, down the toilets and the bath. Plugs in place they ran plenty of water into the basin and bath. The same routine was performed in the downstairs toilet and basin and in the kitchen, the same thick powder was used and the plug was fixed. "You wash the cups, Lady, and use plenty of water." I did as I was told and stood awaiting their instructions. Suddenly came a yell. "OK, Lady, kitchen sink." I pulled out the plug and water gurgled down the drain. I went into the lounge. "No seepage there, Lady."

A man came from the cellar carrying a sleeper. "Last one," he said as he marched down the garden and dropped it into the flames.

"We're knocking off now, Lady. It's just gone four." They were collecting tools together. I asked, "What about the bath water?"

"See you tomorrow, ten o'clock. Meantime, get some paraffin and some old rags, and use that as a mat, soak it with paraffin and wipe your shoes, you don't want to tread woodworm all round the house, do you?"

"About the fire?"

"That will burn itself out, we can relight it tomorrow. Bye."

Left alone, I stood beside the gaping hole and stared at the fire.

I began preparing dinner, then thought about the paraffin. I dashed to the hardware store and bought a can, had it filled with paraffin and bought a two-pint can of paint stripper. Back home fifteen minutes later, I rushed around getting things ready and dinner on the table in time. I was soaking some rags with paraffin when Sam came in, relating all that had occurred. He stared at the hole and at the fire still burning.

"Well, I suppose they know what they're doing," he said moodily. He asked how my day was and after dinner he inspected my paper scraping.

"It's worry and hard work for you, Belle, but we'll get over this hurdle. We've got over other difficulties, you'll see."

For some time now, Sam had been wearing a new type of hearing aid. A mould in the ear led to a small battery holder that lay behind the ear. It was what Jim told us about ages ago. Sam had enquired from his doctor and had been referred to Oldchurch Hospital, Romford, and had been fixed up there with batteries and a replacement book. He had been wondering where to get replacement batteries. Next day, Friday, sharp at ten the workmen arrived, and with them came another man. I noticed immediately that he was wearing a hearing aid similar to Sam's. They set to work and soon relit the fire. I heard them talking as they scraped away more of the damp earth. They asked me to flush the outside toilet and basin. Still no seepage. I was in despair. The water was seeping, I thought, maybe from a cracked underground pipe… perhaps something to do with bombing. "Was there much bombing round here?" I asked.

"Nothing to speak of. How about a cuppa?" one laughed. It was after eleven o'clock. Tea made, they sat cosily chatting.

"The last resort is the bath," one said. "If that's not it, it could be an outside drain pipe, perhaps leading from the manhole."

I suppose they sat chatting for half an hour… and they call this working hard, I thought sarcastically. They asked me to empty the bath. I crossed my fingers as I climbed the stairs. The bath was almost half-filled. I pulled out the plug and going slowly down to the lounge, I heard a loud, "That's it. Got the bugger." Water in a colourful iridescent hue was streaming through between the piers and using a small shovel they sloshed the water quickly into a bucket. So, for a long long time water from the bath had seeped though, but from where? Relief flooded over me, I felt like crying. They went to the sink outside the kitchen door and pointed out to me the cement had worn a thin crack where it had joined the square iron sides of the drain. With a hammer one man broke away the cement to reveal a gaping hole where over the years the earth had been washed away. "Nothing to worry about now, Lady, Bert here'll fix that for you tomorrow." He proceeded to give Bert instructions, and turning to me, said, "This calls for a cuppa, don't you think?" I quickly agreed.

It was 1.30 and we were all happily chatting and laughing. I heard Sam's key turn. "He always finished work early Fridays." I rushed to meet him. "They've found the leak," I said excitedly.

Sam looked round at the men seated and drinking tea. He gazed at Bert saying, "Where do you get your hearing batteries?"

"London Hospital, Whitechapel." I was pouring tea for Sam.

"Sorry to give you all this trouble," Sam was saying, "I was beginning to think the worst about this place."

"No trouble, sir. We do get paid for finding trouble spots, we don't like water to beat us and we're pleased to be of assistance," the man, I assumed him to be the foreman, told Sam. "That Rentokil you have is the best. Splash it around those piers; don't stint it. Let the footings dry out thoroughly before you replace the flooring, splash plenty over the new wood and plenty around the boards under the window in the front room and the passage and cellar. That's all, sir, good luck."

Sam thanked him pressing a ten-shilling note into his hand. "Let your men have a drink on me," Sam laughed.

We were so relieved, Sam hugged me. "Let's celebrate. I'll go for some fish and chips, no cooking for you tonight. The chip shop isn't too far along the road." While he was gone I made fresh tea. We thoroughly enjoyed our meal and for the rest of the afternoon watched television. At last we could get on redecorating the place to our liking.

Bert came next morning and quickly cemented closely round the sink, first filling the deep hole with a mixture of sand and cement. He said, "Let that dry for a couple of days and it'll be OK." So we bathed together and left the water in the bath for two days before I emptied it.

We worked furiously over that first weekend. Sam cleaned whitewash from the ceiling of Mum's bedroom. The weather was warm and the ceiling dried quickly, ready on Sunday for a coat of emulsion. In the cellar we found a full can of cream gloss paint and used this to paint all the woodwork in that room. I did the picture rail and skirting boards while Sam did the airing-cupboard door and the room door. Between painting I prepared the Sunday roast. The room was ready for Mum by evening.

After the washing on Monday I made curtains, then after another quick scrub and window cleaning I considered one room finished. Next was the small room that would become Mum's kitchen, and so we worked round the clock. We borrowed a book of samples and selected the numbers of the wallpaper for each room. Prices and wages were rising. Sam was now earning between twelve and fifteen pounds weekly and we were spending as fast as he was earning, and our savings were growing smaller all the while.

On Sunday of the second week I journeyed to Mum to help with the last of her packing and see the removals men away. Knowing they would arrive at the house before we would, I gave them a key and instructions into which room furniture would go. They were extremely efficient and when we arrived had almost finished their job. We made them tea, while Mum went around making sure all her gear was dumped.

Eventually, with the place to ourselves, Mum eyed the hole in the lounge in astonishment. The smell of Rentokil was everywhere. The piers, each one two feet wide, two feet high and two bricks wide on the footings of the cellar top, showed how well built these Edwardian houses were. Mum enquired if we received the deeds yet? I said no.

"You have both paid a lot of money for this place, and there's much yet to be done. Never mind, now I'm here, I can help."

We discussed rent. "Sam thought one pound weekly, is that OK?" Mum agreed. "You have your own meter and once the cooker is fixed you'll be fine. Meantime we'll eat together." We began preparing the evening meal.

Sam was happy now we were together. The light evenings gave time to do small jobs. Mum was pleased with the decoration of her bedroom and with a toilet basin fixed, she thought that a great asset.

"I want to get a new hot tank, Ma, so don't bother putting down floor covering. The plumber will want floor boards up."

Three weeks later a bright copper cylinder and immersion heater and a new bath were installed. That broke the bank and for a while that stopped our gallop. Mum scraped off old wallpaper while I sloshed paint stripper on the marble mantelpieces and the paint scraped off in curls. In the lounge the marble was a beautiful shiny black with pale green and white veins. I scrubbed away at the ornamental crevices then rinsed off with warm water. To cover such beauty with a sage green paint was vandalism. In the front room the marble was creamy white with light and dark brown veining with ornamental scrolls down the side panels. It was hard work but worth the trouble. In the master bedroom, the marble was painted a lavender shade; the tiles at the side of the grate had the same colour. This proved white marble with cream and grey markings and the tiling was sprays of flowers. Sam was full of praise for my handiwork.

"The persons living here must have been nutty to paint over this lovely marble and tiling."

"They did have three children," I reminded him.

"Yes, maybe the kids did the painting," he grinned.

From the wood yard in Hartley Road, Sam ordered flooring, planed one side. He half-filled an old bucket with Rentokil and soaked the ends of the floorboards. It all took time. In a little spare time amid the chaos, Mum did a little piano playing and I must say it really livened up my days. Slowly the house took on a new lease of life. When the deeds finally arrived, we discovered the previous owner was a railway quantity surveyor. "So that's where all the paint and sleepers came from," said Sam.

Mum liked the cream paint and the woodwork of her living-room painted in this colour. She treated herself to a fitted broadloom carpet in a mixture of cream and brown; it looked cosy and warm. Her kitchenette, woodwork white, walls pale grey and a grey carpet pleased her.

Now Mum was fixed up we went to town on our rooms and Mum gave a hand scraping off old wallpaper. By Christmas-time all doors on the landing and passage were painted white and with just the papering of the landing and staircase to do we decided to rest for a while.

Jim and Myrtle with little Tony, now four years old, stayed with us for Christmas and the house came in for much admiration, and so 1965 began.

We read in newspapers that from time to time people were shot while trying to escape over the Berlin Wall into West Germany. There was one point of entry and exit and it became known as "Checkpoint Charlie".

We began papering and painting the landing and staircase. We chose a shaded green paper, which was very effective. Rentokil was splashed around liberally under all carpeting and in the cellar and Sam felt satisfied we had the woodworm under control.

The nation mourned Churchill in 1965; he had been a good leader while World War II raged.

Sam liked watching the cartoons on television, watching Donald Duck he remarked, "The duck's bill is like a soup ladle."

For some unknown reason, I thought about the duck-billed platypus.

A week or so later, I typed down all I could remember about this strange creature of Australia. In a recent paper I had seen a request for children's short stories. I searched and finally found the Sheffield address, counted the words, 504, and sent off my story to Eadon Newspaper Features, titled *Nature's Oddity.* A few weeks later I received a cheque for 7s 6d. I could hardly believe my luck. I had the cheque framed in passe-partout. Sam grinned, "If you can get that cash for 500 words, keep typing and I'll retire."

Sam's sister, May, phoned in the late spring of 1966 to tell us that her mother was not too well. Down through the years she had had bad bouts of bronchitis.

As she grew older, her cough lasted a little longer each time, but she maintained a cheerful ready quip.

During the war she lived with Babs at Totteridge, North London. When Joe was demobbed they started a family, which resulted in two sons. Mrs Bendon then went to live with May, husband Tom and son John (Joan was already married). We made periodic visits to Welling. Receiving May's phone message off we journeyed to Welling to find Mrs Bendon very ill.

She was later transferred to hospital where sadly she died.

Despite Sam's many cracks about his mother's cooking, he was extremely fond of her and was shocked and upset by her death.

May said, "She was eighty-five, Sam, and had enjoyed every minute of her life and could laugh about most things, so let us remember her that way. She could always tell a joke against herself."

Sam was subdued for quite a time, but gradually came acceptance.

The day he remarked, "No one lives forever," I replied, "Shall we put some flowers on her grave this weekend?"

"No," he exclaimed sharply, "graveyards are creepy, I'll never want to see the grave, so don't ask me."

"So you would never come to see *my* grave?" I queried.

"Belle, don't you ever leave me."

"Well, I'm older than you, remember?"

"That's nothing, I never think about that, so…." He trailed off quietly and stood staring at me. "Make a cup of tea," he said.

He went upstairs to Mum and asked her to come down and play the piano to cheer away his blues, and Mum gladly complied and soon he was his usual happy self and life became normal.

Sam saw a poster advertising a supper dance at Wanstead House. All we had to do was find this place and the telephone directory helped. It was within walking distance. Mum was pleased, saying she would wait up until we were home and off we went. Entrance fee was seventy-five pence, including a fish and chip supper. The hall was large and well lit, and crowded with dancers and was licensed. During the interval we each received our supper, which we ate from the white paper with a plastic fork. It was all very jolly. We discovered the many pursuits of this club and while there Sam joined the chess membership club. Chess evenings were held on Wednesdays and off he went each Wednesday evening. He made friends there and soon invited them to our house.

The dances were a regular fortnightly feature during winter, closing for summer.

"Let's have a party for your birthday, Belle."

"Not a birthday party, just a party," I protested. And so we had our first house-warming party. Mum's maxim was, "Invite the neighbours, if they help to make the noise, they cannot complain."

As time passed we read about the "great train robbery" and the amazing escape of Ronald Biggs to South America.

In 1968 Bobby Kennedy, brother of the former president, was shot. He left a wife and ten children. Mother said they were a very unlucky family… well, that was America, too many gangsters around.

In 1969, in July, Neil Armstrong landed on the moon. The television pictures of him walking in slow motion amazed the world. The USA had beaten the Russians in the moon race. I rushed upstairs to Mum.

"What an amazing achievement, Mum; a man on the moon."

She gave me a pitying glance. "You believe all that?"

"Mum, seeing is believing, we are seeing it live."

"If you'll believe that, my girl, you'll believe anything."

"But Mum, it's happening as you're watching."

"Yes, I've also seen the film *The Invisible Man,* and all the tricks cameras can accomplish. Look at him now, hopping around in slow motion." How to make her believe in science?

"There is no gravity on the moon, Mum."

"How do you know that?"

"That is what scientists tell us."

She snorted. "How is he getting back to Earth?"

"By rocket, I suppose. Same as he was sent to the moon."

I lost every argument with her on this subject, no matter what I said or what she read.

Every time we saved money, Sam thought of something for the house.

He dismantled the old railway hut at the bottom of the garden and made plans to build a shed. He mixed concrete for a base, ordered breeze blocks, eighteen inches by twelve, and in no time an eight foot by six foot building was erected and plastered and we praised his handiwork.

"I think he has a love affair with this place," opined Mum.

Meantime I had written another 500-word story and received a 7s 6d cheque. Sam laughed, "Why not try writing something with more words, maybe the pay will be better!"

After a while I thought up a 1,000-word story.

Chapter Sixty-one

Every holiday we spent the two middle weeks of July in Jersey and Sam's Aunt Lil always spent that time with Mum, as they were great friends.

Settling back to normal after the holiday, I prepared Sam's favourite after-dinner sweet, apple pie. He had two helpings.

He woke me about 5.30 complaining of chest pains. We dressed and he sat in an armchair punching at his chest. I made tea and told him to sit quiet. "It's your bloody apple tart, it's giving me indigestion." His face looked grey and drawn.

"I'll call the doctor," I said feeling alarmed.

"I'll go round when he opens in the morning. The pain has eased a little now." He closed his eyes and lay back in the armchair. He seemed to be sleeping. I went to the bathroom and had a quick wash. He was again rubbing his chest as I entered the room. I sat quietly beside him but seeing he was sweating, I gently sponged his face.

"If I make you a little bicarbonate of soda, will you drink it?"

"I'll try anything to rid me of this pain."

At nine o'clock he went to his doctor. "Let me come with you, Sam."

"No, Belle, I'm OK now."

I watched him crossing the road so slowly. The surgery was about ten minutes' walk. I went up to Mum.

"Sam has indigestion, Mum. He's gone to the doctor. I'm very worried, he's looking very grey and walking so slow."

"He's been working so hard. I think he has a love affair with this house, I've said so before. He's doing his work and then as soon as he's finished a meal, he's out in the garden or working on the house. You too, you're both working too hard. For Christ's sake take a rest."

An hour later Sam returned with a letter for a consultant at the Chest Hospital, Victoria Park. I called a taxi and asked Sam what his doctor had said. "He examined me, wrote the letter and told me to go slow. I've had a heart attack." I was shocked and frightened.

He was seen to immediately the letter was handed to the doctor.

Sam was placed in a wheelchair and we were whisked up in a lift.

I waited while he had a cardiogram. Sam was wheeled into a room farther along the corridor. After almost an hour, a doctor came to me.

"You can see your husband now for five minutes. He is a very ill man, Mrs Bendon. He has had a very bad heart attack. With care, we hope he'll get well." He smiled, I suppose to reassure me.

I entered the small room. I was shocked to see my darling.

He was sitting propped up with pillows, his chest had been shaved and on either side of his bed were lockers on which were placed monitors with wires leading to five discs placed on Sam's chest. He looked dazed and was deathly pale. I gripped his hand as he slowly looked at me. I smiled, "You're going to be all right, darling," I whispered, unconvincingly. I watched the white lines on the monitors; one showing long peaks and the other slight wavy lines, with an occasional few small mounds.

"I'll go to the shop and let the family know. I'll come in tomorrow and bring pyjamas." He appeared not to hear me. I kissed him as the doctor entered. He felt Sam's pulse as a nurse came in and seating herself at the table she watched the monitors and began making notes.

Outside in the corridor the doctor told me to bring nightwear, toothpaste and brush and shaving gear, and finished by taking me into an office where I gave all details asked. I walked along Bishop's Road then along the Hackney Road to the shop. How I would remember August 1970. I was praying as I had never before prayed. He must not die, he must live, we were so happy together... were we too happy? I entered the shop, not really aware of doing so and burst into tears. I stammered out the reason for being there. "Sam is in intensive care, George. I was told he's very ill. He looks so grey, I don't think he realised I was there." Edie made tea. "We can visit any time." George said he would take the car, go to the hospital and then run me home.

Returning from the hospital, George told of the talk he had had with the consultant. Sam had had a very serious attack and was now heavily sedated and would have every care. At the moment that was all he could say.

Back home, we related to Mum all that had occurred. She told George, "Sam has been working on this house non-stop ever since they moved in. They've been out dancing Saturdays too. She is just as bad, but I must admit their combined efforts have been rewarding to them both." She finished, "I'm not blaming you, Belle, but you must let up sometimes."

We sat for a while discussing what to do, George making Mum realise that Sam was a man who had to get things done. When he left, I thanked him and said I would phone each day. I felt so unsettled. Mum tried to cheer me. "Try to look on the bright side," she said.

When I began working for myself after opening the salon I paid voluntary stamp contributions on my NI and unemployment cards. After being bombed, for 1942 and 1943, I missed contributions, but began buying stamps in 1944. Reaching the age of sixty, I waited two years before applying for my old age pension. I then received a weekly sum a little over ten pounds – I forget the exact sum. Sam was tickled pink. He laughed.

"I had my head screwed on tight when I married an older woman."

"Do you have any regrets?"

"If I could relive my life over again, I would choose you. You have made my life so happy. Yes, I would do the same thing again."

"You say the nicest things, darling," I hugged him.

I was thinking about his words now and suddenly realised I was entitled to a senior citizen's bus pass. I enquired at the post office and with my pension book and a photograph, I made my way to the council office. Receiving the pass, I made for home. I hopped on the bus like a teenager, and flashing the pass at the young morose-faced driver, I said brightly, "Look, I've just come of age."

"Ha, bloody ha," he said sourly.

"You should live so long," I retorted.

Next day from Sheffield came a cheque for twenty-one shillings for a 1,000-word story. The editor's note said find an agent, but Sam's health was more important to me then.

Now I could ride free on bus and tube, it cost nothing to visit Sam in hospital so I went every day. I left home about one o'clock, arriving at the hospital soon after two and left about four. Each day I watched the graph on the monitors. The peaks now after a week were not so frequent or so long and he was now wired to only one machine and was more aware of me. We spoke little. He said the food was fine and the nurses were so kind, one sat with him all the time. He was shaved and washed, all he did himself was clean his teeth, and everything else was done for him. He said some days were better than others, most of all he wished he were home. He wanted to know what I was doing.

I phoned the shop each day. George had been to see Sam twice.

Mum came with me one day. Sam grinned at her and was pleased to see her. We were told to leave that day as Sam was to be given a blanket bath. He was ten days in intensive care and was then moved into the recovery ward. There were six men in this ward and Sam found them a jolly lot. Some had pacemakers, some had had heart surgery and they teased the nurses. Sam now had a slight colour to his skin.

He was in that ward for two weeks and I was then informed he was being moved to Cobham, Surrey, for therapy, and he stayed there six weeks.

He was brought home by ambulance. Sam told me he had been having exercises and would do them at home, take short walks, and definitely no lifting and he would see his doctor weekly and make monthly visits to hospital.

We did some walks once round the block, the pace was slow and gradually he increased the walks, borrowing a friend's dog while I stayed home. This continued for over three months before the doctor said he could return to work, but no settees.

It was nearing Christmas when he came in from work looking very disgruntled. "I'm starting on settees next week," he informed me.

"The doctor said no lifting heavy things," I reminded him.

"I stuff two chairs, while others stuff a settee, right? Two chairs have four arms, settees have two arms, and I get a few pence more for stuffing four arms to their two, so who's the loser? Me. I already told the governor of my intentions, and he agrees with me. I'm not an invalid and I don't want to be treated like one, so…."

"As the stuffing on the settee gets heavier, promise me you'll ask your brother Joe to help with the lifting."

He promised, I think grudgingly.

We spent a nice quiet Christmas and slowly Sam became his usual busy self and with 1971 came decimalisation.

I spent time explaining it to Mum. "With decimals, Mum, we count in tens," I explained as she listened intently. "There are 100 pence to the pound, OK?"

"When I went to school, 240 went to the pound, so tell me, what's happened to the other 140 pence?"

"One p is now worth two and a half p and five make a shilling."

She gazed at me pityingly. "Five tuppence half-pennies... in my reckoning there's a half-penny over, what happens to that?" And so it went on, over and over again and she finished by saying, "For eighty-nine years pounds, shillings and pence has been good enough for me, so I'll stay with that."

"Mum, the old money isn't legal tender any more. Like everyone else you'll gradually get used to it." But she grumbled and stated that prices doubled overnight and slowly I agreed she was right.

For Christmas 1972 we travelled to Jim's house in Surrey. Their son, Tony, now nearly eleven years old, was doing very well at school. We had a pleasant time, but the journey home was cold, wet and miserable.

We missed the train at Liverpool Street and had half an hour to wait. We were glad to get home for hot tea and cake.

So into 1972, an eventful year, which began so well.

We ushered in 1972 with a New Year party. Twenty-seven relations and friends turned up. With Jim, Myrtle and their son Tony, now rising twelve, came Myrtle's sister Olive, with her husband. Their son, now twenty-three, had made other arrangements. Jean-Pierre Mallett had been in the French Resistance, being much decorated for bravery. He had the Croix de Guerre, Croix de Lorranine avec Palme (equal to our Victoria Cross), Médaille Militaire and Médaille de Résistance. He married Olive in 1947 and their son André was born in November 1949. They had visited our house many times. Jean-Pierre spoke little of his exploits, sometimes he would speak of an incident, using his hands expressively to emphasise a point. Sam once asked him, "How many Germans have you killed, Jean-Pierre?"

He drew a finger quickly across his throat, saying, "I've forgot ze count." This caused Sam to comment, "If you cut off his hands, he couldn't talk." Jean-Pierre was more talkative when he became a little tiddly on wine. We all had a great time and the party quietened down in the early hours and we were sitting to have a bite to eat. Suddenly Jean-Pierre began, "Ze Gestapo he caught two of our people. Zey picked up an elderly lady, one of two, to question 'er. She was good; zey let 'er go. She tell us what she see. Ze torture of zis girl, no toenails and zis man 'anging by ze arms." We listened in silence as he continued. "We decide to get our people out of zis château, we are not clever and lose ten of our workers. Next night it is dark and rains much. We roll grenades through ze gratings of ze château where our workers lie. We hope zey die quickly and we kill many Germans." Tears were falling down his cheeks. "We make many sacrifices, in torture one can only stand enough. Many times I 'ave ze night 'orse... not too much now." He dabbed his eyes as Olive said, "It's nightmare, Jean, I've told you before." She smiled.

"But it is still ze 'orse," he persisted.

Early in January, I bought a pair of red court shoes in a sale. Going home along Leytonstone High Street, I came to a second-hand bookshop. On a bench outside the store were a number of paperbacks. A bright red cover caught my eye; I picked it up to read *Writers' and Artists' Year Book.* Opening it at random, the page heading was "United States Agents". I remembered Sheffield telling me to find myself an agent. I purchased the book for ten pence. I could study it later. I found some interesting items.

My birthday in February came and asking Mum to come out to dinner with us, she suggested we go alone as she didn't feel like getting togged up. I thought this a little unusual as Mum liked dining out, but thought no more about it and Sam gave me a great time. Saturday and Sunday lunches we always cooked for Mum. Sometimes she came down with us, other times she ate alone watching television. On this Saturday in late March, I cooked smoked haddock with mashed potatoes and egg sauce, one of Mum's favourite meals. I called to her but she asked me to bring the meal to her. She told me she didn't feel too good. Asking her how she felt, she snapped, "I don't know how I feel, I've never felt like this in my life."

"Eat your lunch, maybe you'll feel better. I'll make tea and give you a cup after lunch." Muttering her thanks, I left her.

Telling Sam, he said, "Ma is an elderly lady, she cannot always feel on top of the world. As it is I think she's great."

She appeared brighter when I took her a cup of tea and said so.

By six o'clock that evening I was really worried about her. She was sick, so Sam phoned for our doctor. He came immediately. I was with Mum when he entered the room. She glared at him. "We have called the doctor, Mum, let him look at you."

"I want no doctor, I'm fine, they want you, I don't," she stormed.

Nevertheless the doctor felt her pulse; he stroked her face and pinched her cheek. "You're a wonderful old lady," he told her.

Downstairs he told us: "She is of a great age and you must be prepared for anything. Don't hesitate to call me any time."

Mum liked Warnick's Advocaat. Regularly she had two tablespoons each night – in this way she stated none was wasted. She went to bed that night at eleven o'clock, I sat beside her for a while until she told me to get to bed, and she was fine. Kissing her I told her to call me it she wanted anything. She nodded, closing her eyes, and I left her bedroom door open.

I heard her call, the time ten minutes to five. I nudged Sam awake. Going to Mum, I saw she was getting out of bed.

"Help me to the toilet," she said loudly. I draped a dressing-gown round her shoulders. "I'll come in with you," I said, but she pushed me away and bolted the door. I sat on the stairs worrying. I heard the toilet flush then running water as she rinsed her hands. She smiled when she saw me waiting. "I'm fine now, Belle." I helped her to bed then sat by her dressing-table. She did appear brighter.

"If I die," she said suddenly, "there's money in that drawer, enough for my funeral, do the best you can with it."

"Don't talk like that, Mum, you won't die." She smiled. A few moments later Sam came into the room with cups of tea on a tray.

There came a strange gurgling sound from Mum. I crossed to her; there was a grey look about her mouth. "I'll call the doc, Belle," Sam said, "I think this is curtains for Ma." I heard him phoning.

Ten minutes later the doctor came, trousers over his pyjamas. He gently pressed Mum's eyes and asked for a small mirror. This he held over Mum's mouth, then slowly drew the sheet over her head, shaking his head. Downstairs he said, "I'll arrange an autopsy if you wish, her death is cardiac infarct."

I shook my head. "She wouldn't like that, Doctor. Infarct, does that mean cardiac arrest?" He nodded, thanked Sam for the tea and as I apologised for calling him, he smiled and ruffled my hair. "It was duty to come to a patient, Mrs Bendon."

I hadn't taken it in until that moment, then I cried and cried.

Sam tried to comfort me. "Don't cry, Belle, I understand and feel like weeping myself. She was a grand old lady. I think the time she was here with us, she was very happy." I still sobbed but slowly I realised what he said was true. I would miss her piano playing so much.

I had to let Jim know. At 9.30 that morning, I phoned directory enquiries for the number of Jim's next door neighbour. I asked them to tell Jim the news. Washing dishes after breakfast, the phone rang, Sam answered. He said it was the doctor, telling him that if we went to the surgery on Monday morning he would give me a certificate to take to the registrar in Lea Bridge Road to pick up a death certificate and the government grant of thirty pounds towards funeral expenses (this grant was issued to the next of kin at that time, I don't know when it ceased).

Sam continued, "Why not go to see Len in the next road, tell him to let Flo know." This I did. Len could not believe me. "Gracious," he said. "I thought Aunt Belle would go on forever. She was a survivor, I'll take a trip to Walthamstow to tell Mum, we would all like to go to the funeral."

I returned home about an hour later. Earlier Sam had helped me put a clean nightdress on Mum. Now I said, "I'll give Mum a little wash."

"Belle, the undertakers have taken her while you were at Len's."

I began crying as Jim, Myrtle and Tony arrived. I dried my eyes and we began relating to Jim the events leading to Mum's death.

"I didn't think undertakers worked Sundays," said Myrtle.

"The doctor phoned," replied Sam, saying they would call for the body. I suggested Belle see Len to get her away from the house.

Before Jim left he arranged to phone Tuesday, by that time I would know when the funeral would take place. I think I did things automatically. Sam wanted to take time off work to help me. I insisted that he continued working, I could cope. I rushed around doing all the necessary details. Mum had paid for the grave in Motspur Park, to be with Bill. "It's in Surrey," I told the undertaker when I went to have a last look at Mum. They told me they would have to charge distance, and I agreed.

"Mother always wore a double cluster ring, please, I would like that and her wedding ring." Two seconds later the rings were in my hand, so they had already been take off her fingers.

The funeral would be on Monday at eleven o'clock. I notified relatives and friends.

The cost of Mum's funeral was £227, including £20 distance. She had asked George Bendon to book a room in Bethnal Green Town Hall for her ninetieth birthday on the 4th of June, instead the cash paid for her funeral.

I went up to her bedroom. Opening a drawer I found a large purse tied round with tape. In it I counted £220. I was amazed. Had I known that much cash was in the house, I don't think we would have gone off on holiday. Sam's Aunt Lil always came to stay with Mum while we were away and they had become firm friends and as Aunt Lil always said, it was a holiday for her too, despite the fact that she lived just half an hour's walk away.

There were a great many flowers and all invited turned up. We picked up Jim and friends at Motspur Park, and after the service everyone returned to our house for a buffet tea. Everyone spoke in praise of Mum. All decided that she had never paraded her troubles too loudly yet sometimes life must have been difficult for her. All this was said by friends who knew her best. "Ma was a lovely mum-in-law," Sam said, "I'll miss her."

In May, Sam's Aunt Lil was taken into hospital and died in June.

That was a blow to her three daughters and we felt more sadness to overcome. They were all married and they shared Aunt's effects.

In 1973 in our area the slogan said, "Plant a tree." Workman sawed the branches off an old plane tree and with cables round the old large tree attached to lorries driving slowly along it was uprooted. We lost the tree from the corner and outside our house was planted a mountain ash. In other roads, blossoming almond and cherry trees were planted and in springtime the roads looked very decorative.

Flo became ill and her granddaughter moved her to a rest home in Southwark where she died. We attended a requiem mass in Southwark Cathedral. She was buried at Kensal Rise cemetery, a far cry from her origins in Walthamstow.

Apart from all that we still went dancing, sometimes travelling to our old haunts in Bethnal Green and Shoreditch. I had a few clients who were regulars for an iron wave and our lives went on.

In 1976 Sam's brother George became ill with some kind of chest infection. He was admitted to Bethnal Green Hospital and from there he was transferred to Victoria Chest Hospital. Put into intensive care, he made good progress. His wife Edie visited daily, and we visited three evenings a week, always calling on Edie first. On this particular evening, Edie said, "Tell George I'll be in tomorrow evening." In the wards, George was bright and cheerful. "I'm being transferred to the recovery ward tomorrow," he laughed. A young red-haired nurse passed through. "I'm going to make her life a misery when I get into the next ward, she's a real little tarter, I'll show her," he laughed in anticipation.

After some more chitchat we left, promising to see him over the weekend. Back we went to Edie telling her how happy George was.

Next morning, George's son phoned to tell us his dad had died during the night, a massive heart attack. We could not believe our ears. George had seemed so well. He was sixty-eight.

Later that year Sam had complained saying his nose seemed blocked.

His doctor said there were polyps in the nose and it needed surgery. Sam was operated on in Mile End Hospital. With his brother Joe we visited a few times. Sam made rapid progress and was soon home.

US troops were still waging war in Vietnam; sometimes there seemed a stalemate, neither side making progress. Irish terrorists left bombs timed to explode on the mainland and lives were lost.

Chapter Sixty-two

Summer-time, Olive's husband Jean-Pierre died. His funeral was an impressive ceremony in Surrey. The priest said, "This brave man of France buried in a country he came to love." His medals were placed on his coffin, draped in the tricolour of France. Olive kept his medals.

A little later that year Joe's wife Babs was very ill and admitted to hospital. An operation found she had an advanced growth. She died of cancer in March.

After Christmas, not knowing Babs was so ill, we were making arrangements for our fortieth wedding anniversary. We had invitation cards printed and had paid a deposit hiring a hall. When Joe spoke of Babs's death Sam and I decided to cancel, but later, speaking to Joe, he said, "No, Babs would not like to spoil your fun." So invitations went out. Our anniversary date was the 10th of July. As the 8th fell on a Saturday, that date was decided upon. I rushed around ordering, buying and spending like money was going out of fashion. I sent sixty-seven invites, so nearer the date I began making all types of cakes and tarts, getting the delicatessen at the supermarket to slice ham off the bone, to slice corned beef and chicken breast. I ordered various salad items and it was all delivered on the morning of the 8th. My cousin, Doris Munday, arrived early and began making sandwiches. Running Guy's Retreat, a cycling meeting place with her mother, she was great at making sandwiches. The hall was rented from four o'clock until eleven at night. The disco turned up at 4.30. We borrowed glasses from the off-licence where we bought all the booze and a great time was had by all. After eleven o'clock everyone adjourned to our house, friends occupied every room and even the stairs, and all were happy for us. Once I thought of the friends and relations who had passed away and hoped they were with us in spirit. It all quietened down around one o'clock and many left for home. I had insisted on no presents but the house appeared like a florist's, so many had given flowers. Eleven stayed overnight, sleeping on the floor and in chairs. I stood by the cooker with two fry-pans frying sausages, bacon and tomatoes while Sam did slices of toast.

By 10.30 the house was quiet, all had left. The sink was full of dishes and the place was a shambles. "Where do we start?" I asked.

"Let's have a quiet coffee," answered Sam. Sipping coffee he said: "Thank you, darling, for everything. Tell me, however have you managed to put up with this deaf old bugger for forty years?"

"I've put up with this deaf old bugger for forty years because I've loved him and if needs be, I'll put up with another forty years," I grinned.

"By that time I'll be a miserable deaf old sod," he laughed.

"No you won't, because we'll both be kicking up daisies."

"As long as you're there I'll be a happy old skeleton. Come, let's get the house tidy, then we can watch telly."

We collected the debris into plastic sacks. I dusted, he pushed round the vac. It took us three hours to get the house ship-shape. By that time we were both tired. We had been having snacks as we worked. We had beans on toast for tea and a little later tumbled into bed.

He said, "After all the excitement, to go to work is an anti-climax." He waved me a cheery goodbye.

In late September I noticed my ankles becoming very swollen. I was worried and saw my doctor who told me I had slight oedema. I had never heard of this. "Is it contagious?" I asked, scared.

"No, it's another word for water retention, we do not know the cause. I'll give you some pills that should clear the trouble."

I took the pills for a month and the trouble cleared.

Early in 1979, immediately after Maureen's daughter married, Maureen divorced Jack. She had tolerated his affairs for some time and now had had enough. She said she was happier not having to wonder about him.

Between the household chores and some hair waving, I was scribbling short stories. In 1973 I had found an agent through the old *Writers' and Artists' Year Book.* First I phoned and was granted an interview and met Mrs Rosemary Gould at Laurence Pollinger of Maddox Street, London. We agreed a ten per cent cut of cash paid for manuscripts placed. Mrs Gould was a great agent. Naturally I had rejections, which I put aside for revision later. I thought about Aunt Agnes and Aunt Minne and decided to write about them, but naturally I changed everything about them. The story ran around two young sisters and the manuscript was sold to *True Stories* for fifty pounds. Sam was tickled pink, saying, "With your brains and my money we'll go places and do things."

Every week we went to dances, travelling sometimes to the old haunts in Hackney, Bethnal Green and Shoreditch.

Chapter Sixty-three

In July of that year we went to Ibiza. We admired the marble flooring in the reception hall and the slatted marble staircase set in wrought iron. The room was large and had a small balcony outside French windows, but the flies really put us off, they were everywhere, fat blue-bottles, though I must say the dining-room was fairly free of them.

I bought a spray, having difficulty telling the assistant my needs. Spraying the heavy curtains did keep some of the pests away.

We had a great time there, having an afternoon siesta and found life really began about nine o'clock at night and went on into the early hours. Even the refuse collectors began work at ten o'clock at night and the streets were always crowded. Sam marvelled at the crude electric bulbs strung across the streets. We watched building workers pouring cement from buckets into hollow columns that were to prop up flooring, so different from the brick buildings in this country. We never went to Spain again.

After a week or so Sam complained about breathing difficulty. I wondered if he had picked up some kind of bug. His doctor told him the polyps in his nose needed surgery. He was admitted to Mile End Hospital at the end of August. I visited each evening, sometimes with his brother Joe. Home after two weeks, our lives rolled along happily.

I began to feel very tired and wondered why. It was nearing Christmas and I was busy sprucing up the house ready for a party.

I began swelling, my body and legs and arms became bloated. The doctor gave me pills and more pills but it made no difference. I became too weak to climb the stairs to bed. Sam brought a single bed into the breakfast room. The party was cancelled and after Christmas the doctor insisted I went into hospital. When I refused he said, "You have acute bronchial pneumonia, you must go into hospital." The doctor left quite angry.

Sam said, "You must go into hospital, Belle, you must." I saw tears in his eyes, so I consented. He phoned the doctor and ten minutes later an ambulance was at the door. "Where are you taking me?" I enquired of the men. "Southend General," they replied cheerfully.

"Please don't take me there, it's too far for anyone to come to see me. The rain streamed onto my face that cold January evening of 1980. Sam held my hand, telling me not to cry, he would be able to manage. All I had to do was get better then I would soon be home with him.

In the November of 1978, when he was sixty-five, he'd said he'd retire. I had told him that if he felt well enough to make the journey, why not continue working? I was sure he'd get bored at home. Now, on the way to the hospital, he said, "I'll give my notice in at the end of the week, I'll keep the place tidy while you're away and I can take care of you when you return home." He smiled at me reassuringly. I felt too ill. I wanted to be back in my home… how long would I be in hospital I wondered?

I was put into intensive care and cried when Sam left.

Next morning I was weighed. "Ten stone three," I heard a nurse say. "What do you usually weigh?" I was asked.

"Somewhere around eight stone five or six," I answered.

"That means all this excess weight is water," the nurse replied.

The doctor came, examined me, poking and prodding different areas of my body and limbs. He left my ward, and two nurses bound my arms and legs in a type of stocking mesh. I was given antibiotic pills then six small white pills, two bluish ones and one brown one and was told I must drink six pints of water daily. My intake and output of liquid would be measured daily. "If I'm full of water," I enquired weakly, "why must I drink all this fluid, won't it make things worse?"

"The doctor hopes it will wash out the infection. Did you know you're on the point of drowning? Don't look so scared." She patted my head and left me. I was more ill than I thought. Then I fell asleep. I was awakened some time later and told to drink two glasses of water. She watched me then wrote notes on the graph hanging at the end of the bed.

Sam came each evening to see me, telling me I was in Chingford Cottage Hospital and I thought I was in Southend General.

Each morning I was dosed with all these pills. I just had a wash from a bowl. In the ordinary way I do not perspire but these pills certainly sweated a lot of water from my system. I was not allowed to bath for ten days, though I was given bed baths. You get no rest in hospitals. I was awakened each morning about five a.m., given a cup of tea, then the pills. Next the ancillary ladies came polishing the floors, and all had to be finished before the doctor did the rounds of the wards.

When my weight reached nine stone I was moved into a larger ward. Ladies there were in for general illnesses and chatted about their home lives. Husbands and children visited in the evening and always Sam came regularly. He brought me bottled water from home. The water at the hospital was drawn from a well, I didn't like the taste. In hospital I formed the idea of a story around the French Resistance. I could write about Jean-Pierre's adventures with the Marquis in France. At my request, Sam brought in pen and paper and I scribbled away. The food was sent in and was never really hot but I suppose was adequate. I began being violently sick at the end of each day, it seemed for no reason. I think the doctor was a little mystified, and I certainly was. I didn't feel too ill. It was decided I should be given a liver biopsy. The doctor painted a space between my ribs on the right side of my body asking, "Can you feel anything?" Finally I could feel nothing. He took a long thin glass-like tube from a paper sleeve and dug it deep between my ribs. It hurt me very much and I said so. He moved the tube about a little then withdrew it. He studied the result for a moment. I asked if I could see what he was looking at. He handed me the tube. All I could see was half an inch of pink worm.

"Is that from my liver?" I queried.

The doctor nodded. "It's not like liver in the butcher's shop," I said.

"No. That liver has been dead a long time, yours is alive. Now listen, you must lie quietly in bed all day tomorrow. You may be in a little pain, but it will pass if you lie quiet."

Next day my right arm felt paralysed and it was very painful indeed. When Sister came round I moaned to her, asking why the biopsy was necessary. "It's to find out if you're diabetic," she answered

"Well, I could have told the doctor I'm not if he had asked."

It all seemed so pointless. I was still being a little sick each day, but despite that I asked to be sent home, and so was discharged after six weeks, with bottles of pills to last a month. The sickness continued.

Sam became alarmed, he said I was losing weight, and when I stood on the scales I was amazed at the reading of seven stone two.

He went with me to our own doctor. I took all the pills with me. Our doctor pushed them around and finally pointed to a very small white pill. "That's a heart pill. I've never known you to have a heart problem." He gave me a cursory going over with the stethoscope and nodded.

"That small pill is making you vomit. You have an immune system, and with anything your body doesn't like it causes you to be sick. In this way those heart pills that your system doesn't need your body rejects. I wish I had more patients like you." The doctor left the room and returned from his dispensary a few moments later.

"These are anti-sickness pills. Take one when you get home and one first thing in the morning. If after that you are still sick, I'll come to you, just phone and I'll be round." We thanked him and following his instructions I never looked back. I had to attend Chingford Cottage Hospital for check-ups each week for six months, taking a urine sample, being weighed and a nurse took a blood sample. Slowly I regained some weight.

Now into 1980 off we went to Jersey in July and once again renewed meetings with holiday friends. We spent lazy days on the beach or visited the other Channel Islands and danced in the evenings. Back home, now Sam had retired, we went everywhere together. He came with me to meet Mrs Gould when I spoke of the idea I had to write about the French Resistance. She asked me to type a 4,000-word skeletal manuscript of my idea. When this was finished I journeyed to Maddox Street. Reading the manuscript through quickly she said, "The idea is good, but get your facts right and weave the fiction in." And for the next two years or so I spent what time I could spare at the Leytonstone Library, Church Lane, swotting up dates in old newspapers. It took ages making notes and fitting items in rotation. I typed and revised and then began again.

My visits to the hospital now were for three-monthly checks, and between typing my novel I submitted a short story to my agent.

Meantime our lives flowed in the usual channel. We visited relations and friends and they returned our visits.

Maureen came to tell us she had met a man at a friend's party. He had two sons, had divorced his wife and naturally was wary of forming a relationship. Maureen too was on her guard. He was boss of an engineering factory. Maureen's daughter was married but there was still her son Marcus to consider. After a short while, Maureen went to work in the office of Allen's factory.

Early in 1981 the tabloid newspapers were full of the Solidarity movement in Poland. On the 6th of June that year, my brother's son Tony married Julie and relations and friends of both sides enjoyed the reception and wished the young couple much happiness in their new life.

On television we watched the wedding of Prince Charles to Lady Diana Spencer. "I'm sure that won't last," remarked Sam. "She's so young and he's been around and dated girls."

"Don't say that. He may be older but they're in love."

He laughed. "I'm willing to bet it has been conveniently arranged." I scoffed at the idea. "Time will tell," Sam replied.

On the 26th of September, Maureen and Allen married. The reception was held at the King George Hotel, Whitehall. About sixty friends and relations sat down to a sumptuous feast. "This will make a gaping hole in Allen's bank balance," commented Sam as he tucked into a large beef steak.

On the 25th of November, my friend Pat's daughter gave birth to a son Michael and a few weeks later we journeyed to King's Lynn for the christening.

About Christmas-time we received an invitation to stay for ten days in Olsberg, Germany. We had met these German people year after year staying at the same hotel in Jersey and we had kept in touch letter writing. They suggested May as the best time for visiting as spring flowers and blossoming trees were then at their best. We accepted with delight and after Christmas began planning for the trip.

In early 1982, the Falklands war began.

Before we started the journey to Olsberg, I warned Sam, "This Falklands, there's a large German element in the Argentine. Be careful what you say about this war. I know, Sam, how you can open your mouth and put your foot in it."

"What? Is it us and them again?"

We flew to Dusseldorf to be met at the airport. The day was warm and sunny. Our friends produced cold drinks from an icebox and we were driven 200 kilometres to Olsberg. Their house was large and roomy.

They drove us to meet their friends, showed us beauty spots, and once we were taken to a party in a beer cellar. Drinking songs were sung and the beer flowed. With them we belted out *Lilli Marlene*, quite enjoyable.

They held a party in the cellar. During World War II, I had read that German families were living in their cellars.

This cellar was like a basement flat. Seats were built round the walls, there were shelves stocked with preserves. A large side room contained a shower, sink and toilet and there was plenty of hot water. I asked if all houses had a similar cellar and was told yes, most of them had large cellars. I thought about our cellar, of years having coal shot down the shoot with coal dust clinging here and there to the whitewashed walls. What a contrast. Needless to say, when they visited us I didn't show our cellar.

In Olsberg at every street corner there were flowers growing. At that time of the year, May, there were mostly pansies and they were mostly all one colour; all white, yellow, lavender and deep purple. And everywhere was so very clean. I couldn't help comparing our roads to theirs. Although our road was swept each day it did not appear quite so spick and span.

Later they came to stay with us for two weeks. We introduced them to our friends and showed them our London. Whatever they wanted to see we took them there. We queued for over an hour in the Tower because they wanted to see the Crown Jewels and we gave them a farewell party, which they thought great.

In July of that year we went off to Jersey. While there I suggested to Sam that we could go to France and journey inland a little to give me an idea of the forest for my book. He wasn't too keen but agreed.

We crossed the Channel by hovercraft to the walled town of St Malo. We walked round the ramparts then made our way to the market square.

Sam was amused to see a small whole pig roasting over a charcoal fire; it was being sold off in slices from the pig as it became cooked through. We had coffee and sticky buns at a bistro and were eyed with some curious glances. We found a car driver with a fair knowledge of English, and with my bad French we started off inland for the nearest forest. The Normandy countryside was lush and green and soon we came to a heavily wooded area with embankments and narrow lanes. This I decided was as far as we needed to go so we returned to St Malo, my head full of ideas for my story.

In 1984 my brother moved to Cissbury Avenue, Peacehaven. As Myrtle was asthmatic I wondered if this was unwise, being near the sea with the heavy mists that could occur.

Jim phoned saying that as soon as he had finished some decorating, we would be welcome to visit. A few months later we travelled to Peacehaven. A wide drive led to the garage and their street door. The bungalow was compact with two good sized bedrooms and a large lounge. Although the kitchen was small, it opened to a large lean-to. This Jim had made his dining-room. The wide windows gave a view of the garden, and a small greenhouse and a garden shed completed the picture.

"It's all you need as you grow older, Jim, I like it very much and wish you both all happiness here," Sam said, and we thanked them for their hospitality and a nice day.

We spoke quite a lot about the bungalow as we travelled homeward.

Apart from plumbing and electrics (these things Sam would not attempt) we did all our own decorating and maintenance.

One Saturday morning Sam had been replacing a slate that had slipped on the roof. Entering the kitchen he remarked, "There's a lot to be said for doing your own maintenance from a step ladder. How about thinking of living in a bungalow? We rattle around in this big house like two peas in an empty can."

"You serious? It's an idea."

"Belle, we're not getting younger, I think we could get a good price for this place. Let's think about it." The phone rang at that moment. Maureen told me tearfully that Allen had died. They had a large garden and Allen had been mowing the lawn. She went to call him for coffee to find him lying beside the lawn mower, too late to help him. He had had a massive heart attack. I listened in disbelief. They had been so happy together in their short marriage. We travelled to Great Missenden for the funeral. Maureen was told that only a heart transplant could have saved his life. Allen had not changed his will since his marriage to Maureen. She stayed in the house with Olga the housekeeper until she could find somewhere to live.

As her son Marcus had taken over the flat where she lived before she married Allen, she decided to get back to the flat. She found an office job, to keep her mind occupied, she told us.

Between household chores and some clients' hairdos, I worked on my novel. I wrote and re-wrote sentences. We spent musical evenings together. Sam was no Caruso but we made a tuneful sound singing. Sam belted out *South of the Border* and *Donkey Serenade* and we had the occasional party. Almost every Saturday we went dancing. It was good exercise.

During 1984 the IRA were busy targeting the mainland, causing loss of life, damage and service interruption in many areas.

Explosives planted in the Grand Hotel, Brighton, exploded during the Conservative Party conference, there were injuries to some MPs and Norman Tebbit, a member of the cabinet, was injured and his wife Margaret has since spent her life in a wheelchair.

Chapter Sixty-four

Returning from Jersey in 1985, Sam began talking seriously about moving. "Let's try for a small bungalow, something like Jim's."

"You're not thinking of Peacehaven, are you?" I queried.

"Heavens, no, I thought about Chingford. That's the place for bungalows. Let's have a day out tomorrow, have a pub lunch; maybe drop in to see Lil Remon and take it from there."

Gazing in estate agents' windows, the prices of bungalows amazed us. The price of a two-bedroomed bungalow ranged from £110,000 to £120,000. "We could never get that for our house," I remarked dismally.

After lunch we obtained keys for a bungalow near Chingford Mount. It was certainly small and very dirty, and Sam turned up his nose.

"That's it. Let's visit Lil." And all we spoke about was rising house prices.

An estate agent valued our house at £80,000. I was amazed.

He said, "You can always drop £500. The place is immaculate; you'll have no difficulty getting that price. We will be happy to handle the conveyancing." He handed Sam his card. "We have people ready on our list waiting to move into this area."

We talked it over and two days later the house was on the market and Sam insisted no sale board be put on the house.

We studied a large map of Surrey and Sussex. Surrey we knew

was costly. I stuck a pin in Sussex; it landed between Crawley and Haywards Heath. We decided to find Haywards Heath.

Enquiries at Leytonstone Station told us, "Get to Victoria Station and it's a straight run from there."

Three days later the estate agent phoned to say a gentleman wished to view the house next day and hoped it would be convenient.

At 9.30 next morning a tall thin man arrived.

"I can have a quick look round now, and may I bring my wife this evening if I think it will suit us? It will be about seven o'clock."

At the appointed time they arrived in a heavy downpour. The lady didn't look too happy, I thought it was the weather.

During the afternoon a Mrs Black, who said she lived in an adjoining road, looked over the house and exclaimed it was just what she was looking for and said she would bring her husband to view tomorrow. Now we had two would-be buyers.

I asked if the couple would like tea after they had viewed. They said if it would not be too much trouble, that would be nice. I left it to Sam to do the guided tour.

Sam showed them round. It was September, they asked Sam if they could see the garden. He let them into the garden and left them. They spent fifteen minutes in the heavy rain. We wondered what they were doing all this time. When they came in I offered them tea. They wanted to know about the next door neighbours, if they had children, loud music etc.

They left after saying they would think it over and let us know tomorrow evening and did we think we could accept £70,000?

Sam told them another person was viewing and we would take the person who could first offer the initial deposit to the agent.

We had a definite sale by Thursday. Now I was on pins to find a bungalow for ourselves.

We set off Friday morning and called in at the first estate agent we came to and stated our wants and were taken to a bungalow in Ashington. To me it seemed miles from the station.

The place was a tip, with four children and a dog, toys and trash were strewn everywhere. I questioned a huge tank in the garden and was told it was for the oil-fired central heating and the price was £56,595. I didn't like that tank in the garden. Sam thought we could do something with it and two days later we had it surveyed and the report was frightening. It seemed the place was riddled with woodworm and had a leak in a pipe under the sink. We soon turned that down. The next week we again journeyed to Haywards Heath, found another estate agent and were taken to Burgess Hill. Another bungalow looking trim went down steps. The rooms were so small and seemed more so after the large rooms of our London house. We went down three steps into a small garden. A high red brick wall faced us with overhanging branches. "Do you think the people the other side of the wall would agree to me lopping those branches?" Sam enquired.

The agent smiled. "They are very quiet people. That is the end of the cemetery."

Sam grinned. "Sorry, no go. If I died she'd throw me over the wall." The agent laughed and we left. We found another agent in Haywards Heath Broadway, Braxtons. We viewed two bungalows and decided on one in Eastern Road. We entered to a lovely smell of cooking. We found the rooms a good size, a large kitchen and lounge, every room had some shade of blue wallpaper, the bathroom had a pale blue suite, the kitchen blue Marley tiled flooring, blue walls, blue worktops and blue curtains. I shivered; I was back years in the pub, blood splashing on my mother's sleeve. "I can't live here, Sam… all this blue. You know it's a colour I dislike."

The vendor gazed at me curiously as Sam said, shaking me, "It has great potential. We can re-decorate." Turning to the vendor he said, "Your asking price is £53,995?"

She nodded, "I'll accept £53,000 if you wish to re-decorate."

"I'll offer you £53,500. It'll be a cash sale and if you're thinking about gazumping, you can forget it. Agreed?"

A surveyor's report told of some dampness that could be overcome. So the sale of our house went to the second viewer and all went smoothly.

I kept moaning about the blue decor. Sam, exasperated replied, "Look how we've changed this house from what it was, it was a dump when we first moved here. Look at it now."

"We were both twenty years younger, Sam."

"So we were. How time flies. Amazing. We'll have to sell some of this furniture, there's no way all this will fit into that place. The bunk beds will have to go, those two large armchairs, the piano and my chess table and that cabinet. We could raise a few pounds."

Sell the piano, I felt choked, yet I realised it had to go.

The bunk beds went for thirty pounds, the chess table and six-inch men for forty and the piano for sixty, other items accordingly.

There was so much to think about, I wrote letters to friends and relations giving our new address. Sam contacted a removals firm who came to assess the cost and distance. They would collect the furniture one day, store the packed pantechnicon in their yard overnight and proceed to Haywards Heath next day and the cost would be £300 plus VAT. We agreed.

Now to find somewhere to stay the night. Sam thought of asking his sister May, then realised she was living in Dorset with her daughter Joan. "We'll find a hotel," I said as the phone rang. It was a friend.

She had received my letter. I told her we were looking for a place to stay the night and she immediately suggested that she would pick us up and we could stay at her house in Eltham. She would then drive us to our new home. "I want to black my nose to see what the bungalow is like," she laughed. "You'll probably freeze in the new place, it's snowing heavily here at the moment, so wrap up. Be seeing you."

To say we were very grateful to our friend Pat was putting it mildly. We had borrowed tea chests from the removals firm and all was ready when the men arrived. We left carpets and curtains and four folding garden chairs and a small wardrobe, and taking the keys to the new owner of our house, in falling snow, we left London. I thought of the piano. No more musical evenings singing with Sam… no more parties… I felt sad and near to tears, that piano had meant so much to me. I said as much to Sam as our friend Pat drove carefully along.

"Never mind, darling, I'll buy you a keyboard."

"Where will you put a keyboard in a bungalow?"

"Under the bed," he answered quickly. I never did get that keyboard. We duly arrived at Pat's house in Eltham, tired, and I felt a little disgruntled. After tucking in to Pat's chicken casserole we all felt better.

As we fell into Pat's four-poster bed with pale cream drapes, Sam laughed, "I'm on cloud nine, so just watch it."

"Just forget fun and games tonight, we have some heavy work to do tomorrow and with the snow, what will the carpets look like?"

"We'll change those carpets for something we like, you'll see."

The week previously Sam had phoned asking the seller of the bungalow if he could bring some plants to put in the garage. The lady had consented and my brother, Jim, had driven Sam with the plants to the bungalow. Now Sam wondered how his geranium cuttings were keeping in the cold garage. As Pat drove along the A272, the rutted snow, discoloured by traffic, looked like Demerara sugar. We turned into Eastern Road, where the snow, almost four inches deep, was cleaner. Pat slowed outside the bungalow. We were surprised to see the removals van in the roadway, still full of furniture. The removals men looked angry. One said to Sam as he got out of the car, "They won't let us unload."

"They? Who are they?" asked Sam.

"The bloke in there said money hasn't been paid."

I thought of the cheque I had paid in for the full amount a week previously. "What do you mean?" I snapped. "I paid in the cheque myself."

We marched into the bungalow. A large man stood by the window, a lady by his side. "What's the big idea?" Sam asked.

"Somewhere along the line, cash hasn't been paid, so I cannot part with the keys and you cannot move in. I'm a policeman and I know I'm right. If you like you can move what you can into the garage but you can't have the keys." The removals men were furious. "We're supposed to be back in Walthamstow by twelve o'clock. We have another job to do." It was now 11.30. They began unloading and rushing things into the garage. Sam was stacking his precious plants on shelves to prevent any damage to them. He was furious.

"You must realise our furniture will not go into that garage. It will have to be left in the drive and if it's damaged by the weather, we will know who to blame." I turned as Sam entered.

"May I move in a bed?" he asked sarcastically.

"Move your furniture in, but you can't have the keys. I live in East Grinstead, this is my phone number. Ring your solicitor, find out from him what's happened and explain the situation here."

Chatting to our solicitor, the conversation was long. Sam said, "He'll phone around and try to trace the delay. Now what?"

The policeman and his wife, I presumed, then left, saying, "As soon as you hear something definite, phone and I'll be back with the keys. Good day." Sam didn't answer, he was too angry.

The removals men worked like beavers rushing in the furniture, dumping it wherever we suggested. Sam paid their bill, £300 plus VAT, in cash. They were happy with the tip, but left grumbling.

We made a tour of the bungalow. There was a bolt on the street door and one on the garden door but nothing on the French windows, and these opened onto the garden. We considered the situation.

"In the tea chest containing the garden tools, there is my plastic clothesline. We could wind that round the inside handles, that is if we don't hear from the solicitor and we don't get the keys."

Soon after four o'clock the phone rang. It seemed that an initial deposit had been paid by a buyer in the chain who had then gone swanning off to Germany for a holiday. Sam phoned the policeman who arrived with the keys. At 4.30 on the 12th of December 1986 we became the owners of the bungalow in Eastern Road. "Nothing seems to go right first time for us, Belle, but we get there in the end." We thanked Pat for her help. She left wishing us health and happiness in our new home.

It was getting dark. By the light from the open French doors, Sam swept snow from the paved patio. We then got in the stuff the removals men had dumped in the garage, just leaving the plants. Sam lit a candle and stuck it firmly to the stone garage floor, thus hoping his plants would survive the intense coldness. There was hardly room to move around in the lounge. "I'll make tea while you fix a meal, Belle, I feel all in."

I opened some tins and soon we were feeding the inner man.

"We'll start on the attic room first, working downwards, and tomorrow we'll go into town, find out what's what and get some shopping."

Taking our shopping trolley, we bought gloss and emulsion paint; we could think about wallpaper later. Walking home, it hit me like a sledgehammer. I was seventy-nine, soon to be eighty; would I feel like climbing ladders and sticking up wallpaper? Oh, well, in for a penny, in for a pound, and when I thought again, I shrugged.

We got going. Wallpaper was measured for each room and the hall. In the shop we looked at pattern books. When we decided what we wanted and paid up, the shopkeeper told us he would deliver.

Slowly things were going to our liking.

On the 18th of December Jim phoned excitedly telling us he was now a grandfather. His son's wife Julie had a boy and so far all was well. The baby was to be called James and was Jim thrilled!

Two weeks previously, through *Yellow Pages*, we had contacted the Sussex Timber Preservation Company. Two men worked from our surveyor's report and treated all woodwork in the front rooms of the bungalow.

That cost £300 and had a thirty-year guarantee. (Anything can happen in thirty years.) They gave Sam the phone number of a good builder when he said he wanted new airbricks, as the existing ones were just a brick's width. This was soon done to Sam's liking and two extra air bricks were fixed too. "Plenty of draught under the flooring now, sir."

Sam was pleased. I don't know what that cost.

Chapter Sixty-five

Christmas loomed ahead, and now we had finished a bedroom and the dining-room. It was Christmas Eve. I went into the hall and saw a small card had been pushed through the letterbox. It read, "Flowers left at No. 17" – but who would send us flowers? We had told relatives and friends our new address and we were not expecting flowers.

I called at Number 17 for the flowers. The door was answered by a short thin lady, who peered at me in the gloom.

"Yes, yes, come in. The flowers are in the conservatory."

I followed her into her house, though a living-room into a narrow lean-to. There were plants growing in an untidy profusion.

She picked up a paper-covered plate saying, "Please come in for a drink." As I shook my head she continued, "It's Christmas-time and surely you need a little relaxation. You're decorating, yes?"

I nodded. "It's kind of you to invite us strangers but as you can see, I am not cleaned up, and we are very busy."

"I'm Mrs Klein, Christiana, and you are?"

"Mrs Bendon."

"Yes, Mrs Bendon, but what do I call you?"

"Belle," I replied, short for Isabelle… for my sins."

"Go bring your husband, he must have a drink with me."

"We're not drinkers, Mrs Klein, just soft drinks." From her

accent she was either French or Spanish. "Don't be too surprised if I return without him."

"Surely he will not refuse at this time of year."

I made to take the flowers as she said quickly, "Leave the flowers, you bring your husband."

It was cold and raining and I was sure Sam would not be too pleased. I related to him her offer. "Honestly, I don't see how we can refuse. I think she's trying to be neighbourly, and it's Christmas."

"Look at the state I'm in. How can I visit?"

"Have a quick wash, I'll get you a clean sweater and I'll find a clean dress. I'm not sure if she's French or Spanish."

He began getting cleaned up, grumbling all the time. "Who sent the flowers?" he asked as we made for her gate. Light flooded from her open door as we entered her gate.

"Merry Christmas to both of you. Thank you for coming." She closed the door and we followed her into a small living-room. A log fire burned brightly and it all looked very cosy. Two small tables showed mixed nuts and some chocolates in small dishes.

"What do I call you, Mr Bendon?" she enquired.

"I'm called Sam," he answered, I thought a little reluctantly.

She pointed to an armchair beside the fire. "Now you sit there and relax and Isabelle, you sit there." I looked sharply at her at the full use of my name, she pointed to what I assumed was a blanket-covered divan. "Help yourselves to nuts and sweets, while I pour drinks."

"We drink soft drinks, if you have some," I said quickly.

"You'll like this, it's grape juice, it's delicious." She poured into small glasses a red juice from a carton. We toasted each other and drank. The juice was sweet and pleasant to taste.

"Mrs Woodward, the person you bought the bungalow from, told me you came from London," Mrs Klein began. "Tell me about yourselves."

"We lived in Wanstead, bordering on Epping Forest, Essex," Sam told her and from his tone, I knew he thought she was being nosy.

Sam asked her if she knew a reliable electrician. "Yes, Mr Towner at Number 19." She would speak to him if Sam told her what he wanted done. Sam bridled, "I'm quite capable of stating my needs, thank you. Electricity and plumbing are things I don't meddle with."

I think she took the hint. He looked at his watch.

"It's nearly eight o'clock. Thank you for the invite, Mrs Klein, but I need some dinner. Thank you again." He stood up.

"Please call me Christiana, Sam." He nodded. I thanked her and we hurried home through heavy rain. Once home he said grinning, "I bet all she found out will be all round the road by the end of the week." We didn't know then that few neighbours spoke to her. That we learned much later.

We spent Christmas resting, watching television and eating. Sam contacted Mr Towner and our electric fittings were fixed to our liking, including wall lights, for which I purchased globes.

Early in January 1987, Myrtle phoned saying Jim was complaining of pains in the stomach. In telling her to make him see his GP she replied, "You know how obstinate Jim can be." I asked her to let us know how he was going on. We spoke of our progress, the decoration was very pleasing to us so far, and we spoke too about the Christmas holiday.

Suddenly I remarked to Sam, "Do you realise I'll be eighty next month? Are we going out to eat as usual?"

"Darling, you don't look a day over seventy."

"Flattery will get you everywhere, but thanks for the compliment."

The first week in February, Myrtle rang to say Jim had been admitted to Brighton Hospital for tests as the stomach pains had continued.

We visited Jim there arriving at the hospital at about 11.45, to be told it wasn't visiting time. Sam explained where we had come from and we were grudgingly allowed to see Jim.

He was at the end of a long ward. He looked ill and had lost some weight. He was pleased to see us. All through our lives I had never known my brother to be ill, apart from an occasional cold. He told us he was having antibiotics and pills and was feeling much better.

While we were there, dinner was served. The sausage with mash and carrots, swimming in brown gravy, did not look too appetising.

"What's the food like, Jim?" asked Sam.

"Well, if you feel hungry you eat it, it's not all that good."

We were asked to leave and saying we would come again, we left.

Myrtle phoned, Jim was home, feeling well, and little James would be christened the second week in March. It was a very jolly occasion and Jim was a very proud granddad. It was great to see Jim looking so well.

A few days later Myrtle phoned again. Jim was in the Royal Sussex Hospital and could be visited any time. This shook us rigid. Myrtle said Jim had been very sick, a thick brownish fluid had come from his stomach and the doctor had immediately sent him to hospital. We visited two days later. Jim was very poorly and hardly spoke to us. We spoke quietly to him about what we were doing. Jim just nodded, eyes closed. The ward was bright and Jim was near a window from which one could see treetops. Eventually we left saying we would visit again.

Jim said quietly, "Don't leave it too long, Belle."

Sam saw a doctor and asked if he knew what was Jim's illness. "An x-ray shows signs of a burst ulcer, we're doing all we can."

We spoke about this on the bus going home, I wanted to know how Jim could have developed an ulcer. "He had a worrying job during the war."

But the war had ended years previously, surely an ulcer didn't take years to develop, or did it? April began with warm sunny days.

We visited Jim on the 17th of April. Myrtle, Tony and Tony's wife Julie were there when we arrived. Jim appeared a little brighter, taking notice. We had arrived at two p.m. and we stayed with the family until six, saying we would visit next day.

"It's a long journey without a car, Sam," said Tony. "Leave it for a couple of days and I'll come for you in my car." This was agreed to.

We were absolutely astounded when Tony phoned to say that Jim had died on the 19th, just two days after we had last seen him.

We arrived for the funeral, Sam asking, "Where's Jim?"

"At the Brighton crematorium," answered Myrtle.

"You're having him cremated, Myrtle. Our mother would not like that. Why not a burial?" I queried.

"Your mother isn't here and it's my choice," she snapped.

We set off for Brighton. It was a beautiful sunny day and to me it appeared no more than a car ride. The car followed no hearse as Myrtle remarked, "Why ride the coffin all the way from Brighton only to ride it back again?" The service was short. I didn't see Myrtle cry.

I thought of the many things we did together when we were small, and I cried, it seemed so unfair. I was the last of our small family.

Back home in our bungalow, Sam tried to console me.

"Try to realise, Belle, Jim is not suffering now." So gradually one comes to terms with the loss of a loved brother.

It was at the end of April, I think. In the Russian Ukraine a nuclear reactor exploded at Chernobyl. There was loss of life and many people suffered from radiation and crops were ruined for miles due to the effects of radiation carried by the wind. I thought about our plants processing nuclear waste at Sellafield and Dungeness. Was that risky?

In early May, Sam asked Mrs Klein if she would sell him a piece of land. For a peppercorn rent, she said, he could have a piece of her land at the end of her ground. It was adjacent to the fenced off property in the next road and for five pence, if he would sometimes cut the grass and hedge, she would agree. The five pence was paid and Sam began to clear the bramble-overgrown plot. It took him ages. He then planted seed potatoes to break up the soil and then behind our garage he planted beans.

This bungalow was the first place we had bought that was centrally heated. The water was hot and constant. We showered each evening after a day decorating. As the warmer days of May approached, a phone call to British Gas brought a very helpful workman. He cleaned the boiler, saying it was sooted up, showed Sam how to expel air from the radiators then went into the loft to inspect the head tank. He suggested we had a yearly three-star service thus maintaining a no-trouble heating system. He produced a docket, which Sam duly signed, agreeing the work was satisfactory and saying a bill would arrive in due course. When the bill came two weeks later, we were amazed. For half an hour's work, the cost was £54 plus VAT. "For sure I was certainly in the wrong trade… and he used our electricity to clean the boiler with his small vac." Sam was quite annoyed.

"Pay up and look happy," I said. "We won't need heat until the autumn. "Meantime we use the immersion heater, so smile."

Meantime we had bought material and I machined long curtains for all windows. Mrs Klein came constantly for Sam to do a job for her. He told me that once in her house she had another job lined up for him and he was getting tired of her demands. He bought a large roll of heavy-duty plastic. He would relay the paving stones in the patio and with the plastic underneath, no weeds could come through the cracks. Later he would build a small lean-to to use as a greenhouse for seeds and plants. He wanted to get that finished before winter. Sam was laying wood-patterned lino squares on the floor and I was up the ladder hanging curtains when Mrs Klein entered. "Would Sam please reach some plates off the wall?" She wanted to wash them and Sam was so tall.

"I can't leave this, you'll have to wait," Sam said shortly.

"Well, how long will you be?"

"I don't know… as long as it takes." She left in a huff, saying, "All my hot water will get cold."

"You're doing more for her than you are for me."

"She's in and out of this place like a fart in a colander and doesn't know which hole to get through," Sam replied.

"That's a very rude thing to say about her," I laughed.

"I could say much worse than that. For her five pence a year for that plot, she's certainly getting her pound of flesh. I'll stop her gallop somehow… all right, I know she's a woman on her own, but….

The kitchen was finished, pale cream walls, the lower half covered with light brown tiling, and the light flooring made me feel much happier. Now all that was left to do was the lounge. Furniture was arranged in place and we could take things slower.

Sam sent to the council for permission to build an eight by ten foot glass-covered lean-to over the patio paving. An inspector told Sam it would have to be built two feet away from the boiler grille, as fumes could be very dangerous. Eventually the lean-to was finished. If anyone came to inspect the work, we never knew. The bungalow was detached and anyone could walk round if we were out.

By June all our decorating ended. One day I was sorting my manuscript of my novel and deciding to do some revision when in walked Mrs Klein, and I dropped many pages to the floor. I was furious.

"Now look what's happened," I said angrily.

She began picking up the sheets of paper. "You writing a story?" she asked.

"Trying to write a novel," I answered.

"I'll take it home and put it in order. Let me help."

I felt I'd been a little ungracious to her and agreed.

"What did you come in for? Sam is showering."

"It's to make arrangements for him to tend my garden when I go to Canada for my holiday. I go for four weeks."

"When you bring those papers back, you can ask him. Four weeks you say you'll be gone? You have relatives there?"

"My son, Alain, lives there with his wife and children, I visit each year. He works for the Canadian Airlines."

Fronting the road, there were hydrangea bushes, and in June there was a profusion of large blue florets that spilled onto the pavement. Sam decided to build a wall. At the end of the road, at the time, there was a builder's yard. He measured the length and height of the intended wall, went to the builders and had eighteen- by nine-inch breeze blocks delivered along with the necessary sand and cement two days later.

Mrs Klein came in with my novel saying it was now in rotation and she had read it and thought it good. I thought she had a cheek and said that I would probably retype and revise it. She wanted to know what Sam was doing with all those bricks. She said she would like Sam to keep her garden watered if the weather was dry while she was away. She would be gone a month. He promised. She left at the end of July.

Chapter Sixty-six

Sam began building the wall. First he cut back the hydrangea bushes. Neighbours began chatting and we realised we lived among friendly people. Sunny evenings he tended Mrs Klein's garden. Between household chores and cooking I retyped and revised my novel, and also had an idea for a short story. Mrs Klein returned mid-September. She had been away six weeks. She brought in a half-filled pint whisky bottle for Sam as a thank you for tending her garden, she told him. He eyed the half-filled bottled and said a dubious thanks. Later he said it had been watered.

The last day of September was sunny and warm. Sam had worked hard in the garden. Just before lunch he had cut Mrs Klein's grass. He spent about an hour after lunch mowing our lawn, and then said he would shower.

I was typing when she came. "Where's Sam?" she demanded.

"In the shower; why, what's wrong?" From her tone of voice I knew something had upset her.

"He has cut the couch grass into my beautiful leeks and that grass takes root. My leeks are spoiled. I'll tell him what I think."

"Be careful what you say. He can dig his heels in," I replied.

She stormed out and a while later I repeated her moaning to Sam.

"That's it. This is a chance I've been waiting for. I'll kiss her goodbye once and for all and finish." As he left, I called after him. "Let her down lightly, Sam. She's upset."

I doubt he heard my last sentence, I went on typing.

He came back a short time later. He was smiling.

"What are you grinning at?" I asked.

"We had a real show-down. To all her arguments I had the answers. All I could hear was her beautiful leeks. Seems you dig a large hole and plant a leek and the leek grows and fills the hole. She only wanted me to pick out the bits of grass that had fallen into the holes. I soon told her where to get off. I've finished doing things for her and have told her. I'll be in and out of the garden tending to my plot. I shall dig up the vegetables I have planted and she can have her ground back at Christmas and that's final. When I told her all that, she began crying, that made me leave sharpish. That's why I'm grinning."

"I'll bet you she'll be in again, trying to get round you."

"Belle, it doesn't matter to me what she does from now on."

"I'm sure she'll find an excuse to ask for your help, Sam."

About mid-October came the night of the hurricane. I woke to the sound of howling winds and a dreadful tearing sound and a loud crash.

In a panic I woke Sam. He looked out of the window and saw a car rolling along the road. The heavy wooden gates to our drive had vanished. In the kitchen I made tea, I was too scared to stay in bed.

"It's a terrible violent storm, Belle. Don't be frightened, it can't last much longer." Even as he spoke came the sound of smashing glass and falling brickwork. I thought I heard a scream.

In daylight we saw the extent of the damage to our property. All our fences were gone and insurers do not pay out for fencing.

After a snatched breakfast we began trying to clear away the broken fencing. Mrs Klein came in almost in tears.

"Please, Sam, I need your help. Half my roof has gone and the tiles have broken the glass of my lean-to. Please help me."

He cut off yards and yards from the roll of the heavy-duty plastic. It opened out to twelve feet wide. This he took into her loft and spread over the rafters. He assured her it was costly, but she said she would pay as she was insured. He told me the rafters in her roof were so full of woodworm he wondered how they held up the roof.

"That loft is full of old cases and boxes, it all needs clearing out. She tells me it all belongs to her son, Alain. I'm getting out of these clothes and I'll burn them, they may be full of woodwork flies and I don't want them in our bungalow." The clothes were duly burnt. The wooden gate to our street door hung drunkenly on its hinges. Sam quickly got rid of that.

And between times I was revising my novel.

Sam bought fencing and concrete stays to replace the fencing blown down during the hurricane. He worked very hard; this was work I couldn't help with. He ordered wrought iron gates for the drive and entrance to the bungalow, and finishing that job just before Christmas he was very happy to laze away the holiday period; and so we came to 1988.

This year would be our fiftieth anniversary. We fixed our break in Jersey for the last week in July and the first week in August.

Sam's sister May's son John's tenth anniversary fell on the 6th of July. May suggested we shared the anniversary. The first week in July we journeyed to Dorset. May brought us a brass ornament of two dolphins, which was much admired. As it was John and Elizabeth's tin anniversary we bought them a chrome meat dish; it was tin-coloured, so….

Around May time I had phoned friends regarding our coming anniversary.

The second week in July we held a garden party and twenty-eight turned up. I did not invite neighbours; I felt we didn't know any well enough. It was all so different from our fortieth. There was no music, no dancing, but all chatted and joked and had a good time stuffing.

We left the birds to clear up the crumbs.

The last week in July we went off to Jersey. We met some old friends and spent some time with our Jersey friend, Madeleine, who had recently lost her husband. While in Jersey we went twice weekly dancing in the Somerville Hotel in St Albans. On this day Sam was kicking a ball around the beach with some other men when he stumbled and began rubbing his calf muscle. I went to him. He said he thought it had been a hard lump of sand. "I'm afraid dancing is off tonight, my leg is painful." I helped him to a deck chair and said I would go to the chemist for pain-relieving cream. This did help and two days later when we left Jersey he walked with a slight limp. He suggested an elastic support might help, and with this aid and some rest the pain eased and he was getting around almost as usual. Sam suggested we forgo a holiday in 1989 as he had spent a lot of cash, buying the gates and building the wall. This I agreed to.

After Christmas we redecorated the kitchenette and we half-tiled all round the walls. It looked great when finished.

In June we went to a tea dance, but after three dances he complained of leg pains, which were so bad we had a taxi home. After two days, he decided to see his doctor and Sam, always in a hurry, kicked the top step and fell. His doctor diagnosed a badly damaged Achilles tendon and said it would mean an operation, and Sam was sent to Cuckfield Hospital.

This hospital was a series of Nissen huts erected quickly during the war to house wounded Canadian soldiers.

Here an x-ray showed Sam's injury as a snapped Achilles tendon. The operation was performed two days later and he remained in hospital for ten days. I visited him daily. He came home with his right leg in plaster from toe to knee and was lent a Zimmer walking frame to get around.

Can one imagine the grumbling…? Told to keep the plaster dry, taking a shower was like waiting for an accident to happen. With his right leg outside the bath and standing in the bath on his left leg and the shower curtain pinned half round his body and a towel round the top of the plaster it was a sight to see, but somehow we coped. The leg was in plaster for three months. Going with him to the hospital, hopefully to remove the plaster, the surgeon at Cuckfield, on examining the injury, suggested another plaster as the repair was not complete. So I listened to Sam's grumbles for another three months.

When finally the second plaster was removed Sam was delighted. He now walked around with the aid of a walking stick.

In November we saw on television Berliners knocking down the hated Berlin Wall that had divided that city for so many years. The jubilations were an amazing sight.

On the 10th of December, Sam's niece, Joan, phoned to say her mother had had a massive heart attack and had died. We were shocked and saddened. Sam loved his sister May, she was such a very nice person. We went to her funeral and that Christmas was a sad time for us. Sam recalled how we had all felt when my brother Bill had died in 1952.

"It's a lousy time to die, Christmas is never the same," he said.

On the 12th of December a Pan-Am jet exploded over the small Scottish town of Lockerby, killing all 270 on board and many on the ground. It was thought to be the work of terrorists placing a bomb on board when the plane landed at Frankfurt, Germany. A sad happening so near Christmas.

War broke out in the Middle East in January 1990. Saddam Hussein of Iraq launched a bomb and missile attack on Kuwait.

Immediately British, US and French troops were sent to protect the oil wells. This war was short and bloody, with Saddam sending scud missiles over Israel. The war finally ended towards the end of February. Allied aircraft patrolled the air space over the border keeping an eye for anything suspicious.

Chapter Sixty-seven

Shopping for Christmas 1990, I stepped into the road and was almost knocked down. The driver of the car swore furiously. I never saw the car, and shocked I stood on the pavement, suddenly realising I could not see the darkish coloured cars. In the shops, assistants picked out my needs. At home I told Sam what had happened, and he came with me to see my doctor; and after a brief examination the result was a cataract growth that would need an operation. Did the doctor know a good eye surgeon?

"There is a waiting list about eighteen months to two years," said the doctor, "I'm sorry to tell you."

"I can't wait two years," I said almost in tears.

"We'll pay," Sam said quickly. "Don't worry, Belle."

"The operation costs about £2,000 pounds," the doctor said.

"What is cash against your eyesight?" Sam replied. "What is the name of the eye surgeon, Doctor?"

"Mr Casswell of Hove. He would probably need to give you an eye test, once or twice. I'll phone for an appointment for you if you like."

On the way home I argued with Sam. It was a lot of money, I kept repeating. Over and over he said eyes are more important than money and if I didn't shut up he would give me a good shaking.

As it was I could see a fair bit if I wore glasses and could see to read, watch television and knit, but to see clearly would be great. So I agreed to have the operation, whatever the cost.

An eye test by Mr Casswell was made in late December, then another in January and the third in February. For each test I signed a cheque for fifty pounds. The operation was performed at the Nuffield Hospital, Hove, on the 18th of March. It entailed a twenty-five hour stay at thirty pounds an hour. I had a room to myself with television and toilet. Prior to the operation, I was given a hospital gown and a pair of plastic knickers. I enquired why the plastic knickers? "Well, you might leak during the op," the nurse smiled.

I woke and pressing a bell asked the time and was told it was 3.50 a.m. "May I have something to eat?" I asked for a cheese roll. It came with a small side salad and a cup of tea. I slept and woke again about eight o'clock. My eye was bandaged and I was groping around. Mr Casswell came almost immediately, took off the bandage and I was amazed how bright everywhere appeared. I asked if the cataract tissue would grow again and was assured it would not. He then said the sight nerve of my left eye was damaged. I remembered then, years ago, how an over-hanging branch of privet had pierced my eye when hurrying home during heavy rain. So for many years my right eye had been working alone.

When Sam came with our neighbour to take me home, it was time to settle the bill. The Nuffield receptionist presented it. I stared at the figure, £997. I realised the room cost £500, but what were the other figures for? I was told they were for the gown, for the knickers, the cheese meal and a breakfast of coffee, toast and marmalade and nursing attention. I signed the cheque feeling overcharged, but I could see clearly and I thought I had sight for the rest of my life. I was so happy to be home. I noticed some dust on a cabinet and said, "Just look at the dust on this polish."

Sam said laughing, "That's the worst of it, you being so well educated and saying you can write your name in the dust." He hugged me.

A few days later the bills came in the post. £700 for the operation and £180 for the anaesthetic. Oh well, to be able to see clearly it was worth the money.

Between times I was revising my novel, which was going well. Later in the year my sister-in-law, Myrtle, phoned to say that Tony's marriage appeared to be breaking up. She said Julie was always going off on a course and leaving Tony to care for James, their child. "Tony has a job to hold down and James must attend school, what will happen I don't know." What could I say but offer sympathy? Tony began divorce proceedings and the divorce was made absolute in January 1992. What my mother would have said I cannot imagine.

We travelled around visiting or staying with relations or friends. We went on our holiday and renewed friends met in Jersey and we kept up our dancing from which Sam got a lot of pleasure.

On the morning of the 16th of February I woke to a world of pale brown fog. I groped my way to the kitchenette. I told Sam I couldn't see, everything was a blur. He stared, saying, "What do you mean, a blur?"

"Everything looks foggy, misty, I could see better than this before I had that operation. Honestly, Sam, I don't understand this fog."

At just after nine o'clock he phoned Mr Casswell, relating my news, and the specialist told him to bring me to his consulting rooms by nine o'clock the next day. Our neighbour, Tom, agreed and we arrived in Hove on time. Mr Casswell saw me immediately and after a short eye examination lasting a few minutes said, "I can do nothing for you." Six words. I could have hit him. "What about laser? We can pay." He shook his head.

"Laser goes straight and the eyeball is curved. It is scar tissue behind the sight. My receptionist will tell you the cost."

Sam wrote the cheque for forty-five pounds. Had I had my

wits about me I would not have paid his fee. So here I am, now registered as partially sighted. I cannot see to read or sew, crochet or knit. This I have tried but if I drop a stitch I cannot see to pick it up. I have a lady from the Blind Association come to do sewing for me and we have become friends.

Sam takes me shopping, he cleans the vegetables for me and digs the eyes from potatoes after I have peeled them and is helpful with some cooking. He helps with the washing and will iron straight bits but my undies and his shirts he leaves to me, so I do the best I can.

Before losing my sight I had been trying to find an agent nearer home. My novel was nearing completion. I hung on to the short story I had written. Agents I contacted by phone wanted religious items or science.

I was lent an easy reader through Social Services. This works by enlarging print to three inches on the television screen. I was reading part of my novel, not knowing Sam was watching too, and he said suddenly, "That's very good, Belle. Do try to get it published when it's finished."

"I thought you were not too interested. I have yet to find an agent. Mrs Gould died some time ago and there isn't one near here."

I am not a touch typist so now I learned where all the letters of my typewriter were and memorised them, thus enabling me to continue writing.

I tried more revision on my novel, but decided to leave well alone, but this way the ending was not as well as I would have liked.

At the end of June 1994 our central heating boiler broke down. Contacting British Gas the cost of a new boiler was quoted as £1,200. Sam hit the ceiling but realised a new installation was necessary and the work went ahead. On the 24th of July the work was finished. It was an extremely hot day and testing the new boiler, heating was on full blast. We perspired buckets.

The agent persuaded Sam to pay £365 for a five-year three-star maintenance. It seemed a good idea as we had been paying £58.50 a year and we would have no worries until 1999, the cash was paid and all settled.

A few weeks later, Sam came in from his garden. "I'm knackered, Belle. I'll have a shower, get rid of some of my aches and pains."

"You're working too hard. You cannot do at eighty-one what you did at sixty-one, so take it easy." I grinned at him.

"Goodness, I can't do at eighty-one what I did at eighty."

I busied myself preparing dinner and a while later I heard him come out of the bathroom and flop onto the settee. I dished up dinner and called him. He stumbled in the doorway and fell against the sink unit.

Our dinner was keeping warm in the oven. He dragged at the table to get up and cutlery and sweet plates crashed to the floor. I tried to help him, his speech was slurred and it was impossible for me to lift him. "Stay there, Sam, I'll get Lesley." I left him and rushed to our neighbour. Lesley came in with his wife and while he phoned for our doctor, his wife and I tried to make Sam comfortable with some cushions.

As it was Saturday afternoon, it was our doctor's locum who came. His examination revealed Sam had had a mild stroke. I was shocked to hear this. This young doctor phoned the hospital for instructions. He told me to get Sam to bed, keep him quiet, and he was to stay there for a week. Saying he would return shortly the doctor left. We managed to get Sam to bed. I was almost in tears seeing my big man so helpless and all the time he was trying to speak but we couldn't understand his slurred sounds.

The doctor came back within an hour and left some pills to be taken thrice daily. I phoned Sam's relatives and throughout the week they came to see him. Gradually he recovered his speech. His left side was mostly affected and the little boy next door lent Sam a squeezy ball to get some grip back into his left hand. It took time and patience, something Sam didn't have much of, but slowly he became his old breezy self and I was very pleased to see him happy again. I couldn't do enough for him. I insisted he slowed up, worked less hard in the garden and on sunny days he did relax in a deck chair reading. I waited on him to the best of my ability. One day he said, "I don't think I'll ever regain the strength I had in my left hand despite all the squeezing with this ball."

"You have worked hard all your life, Sam. It's time you sat back and surveyed the world from a deck chair." He looked at me, his face rather grim. "Belle, don't ever leave me." I stared at him.

"Whatever made you say that…? As if I would. We still love each other and I'll always be beside you, so don't say stupid things like that."

From then on he came shopping with me. For some time a kind neighbour had been shopping for me, and it was great to get out shopping for ourselves. We celebrated birthdays and anniversaries at The Fox and Hounds, it was near enough to walk there and the atmosphere was friendly.

Nearing Christmas I began writing cards, with Sam helping by reading out addresses. I began slight stomach pains but ignored them. Suddenly I became violently sick. I hadn't had a bilious attack for years. Then came awful diarrhoea. What had caused this I had no idea. I couldn't keep down water and became very dehydrated. Sam insisted I call the doctor but I refused. I managed to gut the Christmas chicken and gave instructions how to cook it. I couldn't face food and asked Sam to make me a lemon and honey drink. That was the first thing I had kept down. I had not eaten for over a week. Sam eyed me with some concern.

"You have lost weight, Belle. Get on the scales."

My weight was down to six stone twelve. I had lost ten pounds.

Very gradually I regained a little weight, but seemed to stay around seven stone one or two, but felt well.

After Christmas I sent off a deposit to the hotel to secure our reservation for the 8th of July 1995, and life went on as usual.

The events of the week beginning the 12th of June will remain in my memory as long as I live. On Monday I began the weekly wash. Sam said he would defrost the freezer. We had been letting it run down and the few items left were transferred to the fridge. By lunch-time, washing finished, we had lunch and both had an easy afternoon. On Tuesday we went shopping to fill the freezer, spending over twenty-two pounds. That was that.

On Wednesday, about two o'clock, I asked what he would like for dinner. "I'll get some chops from the freezer and how about some fruit salad for a sweet?" He went to get the chops and came back fuming.

"What do you know? The bloody freezer has blown up."

"What do you mean? I've heard no bang," I answered.

"There's water all over the garage floor, come and see."

It was as he said. "What about the goods we bought yesterday?"

"I'll ask Lesley if I can put things in his freezer." He ran out and a few moments later returned to say that Lesley was going on holiday but Annette, another neighbour, would help. Meantime I had packed goods into plastic bags and we thanked Annette for her help. The weather was very hot and I wondered if the meat and fish would be edible. How long had the freezer not been working correctly?

We dried up the water. "This afternoon we'll buy a new freezer. This one's had it. I'll see how much money we have in the house and we can write a cheque." We went to Iceland and selected a freezer of suitable size and width to fit the space we had. The assistant said it would be delivered early next morning. Walking slowly from the shop, Sam said, "Let's get a cab home."

"It's such a lovely day, Sam, let's walk, we need the exercise.

Half-way along the Frankland Road he wanted to rest and we stood in the shade of a tree. Had he told me he felt tired, we would have taken a cab. At home I made tea. The sun blazed down. "I feel better now," I said. "When the freezer comes tomorrow I'll get the stuff from Annette and all will be settled and you can take it easy." He laughed.

"Tomorrow I'm spraying those chrysanths, they're full of white-, green- and black-fly."

"What, no red ones?"

"You taking the mickey?" I shook my head laughing.

"And on Friday, I'll sweep the chimney ready for the winter."

A loud crash woke me during the night. "Someone is breaking in, Sam, wake up." I reached to wake him but he wasn't there. I got up and groped for the light switch. In a blur I saw Sam lying on the floor, blood beside his head. I must get help. I shook him roughly, no sound and no movement. I knew the third number in the right side on the phone was nine. When the voice answered I blurted, "Please help me, I cannot see clearly. My husband has fallen out of bed and I don't think he's breathing, please help me." She asked, "Where do you live?" I gave our address and she said an ambulance would be there shortly. I then dashed along and roused Lesley and his wife Jennifer. The ambulance arrived and the medics quickly wrapped Sam in a blanket. They laid him on the bunk saying they were taking him to the Princess Royal Hospital.

"Get dressed," said Jennifer, "and we will take you there."

Arriving at the hospital, I sat with my neighbours. I asked the time. It was ten minutes past four a.m. A doctor beckoned me and I followed him into a small anteroom. Sam lay on a trolley. They had taken out his dentures and his cheeks looked so sunken. "He is very very ill," the doctor informed me. "He has had a massive stroke. Has he been in hospital before this?" I gave them the list of hospitals Sam had stayed in and the reasons. Thanking me he said there was nothing I could do,

Sam was in good hands, I should go home and try to get some sleep. Sleep… sleep?

It was impossible to sleep so I did some housework, my thoughts being "I know he is going to die, I know it, I know."

Next morning I phoned around his family and our friends.

When I rang my sister-in-law she replied, "Now you know how I felt when Jim died." Thank you, Myrtle, for your sympathy.

Sam's nieces came and we visited the hospital and I was told Sam was in a deep coma. With his dentures in place, his cheeks were not so sunken. I gave the nurse his hearing aid, but she said it would not make much difference, she doubted he could hear.

We could visit any time.

I felt lost without him, and when the nieces left, felt so alone.

Friends and relatives made enquiries every day and daily I phoned the hospital and the reply was always the same. "There is no change."

At 9.30 next morning the new freezer arrived. With fingers crossed, I said, "We didn't expect such an early delivery. My husband is taking a shower. Will you fix the freezer?"

It was soon in place and with a generous tip and the old freezer they left. I gave the freezer a wash out with bicarbonate of soda then went along to Annette for our items she had kindly frozen for me. I related to her the hospital message and thanked her for help and sympathy.

Stacking the goods in the freezer, I wondered if the fish and meats would be safe to eat. How long had the old freezer not worked?

I lived on various tinned food on toast. Every morning about 9.30 I rang the hospital, with always the same reply: "There is no change." A few times kind neighbours took me to visit Sam. Always he just lay like a log, a tube strapped to his hand for intravenous feeding. I wanted to stay with him, but had to leave when the neighbours did.

Myrtle phoned asking to spend the weekend with me. I was so pleased and she promised to come Friday afternoon. Friday morning she rang, she had an asthma attack and could not make the journey. I was so disappointed. I had thought she would take me to the hospital and we could sit with Sam for a few hours. Sunday the 25th of June the sun shone brightly, the promise of a warm day. It was Sam's niece Joan's birthday.

At 9.30 I rang the hospital, the reply as usual was the same. "There is no change in Mr Bendon's condition."

It was just after twelve o'clock when Joan arrived at my back door. Surprised to see her, I asked, "Anything wrong, Joan?" She replied brusquely, "Uncle Sam died this morning." I stared at her in disbelief, then at Allen, her son, standing behind her. He nodded.

"How do you know? Why hasn't the hospital told me? When I phoned this morning they said there was no change."

She replied, "I told the hospital if the worst happened to ring me, as a policeman telling you might give you a heart attack." Well, her manner of breaking the news could not have been more blunt. To my dying day I still think the police would have been kinder. The tears came a little later. I just could not believe my dear old villain had left me.

How could I cope without him? For two years he had been my eyes, helping me with shopping, helping me with cooking, helping me with the weekly wash. Selfishly I could think of nothing but "how would I get by?"

Joan shook me: "Listen, Auntie, I'll stay with you and take you to get things arranged. It's Sunday, so today we can do nothing, so we'll start tomorrow." I was in a daze so left it all to her. I didn't know where the offices were or where to go. With the aid of *Yellow Pages* she drove me to the different offices and filled in forms for me to sign.

I was rushed to shop for black clothes and the funeral was arranged for Friday. Four days... four days, my gentle, caring man for fifty-eight years was gone forever. Relations and friends attended. There were so many neighbours in the church, I never realised he was so well liked. The day was sunny and hot and everyone spent time chatting and reminiscing in the garden. I looked around and whispered, "It's more like a party, Sam, but I'm so unhappy... why... why me... why?"

Later there was just Joan left with me. "I'll have to leave tomorrow, Auntie. Will you be all right?"

"It will be a different kind of living, Joan. There are many worse off than me. I can grope around. I don't know what I'll do at the moment. Maybe I'll sort over his clothes and send them to Help the Aged. I cannot wear anything, sweaters or cardigans, everything is much too big, someone will benefit I hope." She left Monday morning.

I roamed round the bungalow like a zombie. Everywhere was so quiet.

I must have some sound. I could not cope with the silence. I switched on the radio to be greeted with a burst of laughter and applause and somehow felt a little calmer.

All the food that had thawed and had been re-frozen Joan had consigned to the dustbin. "Food, once thawed and re-frozen, is dangerous to eat," she said, so after registering Sam's death we shopped to re-stock the freezer. "You have plenty of food to choose from, Auntie, so do eat and keep well. You haven't eaten much this past week, so do eat."

Chapter Sixty-eight

Seated in the kitchenette, I stared at the pale blur of the gas cooker. I felt suicidal. This new type of gas was not so potent as the old type… it just made you very ill… this I had heard from somewhere.

Do something, I told myself. I entered our bedroom and then began taking his clothes from his tallboy. Carefully going through all the pockets, I found some handkerchiefs and altogether £4.27 in cash. There were many clean hankies. His clothes made a large neat pile on the bed. Partly I opened a medium-sized tin box. It contained cuff links, tiepins and a folded handkerchief. I unfolded the hanky to see a black mascara stain… immediately my mind went back to that October dance at York Hall. His proposal of marriage and my tears accepting… all these years my dear romantic old villain had kept this souvenir. Then I remembered packing the tea chest when we moved and that same tea chest had been salvaged from the ruins of our bombed house. My tears fell. All the heartache of the past two weeks, all the memories of our years together. I sobbed as I lay among his clothes until, drained of every emotion, I began folding and packing the gear into plastic bags.

Our greengrocer's shop was next to the charity store, Help the Aged. I phoned him and he agreed to collect and came immediately.

"Please tell them, suits are forty-four-inch chest and inside leg thirty-three inches."

I hoped his clothes would benefit some pensioners. His cuff links and tiepins I gave to his relations.

I wanted to keep his garden ship-shape and I couldn't see a weed from a flower. Neighbours recommended a gardener and if I needed any repairs someone knew a person who could be trusted to do a good job.

The supervisor from the Blind Association found me a volunteer who would take me shopping and we became friends. Then she became ill. I was then introduced to a lady from the Care Association, and to this day she still takes me shopping and is so friendly and helpful.

Neighbours read my mail to me, and in this way I keep in touch with distant friends and relations. The telephone is invaluable.

Finally I was persuaded to attend Age Concern. Here I have made many friends. Most have lost a loved one and for one day weekly, I get away from my own four walls.

It takes a very long time to come to terms with a different way of living… making my own decisions, no one to discuss or question. Constantly I tell myself there are so many people worse off than I am.

I remember Sam asking me to try to get my novel published. Entitled *The Lengthening Shadow*, it was published on the 24th of July 1997. I think he would have been pleased for me.

Finally, to keep me sane, I decided to write this autobiography, to show where there is life there is hope.

And now?

The small green plush teddy bear compact costing 5s 6d (27.5p) in 1929 was sold for £480 at Sotheby's Auctioneers, Billinghurst, Sussex, Christmas 1996. And at Bellings, also of Billinghurst, the chrome and green enamel compact-cigarette case costing just 7s 6d (37.5p) sold for £12, the pearl lighter also sold for £12. I never knew what that cost.